THE MAKING OF SOCIOLOGY

THE MAKING OF SOCIOLOGY

Dr. S.S. Ralhan
Dr. S.R. Lambat

Commonwealth

The Making of Sociology

Edition : 2024

ISBN 81-311-0045-6

Published by :
COMMONWEALTH PUBLISHERS (P) LTD.
4831/24, Govind Lane,
Ansari Road, Darya Ganj,
New Delhi - 110002
Ph. : 23272541, 23242541
e-mail : commonwealthpublishers2016@gmail.com

Distributed by :
ARJUN PUBLISHING HOUSE
4831/24, Govind Lane,
Ansari Road, Darya Ganj,
New Delhi - 110002
Ph. : 23272541, 23242541
e-mail : arjunbooks2001@gmail.com

Laser Typesetting by :
Dimple Computers
Delhi

Printed at :
Milan Enterprises
Delhi

PREFACE

This book surveys the major contributions to the making of sociology during the nineteenth century. We have studied the chief theoretical systems produced by scholars in continental Europe, Britain and the United States and, by this time, their wide ranging agreement about the nature and elements of the subject, and its importance for both understanding and dealing with the problems which men faced in the period of modern science and industrialisation must be clear beyond doubt.

In a way the present book highlights the history and development of sociology as a regular discipline. It is hoped the book will prove to be of immense value to researchers, educational planners and the layman alike.

Dr. S.S. Ralhan
Dr. S.R. Lambat

CONTENTS

1

THE COMMON-SENSE ROOTS OF SOCIOLOGY

Science begins as critical reflection upon common-sense. Common-sense is not to be understood however as the lowest common denominator of simple-mindedness amongst all men. It is already a set of rudimentary theories about experience; a set of assumptions: of virile, shrewd, penetrating insights into the nature of things; but expressed only in the rough-and-ready words of everyday usage. Sometimes these words are more pungent and articulate than more sophisticated expressions might be (sophistication, too, has its dangers for accuracy!), but sometimes they are limited and insufficient. Already, in common-sense, we know that all aspects of nature are intricately interconnected and interwoven with each other; and that some events, in particular, seem always to cause others - but it is when we need to know what exactly these inter-connections are, what events exactly cause others, that our common-sense experience often fails us. Consequently, we are compelled to think more critically and analytically about our ideas and about the nature of the facts we experience, and we have to devise systematic methods whereby the various factors involved in the situation we seek to understand can be isolated, distinguished, and measured, and whereby our theories about their cause-and-effect relationships can be tested. These methods of critical analytical thought, careful observation, recording, and description, and this testing of theories against the facts, are science; and the pursuit of these methods leads to the elucidation of 'laws' - the discovery of regularities of interconnection between phenomena - which make the explanation of events possible.

Common-sense is not, therefore, different from science, but is science in embryo. And our common-sense and scientific interests in the facts of our experience, stem always from two characteristics of human nature: practical need, and curiosity. We are driven to seek exact explanations because, frequently, we must: as when we wish to quell an epidemic, ensure a clean water water supply, grow enough food for survival, build enough houses for the shelter of our population. But also we seek explanations because we are inquisitive; puzzled. We simply want to know. The excitement of curiosity, puzzling, searching and then discovering, is one of our most absorbing and rewarding experiences. Once a problem is there—we find it difficult to leave it alone until we have solved it. And since all aspects of the world in which we live excite us to inquiry, our common-sense and scientific activity leads us to desire not only partial understanding, but also an entire knowledge of nature: of the universe as a whole and the place of man within it. The various sciences - astronomy, physics, physiology, biology - all provide us with a knowledge of particular aspects of the world, but they are all complementary contributions towards our desired entirety of knowledge.

Of course, the similarity of common-sense to science does not mean at all that science is limited to, or circumscribed by, those aspects of common-sense from which it arises. Clearly in its reflection and sophistication it goes far beyond the assumptions of common-sense and frequently shows them to be provisional, limited, inadequate, false. But this does not mean that the two are essentially different; only that the more adequate stems from the less adequate and comes to replace it.

All this is simple, clear, undeniable.

A. N. Whitehead expresses this relation between science and common-sense in a very simple and colourful way, showing how its most sophisticated abstractions stem from our most ordinary experiences.

'Consider', he says 'how all events are interconnected. When we see the lightning, we listen for the thunder; when we hear the wind; we look for the waves on the sea; in the chill autumn, the leaves fall. Everywhere order reigns, so that when some circumstances have been noted we can foresee that others also will be present. The progress of science consists in observing these interconnections and in showing with a patient ingenuity that the events of this ever-shifting world are but examples of a few general connections or relations called laws. To see what is general in what is particular and what is permanent in what is transitory is the aim of scientific thought. In the eye of science, the fall of an apple, the motion of a planet round a sun, and the clinging of the atmosphere to the earth are all seen as examples of the law of gravity. This possibility of disentangling the most complex evanescent circumstances into various examples of permanent laws is the controlling idea of modern thought.'

No-one, I believe, could possibly fail to understand the characteristics of science in so far as it is concerned with our understanding of the natural world. Nor would anyone deny its claims, or the validity of its endeavours.

Why, then, is there doubt, criticism, and even bitter denunciation when these careful methods of science are employed in seeking exact knowledge about the nature of man and society?

Sociology is the scientific study of human society, or - to be more modest and detailed - it is the attempt to study as scientifically as possible all the known forms of human association: their nature, functions, interconnections, and patterns of change in various types of society.

Why should this science scientific endeavour raise so much argument and bitterness? Not, we shall find, from the antagonisms of common-sense. If we consider our common-sense assumptions about our life in society, we shall find that such criticisms of sociology are not rooted in any uneasiness or hostility of common-sense at all, but from sophisticated scholars who have allowed their attachment to their own subjects, or their own interests and motives, to blur their clarity of mind and judgment. Common-sense tells us quite distinctly and convincingly - and again from both paractical need and curiosity - that the attempt to achieve a science of society is both necessary and important.

In order to see this clearly, let us set out, in an orderly way, what our common-sense assumptions are. Such a process of clarification is a first step of scientific inquiry, and we shall find that, already, in the requirements seen to be necessary by our common-sense ideas, we have a fairly clear idea of what components a scientific study of society should consist. Our common-sense assumptions already tell us what sociology would have to be like in order to satisfy the kind of thing that we already know roughly - but would like to know more exactly.

1. The Necessity of a Scientific Study of Society

As soon as we stop to think about it, it is obvious that we possess common-sense views about our own nature, and about the historically changing society in which we live, as much as we do about the world of nature. And we also see quite clearly the necessity of going beyond our common-sense ideas to a more careful investigation, if we are to ensure that our supposed knowledge is going to be really reliable.

At least three things convince us of this.

(a) *Practical need*

As soon as we become involved in particular conflicts with other groups in society; as soon as we are bought face to face with particular social problems; we are at once made aware how little we really know about social reality, and at once realise that a more painstaking study of the facts is necessary.

Consider a few examples:

We would like to eliminate from society war, poverty, crime and delinquency. We are often hotly indignant when we encounter the intractable inequalities of opportunity in society for children who, no matter what their abilities and qualities might be, happen to be born into different social classes or different 'races'. We would like to improve matters; to remove these obstacles to social justice; and would therefore like to know the underlying causes of these social facts. Then, on the basis of this knowledge, if we could get it, we would like to formulate effective social policies and institute political reforms.

As soon as we embark upon this more careful investigation, however, and upon this well-intentioned activity of social reform, the more we are driven to see the great complexity of these social facts and the order of society in which they exist. In spite of all our efforts, both intellectual and practical, we find it extremely difficult, if not impossible, to alter the social facts which we thought were simply a product of individual intention, or evil, or misunderstanding. It turns out to be far more difficult to eliminate war, poverty, crime, and differences of class, status, and educational opportunity than we had imagined. Some of the characteristics of society turn out to be as intractable as the 'stubborn facts' of nature.

What is certain is that we find it absolutely necessary to probe far beyond our common-sense ideas; to devise far more rigorous methods of thought and practical investigation; in the effort to establish reliable knowledge on the basis of which to act. For we quickly learn that we can only effectively change the nature of society to approximate as closely as possible to the ends we desire, if we know what that nature is.

Just as we can only convert water-power into electricity to improve the material well-being of a nation, when we know the 'laws' - the regularities of interconnections - of the physical factors involved; so we can only change social facts when we know the 'laws' - the regularities of interconnections - pertaining to them.

Several important points are to be noted here.

(I) Moral Feelings — Much of our concern to think about society (i.e. many of our 'needs') stems from our moral feelings; our feelings of moral indignation; our desires to eradicate injustice and to establish justice.

(II) Moral Feelings in Themselves not Enough — But we know that moral ideas and good intentions are not in themselves enough. Without knowledge and power we cannot make them effective. Also, we find that, without knowledge, they often pave the road to something other than a good society.

(III) *A Science of Society not in Disagreement with our Moral Persuasions, but Additional and of Service to Them* - The development of a scientific study of society is not in disagreement with our moral persuasions, does not contradict them, is not incompatible with them; neither does it replace moral concern and clear ethical thinking, or render them unnecessary. It is something additional to them and clearly of service to them.

(IV) *Moral Concern Insists on Scientific Accuracy* - Moral persuasions and practical needs do not - as critics have often supposed - make it impossible for a scholar to be careful, honest, exact, impartial, 'objective', in his pursuit of scientific truth. On the contrary, they insist upon it. We can only hope to achieve our humane ends if we rest our social policies upon the truth, and not upon any kind of distortion of it. Subjective feelings, subjective passions do no necessarily make a scientific study of society impossible. It is just some of these feelings which enjoin it. Certainly some unconscious values and assumptions may lead us to bias in our theories - but (a) our efforts should always be towards the impartial self-criticism which would make such grounds of bias conscious and clear, and (b) such initial bias does not matter crucially so long as our ways of testing our theories are reliable, clear, and always open to the scrutiny of other investigators. Conscious distortion of scientific work - in human sciences and 'natural' sciences alike - is likely to arise not so much from passionate feeling or ethical conviction, as from a lack of integrity, or a lack of rigour in one's methods of investigation.

(V) *Knowledge Enables us to Act more Effectively 'Causal Determinacy' does not Preclude Purposive Action* — It is already clear, in our common-sense, that there is no inconsistency (as, again, some critics have supposed) in thinking (a) that there are definite 'laws' of social facts (i.e. regular interconnections between them), and (b) that, by knowing them, we can act in such a way as to change their manifestations. When we know the 'laws' of the tides, we can calculate the strength of sea-walls necessary to prevent the erosion of the coast. We do not change the laws; but, knowing them, we can act to prevent them having particular effects. Similarly, when we know the 'laws' pertaining to the formation of class and status in society, we can so organise our political constitution, our distribution of income and property, our educational system, as to prevent the occurrence of rigid class boundaries and intractable class conflicts. The 'laws' are not changes; but, knowing them, we can act to prevent the effects we think undesirable and to ensure as closely as possible the consequences we want.

(VI) *In Socicty something more than the Wills of Individuals is Involved* — It is also clear in our common-sense that, in looking for the explanation of some social facts, conditions, and problems, we must look for something more than individual wills and intentions. This is not to say, by any means, that we believe that individuals cannot, and do not, make individual choices or have individual intentions, and that these can never be effective. It is not at all to say that men do not possess some measure of "free will' in that they can exercise conscious choice and act deliberately and with clear purpose. It is only to say that in many human situations something more than the wills and intentions of individuals is involved.

If, then, we find that some sociologists (men who have reflected upon these common-sense concerns and problems, and who have tried to develop more precise methods to get at the truth about human nature and human society) are inclined to say that social explanations must go beyond propositions about the motives and wills of individulas, and that we can only act effectively to change human nature and society if we know the 'laws' of society and the nature of the group conditions within which men exercise their will, we shall not think them absurd, or 'metaphysical' in any derogatory sense. If people object to these ways of talking, it cannot be on the grounds of common-sense. It can only be that they themselves have become confused by their own sophistications. There is nothing unclear about this way of thinking.

It is also quite a clear understanding in our common-sense that the necessity for a scientific study of society has become more urgent as society has become larger and more complicated, and as the growth of knowledge in all spheres has given rise to a wider range of doubts and a more insistent questioning of traditional beliefs and assumptions. In our modern industrial society - which has grown so rapidly and spread so quickly to all parts of the world during the past two hundred years - our needs for a science of man and society (needs both practical and of curiosity) have obviously become greater. Our problems have become more numerous and more pressing and, in the prevailing confusion about 'supernatural' and all types of 'traditional' authority, hitherto taken for granted, we are also driven to a clear awareness that the solution of our problems now depends upon us; upon our own responsibility. If we do not solve our problems in society, no-one else will!

We are quite clear that, during the past two hundred years, a more careful way of studying society has been made necessary by the facts of social change themselves. Sociology is the subject peculiar to the characteristics of the modern human situation, the modern predicament of man. And we feel, in terms of our common-sense convictions, that it is essentially a humanistic subject: not only in that it is of broad human concern and interest, but, more fundamentally, because it is the subject necessarily connected with our growing awareness that, in this new situation, we ourselves are responsible for the making of our own destiny. It the past, men have believed they could rely with confidence upon an authority outside man—the power of providence, or God; but now, whether we like the situation or not, we are faced with a clear consciousness of responsibility for the direction of our own social and individual affairs.

Again, then, if we find some sociologists speaking as passionate humanists, speaking with zealous concern and anxious persuasion, inspired both by moral enthusiasm and by intellectual conviction of the great significance of their subject for contemporary human problems, we shall not find it surprising—for this is attendant upon the emergence of the subject itself, and our common-sense clearly appreciates this. The fact that a subject is 'scientific' does no mean that it is not 'humanistic'. Indeed, the distinction between sciences and 'humanities' seems an absurd distinction in some respects.

(VII) *Reflection on Terms and Concepts Necessary* — It is also clear, if we believe that scientific activity involves the devising of more precise methods of investigation and the testing of theories, that sociology must necessarily weigh its terms and concepts more carefully, more reflectively, than is usual in common-sense, and that, when necessary, it may well be driven to the invention of new terms. It is clear to us, for example, as soon as we start arguing about a topic like 'Christianity', or even one division of the 'Christian Church' (the 'Roman Catholic Church', say, or the 'Baptists') that these simple terms become quite inadequate. For 'Christianity' is far from being the relatively simple unity that our initial common-sense notions sometimes suppose. The ' Baptists', for example, are very differently organised in Coleford in Gloucestershire than they are in the United States of America. 'Roman Catholicism' is not the same in the West Riding of Yorkshire as it is in Ireland or in Italy. Our words have therefore to be examined scrupulously, and no-one will object, therefore, if we begin to use words like 'founded religion' (as distinct from other 'traditional' kinds of religion), 'episcopalian organisation' or 'sect', or 'denomination' (and many others) in our attempt to become clear in our grasp of the facts.

Our common-sense would have no objection at all to a careful analysis of our language, or an invention of terms, if this were for the purpose of useful clarification. It would object to such an exercise of preoccupation only if it were seen to be useless, leading not to clarification but to confusion; to unwarranted and pointless obscurantism.

(b) *Curiosity*

Quite apart from the practical needs which prompt us to examine more deeply the nature of society we are also led to such inquiry by curiosity itself - or, to give the matter the degree of concern which we feel - by our need for personal understanding.

One immediate aspect of this point is the supposed distinction between 'natural' and 'human', or 'natural' and 'social' science. It is clear that common-sense does not make this kind of distinctions at all. It is made only by scholars of various kinds. In our own common-sense awareness of our predicaments in the world, we have a far more mixed up and bewildered experience, but, on the other hand, an experience which has a far greater unity than these distinctions would suggest.

We feel ourselves to be both of the world and not of it; in tune with it and in conflict with it; in harmony with it and hostile to it; members of it and strangers in it; and all this simultaneously. We feel sometimes with deep satisfaction that our own nature is deeply rooted in nature itself. The whole living universe of stars, earth, skies, trees, is in some curious but definite and tangible way linked with, indeed knitted into, our own nerves, veins and flesh. We are all creatures of nature. We are all of the one body of the universe. It cannot be otherwise! On the other hand, we so often and so obviously feel at odds with nature! The most urgent improvements of our condition (such as vaccination against fatal diseases), and the most sublime qualities of our artistic and social achievements (the novels and symphonies which move us, the forms of government or religion which have given us a basis for co-operative, peaceful and creative living), are certainly not simply given to us. They are not simply there, to be found by us, in nature. They are outcome of thousands of years of cumulative effort and struggle. They have been won by unceasing battle with the elements of nature (storm, wind, flood, fire, plague) and with bewildering and sometimes distasteful elements of society (social distinctions, racial differences, wealth, privilege, power). We are at war with nature, just as we find our deepest peace in our communion with it. We are at war with society, just as we find our most satisfying purposes as members of it.

And we are different from all other creatures in nature in that we are members of a historically developing social heritage which transmits the cumulative achievements of our ancestors from one generation to another. And it is quite clear in our common-sense experience that our own individual nature is largely an outcome of the complex influences of this social tradition itself.

I speak English. I love the diatonic harmonies - in their simplicity and in their intricate developments - of Vaughan Williams, Stanford, Herbert Howells, Ivor Gurney, Peter Warlock. I find some of my deepest moral experience couched in the phrases of Shakespeare, Wordsworth, Emily Brontë, Blake and others. And I have these personal experiences not simply because I was created in this way as an individual soul, but because I was born in England. Had I been born in some other society and brought up within the many subtle influences of another social tradition - my individual nature would have been different. If I had been born in India, I would have spoken a different language with all its many different connotations of experience. I would have enjoyed quartertone harmonies in music; and found my moral experience couched in terms of, say, the Vedic hymns, or the requirements of a particular 'caste'.

It is perfectly clear, then, that if we are to understand our place in the world we must also understand our place in society, and the place of our own tradition within the wider context of history and of the natual world. To put this in another way, it is quite clear to us that a careful study of society is as necessary a part of our full understanding of the nature of the world and our place within it, as is any other science or any other branch of human thought.

Indeed, there is a second consideration of common-sense which inclines us to think that a science of man and society is especially central and fundamental in its importance. This consideration is simply this:

All the knowledge of the world and man's place within it which we can establish is necessarily and unavoidably human knowledge, stemming, as we have seen, from the practical needs and the curiosity of our own nature. It cannot possibly be otherwise. Nothing is more obvious to our common-sense than that the kinds of knowledge - ordinary, religious, scientific, philosophical - which exist at any time in any society are: (a) themselves social facts of that period, and (b) inescapably characterised by the level of development of that society. In short: human knowledge and its growth necessarily form a part of the subject-matter of a science of society; and all the various kinds of knowledge should thus find a coherent statement of their nature, development, and interconnections (with each other and with other social circumstances) within the over-all account provided by a science of society. The science of society - providing within itself, as it does, a perspective of all the other sciences—is also a study of the several ways in which man has conceived the entirety of nature. All knowledge - of the world, of nature, of God - is human knowledge; it takes the form of systems of records, doctrines, theories, in societies. And therefore the science of man and society is of the most fundamental importance for understanding the development of man's many conceptions of nature: those sets of concepts, assumptions, ideas, theories, which - at any one time - actually comprise nature for him.

This is not to say, by any means, or in the slightest degree, that sociology is in any sense superior to other sciences. All sciences are equally necessary and important in providing knowledge about particular aspects of the world, and, taken together, in providing a full picture of our natural situation as we see it. It is only to say that sociology, because of its subject-matter, has a peculiar significance of quite a fundamental and central nature that other sciences do not possess: that of throwing a perspective of inter-connectedness over all human activities.

In order that our understanding of nature and man can be complete, therefore, a science of society - sociology - is obviously necessary to us.

Something else must be noted, finally, with regard to this distinction between 'nature' and 'society'. Many scholars have drawn this distinction between the 'natural' and the 'human' or 'social' sciences very strongly. Indeed, they have gone so far as to maintain that it is improper to use the word 'science' in connection with the study of man and society at all. Sometimes they have claimed this because of religious beliefs that man possesses spiritual qualities which are quite distinct from the other characteristics of the 'natural' world. Sometimes they have believed that individuals possess 'free will', and that this renders any attempt at generalization or prediction about human behaviour impossible. And sometimes they make this claim believing that the nature of man, both as an individual and as a member of society, is so complex that, as a subject of study, it defies all hope of manageable, measurable treatment, and so cannot be dealt with in terms of 'scientific method' at all.

Now, clearly, our common-sense tells us that something is wrong with these distinctions, between 'natural and 'human', or 'natural' and' social', and that, in some way or other, these scholars must be muddled and mistaken. At the same time there seems to be something in what they say. The matter is not very clear.

Common-sense experience tells us without any doubt whatever that 'man' and 'human society' are just as much a part of 'nature' as, say, ants and ant-hills, or as bison and their herds. 'What is 'unnatural, or 'non-natural' about man and his relationships which should make it necessary to regard our study of them as being something other than a 'natural' science? There is, of course, nothing. These several objections rest upon simple confusion.

The religious objection is obviously, at bottom, purely a disagreement about words. Whatever one believes about God and man's relation to him it is clearly arbitrary whether we use the word 'nature' to refer to everything that exists including God and the human spirit, or to everything that exists apart from God and the human spirit. If God is responsible for that nature of the created world and man within it, and is active in the world (even though he himself may transcend his own creation and possess qualities that go beyond it) it is difficult to see in what way a 'natural science' of man and society could be thought faulty or inadequate - whether we use the word 'natural' narrowly or all-embracingly. The strongest criticism that could be made on these grounds is that such a natural science of man could not explore all the dimensions of man's nature and of reality; but no-one would have any objection to this. At the same time this criticism could not possibly controvert, nor would it undermine or lead us to doubt, any knowledge about man and society in nature which such a science did demonstrate.

Presumably God, if he exists, is the ground of creation of all his creatures other than man, too - foxes, trees, woodlice, volcanoes, vermin and viruses - and if a scientific study of these can be termed a 'natural science', why not a scientific study of man? Of course, theologians may well claim that this is naive (theologians always do claim that their critics are naïve—it is one of the few kinds of criticism left to them), but this is not so. The fact is that even man's so-called 'knowledge' of God, or his knowledge of 'revealed truth' (i.e. of those 'non-natural' or 'spiritual' qualities which are supposed to be beyond the reach of a scientific study of man), are only experienced within the context of human feeling and human thought and can only be expressed in human terms of communication. Nothing can be known or experienced by man excepting through the medium of his own nature. Theological dimensions of knowledge, which claim to be additional to that of science, turn out, therefore, to be propositions about human experience—as all else. Furthermore, its purported 'knowledge' is in no sense superior to that of science. It cannot be held to be a ground of superiority that it does not possess the same ground of demonstrability. The truth is that this particular objection is an outmoded theological quibble which is not now worth our consideration. Let us note very clearly, however, that this is not an 'anti-religious' position. If God does exist and has created the world, there is no reason at all why we should not use scientific methods in order to secure as full a knowledge as possible of man's nature and place within it.

The objection resting upon the existence of 'free will' we shall return to, in more detail, later. Here, we need only note our common-sense conviction that man, differently from other animal species, is capable of establishing a knowledge of his nature and circumstances and, on this basis, of exercising personal choice and acting in a progressive way to achieve his ends. This capacity is part of man's nature. There is therefore no reason whatever why a study of man which takes this fact into account should not be called 'natural'; and, even if this fact should prove to make exact study difficult, our problem is only this: to make our scientific study as exact as possible, and only to claim that which we can demonstrate.

The third objection - concerning the great complexity of human society as a subject for science—clearly does make an appeal to our common-sense. If we want to study what happens at the boiling points and freezing points of liquids, it is a relatively easy matter to set up tests in a laboratory and to alter the temperature of the liquids until our knowledge is established. If, however, we want to study the causes of 'crime', or the factors which give rise to feudal societies', clearly the facts are incredibly complicated and we cannot put them into a laboratory to observe them. Indeed, it is extremely difficult not only to examine the isolated factors involved, but even to be clear whether there are distinguishable factors to be isolated at all, or, even when there seem to be such factors, whether we can manage to isolate them sufficiently for anything approximating to a testable explanation. It is all very complicated, and, no matter how careful we are, it seems likely that our findings are likely to be much less precise than, say, our findings about the liquids. Our common-sense feels very firm, indeed, adamant about this, and, of course, no social science worthy of the name would wish to deny it.

But the fault, here, lies again in a confusion.

Many people have come to equate the terms 'natural, and 'scientific' and 'exact'. 'Natural' sciences are those which can be exact, (which have, say, the exactitude of mathematical calculability.) 'Human' and 'social' studies are not 'natural' or 'scientific' because they are relatively inexact (they do not permit of mathematical calculability). And this, incidentally, has had the effect of firing some social scientists with the zeal to attain mathematical calculability in their subjects at all costs, simply so that they can claim to be 'scientific'. But this is to take part in a spurious competitive charade. And it rests upon quite erroneous reasoning. Indeed, it is not reasoning at all, but stems from a basic misconception.

Since varying aspects of the natural world have differing degrees of complexity, the scientific study of each of them will require different methods and will result in differing degrees of certainty, but - whatever their degrees of exactitude—they will all be different departments of 'natural science'. And whether the subjects are scientific or not has nothing whatever to do with whether their results are equally precise, but only upon their nature and the methods they employ. Even if a scientific study of some subject or problem yields no positive results at all, it will still have been the scientific method which resulted in these findings, and it will remain for critics to demonstrate what better and more fruitful methods could be pursued in their place; indeed, upon what criteria they themselves rest the supposedly better 'knowledge' that they may profess. But why the 'human' and 'social' sciences should be specially selected for this criticism is very difficult to understand. For all the so-called 'natural' sciences have very differing degrees of exactitude among themselves. Biology cannot achieve the exactitude of chemistry. Physiology cannot achieve the precision of physics. But no-one would argue that biology and physiology were not sciences. The subjects employ scientific methods to establish testable knowledge - and the results are the most exact that the nature of their subject-matter permits. Later, we shall see that philosophers and scientists have long been aware of this. It is nothing new.

There is one other point that common-sense suggests, which might here be posed only as a question.

Is it really true that the phenomena of man and society are more complicated and more difficult to study than those of other sciences? In our common-sense experience there is at least a lot that inclines us to think that the reverse might well be the case, and that the study of man and society - though certainly complicated - might well be simpler than the other sciences of nature. Might is not be that too much fuss is being made about the difficulties involved?

It is clear to us that we cannot put people in laboratories with either ease, moral conviction, or even prospects of success, in testing theories about their behaviour. Social facts are certainly more imponderable, more unwieldy to handle, than are some other facts of nature. At the same time, some sciences seem simple to us now only because they have been reduced to order after long ages of thought. We are told, for example, that astronomy is a simple science. But if we were to face the bewildering array of the heavens and the earth without the accumulated observations, calculations and techniques of the past (without telescopes, for example), would we find the task of explaining the courses of the starts and planets simpler than explaining the causes of social conflict in our locality, or even between nations? At least the basic nature of social institutions - such as property or marriage or education - can be found by examining legal and other documents and by understanding their meaning for us. And even when institutions are different in other societies, the people there are men and women like ourselves, and, with study, it does not seem difficult to understand the ways in which they act and feel. Indeed, sometimes we are astonished at the similarities between them and us despite institutional differences. Social rules and arrangements are at least evident to us, and many of the complexities are due simply to the fact that there are a lot of people and documents involved, and the 'testimony' we can get is of very variable reliability. The understanding of the principles of genetics in heredity, however, or the knowledge of the ways in which viruses cause disease, were exceedingly difficult to explain because these fact were hidden from us, unitelligible to us, unknown. The very existence of genes or viruses was completely beyond our expectation. Similarly, if we think of what is involved - let us say in neuro-physiology - in attempting to unravel and track the many interconnections of the brain cells and other nerves in the body, we are far from being fully convinced that this is less difficult than tracing the interconnections between social institutions.

We would not feel confident in asserting this on the basis of common-sense without further thought; but we would at least feel it sufficiently a matter of doubt to raise as a question.

Might it not be that sociological analysis is a relatively simple matter of clarifying - by means of careful thought, analysis, and investigation - the networks of institutions in various societies and understanding the courses of action which men pursue within them? And might all this talk of complexity have arisen because sociologists had to sound more profound since they were doing what everyone else thought fairly self-evident? In common-sense, we suspect that it might be so. We suspect that unnecessary mystification might have crept into the whole matter. And we suspect, after a little thought, that the difficulties of being clear about the nature of a science of society may possibly be because the subject has only been developed recently (historically speaking), whereas other subjects (like astronomy and physics) have been studied scientifically over a much longer period of time. This, at any rate, is a question which we would like to see considered.

Many and complex arguments have been conducted in the past about 'natural' as against 'human' and 'social' sciences. We can ignore most of them. A subject may be called 'scientific' when, reflecting upon common-sense assumptions, it then goes beyond them carefully analysing experience; carefully clarifying its concepts and procedures of thought; carefully observing, recording and describing the facts about which it seeks to establish knowledge; clearly stating theories about them, and, at the same time, making clear and explicit the conditions whereby these theories can be subjected to test. Each science may be named according to the range of facts it studies. The words 'natural', 'human', 'social', need not enter into the matter at all. Sociology is a valid science of all forms of society, just as biology is a valid science of all forms of organic life.

There is, then, no problem here.

(c) *Testing existing theories*

There is a third important element of our common-sense experience which obviously makes necessary a scientific study of society—and that is the existence of many theories about the nature and destiny of man and society, each of which not only claims to be true, but also continuously, and sometimes hotly, clamours for our attention and allegiance. Furthermore, these theories challenge us with extremely important decisions, for, in supporting one or other of them, we are not only acknowledging the truth of one and the falsity of others, but are aiding or constraining some of the most important struggles for power in the world about us.

Sometimes these are total 'world-views': as ambitious, if not more ambitious, in their scope than even the most grandiose sociological theory ever presented, and asking for our commitment to them on far less adequate grounds.

There are, for example, the varieties of 'Christianity', which offer a total world-view of the author of the universe, the creation and destiny of the world, the sinfulness and salvation of man, and a detailed theory of civil society. Similarly, all the other religions of the world claim the truth and significance of their enormous theories of the universe and man and the nature of spiritual reality. In addition there are the total world-views of a pseudo-philosophical and pseudo-scientific nature like Communism - offering, in the same way, theories about the entire nature of reality, and, within this context, total theories about the origins, growth, and destiny of human society. And, far less imposing than such systems of thought, are what one might call (if it were not for their grave seriousness) the 'comic-opera' theories of society - such as Mussolini's directives for 'Fascism', or Hitler's struggle for 'National Socialism'. How, we now ask ourselves in amazement, could men ever have taken seriously a 'credo' containing such fantastic, reiterated phrases as 'Mussolini is always right'; 'The Duce is always right'? Surely, we now think, men must have been demented to accept such nonsense? Yet millions of men were, and are swayed in this manner.

All these 'theories' are far more grandiose, and rest on far less reliable evidence than any theory proposed by sociology, yet the greater part of the human race accepts one or other of them. And here, it behoves the critics of sociology to examine self-critically those positions of thought and belief other than sociology which they themselves accept. Do they submit their 'Christian' or their 'Communist' theories to the same critical tests which they require of sociology? Many who reject a sociological theory - say that of Spencer - because of doubts concerning its validity or sufficiency of evidence, are ready to embrace a far more pretentious world-view on far less adequate foundations. Many who will not accept what Durkheim says about suicide are quite ready to accept what religious 'authorities' say about the 'Trinity', the 'Crucifixion,'

'Reincarnation,' Nirvana', and even ecclesiastical injunctions about the use of 'The Pill'. Unless these questions of the 'criteria' of knowledge are examined carefully, this is, of course, sheer perversity.

Then there are the more limited creeds concerning specific social problems: like the belief of the Calvinistic church of South Africa that God created white and black men quite distinctly different from each other, and that the organisation of society should reflect his will; or the theories of political parties about 'laissez faire' or 'collectivism', and the like.

As we well know, such theories - large or small, limited or allembracing; many of them ill-founded - are legion. They continually, in our day-to-day lives, seek our support, and they exercise a great deal of power in society.

The sole point upon which I wish to lay very great emphasis, and it is something which we encounter in all our commonsense be-wilderments and deliberations, is this:

In the face of these competing theories - theories which are of vital importance in that human happiness or misery to some extent depends upon our acceptance or rejection of them - we are in need of some reliable basis of judgment. We need a body of well-founded knowledge which will, at least, give us the necessary basis for testing these theories, for adjudicating between them. Unless we pursue those methods which will establish the most reliable knowledge about human society it is possible to attain, we shall have no grounds whatever on which to exercise reliable judgment. And unless we achieve clear and reliable ideas about the validity and adequacy of methods of study themselves, about what constitutes good evidence and grounds of testability; we shall not even be in a position to know which, amongst all these theories, is at least the most responsible and reliable in the procedures it adopts, and the claims that it makes.

Two points are worth nothing and realising very clearly here.

(i) The development, the clear statement, and the wide dissemination of a science of man and society is of the greatest urgency and importance not only from the positive point of view of giving us new knowledge and new theories; but also from the negative point of view of demolishing theories which are false; of giving us a mode of critical analysis which we can readily use to test any theory which people put before us, or seek to impose upon us. To my mind this negative contribution is of the greatest positive worth. It is a very considerable step - to know how to climate error; to be able to clear the ground of rubbish - whether old and hallowed or new and brash - even though we may not yet be in a position to replace it with a new building. At least we shall be able to see clearly within the range of our known uncertainties instead of continuing to be misguided by 'certain' attachments to what is obsolete and useless.

(ii) The second point of interest here is that, willy-nilly, these various religious and ideological theories, in their competition for people's allegiance, all drive men increasingly to the necessity of scientific investigation. Indeed, their moralising zeal finds it difficult to deny its worth. If these theories claim to possess the truth, then they should not fear or disapprove of, but should only encourage, any scientific activities which aim at seeking and demonstrating the truth more clearly and more fully. One clear sign of the bogus nature of any such group or theory is that they discountenance, discourage, or forbid the pursuit of free inquiry. But since, fortunately, several such groups are competing with each other, perplexity increases and the need for extending careful scientific study becomes ever more apparent.

In facing the claims of existing theories, then, (quite apart from proposing theories of its own) social science has to clarify the criteria of validity and truth and the procedures for ensuring these in studying the nature of man and society, and this, too, is a necessary and extremely useful function of which our common-sense misgivings and disturbances completely convince us.

Sociology, then, according to common-sense, is a necessary science. For a wide range of purposes, we need it. But let us now analyse our common-sense assumptions still further, to see what they imply about the subject-matter of this science, and the kinds of method that it seems to dictate. Our common-sense assumptions may contain more than we suppose.

(2) Common-sense Assumptions about the Nature of Man and Society

(a) *Order and regularity prevail in society as they do in nature*

Remembering the way in which Whitehead described the regularities of events which we perceive in nature; the constancy and order of the connections between them; our common-sense experience equally impresses upon us the fact that order, regularity, constancy of expectation, also prevail in society.

Sometimes, hearing critics attacking sociology on the grounds of the unpredictability of human behaviour, one would think that, from their point of view, human society was an ever-changing scene of completely spontaneous, arbitrary, and always varied individual behaviour. On the contrary, however, our common-sense experience of social life is that it is characterised (sometimes depressingly) by repetition, by a continual 'sameness', and, furthermore, a sameness that most people cannot avoid. Indeed, within this routine pattern of activities, we find that individual men and women, in their personalities and behaviour, come to be characterised by deep-rooted habits and almost unalterable ways of doing, saying, and even thinking things.

We do not find, in our everyday life, that everything in human nature and society is completely arbitrary and spontaneous, differing from day-to-day. We do not find Mr. Smith going to work at 9.00 a.m. on one day, 10.00 a.m. the next, and 3.00 p.m. the next; or taking a holiday on Monday, or Wednesday, or Friday, or all three - quite arbitrarily during each following week, simply according to his whimsical feeling as to whether he wants to go fishing, or go to the cinema. People do not and cannot choose, solely according to a momentary personal whim, what time they will go to work. It is, in fact, just the reverse. People have, and for definite reasons, to start and finish work together; so that every morning we shall find millions of Mr. Smiths standing on the platforms of their same local stations at exactly the same time, all contributing to the 'rush hour' in our towns and cities. Usually, too, Mr. Smith will not only be there at the same time, he will be wearing the same kind of clothes, carrying the same kind of newspaper, in the same kind of way, saying the same kind of thing to the self-same companions - or, perhaps, being predictably the same as ever in that he does not speak to his travelling companions but blocks them from view by his open newspaper, and then, after having read the main articles, settles down to the crossword puzzle - in the same corner of the same page! Regularity is the rule. The man who has the 'Mail' on Monday, the 'Mirror' on Tuesday, the 'Times' on Wednesday, the 'Telegraph' on Thursday, and sits in his carriage on Friday with no newspaper at all—naked to every suspicious eye - is not only an exception: he simply does not exist! In the same way, we find that the way in which children are registered at birth; the way they are 'christened'; the ways in which they are educated; the ways in which people get married; the ways in which they vote, worship, bury their dead... are all charaterised by a very marked order, regularity, repetition.

Now this does not mean at all that, in our common-sense experience, we believe that people could not behave differently if they tried. We do not think they are all 'determined', like parts of a machine. All we are saying, and all that we need to say, is that, almost invariably, they do not behave differently. On the basis of this regularity it is quite obvious (and it is testable) that we can both know and predict what people will do. This is nothing akin to fortune-telling. Neither does it make any metaphysical assumptions about human nature being 'determined' or 'free'. It means only that we can know so accurately the pattern of institutional rules, procedures, expectations and constraints in which individuals are involved that we can say that they will behave in certain predictable ways. Indeed, if they do not, we shall have to look for a special explanation.

Without wanting to press the matter too far at this stage, and without wishing to imply even the vaguest suggestion of 'determinism' (which, in fact, I would want emphatically to reject), it is surely true, in our common-sense experience, that we find individuals predictable even at a much more intimate level than the broad regularities of social behaviour which we have been considering. People do become habituated to certain modes of thought, feeling, speech and behaviour, and manifest these habits even in spite of themselves. A husband and wife come to know each other so closely that they can tell almost exactly what each of them is going to do, say, or even think, in response to particular situations. They can, and do, predict one another's reactions, and, indeed, even if they do this openly, whether jokingly or otherwise, and even if the other is fully aware that his or her response has been predicted, they will, nonetheless, still find themselves slipping into the predicted habits in spite of themselves. Indeed, it is when the exceptional reaction takes place which they did not predict, and did not expect, that close partners look up and 'take notice' wondering what is wrong.

People - though being able to exercise choice in their conduct, and to do much by way of self-discipline to shape and govern their own characters-are, nonetheless, not super-human. They live within a social context and comply with its demands. In many ways they are quite predictable, and it is, if properly understood, a necessary corollary of character-formation that they should be so. Furthermore, it is difficult to see why anybody should be distressed that this should be thought to be so. To hear the bitterness of some critics, one would think it was degrading or humiliating to human beings to maintain that they were predictable; instead of being, on the contrary, a simple recognition of their humanity, and an accommodation to the reciprocal requirements of human life. A humanity, we may note, that, curiously enough, critics admire when it is displayed in novels or plays. In a novel, we come to love a character because we come to know him : so intimately that we know exactly what he will do if such and such a thing happens. We know that, in 'War and Peace', Pierre will be forever wandering round Russia through some vague feeling of wanting to see what is going on. And when that event does happen, and when the character does react as we had expected of him, we have warm sense of affection for him. We love him because we know him so well; and consequently we understand and forgive, with humorous affection, all his little foibles. When Charles Diokens has Ebenezer Scrooge snarling at the world in general in every third paragraph, or has Uriah Heep squirming his way repulsively through every third line, we think, with admiration and affection, what a fine portrayer of human character he is; but if a sociologist assumes that we can arrive at clear, testable descriptions about the regularities of human society, he is thought to be guilty of dehumanising the race. Again, there is some kind of perversity among critics here.

At any rate, our common-sense has no difficulty whatever either in recognizing or in admitting these matters.

There is a further fact that common sense knows very well.

Though it is true that all people could behave differently if they set themselves out to do so (that is to say, if they chose to be as unduly perverse as the critics) it is clear (a) that social chaos would ensue, if they did, and consequently this spotaneous variety could not continue for long, and (b) that, in fact, the nature of social necessity is such that they would have either to submit to a certain modicum of conformity with the accepted regularities of community life, or be put into prison or otherwise constrained. And even the ways of being constrained and put into prison in any society are predictable and regular.

If, for example, Mr. Smith stopped away from work whenever he felt the slightest inclination to do so - his inclination being the only excuse he offered to his employer when questioned about his behaviour - we all know that Mr. Smith would not keep his job for long. This, again, is a prediction that can be readily tested by anyone. If, in Britain, given the nature of British institutions, a man openly married three women at the same time, or decided not to bother registering the deaths of his relatives but simply disposed of them under the rubbish heap at the bottom of the garden, or undertook some similarly unusual forms of behaviour; we all know that he would soon find himself in either a penal, or a mental institution. And that, with little doubt, is where he ought to be.

Indeed, the constraints of society are such that we can even predict, with reasonable nicety, which kind of individual eccentricity and deviance will be permitted, and which kinds will be forbidden and prevented, either by social disapproval or by the very heavy hand of authority.

(b) *Society is something more than a collection of individuals*

The experience which we all have of the rules, obligations and constraints in social life makes another important fact quite clear: social institutions are something more than the individuals who are constrained by them.

This, again, is not to belittle individuals at all. It is simply to recognise that the rules and the social organisations which constrain our behaviour are, in a very real sense, there; independent of ourselves and of any other individual. Their existence is not just a matter of our feelings about them, or of any other individual's feelings about them. They exist in the general organisation and the collective conditions of society. And they exert definite constraints upon us; playing an extensive and important part in influencing our behaviour and, more deeply, in shaping the innermost nature of our personalities.

For the moment, we need not ask how or why these institutions came into being; how they have come to be what they are. What is certain is that, in our common experience, they are there: in legal and constitutional rules and precedents, in established governmental procedures, in the ritual of religious worship and the organized hierarchy of the clergy, in the routine administrative rules and practices of civil service departments and local government authorities, and the like, together with all the symbols which clothe them: the Crown of the Realm; the Wigs and Robes of Judges and the Court Procedures themselves; the Cross of Christ, the magnificence of Cathedrals; the music and the liturgy of services, and so on. And they must be investigated, known, and taken into account as the definite institutional fabric of society in any explanation of the approved regularities, or the 'frowned upon' irregularities, of human behaviour.

It seems clear to us, then, even at the level of common-sense, that we cannot understand and explain the many institutional regularities of a society simply in terms of the personalities of the individuals who happen now to be living within it. The social heritage has a definite, historical nature. On the contrary, it seems true that we can only fully understand the lives, personalities and characters of the individuals now living within it by taking into account the many-sided influences upon them of this social setting of their birth, upbringing, and pattern of adult obligation.

This also makes it plain to us that Psychology - 'the scientific study of experience and behaviour', and Sociology - 'the scientific study of human society' are essentially linked in some way. Perhaps, even, they should not be separate studies at all.

It also makes it abundantly clear that any full explanation of social change must be very difficult indeed to achieve. It is clear, at least, that both social institutions and individuals have to be taken into account. Obviously, to some extent, social institutions have themselves in the past, been shaped by individuals in their relations with each other, and by their joint, group activities. But these individuals, too, in their own time, must have been influenced by the social and cultural setting of their own lives. It is obviously difficult to disentangle 'psychological' and 'social' factors. Certainly, no simple conceptions of social 'causation' could possibly seem to be adequate. A very careful and detailed analysis is clearly necessary.

One point we might make especially clear in concluding is that - of course' we are not saying that something called 'SOCIETY' exists like the material structure of some building in total independence of the people who live within it. The regularities of social rules and organisational procedure which are laid down in law, government, religion, and the like, persist because they are practised and carried on by generation after generation of people who become, as it were, living bearers of their social heritage. The institutional regularities which are something more than individuals thus come to be embodied in the collective life of individuals in their associations with each other. The two are very closely knit together, though they are not to be equated with each other. Clearly, if we use the word 'structure' of social institutions within which, or in terms of which, individuals live their social life, we are referring to something definite - though not entirely independent of individuals. If, therefore - when we make this point - someone were to charge us with the error of thinking of 'Society' as being something of a metaphysical nature, totally 'over and above' individuals, and actually existing in some form totally separate from all of them - they would be making a false caricature of our position.

At the same time, it is interesting and chastening to think that, frequently, in the ruins of times past, in the records of civilisations gone to their destruction, it is the evidence of the institutions of a people which remains. The individuals are the dust and air that blow about the walls which they built. In the structure of these derelict buildings, in the artefacts, the documents, the legal codes, the records of contracts made according to fixed procedures, lies a knowledge of the institutions within the framework of which a community of people lived their social life. And it is within the context of this knowledge (when it is at last elaborated) that we are then able to begin to conjecture as to what sort of ideas, emotional attachments, aesthetic experiences, these individuals may have had. Thus, an Egyptologist like, say, Sir Flinders Petrie, does not write initially about particular persons who were fan-bearers or matspreaders or clerks to the Pharaoh; he writes a book (based on the study of scripts, ornaments, buildings and paintings) on *The Social Life of Ancient Egypt*, and the book gives an account of the framework of institutions of that ancient civilization. Only within this reconstruction of a society do we begin to catch the flavour of the feelings, ideas, actions of the individuals who lives there.

> 'My name is Ozymandias, king of kings:
> Look on my works, ye Mighty, and despair.
> ....Round the decay
> Of that colossal wreck, boundless and bare,
> The lone and level sands stretch far away.'

So wrote Shelley. Ozymandias is gone, as are all those who once gathered in multitudes beneath his sway. But some ornament, some piece of wrinkled parchment, some weapon, some stone or clay tablet of a legal transaction, has outlived them; and it is from these that a reconstruction of the 'society' may be possible; by means of which we may then come close to the feelings and thoughts of the actual individuals who experienced them.

In some curious way which we cannot readily understand or express, a 'society', an interconnectd network of social institutions, is the shared creation of many generations of individuals, which has come to have an existence, a power, both massive and subtle, with even something of sanctity about it, which then cumulatively goes into the shaping of the nature of subsequent individuals. What, for example, is patriotism, if it is not a love for our social heritage - something more than and greater than ourselves as individual's - which made us, in large part, what we are.

In some way, society helps actually to create and enrich, as well as to confine and constrain, our innermost individuality. Society, somehow, is a creative reality. It is a distinct creative process in nature. It is a cumulative historical creative process without which the nature of humanity cannot be understood.

(c) *But society is rooted in basic aspects of our human nature.*

Having said that social institutions are certainly something more than individuals, we do nonetheless feel very strongly, in our common-sense awareness, that many human associations are natural: both in the sense that they spring from those inclinations, impulses, emotions, needs, with which we are by nature endowed; and in the sense that our own individual nature seems to need them for its own fulfilment. We feel that we could not fully be individuals excepting in the context of continuous social commitment. To some extent to be natural is to be social. For us, at any rate, whatever may be the case for other creatures, to speak of the individual as something separate and distinct from the social seems itself to be false. It seems, somehow, to violate the actuality of our experience. The two terms - natural and social - embrace each other. To be human means both.

For example, from the beginning we have parents, brothers, sisters with whom we develop a deep and abiding bond (though by no means only harmonious). Later, we ourselves desire, and get involved in, sexual mating, and - having children - feel love and feelings of protection for them, and a sense of identity and intimate responsibility which is difficult to describe, but which gives us a concern for the continued security and stability of the basis of social life which we hope they will enjoy. And we are not members only of one or two families - but of a much wider community of families with whom we have to co-operate in the economic tasks of earning our living, in the governmental and legal tasks of deciding and upholding rules and judging the people who break them. We also experience a moral need. We feel duties towards our own kin, and a powerful sense of justice or injustice with regard to the ways in which they are treated by others or by the community in general; we naturally need rules of reciprocal conduct whereby mutual right-dealing may be assured and disputes resolved.

According to our common-sense experience, then, society is natural. All these elements of social organisation are necessary aspects of our natural life. We have no difficulty in understanding or explaining this. It is obvious to us. Indeed, if anyone maintained that society was not naturally attendant upon the satisfaction of our many needs, we should require an explanation of this point of view from them, and we think they would be hard pressed to find one. Society may have become so complicated as to perplex us in many ways; some groups may have become more privileged and powerful than we think warranted in terms of social justice, so that we may feel opposed to society as it is; but whatever disagreements, problems and conflicts we experience within it at present, we know, fundamentally, that co-operative activity in society is natural and right for us, and that total isolation is unnatural, intolerable, and, indeed, inhuman, No individual could possibly fulfil his natural impulses and propensities without associating with others.

It follows, then, from our common-sense experience, that some of our associations and institutions can be readily understood and explained to a degree, in terms of our natural, instinctual and emotional needs, the interests, purposes, and ideals related to them, and the kinds of social regulations and more general interests and purposes which they entail and which go beyond them. If any sociologist therefore speaks of the 'functions' of social institutions in terms of the needs or purposes they serve, or the ways in which they are linked together in their working, we shall find no difficulty whatever in understanding this. If, for example, it is said that one 'function' of judicial institutions is to resolve disputes, or that one 'function' of governmental institutions is, in a formally agreed way, to take decisions centrally which are to be binding upon all, we shall find this a perfectly straightforward and sensibly way of speaking. It is a perfectly clear idea. Indeed, if anyone maintained that institutions could not be understood, in part, in terms of their 'functions', the needs and purposes they served and the ways in which they worked interdependently, and that this was being 'teleological' and 'unscientific' because it was an error to think that institutions and individuals sought to fulfil certain 'purposes', we would not be puzzled - we would be flabbergasted. Whether it was described by the word 'teleological' or by any other confusing word, we would be unable to see anything wrong with it. Men are prompted to communal action by needs; they do act in accordance with purposed; they do participate in, and, indeed, create institutions and associations which further their purposes. This is a plain fact that we cannot and will not relinquish. And we shall expect and scientific sociological analysis to take it adequately into account. If it does not - we shall think there is something wrong with it.

(d) *Society is essentially a historical process*

Society, as we have said, is in many ways natural to us, but is something more than ourselves as individuals. It is something which has a 'traditional power' of its own and which constrains us in our behaviour and character - not only in the sense of forcing certain rules upon us, but also by persuading us of the worthwhileness and rightness of certain values and obligations.

But in common-sense we have no difficulty in explaining or understanding this. Is quite obvious that as a community, over many generations, encounters problems, challenges, difficulties, both among groups within it and with other communities outside it, its social institutions come to possess definite characteristics which are upheld by each generation as being matters of proud achievement. Whether all aspects of the social tradition are pleasing to all its members is another matter; indeed, this would be very unlikely. Some may be a matter for pride among certain social classes and for disgust among others; but still - the historical continuity of the institutions of the community as a whole is not in any sense difficult to understand.

The essential point here, then, is that - in our common-sense - we know, without doubt, that human society is essentially a historical process and can only be understood as such. If someone tried to explain social regularities without taking past history into consideration, we would immediately think that there was something very odd, something lacking - indeed, something perverse - in his position. We would think that such a person could not properly have understood the nature of the facts he was studying. Our methods of studying society, then, must be in some way historical. They must enable us to investigate society as a set of changing, growing, developing social institutions and social traditions.

Our common-sense convictions about this point are so powerful and immediate as to entertain no denial. When we see, for example, the ceremonial attaching to the British Monarchy, or the ritual procedures in the election campaign for the President of the United States - we know completely that these traditions cannot possibly be explained without a knowledge of their nature and changes in the past. Similarly, when we see the conflicts between Trade Unions and Employers in relation to a 'Prices and Incomes Policy' of the Government; or the revolutionary conflicts that have burst upon institutions of higher education in France; we know that these cannot be explained unless we have a knowledge of how and why these institutions came into existence, and how they have changed in changing circumstances to become what they are now.

This fact of historical development also gives us a clear ground for understanding the obvious differences that exist in social traditions throughout the world. Our common-sense awareness of the fact that the family, the religion, the form of government of, let us say, China, are different from ours, is readily understood in that we know that the people of China have had a set of geographical conditions and historical circumstances very different from our own. Different social traditions are bound to develop when communities confront different kinds of situations. Though we cannot possibly claim to know the details of the historical causes of these differences, there is no obscurity, no insurmountable difficulty in our minds concerning this point. We know very well that our own society has changed even in our own brief lifetime, and that it is impossible to understand the nature of our society now without knowing of the problems, conflicts, and disturbances which we ourselves have experienced, which our parents experienced twenty years or so before we were born, and which have brought about these changes. For example, many present characteristics of our society are an outcome of the last war; the problems of the war itself and the post-war period; and any explanation of the nature of society now must take these historical facts into account. And if this is true of our own period, it is very likely to be true of any other period, and of any other society.

Again, then, if anyone tries to explain social institutions without taking history into account, we shall want him to explain how he can manage to do so, and on what grounds he should want to try.

(e) *We expect societies, nonetheless, to be basically similar to each other*

The fact that, in common-sense, we feel it necessary to understand the differences in societies, is one aspect of another of our deep-rooted assumptions, namely: that all human societies must be basically alike. They must have something in common with each other. They must have some basic similarities in their forms of association as well as differences of detail. They must encounter the same basic problems - even though these may well have been experienced in the context of different circumstances and have developed differently. This common-sense assumption is rooted in the very simple fact that, despite historical differences, we are all human beings; members of one biological species. Consequently, we expect our own natural needs, problems, concerns, and ways of dealing with them to be shared by men and women everywhere.

For example, we expect all communities to regulate sexual behaviour; to protect young children; to care for old people; to have some form of marriage for the foundation of the family groups in society. We expect all peoples to instruct their children in the skills and knowledge they themselves possess, and to educate them in their values and beliefs. We expect all peoples to establish some form of government and some procedures of law for taking central decisions about matters of common concern and for interpreting and applying these decisions with regard to particular disputes between individuals and groups. We expect all peoples to divide the many jobs of the community amongst themselves in some systematic way; to allocate different jobs to different people in accordance with some notion of their general fittedness for the work. We expect all peoples to devise rules of property - making clear the rights and responsibilities of legitimate control over the material things of society, and guaranteeing a security of possessions to all.

Different societies, with different historical traditions, will have different ways of dealing with these problems; their institutions are likely to have forms which are different from our own; but the needs and the problems underlying the institutions are the same everywhere, and because they are outcome of our universal human nature.

We expect universal similarities in human societies, then, despite some differences; and it is a simple common-sense matter to see how this assumption can be tested by comparing societies (both of the past and of the present) the world over, and by gradually achieving a more detailed and precise analysis of what human needs are, and what institutional provisions are made for them. Analysis and comparison are therefore essential procedures in any reflective and careful method. There is nothing difficult or un-clear about this.

With reference to this assumption, too, we often feel - in terms of our common-sense - very suspicious of some of the claims which seem to be made by some modern social anthropologists that human nature, human experience and behaviour, is not only widely different among societies, but is infinitely variable. When some statements seem to say that in some societies sexual behaviour is not regulated at all; that there are no rules of private ownership whatsoever; that children are not loved and cared for but often killed without concern: that no forms of Central Government and law exists whatsoever; and so on . . . we feel, even though the anthropologist has the evidence, and we have not, that they must be somehow mistaken. We are perfectly ready to agree that human beings may differ to some extent, even to a great extent, in their modes of behaviour and their varieties of social feeling and regulation, but - and about this we feel convinced - not so much. We cannot believe that human nature is infinitely malleable. We cannot believe that the variations of society can be such as to eradicate basic elements of our human nature, and the common kinds of need for social regulation to which they give rise. The varieties are at least, we think, bound to be variations upon certain very fundamental and common themes.

(f) *Societies do exist as distinguishable wholes*

So far, we have been considering the various associations and institutions of men and communities in the widest and most general way, but this question of similarities and differences between distinct historical societies leads us to another common-sense assumption which, with unmistakable clarity, we possess. It is very simple, but it is also very important, and must be noted.

It is: that societies, as total systems of interconnected institutions, do exist; that they are entities which can be clearly distinguished from each other even though some of them may well share, and have shared in the past, common cultural features and influences. We do not have the slightest difficulty in thinking that France, Germany, Great Britain, Italy, are separate societies, having systems of social institutions with distinguishable characteristics, in spite of the fact that they have all been shaped in important ways by the same elements of culture, thought, beliefs, and even by common institutional developments such as the Christian Church and earlier common institutions of 'feudalism'. If we were pressed on this, we would probably say that the chief factor leading us to distinguish one society (as a whole) from another is the fact that it is a separate independent political community. Its members acknowledge a common allegiance to the one central political authority and not to other authorities outside. They abide by the laws which apply to them all, and consider themselves citizens of this one society, accepting the rights and duties which these laws entail. And this, of course, does not prevent us from being able to distinguish differing 'cultural groups' or 'regions' or 'local traditions' within the same single society. Wales, Scotland, and Northern Ireland have certain distinct differences from England, but all constitute , in a very firm allegiance, the single society of Great Britain, which is an entirety distinguishable from other nations, and has a system of institutions whch the people of all these 'regions' share. In the same way, we would recognise 'culture areas' going beyond the political community.

A few important points are well worth disentangling here.

The first (of the very greatest importance) is that we recognise clearly, in our common-sense, not only that the many associations of men are characterised by order and regularity; but also that this order is one simple aspect of the fact that all the parts (the particular institutions) of a society are intimately interconnected with each other; mutually influencing each other in the ongoing process of social life; and coming to be pervaded with the same general character. We see quite clearly that the many associations of a community form an interconnected pattern; a system; and the total system is what we call the society.

Thus, in Great Britain, the form of central and local government administration, of the law, of property and economic organisation, of education, of communications, of the Churches, of marriage and the family, and all other associations besides, are inextricably interwoven. So much is this so, that we know quite well that it is impossible to understand any one of these excepting in the context of the others. We cannot understand the law, or, let us say, the institution of marriage, excepting in relation to government, religion and morals. We cannot understand the educational system excepting with reference to social classes, private and public sources of wealth, religion and the welfare policies of government. The same is true of all other institutions without exception. Again, too, history reinforces this point, for this is a system of institutions because they have all developed together in the closest relationship with each other throughout the experience of many generations. It is clear, because of this close interconnection, that if change occurs in any one of these institutions it is likely to bring about some sort of change in the rest.

On the basis of our common-sense, then, we clearly expect that a full understanding of any one social institution must involve the understanding of the whole society of which it is a part. Sociological analysis must be an analysis of systems of social regularities: and no account of a separate institution or a particular social change can possibly be adequate unless it has been investigated within the context of such analysis. What we are really saying here, in short, is that it is our awareness of the existence of total systems of social regularities which makes sociology necessary as a science. The existence of societies, of social systems, and what this implies for seeking knowledge of any aspect of them, is the crucial fact, the distinctive point of departure, the distinctive orientation of sociology as a subject.

If, then, sociologists, in pursuit of clear analysis, liken a society to an 'organism', and speak of the 'functional interconnection of institutions in the social system as a whole', it will be perfectly clear to us what they mean. There is nothing obscure about it. We actually find it in our experience. Our common-sense tells us that this way of thinking about the nature of society is necessary.

A further important point is that it is quite clear to us that if we are to compare examples of social institutions carefully, in order to understand their nature - we can only do this reliably by taking into account the total societies of which they form a part. Since we cannot understand a single institution in one society without considering its characteristics and place within the whole system of which it is a part; so we cannot compare the same institution in different societies without taking the differences of these total social systems into account. This clearly presents a very great problem indeed: how are we to manage comparative studies of this kind ? And it leads us to a further consideration.

(g) *In common-sense, we distinguish 'types' of society*

As soon as we stop to think about the matter, we find that it is, in fact, common-sense practice to compare and contrast social institutions within the context of total societies, and we try to manage this in our rough and ready way, by dividing societies into types.

For example, if it is discovered that the Soviet Union has put a space capsule into orbit successfully, but that this had received no mention in the press before the event, we say: - 'Ah' yes. That is typical of communist countries (societies). The government will only release news which is beneficial for its own purposes. If the launching had been a failure, we would have heard nothing about it. 'In democratic countries (societies)', we might continue, 'the failures are as widely publicised as the successes. It is thought that the people should know the truth of what is going on and so the government is continually bombarded by alert criticism from the press.'

We obviously believe that different 'kinds' of society have 'typically' different institutions, and that the entire network of institutions, in the one type has an over-all character which is qualitatively different from that of the other. We speak of 'totalitarian societies,' for example, to include Fascist as well as Communist societies, and to distinguish them from 'liberal' societies. We also speak - when we are comparing different ways of life - of 'capitalist' societies, 'feudal' societies, 'primitive' societies, and so on.

It is quite clear from this that we believe that societies can be classified into types according to certain very well marked characteristics; and also that illuminating comparisons of them can be made, giving a sharper understanding of their distinctive institutions, and providing us with a certain basis of judgment. In our heated day-to-day arguments, for example, we compare the educational system, the families, the religions, of these different types of society. If sociologists pursue this same method, then, trying to do more carefully and methodically what we already see the necessity of doing approximately or roughly in our everyday arguments, we shall readily see both the point and the good sense of their efforts.

It is worthwhile to draw attention to a further point here.

Often, we find that we do not compare societies only as 'total' types, which differ altogether in all their institutions. Sometimes, we compare them because of the dominance of one or two specific characteristics which seem to us very important. For example, we may compare societies which are chiefly 'Roman Catholic,' societies with societies which are chiefly 'Muslim'. These societies may, in other respects, be similar to each other. They may, for example, all be peasant societies in which sudden wealth has been produced for small minorities by the discovery of oil, and in which vast industrial changes are just beginning. But we may select the one dominant characteristic, the religion of the societies, because we feel it to be relevant to the particular problem which we have in mind; in this case, perhaps, the different attitude of the people to social and economic change. Similarly, sometimes we may compare 'capitalist' or 'socialist' societies for some purpose (for example, the development of technology, or bureaucracy, or managerial élites') and may ignore the fact that some are Roman Catholic, some Muslim, some Jewish, and the like.

The point which is worth very considerable emphasis here is that, even in our common-sense, we do not think it always necessary to think of our 'types' of society in terms of an exhaustive description of all institutions. We think it useful, sometimes, to distinguish 'types' in terms of one selected feature which, we have a strong suspicion, is the most significant feature for the kind of understanding we are seeking. This means, too, that we do not suppose, in thinking about the problems of human societies, that we must set up a rigid set of 'Types of Society' which - for ever after - will be the only basis, the true basis, of comparative analysis. On the contrary, we think that the distinguishing of 'types' of society should be left fairy flexible, since it will depend a lot on the problem we are concerned about. A social scientist can be left free to clarify his own particular 'types' for his specific purposes of explanation at the time. The test of whether the 'types' he constructed were worthwhile would simply be the degree to which they proved useful in leading to more satisfactory explanations.

(h) *Existing societies and social institutions have developed from a simpler, primitive condition*

It also seems obvious to us (whether or not it may be proved by more sophisticated study) that all the complex civilisations of man, all the highly complicated modern societies which employ such sophisticated levels of knowledge and skill, must have developed through some long historical process of struggle, conflict, and effort, from earlier, smaller and simpler groups which were very primitive in their conditions. By primitive, we are perfectly clear what we mean. We do not mean anything derogatory or blameworthy: we mean 'simple', 'rudimentary', 'undeveloped', not possessing the cumulative achievements of civilisation. For example, a mud hut in some ancient encampment, the summer tent of an Eskimo tribe, or a rural labourer's cottage in eighteenth-century Britain, are thought of as 'primitive' dwellings when compared with well-designed and well-built houses of today incorporating modern technical skills. But this applies, we feel, not only to material things, like houses, but also to social arrangements and forms of social organisation. For example, we think that economic organisation, the division of labour and rules of property, must have been very simple in the earliest human groups of hunters and food gatherers; and that their language, their education, their communications must all have been a matter of direct face-to-face contact. Their government, their laws, their ways of resolving disputes, indeed, even their very conceptions of justice, must, we suppose, have been very simple compared with those of later, larger, settled civilisations and modern industrial societies.

This, at least, is what we are strongly disposed to think. And there is plenty of evidence in ordinary (non-sociological) writings to show that, in general, people do think that not only material things, like tools, weapons, and vehicles, but also social institutions, have developed to meet new contingencies. A good example can be seen be in a small, straightforward history of Methodism, written in 1903. The author, W.B. Fitzgerald, writes as follows:

> 'The circuit, like every other part of our organisation, has had a gradual development. And just as in the Northrop loom, with its electric motor, its delicate adjustment, its lightning speed, and its shuttle changing automatically when the thread is spent, you can still see the old handloom of a hundred years ago; so in the modern compact circuit, with its up-to-date methods and economy of power, you can see a distinct relationship to the simple arrangements necessitated by the spread of Methodism in the middle years of the eighteenth century.'

The writer's meaning in this paragraph is perfectly clear and sensible. Again, then, if we find sociologists attempting to uncover, describe, and make clear, the nature and the developments of social institutions (and even of total societies) which have taken place, we shall find nothing questionable in this. It will not puzzle or confuse us, but will be seen at once to be necessary.

Two other matters are also clear in connection with this.

Firstly, we are all persuaded in common-sense (just as Fitzgerald assumed that he could give us an understanding of the present organisation of the Methodist Church by making clear the nature, and reasons for its past developments) that we cannot possibly have a full and correct understanding of the institutions of the present, unless we know the ways in which they have developed from the past. We feel that we understand the nature of the Trade Unions as they are now much better (including the attitudes of individuals within them) when we know how and why and in connection with what struggles they originated, and how they have developed in the growing complexities of industrialisation. We feel we understand the nature of the political parties now much better if we have a knowledge of their historical development. And the same is true for any social institution. Furthermore, we know that we can take far more effective active now in seeking to change these social institutions (if we do wish to change them), if we have this full knowledge of their past development as well as a knowledge of their nature in the immediate present. We have already noted this point in insisting earlier upon a historical account of social institutions, but here there is the additional consideration that we need not only an account in simple terms of chronological sequence, but also an analysis of the cumulative developments as institutions come to deal with different and more complex problems. This notion is not easy to distinguish from the idea of 'progress', and we must come back to it later.

We believe, then, on the basis of common-sense, that we can only fully understand the present nature of society, in order to act reliably and effectively in relation to it, if we have an understanding of the social developments of the past. With this knowledge, we have a perspective within which we can make reliable judgments; without it, we are looking only at a final picture, without any understanding of how it came to be what it is and what its many dimensions are.

But secondly, we find that we are interested in how things began and how they developed simply because we would like to know. A knowledge of this kind enables us to have a perspective, a clear conception of our own place in the ongoing process of nature and civilisation. It gives us a direction and a set of purposes in the context of past human effort. To state this as simply as possible for the moment, there are at least some of us who like to have a 'world view' within which we have some understanding of our nature and our destiny. As full a knowledge as possible of the development human society from its origins up to the present time gives us a necessary part of such a 'world view'. This is a highly unfashionable point to which we shall return later: but, for many of us at any rate, it is important.

We might note, however, before leaving these considerations, that in connection with them, any science of society is immediately faced with a very serious criticism. If so much knowledge of a historical and comparative nature is needed to understand our present-day institutions, our knowledge must always be incomplete. It will always be impossible for individuals or groups to know so much.

Common-sense has only one view about this criticism. It must concede it. It is true. Our knowledge must always fall far short of completeness. Even so, we shall see that even this obvious and very clearly known inadequacy of our limitations can be turned to very great advantage in laying down certain rules of method. It has long been said that a knowledge of our ignorance is the beginning of wisdom. And it has not been commonly understood that when Socrates made this the centre of his teaching, he was not speaking simply of his own limitations - he was making clear the perennial condition of man. Putting the matter very minimally, we can be liberated from making great mistakes in attempting the impossible - if we know it is impossible. Knowing what is, and is not, feasible, we can provide ourselves with rules of procedure which will delimit and sharpen our knowledge accurately. Furthermore - knowing the limitations of our knowledge - we are able to formulate sound criteria of judgment.

(i) *In common-sense, we believe in progress*

Just as we believe that social institutions have developed, so, at least in many cases, we believe they have improved. And therefore just as we find it necessary to think of human society in terms of development, so we also find it sensible to think of it in terms of progress. We are, of course, not so foolish as to think that things inevitably get better. We know only too well that quite unforeseen problems can arise: as, for example, unemployment as a result of technical progress. Neither do we think that everything improves simultaneously, in a single ongoing sequence. Frequently, as in the example just given, we know that an improvement in one aspect of social life may give rise to what seems to be retrogression in another. There seem always to be losses as well as gains. But, on the whole, we are inclined to believe that our own society is in many ways better than that of our parents' or grandparents' day, and certainly much better than the simpler societies with their very limited resources and knowledge. It is better to have our teeth out with rather than without a pain-killing injection. It is better that all children, rather than only a small privileged minority, should be educated. It is better to drink clean rather than contaminated water. It is better to work eight hours a day for five days a week in safe and pleasant conditions with regulated meal-times, than to work eighteen hours a day for six days in harsh, dismal, insanitary and unsafe conditions with no regulated meal-times at all. It is better to be healthy during a long life than unhealthy during a short one. It is better to have some democratic representation in government and to be protected from arbitrary power than to suffer tyranny - whether from kings, nobles, bishops, or employers. The list could be endless!

It seems a feasible question, then, to discover what improvements in their various modes of social life men have achieved, and what can be done to consolidate these gains for everyone and to make matters even better still. Clearly the increase of knowledge about nature and society has given man a greater degree of control over his environment and his affairs; over his own destiny. It is instructive to know in what ways he has used this knowledge for good or ill, and what kinds of improvement it at least makes possible. If it could give us a balanced pictures of this kind, sociology would clearly perform a great service in enabling us to direct our efforts to worthwhile objectives. Sociology could be one useful subject among others which could enable us to 'learn how to learn from our experience'.

What is certain is that the question of social progress or social deterioration is always a matter of controversy, and has especially been so during the past two hundred years, during which industrialisation has disrupted the long established traditional societies of the past. Since consciously directed progress has become a possibility there have always been those reformers who thought they could improve things, and those conservatively inclined traditionalists who were convinced that the golden age was being ever more rapidly torn as under and destroyed. This controversy is with us, now, in every generation. At the very least, then, it would be a good thing to have the issue clarified; to provide ourselves with a body of knowledge which would give us a basis for careful discussion and reliable judgment. It would be a great gain if sociology could only provide us with a sound perspective for judgment.

(j) *Common-sense needs science. Scientific method is the only way to answer the questions to which common-sense gives rise.*

There is one final assumption of common-sense which is quite a decisive matter.

Once questions have been raised by a disturbed awareness of the insufficiencies of common-sense (i.e. about our knowledge of social institutions, social development, types of society, social progress, and the like), it is clear to common-sense that there is no other way of resolving them excepting by careful reflection, careful observation, the careful statement of theories, and the testing of such theories against the facts we are trying to explain. In short, common-sense knows perfectly well, and is perfectly ready to admit, that science is the only way of exploring and answering its doubts.

Once this matter is put, it becomes perfectly clear that the attempt to establish rigorous scientific methods of investigation is absolutely unavoidable for both the proponents and the opponents of sociology alike. The assertions made by critics against sociology require (if they are to be preferred to the generalisations of sociology) the same kinds of supporting evidence, the same methods of testing, as do those generalisations themselves. For example, if some critic argues with us that there are no regularities of institutional behaviour in human society; that human behaviour in society is completely unpredictable; that it is impossible to classify 'types' of society in order to compare social institutions for a better understanding of nature, and so on; this critic must not only assert these things, he must demonstrate that his generalisations are valid and true. And he must do this by showing us that the facts give better support to his propositions than they do to those of the sociologist.

If it does not sound too dialectical, what this amounts to is that once the common-sense assumptions about man and society are questioned, sociological theory has necessarily to be employed even in order sufficiently to criticise (and perhaps deny) sociological findings. The simple truth is that once the issues have been raised, the subject cannot only not be rejected, it cannot be avoided.

The only thing to do, whatever our dispositions towards the subject might be, is to develop it as honestly, clearly, carefully, and rigorously as we can - and see where it gets us. If its methods and findings are proved to be valid, true, and useful in answering the questions we pose, then they must be accepted by both practitioners and critics alike - just as they must be rejected by both if they are invalid, useless and false.

Summary of Common-sense Assumptions about the Nature of Man and Society

In our common-sense assumptions, then, the following persuasions are clear:

(1) That it is sensible to reflect critically upon our common-sense ideas about society and social problems and develop scientific methods of study (careful analysis, careful observation, the careful statement and testing of theories) in order to establish more precise and reliable knowledge than common-sense itself can provide.

(2) That, once this has begun, even critics must adopt it, since the only kind of knowledge about society which can rightly be preferred to that of sociological science will be that which, itself, rests upon more reliable grounds.

(3) That sociology is necessary from the point of view of:

(a) practical need,

(b) curiosity and the desire for understanding,

(c) the testing of those important and influential theories about man and society which already exist.

(4) That sociology, in its development as a science, can rest firmly on the facts:

(a) that there is order and regularity in social life, the nature of which can be increasingly clarified by careful study,

(b) that this order entails definite rules, procedures, and forms of social organisation which are other than and more than the nature of individuals, and which are know to exert considerable influence upon the behaviour and personalities of individuals,

(c) that these associations are rooted in human needs and purposes of various kinds, and are interdependent in their operation in society as a whole, and that these functions could be further clarified by careful analysis and comparison,

(d) that society is essentially a historical process, that different historical circumstances give rise to different social traditions, and that the science of socicty must therefore incorporate appropriate historical methods,

(c) that socictics must be basically similar to each other despite some historical differences because of the universal featurcs of human nature, and that this gives a firm ground for expecting that significant and useful comparisons between socictics can be made, and that universal generalisations are possible,

(f) that societies exist as distinct entities, as entire systems of interconnected institutions, and that particular institutions can only be properly understood in the context of such systems,

(g) that societies do not seem infinite in their variety, but can be divided into 'types' so that they can be classified and compared in order to seek general truths about the nature and functions of their institutions,

(h) that society and its many institutions have developed from simpler forms, and that sociology should study this process of development in order fully to understand the present, and in order to act effectively in relation to it,

(i) that it seems very probable that human society has progressed in certain ways, and that it will be useful for the direction of our efforts if we can be clear what the grounds of these improvements are, what improvements have in fact been achieved, and what others might still be made.

Finally:

(5) Scientific sociology need suffer no anxiety as far as critics are concerned, for these critics themselves can only be considered seriously if the methods they employ can be shown to be more reliable than those employed by sociology - in which case, of course, sociology would itself accept them since it seeks, in fact, the most reliable methods possible. Sociology can therefore only welcome serious criticism; indeed it should look for it.

As far as criticism of an ill-informed kind which is what most criticism of sociology is: this may well be irritating, but it can be safely ignored, excepting when it has such telling influence as to misrepresent and despoil the development of the subject (which, unfortunately, is frequently the case in educational circles), in which case it must be attacked - root and branch.

Sociology, then, is the scientific study of all forms of human association: their nature, functions, interconnections, and patterns of change, in various types of society. Beginning with reflection upon common-sense assumptions, and thereafter employing analytical, observational, classificatory, historical and comparative methods, it seeks to establish testable knowledge, testable theories, about these associations.

In what follows, we shall find that all the major contributors to the making of sociology have concentrated upon a refinement upon these initial reflections upon common-sense. All have contributed to the clarification of one or other aspect of them, and therefore, taken together, they have created a more exact, satisfactory, and useful system of analysis than common-sense itself possesses. But this still remains a system of analysis which, when carefully stated, common-sense can readily understand

and approve, because it remains firmly rooted in its own assumptions.

Some Reservations of Common-sense

In concluding this survey of our common-sense assumptions, and in order to be completely fair in our presentation of them, we should note a few misgivings about sociology which we also feel. Some of our common-sense assumptions are critical of sociology, as well as being in support of it.

Though all we have said so far seems plausible, there are two or three reasons why we have some initial and serious doubts about the possibilities of creating a satisfactory science of society.

(a) *Is the subject-matter of a science of society manageable*

The first of these stems from our rough-and-ready awareness of the difficulties involved. To speak of 'all forms of human association known to us', in the same way as in biology, we speak of 'all known forms of living organism' is, without doubt, perfectly clear, but, when one stops to think of what this involves, one is staggered and overwhelmed by its extent and its detail. It seems, in fact, to involve the entirety of human history: the nature of human groups and communities, their manifold rules and social arrangements, from the simplest and earliest hunting and food-gathering societies throughout the whole detailed and diverse development of all the historical civilisations. . . Egypt, Babylon, India, China, Greece, Rome. . . up to and including all the societies of our modern industrial age. Now it is very clear to us that, for any one of us to know in any detail, even one society, even our own society, is a job which outwits and defeats us. We do not know completely all the details of even the county, the town, the village, indeed even the street or the family in which we live, and we are doubtful whether we ever could. Surely, then, to speak of a science of all human associations is being over-ambitious almost to the point of megalomania?

There are one or two ways of meeting this objection, but, at this point, it will be wise to let it have full weight, for there is no point whatever in denying the extraordinary difficulties experienced by the subject in dealing satisfactorily with its subject-matter. Indeed, it is best to realise these difficulties to the full and never to lose sight of them. In this sense, modesty is always the only correct attitude However, two points may be made which are themselves of a common-sense nature and which serve at least to allay our first fears arising from what seems a very real and fundamental misgiving.

The first point is very simple and clear. The definition of the 'universe of discourse', the 'range of subject-matter', dealt with by a science does not rest upon the question as to whether one individual is capable of comprehending it all. The definition is that of the total distinctive area of the subject covered. Within this area of course, and of necessity, individuals will have to specialise. All sociologists can agree about the entire theoretical scope of their subject though each of them will satisfied to devote his attention and efforts to that particular set of problems which interests him.

The statement that biology is a science of 'all forms of organic life' does not fill us with an immediate sense of the impossibility of comprehending all the many living species in nature, for we know well enough that, though all biologists have a commonly shared outline of the nature, boundaries, and methods of the whole subject, they each of them concentrate upon those problems which interest them. All of them may share the general classification of species, but within that classification they will concentrate upon, let us say, the 'arthropods', or, like Fabre, on the detailed study of insects, or even upon very specific responses which one species may have to a very specific aspect of its 'habitat'. In exactly the same way, sociologists may share a general classificatory schema of the societies which have existed and now exist, but, within this context, they will each concentrate upon that society, that kind of society, or that aspect of society which interests them. Some may be interested in the development of various political constitutions in the Greek City States; some in the relation between morality and law, or religion and education, in an early period of Egyptian society; some in the relationship between myth and social and ecological control in an early period of Babylon; some in the changing nature of the institution of 'property' in twentieth century Britain; and so on. There is clearly, then, no problem here in terms of the sheer size and complexity of the subject-matter: for no-one would expect any one person to have a knowledgeable grasp of the whole. The definition of a subject does not depend upon that.

The second point need be reiterated only briefly here, though it will be seen to be of considerable importance later. It is simply that a clear recognition of our limitations may be the very firmest foundation for attaining clearly such a degree of certainty in our knowledge as is possible. Knowledge of our shortcomings is of positive value. It can be liberating in our studies, and can secure accuracy by ruling out those efforts which are shown to be beyond the bounds of possibility and leading us to concentrate upon sharpening, as clearly as we can, our methods of studying that which lies within them.

(b) *Confusion about the relations between sociology and the other social sciences*

A second source of misgiving in our common-sense (whether justified or not) is that, though all that has been said concerning the necessity of sociology seems plausible, we are still doubtful about its claims for one particular reason. The impression we are given is that there are already many social sciences which study just the sort of questions which we have raised. Political science studies forms of government and other political associations. Economics studies the market-relationships of men in the production and distribution of wealth. Criminology studies the 'deviant' behaviour of men in society and those institutions which detect, and punish, or treat it. Jurisprudence studies the systems of law in human societies. History studies the ongoing nature of social change and development in the way we have been speaking of it. What, then, remains for sociology to do? Is it not the case that all social institutions and all social problems are already studied by special sciences and that therefore sociology, as a how science of society seems not only unnecessary, but also unnecessarily confusing?

Here, again, we will leave this impression and misgiving of common-sense to have its full weight until we come to deal with it later. It is obviously a question to which we must give a careful and satisfactory answer.

Meanwhile, having made clear those assumptions and questions of common-sense which are at the root of sociology as a science, we can now clarify the science which has developed from them.

Sociology, however, has its roots not only in common-sense, but also in those subject which, before its own foundation, had speculated about the nature and problems of man and society. In order to be aware of the distinctive nature and contribution of sociology itself, it is obviously necessary to have a perspective and estimation of those kinds of theories which had been elaborated and adopted by men before sociology arose.

2

EARLY SOCIAL THEORIES

If sociology is so strongly rooted in our common-sense assumptions and in the practical needs and inquisitiveness of our nature, it would be very surprising, indeed inexplicable, if we were to find that theories of a sociological nature had emerged only in the modern world. In fact, there have been 'theories' of man and society almost as long as man has existed, though some of these, in the form of early, simple myths, must have been very rudimentary indeed, differing in character very considerably from what we would now call a 'scientific' theory. Even so, in the simplest myths that we know, some of the same ingredients are there: the effort to achieve a total picture of man's situation in the world, in the context of which both 'society' and 'individual' possess meaning and significance.

It is obviously impossible to give an account of all of the kinds of social theories which preceded scientific sociology, but it is worthwhile to attempt a brief assessment of their nature and the achievements which they embody, and to see them in some perspective, for several reasons which are very important.

The first is, that it is only if we have some such perspective on the nature and development of human thought and speculation on social matters in other times, and in other social conditions, that we shall be able to appreciate the significance of the emergence of sociology proper—as a science of society, in the modern industrial world. For though sociology did not spring to birth by some isolated process of special creation, but was rooted in these earlier traditions of thought and feeling, it is different from them in very important ways - which we must understand as clearly as possible.

Secondly, it is wise to remember continually that sociology is not just a modern innovation, a twentieth century expertise, but the culmination of a broad, perennial concern with fundamental questions concerning the nature and destiny of man. Sociology severs its connections with these earlier roots only at its peril: at the risk of dehumanising itself and becoming nothing more than a set of professional techniques (of investigation and action) which many people are already beginning to fear; a set of techniques for salesmen, market researchers, social workers, and the like, whose intellectual horizons are parochially confined to a specific utilitarian end.

Thirdly, bearing in mind that many early social theories were philosophical speculations as distinct from scientific theories, it is worthwhile to remind ourselves that these are not as clearly and distinctly separable as we are now-a-days inclined to suppose. 'Philosophy' was a love of knowledge, just as 'science' is now thought to be. The early Greek philosophers laid great stress on the fact that their subject sought to distinguish 'knowledge' from mere 'opinion' or 'belief'. It was certainly not only knowledge of material matters of fact which they sought, but of other questions and other dimensions of human experience also, such as the nature of mathematical 'forms' or of moral 'ideals', and this raises important questions for us.

Clearly, on the one hand, knowledge entails more than the particular kind of knowledge which science itself attains. In this sense science is simply one kind of knowledge: that which permits of empirical testing. It is the most simple category of knowledge within the wider subject of philosophy. And it may well be that, in our own time, we are in danger of interpreting 'science' itself too narrowly, in such a way as to impoverish both it and ourselves by losing sight of its place within the wider context of philosophy, or indeed even denying that there is such a wider context. It may be that, in general, we are tending to lose sight of the imaginative range of 'science' and coming to think of it - falsely - in narrow terms of utilitarian technology.

There is an important sense in which the very nature and limits of 'science' depend, themselves, upon philosophical clarification, and that, without this, there is a real danger that 'science' might be misunderstood and impoverished, even among practising scientists themselves. There is a danger that science might even come to be taught as a practical technology only. In short, science rests, essentially, within a context of philosophy, and to pluck it from this context and to consider and practise it independently of it, is highly questionable. This is true of all sciences - including sociology.

But also, philosophy aside, even religious myth and the works of art and literature have their own oblique ways of evoking our appreciation of truths of the human situation which are additional to, and which are not quite like, the more mensurable propositions of science. It may be that it is we (i.e. scientists) who are in danger of becoming the philistines in this quest for 'truth'. It may be that we are blinding ourselves to the wider exploration of truth by wearing only special spectacles of science, which, of course, have their own uses for enhancing our vision in certain directions, but which should, perhaps, be taken off, or replaced by others, for different kinds of view.

It must be remembered, too, that many of these earlier theories were concerned to make as clear as possible not only the facts of human nature and society, but also the ethical basis of what human conduct ought to be. They were, that is, theories including ethical and 'normative' considerations. This also raises questions, some very profound indeed, which make it always important to see modern sociology in the context of its intellectual forebears.

A first question is whether there really is the clear distinction between the study of ethical principles and the study of matters of fact that many modern scholars now assume. Is there really a fundamental cleavage between studying what is, and what ought to be? It is common practice to insist that this is so. But is it? Might not our enquiry into the implications of our compelling experiences of moral obligation lead us to uncover moral ideals which, in fact, exist? Are not ethical principles a species of 'fact'? Do moral ideals not exist? Many would dismiss this question as trivial - but this may simply be a matter of their unreflective dogmatism concerning what we may accept as 'categories' of 'existence'. They may simply be a lot of Dr. Johnson's kicking posts in the street, and deluding themselves that this is an argument.

It may be, for example, that, in witnessing the factual struggle for the equal rights of negroes in the United States; the factual struggle against what is considered to be injustice; we can discover, by careful, analytical thought that certain principles of equality in political citizenship, and of impartiality in the making and treatment of claims in society, are essential ingredients in the idea of justice. Now this may well be a fact which must be taken into account in exploring certain kinds of social conflict. And I am not saying only that this may be an operative ideal which is at work (as a 'norm' or 'convention') in a particular society, but that, in fact, it may be a universal feature of the ideal of justice and, therefore, that none of the struggles of men against arbitrary power in any society may permit of explanation or understanding without taking it into account. It may be impossible to explain the facts of social conflict, without a clear knowledge of the facts of the ethical entailments of the feelings of 'injustice' among subjected groups, but the uncovering of these facts is a matter of reflective philosophy rather than of empirical science. The philosophical understanding of 'what ought to be' is a necessary element in the scientific explanation of 'what is'. It is, therefore, at least possible that early philosophers were right in thinking that ethical concepts were a necessary part of social explanation and, if this is true, then philosophy continues to be a necessary part of the social scientist's equipment.

Furthermore, it may also be, as early philosophers thought, that knowledge is not only a matter of intellectual apprehension, but carries with it certain kinds of commitment and obligation : of maintaining qualities of integrity; of seeking and sustaining truth; of insisting upon the freedom and the procedures of enquiry necessary for this; even, perhaps, of denying the rightness of certain kinds of action because they rest upon falsehood. It may be, then, that sociological theory, and any other scientific theory, may carry with it more connotations of an ethical kind than we are ready to admit, and than appears to be the case on its 'scientific' surface.

Whatever we may think about these matters, it is certain that we should be wise to understand as fully as we can what the philosophers and other early social theorists actually said before shrugging off their systems of thought, and a fashionable stereotype of the nature of their activity, too easily.

If this is thought to be outlandishly unorthodox in the present-day context of thought in social science, it might be well to bear two points in mind.

Firstly, all sociologists until the last few decades (and I believe the same could be said of the greater number of sociologists today) have been concerned with sociology because of their ethical concerns. They have been humanists first, and sociologists second, or, to put it minimally, their sociology has been one part of a much wider concern to understand the human situation and to act in relation to it.

Secondly, we might stop to ask ourselves why, now-a-days, we are sceptical about ethical principles as such, but why, as scholars, we insist upon a commitment to truth in scientific inquiry before everything. There is nothing in science itself to oblige us to do so, unless we regard the persuit of truth in science itself as an ethical matter. And this, in fact, is what we do.

Why do we take the ideal of scientific integrity itself for granted, as being something beyond question, whilst thinking of all other moral ideals as being 'relative' in some sense, and always a potential source of 'bias' in our scientific activity? Without wishing to be too dialectical, might it not be possible that the scientific insistence upon the pursuit of truth by certain procedures alone, is itself a 'bias' in intellectual matters?

It seems to me, at any rate, that we are in great danger of rushing into a very glib and superficial conception of what sociology is aiming at, and what its nature is, if we do not have a good understanding of the insights of earlier systems, of myth, religion, and philosophy. Later, I hope to show that sociology is, quite fundamentally, a humanistic and ethical activity, and must falsify its nature and be a social danger in consequence if it tries to avoid or deny such a role.

I think this consideration so important as to be stated very strongly indeed. I believe it to be true that many modern approaches to social science, because they do not properly appreciate this necessary and continuing philosophical context, are much more superficial than the philosophers whom they have supposedly superseded. There is more knowledge of human nature and human society in a few pages of Plato, or Hobbes, or Spinoza, or Hume or even of Montaigne, than in whole volumes of modern social science. And frequently it is those who pride themselves on their 'scientific advancement' who are least informed about these theories of the past. In my view 'scientism', and a glib assumption of its 'modernity' and 'superiority', is one of the very greatest dangers facing our subject; one of which we have continually to be aware.

A further point of great importance is that a study of these earlier theories of society shows - whether they were myths, religions, political theories, or philosophies of history - that they were not only theories intellectually held by scholars or priests, but were also important ideologies of the societies in which they existed; focusing the feelings and commitment of entire communities upon certain values and certain ends. The point here is this : though sociological theory now strives towards the achievement of a scientific basis, it cannot, even if successful in this, avoid this same kind of ideological role in our own time. Modern sociological theory has emerged partly because these earlier theories of society have been seen to fail. Its own birth, its own nature, are rooted in criticisms of them. It therefore becomes an important basis, or at least a necessary part of whatever ideology modern man adopts. Modern man may, as Jung put it, be 'in search of a soul', but he is also 'in search of a sociological theory' appropriate to his own time and conditions, and perhaps the two are more closely linked than appears at first sight.

Sociological theory provides a picture of man's place in the world as much as any other theory in the world ever did. This is its absorbing interest; this is its humane value; quite apart from its scientific pretensions - necessary and of fundamental importance though these are. In sociological theory all earlier ways of thinking about man's history, moral and political philosophy, biology, psychology, religion, come to be critically assessed and fused. Sociology is the new focal subject, the new 'orientating' subject of human enquiry in the twentieth century. And this is not the grandiose claim that it must appear, but is no more than a working out of what was already foreshadowed by earlier theorists and clearly envisaged, for example, by David Hume and John Stuart Mill.

In order to provide, though briefly, a perspective of the subjects within which, and out of which, sociology took shape, I propose to discuss them under four headings: (1) Religion, (2) Moral and Political Philosophy, (3) Philosophy of History, (4) Natural Science and Epistemology. In a final section (5) we can then outline the particular needs which led to the emergence of sociology proper - which drew critically from all these subjects and then created something going beyond them.

A. RELIGIOUS THEORIES

The myths and religious systems which preceded scientific sociology, and which continue to exist side by side with it, are not only theories concerning man's spiritual relationship with God or with some kind of supreme spiritual reality. They are also theories about the nature of man and society in the context of the natural (as well as the 'supernatural') world. No matter how 'transcendental' some of these theories become with regard to their ideas of 'God' or the divine ground of reality, they always contain theories about the actual nature of man, and his place in both the natural world and in society. And they frequently lay down, in addition, rules of a social and moral, as well as of a spiritual kind, which man ought to observe. It is not too much to say that mythical and religious systems of doctrine, feelings, and ritual, were mans' earliest ways of achieving a systematic picture of the nature of things, including himself, and that critical theology, philosophy and science have grown out of these roots.

Sociology has a clear line of descent from them, and is clearly relevant to them. In some ways it remains like them - though it has considerably refined the mature of its theories and its methods. It tends to replace them - since it emerges because of their inadequacy, and, in developing, increasingly demonstrates their inadequacy. And it continually encounters resistance from them since its own way of establishing knowledge, as well as the substantive knowledge it produces, is frequently in sharp conflict with those which they employ and insist upon.

The Simpler Societies

The simpler (non-literate) societies always have systems of myths built about those aspects of their environmental setting which are of supreme importance to them. Most myths, indeed, deal with both the ecological and the social problems which a society experiences.

One good example is sufficient for our purpose.

The Ihalmiut, a group of Eskimoes living in the Canadian Barrens, were almost entirely dependent for their survival upon the seasonal migration of the deer. All the things of importance in their life - their dwellings, clothes, tools, weapons, food - were derived in some way or other from the deer. And we find that their 'theory' of creation centred about the deer. The myth, in very simple form, was this.

Kaila - 'He who is Thunder in grey skies' - prepared the land, created hare and ptarmigan, and then made man and woman. Everything was very still in darkness. The hunters could not see and were hungry, so the woman cried to Kaila for help. Kaila then created fire and it was the woman's task to keep the fire alive. But soon the hare and ptarmigan grew wary of man and his torch of fire, and he again suffered hunger. Again the woman cried to Kaila for help, and he told her to dig a great hole in the ground. Then he told her to make a rope of the sinews of the hare, a hook from the wing bones of the ptarmigan, and see what she could draw from the hole. In succession she gradually caught all the beasts of the earth - but she was not satisfied with them and freed them to multiply over the land. 'She had still', says the story, 'not caught' the one thing which she sought.'

> 'We do not know how long she lingered by the hole, for then there was no winter and no summer, no day or night. But in the end there came a great jerk on the line so that it was almost torn from the woman's hands. The man sprang to help her and together they pulled the sinew

> rope out of the pit. It was a mighty struggle, and yet man and his woman triumphed and so at last beheld the antlered crown of Tuktu - first of all the deer!
>
> The woman cried out with joy and flung her hook away, and the deep hole closed up and vanished. Then the woman spoke to the first deer, saying:
>
> 'Go out over the land and become as many as all other things which live in water, land or air - for it is you and your kind who will feed me and my children and my children's children for all time that there is yet to come.'
>
> The first deer heard, and heeded what the woman said, and so it came about that there were many deer....'

It is a very simple 'theory' which gave meaning to the entire social and individual mode of life of this people struggling in their exceptionally harsh environment and being entirely dependent upon a few natural resources. There were, of course, many other attendant theories in their entire system of myths, but it can be seen, from this central example, how the 'story' links all the main social problems (darkness; cold - and fire; hunger - and food) with a clear picture of man's place in the world of nature as he experienced it.

These elements of myth seem quite unbelievable, simple-minded, even bizarre to our (supposedly) more sophisticated minds. But, as the man who recorded these myths put it:

> 'It must be remembered that the People of the Deer are of their world and know nothing of us and ours, and so what seems like gross unreality to us can remain unassailably real to them. Their beliefs are a product of centuries, and they fit the needs of their life and the shape of the land they live in. They believe! That is the point.'

The myths and doctrines of more complex literate societies were not greatly different in their main components (they still dealt with social functions and ecological problems) though more elaborate in their details.

Ancient Egypt

In ancient Egypt, for example, the Isis and Osiris myth reflected the physical characteristics of the Nile Valley, and signified the ultimate political union of Upper Egypt and Lower (Delta)

Egypt as well as the attendant fusion of all the thousands of lesser deities of Egypt into one pantheon of gods at the head of which was Pharaoh - the one, living, visible, divine authority of the unified society, indeed of the 'world' - in whom ecclecsiastical, military, political and legal authority were all fused.

Within this pantheon most gods were responsible for some social function. SAFEKHT, for example was the goddess of writing; ANUBIS - the guardian of the cemetery; NEIT - the goddess of hunting, always depicted holding bows and arrows. The over-all myth therefore vested all the aspects of social organisation with a divine meaning and sanction, indeed a divine supervision.

The idea which had emerged of the judgment of men at death, and of a life after death, also entailed a theory about the nature of the human soul. A man was thought to consist of three elements : his physical body; 'Ba'- depicted as a human-headed bird whose seat was the 'heart' or abdomen, which could fly from the body, but returned to it for its pleasures; and 'Ka' - the mental aspects of personality, the identifiable intelligent consciousness of the personality itself (a 'double' of the personality), which was something of a spectator or onlooker in its appreciation of the pleasure of life. And the tomb arrangements in ancient Egypt were such as to take account of all these features. Passages were provided so that 'Ba' could revisit the body. A life-like statue was placed in the tomb so that 'Ka' could take up its residence there and see the things which had given it pleasure in life. And, of course, all this necessitated the preservation of the body itself; and even this emphasis upon the physical preservation of the body seems to have been an outcome of 'ecological factors', namely the preservative qualities of the sand of Egypt.

Breasted, for example, wrote:

> 'Experience in the land of Egypt has led me to believe that the insistent faith in the hereafter was greatly favoured and influenced by the fact that the conditions of soil and climate resulted in such a remarkable preservation of the human body as may be found under natural conditions nowhere else in the world. In going up to the daily task on

> some neighbouring temple in Nubia, I was not infrequently obliged to pass through the corner of a cemetery, where the feet of a dead man, buried in a shallow grave, were not covered and extended directly across my path. They were precisely like the rough and calloused feet of the workmen of our excavations. How old the grave was I do not know, but anyone familiar with the cemeteries of Egypt, ancient and modern, has found numerous bodies or portions of bodies indefinitely old which seemed about as well preserved as those of the living . . . The surprisingly perfect state of preservation in which the Egyptian found his ancestors whenever the digging of a new grave disclosed them, must have greatly stimulated his belief in their continued existence, and often aroused his imagination to more detailed pictures of the realm and the life of the mysteriously departed.'

The myths of Egypt, therefore, reflected the physical conditions of the life of the people and provided theories about the unity of society, the importance of many social functions, and the nature of the individual soul in life and in death. They included also a system of laws, and certain moral directives, which defined the nature and requirements of social institutions and laid down rules for the regulation of social behaviour.

As a matter of interest a brief example of such moral rules might be given from the Egyptian 'Book of the Dead' which contains sets of 'negative confessions' by which the individual declared his innocence. According to Sir Flinders Petrie, these were arranged in sets of five, to facilitate learning by finger-counting. The rules are amusing in that they indicate what people might be prone to do in certain areas of social life and conduct, and I have selected illustrations of two or three of them.

Religious Obligations

(1) I have not lessened the bread offerings in the temples.
(2) I have not ravaged the cakes of the Gods.
(3) I have not carried off the bread of the glorious dead.
(4) I have not cohabited in the temenos of the God of my city.
(5) I have not defiled myself in the temenos of the God of my city.

Commercial Honesty

(1) I have not lessened the corn measure.
(2) I have not lessened the palm.
(3) I have not deceived in the fields.
(4) I have not added to the weight of the balance.
(5) I have not made poorer by means of the plummet of the balance.

Other rules which indicate the importance of social and ecological factors were :

I have not turned back water in its season, nor divided by a dam at running water.

I have not driven away cattle which were on their pasture.

I have not netted birds of the records of the Gods.

Social and moral regulations obviously found a clear place in these religious 'theories'.

Ancient Babylon

The same was true of ancient Babylon. Amongst a people whose chief ecological problem was that of extending the boundaries of fertile land, developing and maintaining a reliable system of irrigation, keeping control over the artificially canalised waters, and whose chief disaster was that of flood, their myth of creation was very appropriate.

It was APSU—the god of fresh water, and TIAMAT - the dragon of unbounded salt-water (chaos), the earliest divine forces of the world, who first created a number of lesser gods. These lesser gods, however, began trying to bring order into things. They tried to canalise the fresh water and to drive back the salt-water by extending the land. This interference irritated and then angered APSU and TIAMAT, and they therefore decided to destroy them in order to restore their earlier and untrammelled peace. But the lesser gods rebelled, and engaged in battle with them. One among them - Marduk - was elected chief, and he fought TIAMAT in battle and defeated her. He then 'split her like a flat fish into two halves'. Of one half he made the canopy which holds back the water above the heavens. With the other he covered the waters which lie under the earth.

Then, within this firmament, he fixed the stars, and then created plant life, animals, and, finally, man.

'My blood will I take,' said Marduk, 'and bone will I fashion.

I shall create man who shall inherit the earth.'

It will be seen that in this story of creation - which was achieved in an orderly sequence of six days followed by rest on the seventh - Marduk, the God of creation, was on the side of man. It was he who had defeated the forces making for chaos, and had created an order of the elements of the world within which man could live in security and peace.

In this society, too, we find the myth of the Flood - clearly stemming from the Babylonian experiences of the flooded river deltas. It was not, in this case, however, Noah who built his ark of so many cubits high, so many cubits wide, so many cubits long, but the Babylonian figure—UTNAPISHTIM.

The myth is almost exactly the same as the Judaistic myth of Noah with which we are familiar, and not surprisingly, since the latter seems to be a later version of it.

Again remembering the relation of the Isis and Osiris myth to the political union of Upper and Lower Egypt, it is interesting to notice that this unification of myths occurred at a time when Hammurabi was succeeding in consolidating the earlier Sumerian cities into the unified civilisation of Babylon which then endured for some twenty centuries. And, again, we find that lesser deities were now absorbed or combined into an all-embracing pantheon of the gods.

The Greek City States

The ancient Greeks had their pantheon of gods, too, and their many and beautiful myths. But the Greeks of course, were invading conquerors, and when the Olympian pantheon came to be consolidated, the gods, though certainly possessing social functions, were by no means altogether suited to the settled life of the City State which ensued.

As Gilbert Murray put it:

> 'It is a canon of religious study that all gods reflect the social state, past of present, of their worshippers. From this point of view what appearance do the Olympians of Homer make? What are they there for? What do they do, and what are their relations to one another?

> The gods of most nations claim to have created the world. The Olympians make no such claim. The most they ever did was to conquer it . . . And when they have conquered their kingdoms, what do they do? Do they attend to the government? Do they promote agriculture? Do they practise trades and industries? Not a bit of it. Why should they do any honest work? They find it easier to live on the revenue and blast with thunderbolts the people who do not pay. They are conquering chieftains, royal buccaneers. They fight, and feast, and play, and make music; they drink deep, and roar with laugher at the lame smith who waits on them. They are never afraid, except of their own king. They never tell lies except in love and war.'

It was because of this mythical presentation of the gods as superhuman beings whose vices were as strongly exaggerated as their virtues that philosophers like Xenophanes and Plato began to criticise such 'religious and mythical theories' and to offer what they thought were better theories in terms of qualities of human excellence and reason. Hitherto, theories of God, nature and man had reflected and fitted society, but from this point of reflection onwards, men began, at least to some degree, to 'reconstruct' the gods they believed in, in the image of their own moral, intellectual and aesthetic aspirations. They could not accept that what was divine was of a lower standard of excellence than that of which man himself was aware. They made the Gods in their own image. And as their knowledge improved, so the picture of the Gods improved. It was, in part, in terms of this dissatisfaction with myth and religion that critical philosophy began. Firmer foundations were now sought for theories of man and society.

Examples of these same kinds of mythical and religious theories could be drawn from the history of every society.

Japan

In Japan, the creation myth began with the two fundamental principles in Nature: Male and Female; IZANAGI and IZANAMI respectively. It was they who created the Japanese Islands and their people. The eight chief islands stemmed from IZANAMI's womb. When IZANAMI died and went to the underworld, IZANAGI followed her. But she was in a state of decomposition and warned him against seeing her. But he broke in, saw her, and was polluted. He then rushed back to the earth to cleanse and purify himself. In doing so, he created other gods. The filth cast from one eye became AMATERASU - goddess of sun. That from the other eye became TSUKI-YOMI - the moon god. That from his nostrils became the storm god, and so on. In this way all the Japanese deities were brought into relationship with each other in, again, one pantheon.

Men, as usual, however were unruly. Because of their disorder, AMATERASU sent her grandson, NI-NI-GI, to establish a firm government of the islands. The offspring of NI-NI-GI were the Japanese Emperors. All the leading families of Japan traced their descent from some deity or other, and every aspect of nature came to be represented as a deity. The system of myth, once again, served to unify nature and society.

But what is of greater interest is that this mythical unification seems to rest, again, upon a necessary historical imposition of unity. The Japanese people are not the native inhabitants of their islands, but initially came from the Asiatic mainland and from some Pacific islands. Early Japanese society appears to have been a loose association of tribes, having three chief centres with three chief gods: the Gods of the Sea, the Gods of the Stars, and the Sun Goddess. The myth we have briefly described represents the conquest of one of these tribes - the YAMATO - over the others, and the fusion of all the gods into one unified myth with the sun Goddess as the supreme deity.

China

The religion of China is, similarly, most impressive in the entire interrelated order of nature, society, and the propriety of individual life and conduct, which it presents.

China has, for millennia, been an agrarian civilisation. Its traditional religion - in both doctrine and ritual - rested upon a conception of the Order of Nature. The entire universe, the heavens, and the dependent nature of the world, were characterised by order, regularity, harmony, majesty. All was governed by a law of order in nature. Two conflicting but co-operative principles were fundamentally at work: the male and female principles; but a certain pre-ordained way of creative development was entailed in these forces of nature, which led to harmony, propriety and beauty in its pattern. Man and his society were part of the whole order of nature, and the major institutions of society were there to make the full harmony of human relationships possible.

The Emperor was the father and representative of the people who carried out ceremonials on their behalf and achieved order in relation to Heaven. The continued order of society depended upon his diligence and devotion. From the Emperor down to the lowllest peasant, the family was the important group within which good human relationships were realised and sustained, and the family included not only the living family group, but also the continuous line of ancestors. There was a living interdependence in the family and society between the dead and the living. The whole of existing society, and the whole of its history, was thus permeated by filial piety, and in Confucianism, which is a reflective systematisation of traditional beliefs, this family regulation became the means of achieving and sustaining several specific sets of relationships, with their attendant qualities, which were thought to be of fundamental importance for the natural harmonious fulfilment of both social and individual life.

There were five such relationships and sets of qualities:

(1) Between Ruler and Subject. (The Ruler should possess the qualities of benevolence, care and responsibility, and the subjects that of loyalty.)

(2) Between Father and Son. (The Father should possess kindness and care, and the son filial piety.)

(3) Between Husband and Wife. (The Husband should observe righteous behaviour and the Wife obedience.)

(4) Between the Oldest and the Younger Brothers. (The Oldest brother should possess gentility, the younger brothers humility and respect), and

(5) Between the Elders and the Young in general. (The aged should have a humane and tolerant consideration for the young, and the young should show deference to the old.)

In this system of doctrine and morality there was clearly a theory of nature, society and man, and a theory about those social institutions which were considered essential for achieving the natural order and fulfilment of individual life in society, and for the engendering and development in individuals of those qualities of character which were necessary in order continuously to achieve these ends. Character was seen as the chief aim of government and education, and Confucius was very meticulous and subtle in working this out; showing how the quality of order of the state and the quality of order of the individual soul were inextricably linked with each other. In this he was remarkably similar to Plato. Here, for example, is what he said about the necessity for clarity of language and the importance of knowledge.

When asked what his first task would be in undertaking the control of a prince's administration, he replied: 'The one thing needed is the rectification of names.' For, he argued, without care over words and names, education and ritual would be disordered, laws would not be just, and people would not know what to expect in relation to each other. Clarity and truth were a basic necessity for the right ordering of society.

'The rectification of names,' one of his followers elaborated, 'consists in making real relationships and duties and institutions conform as far as possible to their ideal meanings . . . When this intellectual reoraganisation is at last effected, the ideal social order will come as night follows day - a social order where, just as a circle is a circle and a square is square so every prince is princely, every official is faithful, every father is fatherly, and every child is filially pious'.

And in the 'Great Learning' it was put like this:

> 'The ancients (i.e. the ancient kinds) who wished to cause their virtue to shine forth first ordered well their own states. Wishing to order well their states, they first regulated their families. Wishing to regulate their families, they first cultivated their persons. Wishing to cultivate their persons, they first rectified their hearts. Wishing to rectify their hearts, they first sought to be sincere in their thoughts. Wishing to be sincere in their thoughts, they first extended to the utmost their knowledge. Such extension of knowledge lay in the investigation of things. Things being investigated, their knowledge became complete. Their knowledge being complete, their thoughts were sincere. Their thoughts being sincere, their hearts were then rectified. Their hearts

> being rectified, their persons were cultivated. Their persons being cultivated, their families were regulated. Their families being regulated, their states were rightly governed. Their states being rightly governed, the whole kingdom was made tranquil and happy.'

Clearly, the teaching of Confucius was not only a theory of nature, society and the individual; it contained also an appropriate theory of education.

Summary: The Nature and Elements of Religious Theories

Many other examples of mythical and religious theories could be given, but we have seen enough for our own particular purposes. Though we have been able to describe them only briefly, it is quite clear that all these 'theories' possessed certain definite characteristics.

(1) They were appropriate to the conditions and problems experienced in the societies in which they existed.
(2) They were pragmatically based. They were shaped to deal with concrete problems.
(3) They were empirically based in the sense that they rested upon the facts - both evident and underlying - of the world and society as far as they were known.
(4) They included a justification, almost a sanctification, of the order of society as it existed.
(5) They included an analysis of the nature of social institutions and their functions.
(6) In their proposals for conduct they offered an analysis of the psychology of the individual in relation to the insititution of society. They saw the one and the other as being, at least to some extent, interdependent. In short, these theories all presented a rudimentary analysis of:
    (a) the institutional framework of society,
    (b) the psychology of the individual, and
    (c) 'social' psychology - the influence of institutions upon individuals, and vice versa.

But two quite clear and considerable points must be made before leaving these kinds of theories.

The first is - that though we may readily concede that some of these myths contain valuable insights into human nature, and have much continuing interest and value - in our modern society, characterised not by a simple natural setting or a stable tradition resting upon rural and agrarian conditions, but by a complexity of industrial technology resting upon rigorous scientific methods for the establishment of knowledge, they cannot be retained. They are no longer adequate. Their basic assumptions concerning nature, and the origins of man and society are almost entirely without foundation. But again, to put the matter only minimally, they are couched in terms which no longer have significant meaning for us. The analysis of society and of human nature which they offer are of little value in relation to our own complexities. Their propositions do not approach the most elementary requirements of scientific exactitude. They cannot be accepted. We may like them - as we like fairy stories, or allegories, or any symbolic presentation of stories and ideas which illuminates some aspects of our nature; but we must reject them in the same way. They cannot help us in our own task of dealing with our own situation within the context of our own required standards of knowledge. And when I say we - I mean mankind throughout the world in the modern world; all who have confronted and experienced the new conditions of scientific, technological and industrial change during the past three human life-times or so.

No doubt this will be fairly generally agreed, since I have purposely selected religions which people commonly attribute to the 'pre-historic' or the 'ancient' world.

But the second point of the very greatest importance is this. The world is still, in the second half of the twentieth century, influenced very considerably by inadequate 'theories' of this kind; indeed some parts of the world are dominated by them. All the religions of the world - Hinduism, Islam, Buddhism, Christianity - offer a set of myths of this kind. In a world in which the requirements of scientific knowledge form the basis of their every practical and social activity, the minds of millions of men and women are still in great part immersed in 'theories' of this kind.

Clearly, then, in describing these kinds of 'early social theories' we are not dealing, by any means, with something remote from, and irrelevant to, our own time. These 'early theories' are still with us. They remain very powerful. We have still not struggled out of the trappings of these intellectual infancies. But in struggling to replace these 'outworn dreams of a time outworn' with more accurate and satisfactory theories of man and society, sociology must inevitably lead to some new ideological position for mankind - even if this is only the recognition, from now onwards, of the impossiblitity of a unified, collective ideology. Some ideological position must, necessarily, follow in its train. In these struggles between 'old' theories and 'new', and in our confused considerations of the nature, the place, the worth, and the importance to be attached to each, lie many of our present-day dilemmas. And, indeed, we cannot assume that, having found certain 'theories' insufficient, we can succeed in putting something better in their place. We face very great and grave problems here.

B. MORAL AND POLITICAL PHILOSOPHY

We have seen that among the early Greeks most conspicuously, a criticism of the 'theories' of myth and religion took place at a certain point in their history. The same thing happened in other societies, too. Confucianism was an outcome of critical reflection upon the earlier traditional elements of Chinese religion. Brahminic Hinduism (let alone later philosophical schools) was an outcome of long reflection upon the earlier Vedic Hinduism. Similarly, the founded religions of Buddhism and Jainism were the outcome of criticisms of Brahminic Hinduism. Zoroastrianism arose from a criticism of the traditional religion of Persia. And many other examples could be given. Religion changed by reflection. Myth gave way to philosophy. Theories of nature, society and man, both of a factual and normative kind, came to be worked out in terms of reflection and a critical analysis of experience. Some mode of explanation other and more reliable than that of religious doctrine came to be required.

The richest source of such speculative theories is undoubtedly the long argument of moral and political philosophy which developed throughout the history of Western Europe, stemming roughly from the time and the personality of

Socrates, and the important philosophers - such as Plato and Aristotle - who immediately followed him. The thought and observation, the critical analysis of experience, and the systematic deduction embodied in the elaboration of these theories are such as to compel the utmost admiration. In some respects it is doubtful, even now, whether we have advanced beyond them. What is certain is that one of the best corrections to any naive 'scientism' is a thorough study of these early philosophers.

Theories of the Greek City State

The first theories of man in society stated in general terms (i.e. in terms of analytical and critical philosophy) appeared in the context of the Greek City States. It is worthwhile to ask why this was, and what factors might have been involved, because an awareness of these factors throws much light upon the relationship between the actual experience of the Greeks and the theories themselves. Some factors, at least, are quite definite and clear.

The Greek City States consisted of populations which were, relatively speaking, so small and self-sufficient that their members had little difficulty in knowing each other, in being familiar with each other in reasonably personal terms. As in an English village or a moderately sized city, many people would know each other as persons, or, even failing this, they would know each other as members of certain families. There was a 'familial' sense of belonging to the community. Also, each city state was politically independent. It could support itself economically and defend itself from outside attack, and in large part this was due to the facts of local geography. The territory of each community was usually bounded by mountain ranges on two sides and the sea on the third. This made for ease of military protection. But there were also very considerable differences of altitude in each of these small territories and therefore very differing degrees of climate and kinds of soil. Conditions varied from sub-tropical to alpine, and from pastoral to forested kinds of vegetation. This made possible a wide range of products. Such a circumscribed territory with such a small population living within it, made for a centrally organised communal life in which all the people shared, and in which all participated as individuals.

The central ordering of communal affairs took place about the 'polis' - literally, the most convenient central point of the whole area, and usually an up-raised place from which the entire are of the state could actually be seen. Professor Kitto translates the terms 'polis' as 'central rock' or 'stronghold', and upon this centre was focused the military, commercial, religious, 'political' life of the community, so that it sometimes developed into a town. Kitto says that because of this the terms 'city state' is not a particularly good translation of 'polis'. A better conception is simply that of a community living in its own limited territory and coming to the central stronghold to discuss and manage its affairs; though it should be emphasised, however, that these 'City States' were deliberately and ceremonially founded and therefore had, from the beginning, a strongly symbolised central unity. This intimacy of involvement of the Greeks as individuals and families in their social life accounts for many things, as for example, the extreme extent of their democratic citizenship under some circumstances. Not all political constitutions, by any means, were democratic, but, when they were so, all citizens had the same equal status, and all participated in legislative and judicial duties. Indeed, sometimes the representatives of tribes to the central councils or to the courts were arrived at by 'lottery'; so that it was quite possible for a poor man of lowly origins to sit in judgment upon the rich. The Greek citizens, very positively therefore, came to look upon the central political business of their community quite literally as 'their own' business.

Another important fact was that the 'polis' was founded upon blood-relations. It was a formally founded extension of earlier clans and tribes. Membership was a matter of being born into it. There was consequently, in this most profound sense of being a group of kinsfolk, an extended 'family' feeling about communal life. The Greeks never liked their 'own' business, their own personal and family concerns, to be taken out of their hands - even by benevolent tyrants from among their own number. They realised very well that the power of a second generation of tyrants was not necessarily as benevolent as the promises and good intentions of a first.

Greek life was therefore characterised by an intense, stubborn individuality among a number of people who were all fully and sensitively aware of their own desires and demands upon society, and their reciprocal tasks and duties in the community. They made continuous demands upon each other in a concrete, responsible way, as members of a family do, and one important outcome of this was that the Greek notion of 'goodness' or 'virtue' was therefore, also, always a very concrete thing; something definite and perfectly clear. A good man was reliable in his group, capable of good advice, courageous, intelligent, temperate, capable of sound judgment, impartial, honest, helpful to others, generous, and able to manage his affairs effectively and successfully. The Greeks' idea of virtue had nothing vague about it. They had a clear conception of personal goodness, of qualities of human excellence, which was clearly related to the achievement of a good and just society.

One other important and obvious aspect of this was that ethics was considered the same thing as politics. The life of the polis was the necessary context for the enjoyment of the good life on the part of each individual citizen. The polis gave him the necessary basis for, and the opportunity of achieving, a full, rich and responsible life. The serious debates, religious festivals, dramatic performances, were not highbrow entertainments but 'popular' activities; activities of the people. The Greeks were clear, concrete, mature in their personal and communal life and in their artistic and athletic activities, and were continuously accustomed in all their concerns to serious personal responsibilities. The city was a clear framework for the individual citizens's entire life. His moral conceptions, personal and social, were perfectly clear. He knew exactly where he stood in society, what values to approve and what objectives to aim for.

The Greeks were also, because of this, quite accustomed to what we would now call a planned society. That the members of a community should deliberate upon, and then plan, their social activities seemed to them a perfectly natural and correct thing to do. In politics, law, defence, in all public affairs, everyone played a responsible part, fulfilling his appropriate and clearly seen functions in society, and all these facts tend to suggest that the theories of the first critical philosophers - Socrates, Plato, Aristotle etc. - were not so much their own unique speculations as reflections upon the actual social practices of the Greek community. Before considering these ideas, however, one or two other matters should briefly be mentioned.

The Greek cities were, of course, not isolated, but in touch with each other. More important, however, they were also involved in communications - especially in trading relations - with the larger civilisation that existed round about them in the Mediterranean. This led to complexities of commercial, political, and military contacts with many different peoples and to a changing economic structure at home. In particular it led the Greeks to make quite detailed comparative observations of the customs of other peoples - Egyptians, Persians, and others - as in the accounts of Herodotus. But it also led to the growth of internal conflicts within the city states themselves: conflicts between the new commercial classes and the established agriculture aristocracies. Each city came to contain within itself 'a city of the rich and a city of the poor.'

Finally, a certain development of the political and philosophical life of these communities must be mentioned. With the growing complexity of public life and the diversity of social interests stemming from it, the struggle for power and influence among demagogues, and the pressures for social, economic and political reform, increased. In this context a new kind of tutor came into prominence, the *Sophists*. These men sceptically criticised all moral rules, all principles of justice and righteousness - discounting them as superficial conventions to be calculatedly complied with, rather than being natural in the sense of being deeply rooted in human nature and its needs in society, and requiring, therefore, full commitment and obligation. They taught, in short, how a person could become a successful man of the world. Their teaching was one of expediency and self-interest: how to understand affairs of the world in such a ways as to manipulate people in society successfully, in order to get your own ends. And in this teaching they drew the distinction between nature and convention; insisting that the latter (morality) was only man-made, and therefore 'relative' to those who possessed power, and therefore alterable. It was in direct opposition to this superficial doctrine of the Sophists as they so thought it, that Greek moral and political philosophers developed their own theories.

In connection with this new centrality of the philosophical investigation of human nature and morality, two or three things seem to have been of great importance.

Firstly, the mere existence of Socrates, as a person, seems to have had tremendous and vital influence upon the nature of this early philosophy. His character, his scepticism, his argumentativeness, seem to have stimulated not only enthusiasm, but also both affection and irritation, love and antagonism. Above all, his moral integrity and his intellectual tenacity in pursuing the peculiarly insistent demands of his conscience had a profound influence upon his contemporaries even though he seems to have done little but profess his ignorance about most matters, and - in arguing to demonstrate this - to have shown that most other people were a good deal more ignorant than he in fact, of course, Socrates, as we have noted, was stating the perennial human predicament - of having to exercise sound judgment whilst clearly recognising the horizons of our ignorance - and insisting that the recognition of ignorance was the beginning of wisdom.

Secondly, through Socrates and his arguments against the Sophists, the philosophical enquiries of the Greeks into the nature of the physical world were somehow orientated about the central importance of the study of human nature and moral ideals; an emphasis that was to continue throughout the history of Western philosopy. And thirdly, it is important to note again that the work of the philosophers who followed Socrates was direclty concerned to show that morality in society was rooted in the individual and social nature of man, and was not, in any specious sense, a matter only of convention.

In short, this led moral and political philosophy to become, at once a theory of the facts of human nature and human society, as well as a theory about the ideals in terms of which one could clarify what man and society ought to be.

One final point is worth making. Because of the smallness of scale of the city states and the intensity of their political life, personal ambition became a factor of tremendous importance. Tyrants could spring up quickly and dominate the entire community by their influence. A command of the art of rhetoric on the part of a demagogue could influence the minds of citizens to a marked and crucial degree. This therefore became an important social matter, and a supremely dangerous one. This point is of importance in indicating the urgency to the Greeks of the political and moral questions into which the philosophers looked. Again it is clear that the 'theories' of philosophy were not a matter only of intellectual interest, but also of compelling need.

The Theory of (427 BC - 347 BC)

The danger of tyranny was, to a considerable extent, the starting point for Plato's own theory. He was devastated by the execution of Socrates (the man he most loved and admired) at the hands of the court of Athens (the city he most loved and admired) and his immediate objective in his moral and political philosophy was to attack the decadence of his time, to discountenance the superficiality of the Sophists' teaching and to demonstrate that morality was as much rooted in the nature of things as any other attribute of human nature and that its presuppositions could be elucidated by reason and clearly known. He attempted an account of the qualities of excellence and righteousness in individual and social life at the level of demonstrable knowledge, and sought to lift it from the easy-going and false level of expediency and whimsical opinion. His analysis was both factual ('positive' as we now say) and normative; for Plato believed that to know was a part of striving to become, that no moral endeavour towards excellence could be based on anything less than a knowledge of the truths concerning the nature of society and the individual soul, and concerning the ideals that the facts of our nature and our social commitments were seen to entail.

Using the methods of critical reflection; undertaking a careful analysis of his common-sense assumptions about the psychological and social aspects of human nature; and drawing upon such comparative knowledge about other societies as he possessed; he offered a general theory of man and society in terms of functional excellence. In order to make clear the nature of justice and righteousness he thought it necessary to consider first the factual nature of man and society.

The basic reason for the existence of human society, Plato claimed, is the simple fact that men have many needs, but, as individuals, cannot satisfy them. We are insufficient, as individuals, for the individual fulfilment that we need and desire. Men must therefore live in communities in which different tasks are allocated to those who are best fitted to undertake them, for the purpose of satisfying, in the best possible way, the needs of all. Society is a necessary mutual interdependence of men which achieves a satisfactory division of functions among them.

The origin of a community, he wrote, '. . . is due to the fact that no one of us is sufficient for himself, but each is in need of many things. . . . Men, being in want of many things, gather into one settlement many partners and helpers to satisfy their diverse needs and to this common settlement we give the name of city.'

Plato then enumerated certain basic needs - for food, clothing, dwelling places, and the like - and made clear the division of labour which they required. Obviously, the community must have farmers, builders, weavers, shoe makers, and others who make necessary commodities. But since the most excellent performance of any job, for the benefit of all concerned, is achieved when men can concentrate upon it entirely, a more extensive division of labour is necessary so that these essential workmen do not have to concern themselves with jobs not strictly their own. Other craftsmen are necessary in addition to the first group of workers. Specialist such as carpenters, smiths, herdsmen, shepherds, are necessary to support them with particular materials and special skills.

Plato also thought it extremely unlikely that any community could be so completely self-sufficient as not to benefit to some extent from external trade. Trading required a further group of people: the merchants. Also, 'markets' are necessary even within the community itself. Some intermediaries anticipate the needs of consumers and buy from producers accordingly. These, Plato called the 'shopkeepers'. In addition to all these there are those possessing no special skills, but who are useful for carrying out simple and routine kinds of work, and who hire themselves out as unskilled labourers for wages. A community, on the basis of a simple division of labour of this kind, can live a secure, peaceful, happy life.

> 'Let us consider', Plato argued, 'what will be the manner of life of men so equipped. Will they not spend their time in the production of corn and wine and clothing and shoes? And they will build themselves houses; in summer they will generally work without their coats and shoes, but in winter they will be well clothed and shod. For food they will make meal from their barley and flour from their wheat, and kneading and baking them they will heap their noble scones and loaves on reeds or fresh leaves, and lying on couches of bryony and myrtle boughs will feast with their children, drink wine after their repast, crown their heads with garlands, and sing hymns to the gods. So they will live with one another in happiness, not begetting children above their means, and guarding against the danger of poverty or war.'

Plato conceded, however, when others argued with him, that many people would not be contented with such a simple way of living. Many desire a more luxurious manner of life with more sophisticated commodities and pleasures. Plato then went on to consider the more elaborate division of labour which is necessary if this greater complexity of desires is to be satisfied. Before he agreed to move on to this more elaborate analysis, however, it is worth noting that Plato went out of his way to make it clear that it is in these desires for greater complexity and luxury, and all that they entail, that the seeds of war, social differentiation, and social division lie. It is not, in short, Plato's view that war and extreme social distinctions are necessary accompaniments of human society; only that they are brought into being by what he calls 'the inflamed society'.

> 'I, for my part,' he wrote, 'think that the city I have described is the true one, what we may call the city of health. But if you wish, let us also inspect a city which is suffering from inflammation ... We need one swollen in size, and full of a multitude of things which necessity would not introduce into cities . . . But,' he continued, 'let us only notice that we have found the origin of war in those passions which are most responsible for all the evils that come upon cities and the men that dwell in them.'

Having made this warning clear, he then proceeded to analyse the more complex kind of society which men, with their 'inflamed desires', bring into being.

His account of the ideal constitution of society and the individual was still based upon the division of functions, and the qualities of excellence required for their fulfilment, and he considered society (rather than the individual) first of all, because he felt that the nature and importance of functional excellence would be likely to be so much more clearly apparent there. He began his analysis with the simple question: whom would we approach if we wanted a good pair of shoes, a good saddle, an efficient navigator for a ship, or the performance of any job of that kind? In all cases, he argued, it is obvious that we would go to the man who had the talent and the appropriate training to make shoes, to make saddles, to navigate ships, and so on. These men and only these men could be relied upon to perform that particular function most satisfactorily. People without talent and people without training would lack the requisite skill. Those who perform special skills to satisfy specific needs of this kind Plato called 'the Artisans', and these constitute the first large class of people in his society. Plato also argued that such people will be very preoccupied with performing the skill for which they are best equipped and trained, and to which they have devoted so much of their lives. Their trade will be the basis of the immediate welfare of their families. There is bound to be in short, a certain propriety of selft-interest amongst the artisans; a limited focus of attention and effort, if their function in society is going to be fulfilled with the highest standard of excellence, and if it is going to form a satisfactory basis for their lives.

However, an additional class of people in society is also required which must not be motivated by self-interest or by any single-minded devotion to a specific utilitarian skill. The members of a complex society will unavoidably make claims and counter-claims upon each other; they are bound to be involved in disputes; and if there were no generally accepted pattern of social control for dealing with such conflict, then chaos would result. There must therefore be a group of people in the community who are trained to have a disinterested attitude with regard to maintaining order and justice on behalf of society at large and, of course, to protect society as a whole against outside attacks and insecurities. This second 'class' Plato called 'the Guardians' and he felt that the function of such a class is not simply a negative one of restraining or suppressing the artisans, but the positive one of providing a stable and secure basis for their proper freedom and the proper fulfilment of their own functions. In short, such 'guardianship' should be not repressive but liberative to a proper degree.

Plato then argued that still a third class of people in a complex community is necessary, and this follows from the supreme difficulty of the art of government. The guardians, who protect society and maintain order, have to act in accordance with certain ideals and principles of justice and morality, but the recognition and understanding of these ideals, and the wisdom to govern effectively in accordance with them, requires very clear vision, very careful deliberation, and very considerable powers of reason, knowledge and judgment. But the force of Plato's argument may best be seen if we approach it negatively. He put the matter crucially like this.

There are some people, he said, who think that - although it is advisable to go to a skilled cobbler for a good pair of shoes, or to a trained saddle-maker for a good horse's saddle - when it comes to considering the tasks of decision-taking, legislation and administration in government, everyone in society should have an equal say. But this, surely, said Plato, is absurd. If, in the making of shoes, saddles, and other simple manufactures, specific talents and specific training are necessary for the achievement of excellent standards, how much more must this be true with regard to the most subtle and most difficult art of all - the art of government? Surely this art, more than any, requires many-sided talents of the highest order and the most excellent degree of training in the understanding of all aspects of human nature and society than can be provided. There should, then, be a third 'class' of people - 'the Philosophers' - who prove, after many and searching tests, that they possess these many-sided talents and who then devote very large period of their lives to learning the skills of thought and judgment which will give them the clearest knowledge possible of the moral ideals in the light of which the community should be governed, and the wisest basis of knowledge and judgment whereby the best order of society is to be achieved and sustained. But again it must be noticed that the governing authority of the 'Philosopher Kings' is not thought of by Plato as being repressive or tyrannical. On the contrary, for him the 'Philosopher Kings', too, have a positive function: the necessary, rational ordering of relations in society whereby every sector of society can fulfil its proper task, and its proper kind and degree of functional excellence, with regard to the maximum well-being of the whole. Plato went on to give a very detailed account of how he thought that people in a society should be selected and trained for these various functional skills. For the moment, however, it is enough to see that he gave an account of both the factual and the ideal nature of society in terms of certain necessary functions and the highest degree of excellence in the fulfilment of them.

Following this, Plato then considered how far this threefold functional analysis of the artisans, guardians and philosophers in society might be of use in understanding the factual and ideal nature of the individual human soul, and he tried to demonstrate that it was of use in this connection. He claimed that the individual human soul, too, can be seen to consist of at least three important elements, and that these have the same functions that are reflected is society as a whole. First of all there is the desiring element: all the specific appetites by which man is driven and which seek their satisfaction by the attainment of specific utilitarian ends - as, for example, hunger and desiring food; sex and desiring consummation in love; fear and desiring security. These appetites in the soul are the equivalent of the artisans in society, and the activities of the artisans are, obviously, closely related to them. But again Plato insisted that if the appetites of a man, though each having its own proper end of satisfaction were to be submitted to no over-all control whatever, the result would be chaos. In such a situation it would not be the case that a man governed his appetites in such a way that each of them had its proper place, and provided its proper satisfaction in his nature. On the contrary it would be his appetites which tyrannically dominated him. It is therefore necessary, secondly, that there should be some kind of government of the appetites in the soul, and Plato argued that it was the rational element in human nature (parallel with the Philosopher Kings in society), which could give man a clear knowledge of the moral ideals in the light of which he could wisely govern his nature and exercise control over his desires and conduct.

There is also, however, a third element in the nature of the human soul which Plato found it more difficult to be clear about, and this he called the spirited element, (equivalent to the role of the guardians in society). He argued that there is some element of feeling in us - equivalent to what we would now call 'conscience' - which is a feeling but which, peculiarly, seems always to be on the side of reason in supporting some kind of governing order over the sheer anarchy of the appetites. And Plato maintained that the best ordering of the nature of the individual soul is achieved when the rational element, utilizing the spirited element, orders the many desires of the soul (appetitive and others) in such a way as not to suppress and negate them, but to achieve a sustained balance or harmony, within which each of them can satisfactorily fulfil its own appropriate functions with regard to the unity of the whole. This, again, is both a factual and an ideal theory; an account of what the nature and constitution of the individual human soul both is and ought to be.

There are one or two points which must be emphasised before leaving this account of Plato.

First of all Plato discussed the political constitution of society in terms of some blend of the democratic element (the artisans), the oligarchic element (the guardians), and the monarchic or aristocratic element (the philosopher kings), and his argument was that the monarchic or aristocratic constitution, in which the philosopher kings exercise authority in governing the artisans with the aid of the guardians, is the best one; that is to say - it is the constitution most likely to achieve that over-all harmony within which each group can most satisfactorily and happily find its appropriate fulfilment. In short, Plato was anti-democratic on reasoned grounds.

Secondly, it is worth reiterating that Plato's ideal model of society and of the individual soul rested essentially upon his factual analysis of what society and the individual soul actually are. In his view, the understanding of society and the individual required the recognition of ideals which exist; and which are definitely entailed in the nature of human needs; and which are discovered by reasoning. This blend of actual and ideal, of the factual and the normative, is still a matter for serious philosophical consideration and which we have now-a-days all too easily rejected.

A third point worth emphasising is that Plato saw a real dimension of moral endeavour in this clarification of the ideal and the actual. Recognising the nature of intellectual, aesthetic, and moral ideals is not, in itself, enough. With this discovery, this elucidation of reason, there is a positive desire to approximate to these ideals in so far as it is possible, and this means a conscious attempt to order society and one's own nature in such a way as to achieve the ideal constitution that one has in mind. This again may be an element in social and individual thinking that we tend now-a-days to ignore, and with loss to ourselves.

A final point to notice is that Plato was not 'academic' in any orthodox sense. Though he emphasised fully the intellectual investigation of the nature of the actual and the ideal, and, indeed, the importance of 'the life of the mind' as such, he had, centrally, always a practical end in mind: namely the actual effort in this life as individuals and as members of society to approximate as closely as possible to those idealities of which we became aware. Plato never thought for a moment, either, that the 'idealities' and 'harmonies' of which he spoke were in any sense simple to recognise, or achieve, or that they were 'once-for-all' ends that one could attain. The balance was always precarious. And we sought these things in a perennial and vital 'war of the soul' in which man was always involved.

The Theory of Aristotle (384 - 322 BC)

It is worthwhile to make a few brief comments on the ideas of Aristotle but only for our own purposes, to see that, though in some ways similar to and in some ways different from Plato, his theory was essentially of the same nature: still couched within the context of the City State.

First of all, Aristotle's theory was the same as Plato's in that it gave an account of both individual and society in terms of functional excellence. Similarly, he agreed with Plato in wishing to establish that in some sense or other morality is deeply rooted in the nature of man and is not something conventional in any superficial or expedient sense.

Secondly, Aristotle also agreed completely about the importance of clarifying ideals for the purpose of guiding individual and social endeavour. His difference with Plato here was only a difference of metaphysical level. Whereas Plato wished to insist that in some important sense which it is difficult to make clear ideals actually exist; that they are implicit in all the actual forms of nature and of human nature and that reason can discover, clarify, and know them; and that all the actual individuals in the world (trees, animals, men) are in a process of active development, seeking to fulfil the ideal form on which they are patterned; Aristotle wished to argue that it is sufficient to think of ideals as being simply standards recognised and clarified within men's minds in contemplating their experience. He did not think it possible or necessary to give them an 'existential' status beyond this. Even so Aristotle's analysis was still in terms of ideals rooted in certain human needs and in the overall desire for harmony and happiness in social and individual life, and he was not therefore greatly different from Plato in this.

A third point is that Aristotle's theory of man and society was still in terms of a substantive account of 'the good life'. It was still rooted in a careful analysis of human needs and human ends and in the purposive striving for an overall government of individual and social conduct which would harmonize the needs and functions of men and achieve the highest possible degree of excellence.

Fourthly, however, Aristotle was very sceptical about the place and status of the 'Philosopher Kings' in society. Despite Plato's insistence that the 'philosophers' were men carefully selected for their all-round qualities - their physical qualities, their courage, their temperance, their wisdom, as well as for their qualities of intellect proper - Aristotle still argued that philosophers do not necessarily have, and, indeed, cannot possibly get, the practical experience that is required for the successful organisation of social affairs. His own emphasis with regard to the achievement of effective government was upon the importance of the practical sagacity of the man of affairs. The role of the philosophers with their intellectual enquiries should be to explore fully and in detail all the implications of political issues in order to give men of 'practical sagacity' the best context of information within which to exercise their judgment. The philosophers, in short, should serve and supplement this practical sagacity. Aristotle wished to achieve in society the most excellent qualities of judgment resting upon a knowledge of human affairs and he believed the practical sagacity of the man of affairs to be of equal, if not greater, worth than the intellectual competence of the philosopher.

Finally, Aristotle was more empirically and scientifically orientated in his work than Plato, though, to my mind, this can easily be over-emphasised. Whereas Plato critically reflected upon his own experience of the Greek communities, Aristotle urged the undertaking of a careful comparative study of the varieties of political constitutions that existed in the world of his time. He urged upon his students a recognition of the necessity of this kind of comparative empirical study for a knowledge and understanding of human societies, just as he urged it upon students of biology for establishing a knowledge of different animal species. Aristotle was perhaps the most important early scholar to see the necessity of scientific and comparative sociology, as distinct from, or in addition to, the speculative discussion of 'idealities' which underlay the entire thought of Plato. Aristotle was also very 'sociologically' orientated in his analysis of social institutions and their interrelations in society as a whole. He gave clear and detailed accounts of the part played by the family as a social group, of the 'village' as a communal group, and of the functions of particular institutions - such as 'property'- in establishing certain kinds of relationships and qualities in society. And he placed much importance on inter-personal ties such as 'friendship', of which, again, he gave a very full account.

It is quite clear why Comte and others in approaching the making of sociology in more recent times looked to Aristotle as one of their most important 'ancestors'. Aristotle already had quite a clear conception of a science of society - the analysis and comparative study of social systems in order to establish testable knowledge about them; and, within this conception, he had already undertaken a study of some social institutions and relationships in considerable depth.

To summarise: the theories of man and society which were produced in the context of the Greek City State were theories in terms of functional analysis and excellence. They were undertaken to refute the Sophists by showing that morality was not expedient, superficial, or 'man-made' in any specious sense, but that it was as much a part of the nature of things and of the nature of man and society as anything else encountered in human experience. They emphasised normative considerations, but these were thought to rest upon and to be implicitly entangled with actualities, so that they also offered accounts of the facts of human nature and human society. And they emphasised the importance of attaining knowledge and wisdom for the practical endeavour of governing individual, social and political life in seeking to approximate to the idealities which were recognized. These theories were obviously rooted in the characteristics, conditions, and problems of the life of the Greek city states that we outlined at the beginning, and they were to change when the city states themselves changed and declined.

Theories of Hellenistic Greece

Plato and Aristotle lived and worked when the Greek city states were already changing considerably, and when they were on the point of decline. The self-containment of these political communities vanished altogether with the campaign of Alexander which set up an empire of tremendous extent. This empire was itself a very short-lived achievement, lasting little longer than the lifetime of Alexander himself, and quickly disintegrated, but the important result was that Greek civilisation came to be thinly spread over this very wide area. Although certain local centres such as Alexandria, became important, the old self-contained, 'familial' and independent kind of Greek community was not achieved again. There was, in short, a situation and a period in which men had to live without any clear civic and political unity in mind. There was no longer the clear basis for political citizenship that had existed before.

In this context the old conceptions of the good life for both the individual and society, as being almost two sides of the same coin, were no longer relevant. Instead of thinking of personal morality and political obligation in the same terms - of the fulfilment of individual qualities in a life of loyalty and service to the community, people now came to think in much more individualistic terms. They now thought in terms of some 'natural law' or some source of morality and ground of moral obligation which existed 'in the nature of things', over and above the particular state in which one lived. This 'moral law' existed universally, and applied universally to all men, transcending political boundaries. The characteristic qualities of this thought can best be described as individualistic and cosmopolitan, in clear distinction from the much more 'locally orientated' functional excellence in the thought of the Greek city states.

This individualism and cosmopolitanism was expressed in different terms by different 'schools' of philosophy which were founded and developed during this period. The Stoics, the Cynics and Epicureans were all schools of importance, and put forward distinctive points of view, but the Stoics give perhaps the best illustration.

A clear distinction lay at the heart of the Stoics' belief. Some things in the flux of nature were not within the individual's power to control. Some things, however, were within his power. For example, the span of human life, the sequence of human growth, being a prey to accidents, diseases, death . . .all these were things beyond personal control. On the other hand, the individual could control his own behaviour, his own conduct towards others, his own manner of thinking and speaking; the govering and shaping of his own character. Their teaching was, then, that it was sensible to resign yourself to the things that were not in your power (since it was useless to do otherwise) and to concentrate upon governing in the best way possible the things that were within your power. It is the aspect of resignation to uncontrollable things which is now-a-days taken to be the distinctive characteristic of Stoicism but it can be seen that this was only one emphasis, or one side, of their teaching.

The question arose, however, as to what the best or the right way of controlling one's conduct was? The Stoics' answer was that the feature which entirely distinguishes man from the brutes is his capacity for reason. Reason is the universally distinguishing attribute of man, enabling him to elucidate the nature of things, to clarify and know the *Natural Law* by which all things in nature are ordered, and to guide his conduct in accordance with this knowledge. A knowledge of *Nature Law* is therefore the most important thing for us, and each individual must recognise his own responsibility for his own reasoning and the government of his own life.

The Stoics did, in fact, outline a good many rules for personal conduct, and outlined certain principles and qualities of character which reason seemed to uphold, but even so, it will be seen that this kind of teaching had a noticeable lack of content as far as the obligations of men as citizens of the state were concerned. Community life lacked close, centralised cohesion, and therefore the account of the good life was in entirely individualistic terms, and there was a complete absence of consideration of the necessary relations between individual and community which had characterised the theories of the Greek city state. There was no discussion of political constitutions of the Platonic and Aristotelian kind. The Stoic creed was a personal creed, and the same was true (though they were qualitatively different in their details) of the teaching of the Cynic and the Epicurean schools.

Theories of the Roman Empire

During the third and second centuries before Christ, Rome gradually absorbed, together with other territories, the area of the disintegrated Macedonian empire. The modes of thought that were prevalent in Hellenistic Greece became elements in Roman civilisation and continued throughout the period of Roman domination in Europe. The Epicureans, for example, were represented by Lucretius. Cicero wrote treatises on ethics and government using Plato's familiar titles of *The Republic* and *The Laws*. And the representatives of the Stoics best known to us were men like Epictetus, Marcus Aurelius, and Seneca - the first a slave, the second an emperor. The Stoic philosophy is presented most clearly in their writings.

What is particularly important for our purpose is to note that the conception of natural law persisted throughout this period. Roman civilisation did not produce any great original philosophers of the calibre of those who had arisen in Greece. Roman thinkers studied the Greeks and discussed their ideas both clearly and elaborately. Cicero, for example, has a greater range and power as a thinker that is commonly thought. Still, it is true that they made no major contributions themselves. In the main Rome was most noteworthy and important in the development of Western civilisation, including the development of thought, for its contributions in the sphere of practical law and government. The great achievement of Rome was the successful establishment of a wide network of positive law over the many peoples they conquered, and, during this practical process, the achievement of a systematic, reflective, and progressive codification of the law.

One very important aspect of this was the conception of natural law, as a strictly philosophical idea, now received a basis of practical support from the actual experience of the Romans in dealing with the new complexities and problems of law. Jus

Naturale for the Romans was that law inherent in the nature of thing including human nature, which could be discovered by reason, and which in some sense underlay the actually existing network of the civil law. In short, Jus Naturale, was very similar to the philosophical idea of the Stoics, but was thought also to interpenetrate the actual laws of society.

Another important element of law emerged in Roman affairs, however, which was very similar, but not exactly the same. In the early city states of Rome, as in the early Greek city states, membership of the community was a matter of blood-membership or birth, and men were subject to the pattern of custom and law within the community into which they were born. With the extension of Roman administration, however, disputes were brought before the courts between men who were members of widely differing societies and patterns of custom. The lawyers found themselves having to judge claims, counter-claims, and specific cases between members of different communities to whom quite different systems of law applied. They therefore looked for the 'common' element in all these systems as an agreed ground for judgment. A body of 'common' law accumulated, and was known as '*Jus Gentiun*': the 'law of the people'. In the Roman empire these two elements of law, *Jus Naturale* and *Jus Gentium,* appear never to have been quite identified with each other; were never thought to be quite the same; but nonetheless were thought to lend support and reinforcement to each other. It was felt that natural law, discoverable by human reason, must underlie the common strands of law which actually existed in the law of the people derived from all communities. If reason and natural law were universal, one would expect them to assume a certain common form in the institutions of justice in all societies.

In addition, however, there was a third strand of law: the body of constitutional laws laid down by the decrees of the emperors and the edicts of the praetors as and when they came to power; and this was known as civil law or positive law: *Jus Civile.* A close relationship between all these three elements in law was held to exist, even though the relationship was never thoroughly worked out or made perfectly clear.

In the period of the Roman Empire then, the theory of a 'natural law' underlying the ordering and government of individual and social behaviour, received a kind of 'underpinning' from the actual administration of legal affairs.

Theories of Feudal Society

Following the disruption and decline of the Roman Empire, and the gradual emergence of the new order of Feudal society, a new dimension of law - Divine Law - came into being as an ultimate justification of all those other strands of law that had come to be emphasised during the period of the empire. This, of course, rested upon the central importance of the Christian Church in the new pattern of authority. Whereas, before, 'civil law' and the 'law of the people' was justified by 'natural law', which was clarified and understood by reason, it was now believed that, beyond this, there existed the 'divine law' which contained elements not discoverable by human reason.

Christian doctrine came to maintain that whereas reason was God-ordained and could therefore be supposed in its original condition of innocence to contemplate the full nature of the moral law of God, it had been rendered incapable of this by the sinfulness of man and the fall of man from his initial state of grace. This did not mean that human reason was totally incapacitated, and it was still agreed that human reason could, to a degree, clarify certain matters of morality and certain aspects of the will of God, but because of man's fallen nature it had been necessary for god to provide, by revelation, a knowledge of his own nature and of his divine law which reason itself could not now apprehend. This 'revealed' divine law came therefore, to proclaim and insist upon certain idealities and moral principles which went beyond natural law, civil law and positive law.

On the basis of this divine law, but linking with it the rational clarification of natural law which earlier thinkers had achieved, the philosophers of medieval society, perhaps especially St. Thomas Aquinas, outlined an entire theory of the nature of civil society and an entire picture of what 'the good society' was like. This, of course, was cumulatively established and clarified by successive papal encyclicals. Here again, then, was a 'theory' of society which outlined the factual nature of the individual soul and of society, in such a way as also to provide a clear statement of moral and spiritual ideals for man's guidance. But it was this theologically based theory of Christendom which came to be torn asunder with the Protestant reformation and the violent emergence of modern secular nation states.

Theories in the Emerging Nation States

The success of feudalism brought about its own downfall. With the new security which the feudal order re-introduced into the chaos following the disruption of empire, there was a renewal and re-establishment of many of the earlier strands of communication between diverse peoples. Travel between various parts of Christendom was now more possible roads and sea-routes were opened up again. New commercial contacts and interchanges were established and extended, and with this resurgence and growth of inter-communication came an increasing interchange of knowledge and enquiry. A new spirit of adventurousness in all fields of enquiry and activity awoke. This was linked, in practical terms, with the emergence of competing groups of merchants, all seeking to establish new mercantile organisation and their 'national' independence. The universal pattern of Christendom was gradually unsettled and then violently torn asunder. A period of intense conflicts, of an economic, political, and religious nature, brought the disintegration of the feudal order and the emergence of new secular nation states, each insisting upon its own political authority and independence, and upon its own responsibility for its internal organisation an its external policies. These struggles towards independent nationhood were reflected in the emergence of new theories about human nature and about the grounds of moral and political obligation.

We have seen that all the earlier theories of man and society had contained propositions as to what men ought to be like and how they ought to behave. There was always a mixture in them of the fact of human nature and the idealities which human beings ought to observe. One of the most noticeable changes in the new moral and political theories attending mercantilism and the emergence of the independent nation state was that the accent upon the normative tended to be very much diminished, indeed decried, and there was a much greater emphasis upon the positive study of man; the study of the facts. This must not be exaggerated too much - the normative was still very strongly there; but it was stressed very forcefully that 'idealities' were figments and delusions with which those who were in power hoodwinked those who were not, and that the only grounds on which morality could reliably rest were to be derived from a knowledge and understanding of what the facts of human nature actually were.

Machiavelli (1469 – 1527) wryly advocated that statesmen should have done with thinking too much about how men ought to be have and should look more scrupulously at the ways in which they actually do behave. Only if men had a satisfactory knowledge and understanding of the actuality of human nature could they know successfully how to influence others, and gain and sustain power over them for the pursuit of what they themselves thought worthwhile. All this was laid down in his treatise on *The Prince.* Machiavelli, however, was by no means altogether as sinister as he is now made out to be and in his *Discourses on Titus Livius* he gave some account of the moral principles which ought to be the objective of the statesman's efforts. Machiavelli's real emphasis was that 'ideals' and 'principles' are all well and good, but of no avail if one cannot achieve and sustain effective order and government, and for this a thorough knowledge of the ways in which men pursue power is necessary.

Similarly in the work of Thomas Hobbes (1588 –1679) there was a firm insistence upon knowing the hard facts of human nature as a basis for knowing wisely what the most just order of society could and should be. It is well known that his ethical theory was not successful in the sense that he could not demonstrate how his ultimate moral principles were derived from the stark 'facts' of human nature in which, he claimed, there were no moral glimmerings at all. Nonetheless, his theory offered a detailed analysis of the psychological propensities of men which led them to fear others and be in conflict with them, to be in a 'state of war' with each other, and thus to be driven to seek some kind of legitimate civil authority which would minimise this conflict and provide a basis for peace, security and harmony. Many of these observations which Hobbes made about human nature, about both the individual and society, are full of remarkable insight, and again it must be said that he was far from being as sinister in his account of the perpetual prusuit of power on the part of all men, as is commonly supposed. For example, his account of the 'passions' which drive men to seek 'power' include such propensities as benevolence, curiosity, humour and the like, and for him the term 'power' refers simply to the seeking of that degree of control over things and people which is needed to secure the ends which the passions desire. This is by no means necessarily sinister. However, our central object here is not to defend Hobbes, but only to see the kind of theory that he proposed.

One other point that must be noted is that it is with the emergence of the modern nation states that the 'Social Contract' kind of theory came into being. 'Divine law' had come to be suspect, and had to be attacked. With the overthrow of Christendom, however, some new basis of political sovereignty had to be found and this, by these new theorists, was sought by examining the assumed reciprocity of a 'contractual' nature which seemed to underlie all the co-operative behaviour of men in society. Men do, in a political community, seem to act as though they feel bound by reciprocal obligations; as though they had entered into a contract with each other. Why do they feel and act like this? What exactly underlies this 'contractual' behaviour?

Perhaps one of the most important characteristics of this new kind of social theory was that all the metaphysical or theological presuppositions concerning the basis of power and authority were dropped. There was no longer an appeal to *divine law* and *natural law* in the sense that there was something actually there over and above the heads of men, which by reason could be discovered and which gave some kind of 'ultimate' justification to the actual laws of the state. The emphasis was now entirely upon *positive law.* To put the matter simply, law was thought to be what men decided; and nothing else. Law was simply that set of rules which men made to order their social life. This was enough.

Theories in the Maturing Nation States

This vehicle of the 'Social Contract' idea came to be filled with rather different contents as the emerging nation states came to grapple more fully with the making of political constitutions. The detailed elaboration of new patterns of political rights; the detailed working out of constitutional procedures; resting only upon human reason and morality, encountered different problems in different societies. Machiavelli and Hobbes produced their theories in the thick of the rebellions taking place against the order of Christendome; but towards the end of the seventeenth and during the eighteenth centuries, up to the time of the French revolution, those who constructed theories of society were now faced with the positive and continuous task of providing a justification for the details of the new secular political orders. The social contract idea was therefore used with different emphases by different theorists in the context of different conditions.

Towards the end of the seventeenth century in Britain, John Locke, for example, argued, as against Hobbes, that moral principles were not, and could not be, brought into being by the creation of a political society. They were not created with the setting up of a central sovereignty. On the contrary, moral principles were actively involved in the 'state of nature' of men's ordinary feelings and conflicts. Men felt and recognised reciprocal moral duties before any elaborate political apparatus of authority was set up. Furthermore, the political constitution, or the apparatus of the state, which men did set up for the achievement and preservation of a just order in society, was one which they accepted in order effectively to secure the moral principles they already recognised. If, therefore, this organ of government came to deny or to abuse these principles of morality, then the people had a right to overthrow it and to replace it with something more satisfactory. Locke's theory again, however, consisted of a psychological account of the nature of man, both individual and social, from which he then deduced his principles for the organisation of the state.

Jean-Jacques Rousseau also used the social contract theory as a vehicle criticising the *ancien régime* in France during the eighteenth century, and he too used the theory for the strong defence of democracy. He regarded any kind of political apparatus which - whether from size, complexity, or arbitrary privilege - prevented every adult individual in the community from participating in the taking of those central decisions which were to be binding upon them all, as being totally unjustified. He argued therefore for the relatively small political community in which all men could participate as individuals. Again, however, Rousseau's theory included a psychological account of the nature of man and a connected account of that organisation of society which would most lead to the maximisation of individual liberty and individual fulfilment.

It is interesting to notice, also, that even the criticisms of these social contract theories were themselves theories of society in what we would now call psychological and sociological terms. The best example of this is the theory put forward by Edmund Burke, in his *Reflections upon the Revolution in France* as a critique of everything that the French revolution stood for. Burke argued that the 'social contract' idea was historical nonsense and, furthermore, that the idea that the men of one generation could 'rationally' know how to obliterate the institutional fabric of a society and replace it overnight in a revolutionary manner with a totally new social structure, was a matter of political as well as intellectual lunacy, and deeply dangerous. The fabric of institutions in society as a whole, Burke insisted, is a collective tradition which has grown up over many centuries; to which many generations have contributed; and which has come to be a complex embodiment of all the non-rational and prejudicial, as well as the rational elements of a people's experience in confronting and dealing with its own particular historical circumstances. The social heritage consists of a pattern of institutions which are intricately and intimately interrelated, and which are rooted in the most profound emotions and values of a people which simply cannot be fleetingly and momentarily 'understood' by the rational analysis of one generation. The institutions of a nation are ways of living, ways of feeling and doing, not just abstract administrative procedures which can be 'known' by 'reason' and judged against abstract moral principles. And to tamper brashly in ill-considered social reform with any one element of the social heritage might well produce a degree and range of social disorder that was not envisaged and might bring disaster instead of improvement. One stone in a building may seem to fit badly, but if, without care, it is pulled out, the entire building may collapse.

Burke's theory was therefore a very conservatively toned theory insisting that reform, if undertaken at all, should only take place after very prolonged and deliberate thought and careful judgment, and even then very guardedly and never in any totalitarian or revolutionary spirit. Again, however, it is to our purpose only to note that this is really a systematic theory of society: a socio-psychological analysis of what is involved in the cumulative development of social traditions in the institutional organisation of society as a whole.

New Approaches to Social Theory

During the eighteenth century, however, whilst these new kinds of 'national' social theories were being put forward, a qualitatively new kind of approach to the study of man and society was beginning to emerge, was beginning to disentangle itself from the old, and the crucial distinction which was being clarified in these new approaches was that between a scientific and a moral theory. Some thinkers were coming to be clearly aware that a certain scientific body of knowledge at least about the nature of human societies could be achieved, and that it was necessary to achieve it, quite separately from the statement of any moral theories as to what human society ought to become. And this was a movement of thought which grew throughout the eighteenth century and culminated in a proliferation of theories about the establishment of 'social science' round about the time of the French revolution. For our purposes two theorists are particularly significant : Montesquieu and Condorcet.

(a) ***Montesquieu (1689 – 1755)***

Montesquieu was a man of culture and affairs; a man of wide experience as well as a scholar. He travelled in Italy, Germany, Holland, and stayed for something like three years in England. His work had a wide-ranging air of sophistication, and contained much social commentary and satire quite apart from contributing very substantially to serious and scholarly studies of society. In his Persian Letters, for example, published about 1721, he produced a satire on the nature of French and Parisian life and discussed many ideas of the time - for example, Hobbes' account of the 'state of nature' - in an unusual and entertaining way by treating them as they were seen through the eyes of two visiting Persians. His major contribution to the study of society, however, was his book *The Spirit of the Laws* for which he undertook an enormously wide range of reading and research in history, geography, political philosophy, economics and comparative law. The range of this work is best indicated by Montesquieu's full title - *De L'Esprit des Lois, ou du rapport que les lois derivent avoir avec la constitution de chaque gouvcrnement, les moeurs, le climat, la religion, le commerce, etc.*

The central and most distinguishing feature of Montesquieu's treatment was that he now used the idea of 'natural law' not in the old philosophical sense in which it had been used throughout European history, but in the new sense of a scientific 'law of nature'. He now brought to the fore the idea that each society, each social system as an entirety, has its own 'natural law of development', and that it should be the objective of the student of society to uncover and to establish a satisfactory knowledge of this law. He still believed, like all the other thinkers we have mentioned, that such knowledge should be provided for the use of statemen but his major belief, rather like that of Burke, was that a statesman can only legislate wisely if he knows, very intimately, the nature of the society for which he is legislating, and knows the nature and pace of institutional change which is proper to that society. Only if he legislates within the context of this knowledge of social development will his principles and actions of government be soundly based and such, therefore, as to produce successfully the ends he has in mind. Montesquieu, too, was opposed to the idea of the statesman as a kind of idealist who, with certain moral principles in mind, believes that he can totally reconstruct society in a revolutionary manner. The wise statesman governs within the context of the institutional fabric of his society, of which he has gained a profound knowledge.

In pursuing these 'laws of development' of societies Montesquieu insisted upon and actually used both comparative and historical methods in his study. He classified societies chiefly in terms of the political constitutions that they possessed; into republics, monarchies, and despotisms; but in this classification he took into account not only the differing institutional complexes which were appropriate to each, but also what he called the 'spirit' or the 'principle' which was required among the members of society if the institutions were to function satisfactorily. This 'principle' or 'spirit' really amounted to the kind and qualities of education by means of which those values necessary for the functioning of a society were engendered in its individual members. In despotisms the 'principle' necessary to maintain institutional order is always fear. In monarchies, which frequently have a nobility surrounding the monarch, the 'principle' on which social order depends is the instilling of honour. And in republics, which may be democratic when all people share in the tasks of government or aristocratic when relatively few people participate, the principle whereby appropriate social order is secured and sustained is that of virtue. Montesquieu therefore conceived of entire social systems as being collectively different entities but as being the embodiments of certain 'typical' networks of institutions, each of which was sustained by a particular 'ethos' of a psychological nature engendered and sustained by education.

Stemming from all this he also put forward certain political prescriptions. For example, he agreed that if liberty is to be maximised in a society there must be a division of powers between legislative, executive and judicial authorities, and that these powers should be undertaken by different bodies of people. These political prescriptions however, were an additional matter.

It should also be mentioned that Montesquieu saw the total institutional complex of a society as coming to assume the shape it did by a process of adaptation to a specific ecological setting. One of the most important characteristics of a society's environment he thought, was its climate: its ranges of temperature, and the like. He believed that climatic and other ecological conditions exerted a powerful influence upon the psychological nature of a people and that this was reflected in the nature of their social system. However, the social system - the interconnected institutions of religion government, education, family - was seen as an entirety in relation to the entironment and not, by any means, as being entirely subservient to it. Montesquieu quite readily believed that it was part of the function of the statesman to reduce this dominant influence of the geographical environment and society's dependence upon it, and he believed that as human civilisation grew, and as its technology accumulated and advanced, so the social order could have an increasingly determining influence upon the geographical environment, rather than the other way round.

Montesquieu's theory of society, then, was a theory about the development of social systems within their ecological settings, and it involved an entire psychological institutional and developmental analysis of the nature of these societies. In all this he also studied institutions in a way which we would now call sociological and scientific, quite independent of any ethical or metaphysical questions concerning the truth of their values. A good example of this is that he discussed the nature of religion in society, and the social and psychological functions it fulfils, quite apart from the question as to the truth or falsity of any of its doctrines. In all this Montesquieu was remarkably modern and a clear precursor of psychological and sociological theory proper. Like Aristotle, Montesquieu is one of the 'pre-scientific' students of society to whom many later sociologist - Comte, Durkheim and others - acknowledge their great indebtedness. The reason is quite clear.

Perhaps, referring again to his consideration of the division of powers in the exercise of political authority, one final point to be made is that Montesquieu, though he did not make much of this in the entirety of his theory, really had an implicit theory of progress. He hated and despised slavery, domination, tyranny, and it was the maximisation of individual fulfilment that he loved. And his comparative study of 'laws of social development' came to be judged according to this yardstick of measurement. Those social systems which maximised liberty were ' better' than those which did not, and therefore constituted models for political action.

(b) *Condorcet (1743 – 1794)*

This mention of the term 'progress' brings us directly to the significance of the work of Condorcet. It was Condorcet who, more conspicuously and centrally than anyone else, brought the new idea of progress into the centre of all thought about the nature of man and society, and this change of orientation was much more considerable than we are now-a-days inclined to think. In many of the earlier systems of social thought, the prevailing assumptions were those of a kind of timeless eternity. Man, his society, his patterns of historical change, were all seen within the larger context of the divine eternity of things within which he had been created. Some theories, like that of the Italian philosopher Vico, argued that there was a cyclical pattern of change in human societies, but that these cycles of change still existed within the external nature of things as created by God, and were, indeed, ways in which man became ever more aware of the divine scheme of the universe. The new conception of man's place in nature came as biological and historical knowledge increased, and the idea emerged that there was no evidence for the earlier 'cyclical' theories, and that human history could simply be regarded as an on-going process in which change was, no more and no less, a matter of society becoming different from what it had been before. Ideas of cyclical patterns or eternal purposes tended to be abandoned, and it was thought more correct to conceive of human history as a changing creative process in which human civilisation was cumulative and, in many ways, possibly an advancing thing.

Condorcet, even more than Montesquieu, was very much a man of affairs, distinguishing himself in French academic life, but also, with the French Revolution, involving himself very considerably in political activities. He became responsible, for example, for state education in the early years following the Revolution, and in 1792 it was he who put forward a scheme for State Education. His concern for clarifying the nature of progress in human society had therefore very practical implications for the making of policy in the context of the new political constitution of France, as well as being a matter of theoretical interest.

His main work, and probably his most influential work after his own time (it was published posthumously), was his *Sketch for a Historical Picture of the Progress of the Human Mind*. In this book he analysed the stages of advancement of human civilisation from a 'sub-human' or near animal condition to the possibility of an enlightened and virtuous society which had as its objective individual fulfilment and happiness. And in all this he tried to show how the advances of mental experience as experienced by individuals, were closely associated with, and considerably dependent on, the conditions of society at any particular time. In short, his account was an analysis of the progress of mankind from its original 'animal' state towards the most perfect fulfilment of human potentialities, emphasising throughout the close interdependence of individual and society.

Condorcet maintained that there had been nine great and distinguishable epochs of social development in history. First of all, mankind must have lived in simple hordes. Their economic activity must have been that of hunting, fishing, food gathering, and they must have come to possess some central customary authority, some systematic kinship relationships, and a language - no matter how rudimentary. These, he thought, were the crucial necessary elements for the foundation of human society. A second stage was when men accomplished a pastoral economy - their livelihood depending upon the keeping of large herds. At this stage propery as a social institution emerged and, correlated with it, social inequality and slavery. But these developments were responsible, at least, for a certain amount of leisure amongst certain groups of the population, leading therefore to a new development of other aspects of culture, including inventions and the beginning of science. A third stage was when mixed agriculture was accomplished as a basis for the economy. In these societies wealth was greater; the degree of leisure enjoyed by the population was therefore greater; and there was a better, more efficient, and wider-ranging division of labour. But, perhaps more crucial, there was the emergence of literacy. The development of alphabets, written knowledge and records, meant that history proper and clear perspectives of historical consciousness in societies could begin. The fourth and fifth stages were more or less descriptions of Greek and Roman civilisation respectively and gave a detailed account of all their scientific, philosophical, technical and artistic advances. The sixth and seventh stages were those of the Middle Ages; the first being more or less the founding of the feudal order, ending in the crusades; the second referring to the development of feudal society ending with the invention and effective use of printing. The eighth stage covered the period from the invention of printing to the emergence of modern critical philosophy marked, for example, by the 'Systematic doubt' of Descartes; and the ninth stage covered the period from this to the French Revolution. In this final stage Condorcet discussed the gradual extension of scientific knowledge about all aspects of the world and society; the gradual culmination of the scientific approach to the study of a society; and, following this, the conscious reconstruction of the institutions of society on the basis of a clear moral philosophy and clear scientific knowledge.

The tenth stage to which Condorcet devoted himself very considerably was, of course, the future of mankind which was just beginning to be consciously created in his own time. He believed that the conscious reconstruction of society would focus upon the elimination of inequalities between nations, the elimination of inequalities between social classes, and, parallel with this, upon the perfecting - physical, intellectual and moral - of individual human nature. All this meant an elaborate statement of human rights in order to secure and maximise individual freedom in the social order.

Condorcet maintained that no end to the possible progress of mankind could be foreseen; that no limits, could be set upon it; but that perhaps the most important vehicle for the achievement of advancement was that of education. He also, with a kind of rationalistic optimism (though by no means a naive optimism) thought that the kind of feeling that had hitherto been organised by religions in society, about their symbols, rituals, and doctrines, could now be adequately organised about certain important humane ideals and so organised with equal efficacy in the service of human liberty and human improvement. In all this he thought that education could achieve an extension of human sympathy, of social feelings, and reciprocal social concern.

These then were the kinds of social theories presented in the on-going development of moral and political philosophy, and in our discussion of them, two things, at least, have become very clear.

First of all, these theories possessed the same characteristics as the 'religious theories' which we outlined earlier. They can all be seen to have been appropriate to the conditions and problems experienced in the societies in which they were elaborated. They were all pragmatically based; shaped in order to deal with these pressing social problems. They were also empirically based, presenting an account of the facts of human nature and society. But, related to this, they also sought a moral ground of justification of some kinds of social organisation as against others. They all included an analysis of the nature of social institutions and their functions, but they also provided an account of the psychology of the individual - clearly believing that this was closely bound up with the pattern of social life and values which the individual experienced in the community.

The difference is only that these theories were constructed on the basis of critical philosophy, whereas the religious theories were a matter of accepted traditional belief, but it is of great interest to see that, in both kinds of theory, the same components were involved. It is almost as though these appear to be essential components, which any satisfactory theory must, in some way or other, take into account.

The second point, however, is that we have also seen quite clearly that, in the time of Montesquieu and Condorcet, and mirrored especially in their work, these theories of moral and political philosophy were moving towards a clearly seen need for a much more scientifically based approach to the study of man and society: an approach which would be much more systematic and widely inclusive in its comparative and historical studies; much more scrupulous in its ways of accomplishing generalizations and in its clarification of the criteria of its knowledge; and much more careful in its distinction between the study of facts and the statement of values, and the problems involved in considering both with reference to prescriptions for practical application and the making of political policies. These were dimensions not sufficiently pursued before, and it was these kinds of preoccupation within these the theories, which led quite directly, shortly after the French Revolution, to the conscious and deliberate attempts to create sociology - a 'science' of society.

C. PHILOSOPHY OF HISTORY

There was one other field of philosophical enquiry which produced some very interesting theories about man and society, and this, though to a certain extent distinct from moral and political philosophy, was closely and significantly related to it. This was the Philosophy of History.

'Philosophies of history' differ from specific theories within moral and political philosophy in the sense that they offer a total account of the place of man and society within the nature of things. The place of man and the development of historical society within the entire scheme of things is rendered 'intelligible' in these systems of speculation, whereas moral and political philosophies tend to be relatively limited accounts of the relations between individuals and the state, and of the ethical principles on the basis of which these relations ought to be organised. There is a perennial desire among men to believe that nature, in its entirety, embodies some kind of purpose which gives meaning and significance to the life of individuals and to the complex events of history.

When men see the tragic wars, the conflicts of power, the changing panorama of human affairs in history, in which so much that is deeply felt, noble, and sublime, encounters so much that is evil and abhorrent, it seems an agonizing thought - that all this is nothing more than a dance of transient puppets in a meaningless play. There is a desire to believe in some deep-rooted value and meaning in it all.

Philosophical enquiry into whatever meaning and significance might exist stemmed quite directly from some of the religious theories we have mentioned, and from certain religious persuasions about the nature of man. If God had created the world and man with certain underlying purposes, then these purposes should be revealed by careful study. And even if there was no such ultimate divine purpose, it could still be maintained that since man was in part a rational and purposive creature, the historical story of his life and development in the world would reveal the meaning and purpose of his struggles. Some philosophers, therefore, attempted a detailed examination of the events of history in order to trace the meaningful pattern in them, and these theories were, and remain, among the most interesting that emerged before the development of sociology.

Here I shall concentrate chiefly upon the ideas of Hegel, because it seems to me that his is a philosophy of history which rests most clearly upon what we would now call sociological assumptions, and also, an understanding of his system of thought is essential for any subsequent understanding of the sociological theory of Marx, Hobhouse and others. It is of interest, however, to see how sociological insights pervaded the ideas of one or two other scholars who preceded Hegel.

G. B. Vico (1668 - 1744) : The New Science

The work of Vico is quite astonishing in its range and detail, but also, more paricularly, for the many insights it contained which clearly anticipated a systematic science of human society.

Vico saw quite clearly, for example, that it was impossible to understand the nature of human personality without studying individuals within the context of the society of which they were members. He was quite clearly aware of the 'social psychological' dimensions of society and their importance for the making of human individuality. Also, he emphasised religion as a particularly important social influence in this respect. Religion sustained and transmitted the important ideological elements of a community and provided the basis for social cohesion. Vico also insisted clearly that societies and their cultural traditions were slow, cumulative, historical processes and that it was therefore necessary to employ a historical method in seeking an understanding of them.

In order to accomplish such a vast account of man and his social developments in history, Vico deliberately undertook careful comparative studies. He was forced to conjecture about the nature of 'primitive peoples' and their mentality (he emphasised language, mythology and religion as the basic elements in the emergence of the earliest societies); but he then went on to collect and study documentary evidence (from classical literature, biblical studies, and the like) in order to describe and analyse with reliability the subsequent patterns of social change and development.

Following these studies, Vico put forward a theory of social change which was in part repetitive, in part progressive. He thought that all the epochs of civilisation were characterised by a cyclical pattern of change through three stages. Firstly, there was a stage in which explanations of society and its origins were couched in terms of the 'divine'; there was a dominance of feeling and emotion as distinct from reason, and political organisation was 'theocratic'. Secondly, there was a stage in which explanations were couched in terms of 'heroic human action and values'; poetic imagination and insight were the dominant characteristics of thought, and social organisation was modelled upon aristocratic excellence. The third stage was one in which explanations of society were couched in purely human terms, resting upon straightforward matter-of-fact knowledge, and entailing an extensive range of political freedom under various forms of monarchies and republics. However, this historical change from epoch to epoch - though each epoch was cyclical in itself - took the form of a 'spiral' of progress. Each epoch, though cylical in its own pattern of change, rested upon the achievements of earlier epochs. Each subsequent epoch therefore moved the human mind to a new and progressive level of fulfilment; achieved a richer awareness of reality and of the nature of human destiny within and in relation to it.

In this way Vico tried to show that the entire process of human history was intelligible as a process of the coming to maturity of the human mind in its understanding of nature and God. And this maturing of the human mind, he showed, was attendant upon the achievement of better and more appropriate social institutions. The achievement of enlightenment in human mentality was in large part a collective matter; a matter of the collective advancement of 'mind' or 'spirit' in which all individuals could participate and share.

In this way, too, Vico tried to demonstrate the hand of God in society and history and the way in which man came to an even more enlightened and deepened understanding of the nature of God and the world.

A final point of great interest is that, in all this, Vico introduced the idea that a study of man and society in history was significantly different from a study of other phenomena in the world in the sense that it involved subjective understanding in terms of meaning as well as a simple set of statements of an 'objective' kind about the external qualities of things - trees, rocks, animals, stars and the like - such as the other sciences of nature could achieve. In this Vico undoubtedly foresaw the emphasis by Max Weber and other German scholars upon the distinctive differences of theory and method between the 'natural' and the 'human' sciences which were, of course, only developed fully much later.

Immanuel Kant (1724 – 1804) : A Universal History

Kant, of course, is chiefly known for the exposition of the 'critical' philosophy which has influenced modern thought so profoundly. His major contributions lie in the theory of knowledge and in his attendant discussions of moral philosophy. His contribution to the philosophy of history is, by comparison, very slight. It is put forward in one quite short essay: *The Idea of a Universal History from a Cosmopolitan Point of View*. However, Kant's contribution is of considerable importance as an example of a kind of philosophy of history which does not rest necessarily on the religious or theological persuasions of men like Vico and, later, Hegel.

Kant, again like all those who were interested in the philosophy of history, began his essay with the fundamental question as to whether history could be thought to be completely meaningless, or whether it entailed some kind of direction; some kind of moral and intellectual meaning for man. His answer seems, at first sight, curious. He decided that a certain pattern of purpose was working its way out in all the complex events of human history, but without any clear consciousness or fore-knowledge on the part of all the individuals concerned. In short, he thought that a purposive plan was taking place in history 'over the heads of human individuals'.

The basic cause of all this, the basic factor underlying it, is what he called the 'unsocial sociability of man'. He maintained that human nature in society is paradoxical. Men need each other and are bound to enter into social relations with each other in order to fulfil their many needs, but, simultaneously, they resent the extent to which others intrude upon their privacy. They must enter into social relationships with others, but they also want to keep them at arm's length. Men cannot do without each other, but they want to keep each other at a distance. Both sociability and unsociability are necessarily involved in the fulfilment of human needs and purposes. It is this peculiarly conflict interdependency of men, said Kant, which gave rise to the origin of human civilisation and to the whole complex pattern of historical conflict, co-operation, change and progress.

Kant believe that it was in the experience of these conflicts and in each institutional resolution of them that society developed and that an increasing fulfilment of what is potential in human nature gradually took place. In the long-run this pattern of change must move mankind not only beyond families, clans, and tribes to the creation of large-scale nations and federations of nations, but also to a completely global society, in which men the world over will be bound to recognise the necessity of world government and some kind of international organisation which caters for the claims and counter-claims of societies and groups throughout the world.

The ultimate purpose, or plan, which is being worked out in human history is, therefore, the achievement of a government or society which, in his words:

> 'Combines with the greatest possible freedom, and (in consequence) antagonism of its members, the most rigid determination and guarantee of the limits of this freedom, in such a way that the freedom of each individual may coexist with that of others.'

Also, Kant wrote :

> 'The history of the human species as a whole may be regarded as a realisation of the secret plan of nature for bringing into existence a political constitution perfect both from the internal point of view and, so far as regards this purpose, from the external point of view also : such a constitution being the sole condition under which nature can fully develop all the capacities she has implanted in humanity.'

This is an all-too-brief account of Kant's ideas, but sufficient to show their relevance for and similarity with the much more fully worked out ideas of Hegel, upon whose work I think it is best to concentrate.

G.W.F. Hegel : An Idealist Philosophy of History

There is no doubt that the most impressive statement of a systematic philosophy of history, and that which brings the subject most clearly to the brink of modern sociology, is that of Hegel. And Hegel's work is best introduced as the greatest exposition of an idealist philosophy of history. Two points are worth making immediately about this word 'idealist'.

The first is that the term idealist in speculative metaphysics does not mean that the philosopher believes in, or postulates, certain moral ideals, or ideals of any other kind (aesthetic, intellectual), in human experience. A 'materialist' can believe in moral ideals and incorporate them into his system of thought, just as legitimately as an idealist or anyone else. The crucial distinction is that an idealist philosopher is one who believes in the primacy of spirit or mind in the universe. Spirit and mind (or God), is, for him, the ultimate reality, and the entire fabric of nature, material and otherwise, is held to stem from, to be rooted in, to have been in some way created by, this primary spiritual reality.

The second point is that anyone who believes in the existence of God, and believes that God created the world and man - and is therefore in some sense immanent in nature, must have an implicit philosophy of history of the same kind as that held by Hegel. If they are not clear about this, it is only because they have not worked it out. They have not made fully explicit what is implicit in their beliefs. Hegel's philosophy of history is therefore of very considerable interest as one detailed example of an 'idealist' position.

It was Hegel's belief in this primacy of spiritual reality (indeed, for him, it was more than a belief, in that he was convinced that it permitted of rational demonstration) which enables us to understand what would otherwise be a baffling element in his system.

Believing in this primacy of spirit and mind, Hegel went on to maintain that all the many processes of nature, including all those of human society and history, must be 'intelligible' in terms of it. They must be an embodiment of the progress of God or the 'World-Spirit' in the developing creation of the world. They must manifest a rational direction and pattern, and a study of them must discover and reveal the meaning and purpose of spirit or mind itself.

There were thus two important and connected strands in Hegel's system of thought. First, he discussed the nature of logical development itself, the way in which the processes of thought disentangled its problems and moved ever more closely towards the truth, and secondly, he related these logical processes to the actual events of nature and history.

The process of logical development; the logical procedures whereby mind moves towards the truth and ultimately discovers it by exact clarification; he termed the 'dialectics' of thought, and his account is similar to the procedures of argument used by the early Greek philosophers. In any discussion or deliberation about the truth of a certain question, we begin with the statement of a proposition about it - a thesis. Every such proposition, however, encounter's its opposite. Indeed, logically speaking, every thesis entails its own possible contradiction. As Hegel put it, every thesis has its antithesis. These two contradictory statements are then scrutinised and a partial resolution of them is arrived at. This is the synthesis of the two originally conflicting statements. This synthesis, however, then becomes the new thesis for the next stage in the argument. This too will have its own antithesis, and so, in this on-going dialectical way of argument, all the aspects of the question will come to be exposed, explored and clarified, and, progressively, we shall have arrived at the fullest truth possible of the matter under discussion.

Because Hegel thought that mind or spirit (what he called the 'Zeitgeist': the 'World Spirit'; a term which includes the notion of creative will) was a real substantive entity, and that Reason was an actual substantive force working its way towards the creative actualisation of truth in the world, he believed that these dialectics of thought and logic were actually at work in the physical order of events in the world, and he therefore identified the dialectics of Reason itself with the dialectical processes of nature and the dialectics of history. The phenomena of the natural world and of human history are themselves interpenetrated by substantive Reason and are themselves the manifestations of the dialectics of Reason working themselves out in the actualities of existence.

Now this idea that reason is a substantive entity, an actual reality in the concrete world of events, seems to us in our present climate of scientific thinking a very curious idea, and in order to make it perfectly clear how Hegel himself conceived it we might look at one or two quotations.

First of all, for example, Hegel wrote, when trying to make clear what 'the Greak Anaxagoras' meant in his statement that 'reason governs the world'.

> 'It is not intelligence as self-conscious Reason, not a Spirit as such that is meant; and we must clearly distinguish these from each other. The movement of the solar system takes place according to unchangeable laws. These laws are reason, implicit in the phenomena in question. But neither the sun nor the planets, which revolve around it according to these laws, can be said to have any consciousness of them.'

HEGEL: AN IDEALIST PHILOSOPHY OF HISTORY

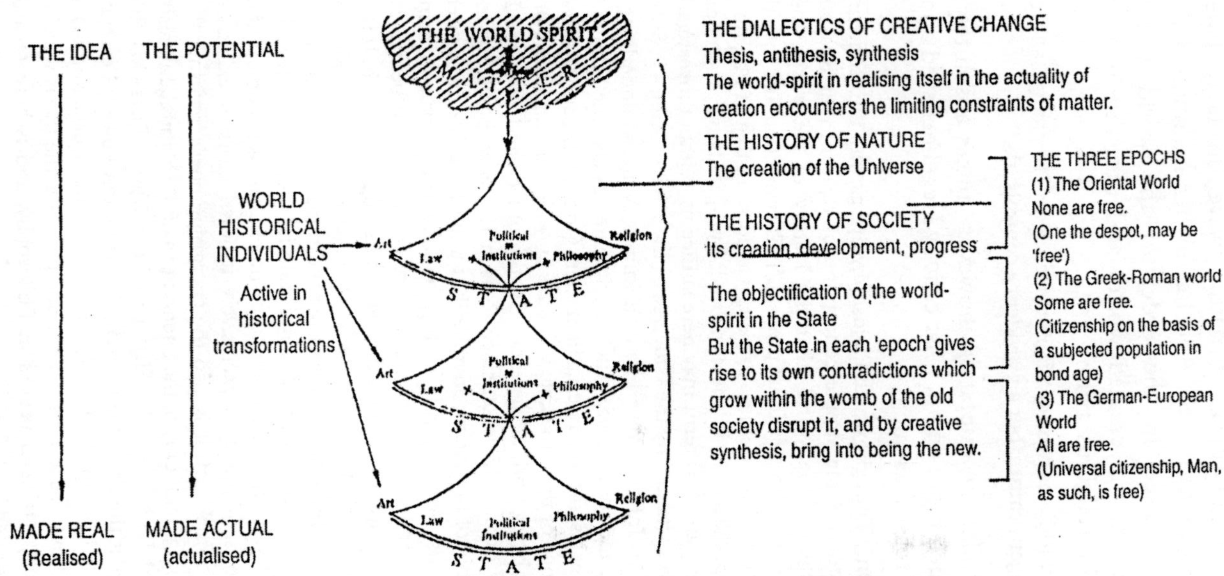

The realisation of the will of the world-spirit in institutional, moral actuality: in the *'totally'* of the Staie. The 'whole' is greater than the parts. The parts realise their character within the whole.

'Progress': The emerging freedom of mind and spirit. The joy of mind and spirit in the fully conscious realisation of its accomplished, created actuality of the world. The *conscious harmony of mind, spirit, nature and society.*

It is perfectly clear from this that Hegel believed that the 'laws' or 'regularities' of nature were, in fact, aspects of substantive reason itself. And he further maintained that this reason actualised in the order of the world was divine providence in the created world, and that this had become manifest in 'religious' truth.

> 'The world', he wrote, ' is not abandoned to change and external contingent causes, but a providence controls it'.

The following quotation, however, makes absolutely clear, and in much more detail, what exactly Hegel believed about the nature of reason as such.

> 'The only Thought which Philosophy brings with it to contemplation of History, is the simple conception of Reason; that Reason is the Sovereign of the World; that the history of the world, therefore, presents us with a rational process. This conviction and intuition is a hypothesis in the domain of history as such. In that of Philosophy it is no hypothesis. It is there proved by speculative cognition, that Reason - and this term may here suffice us, without investigating the relation sustained by the Universe to the Divine Being - is Substance, as well as Infinite Power; its own Infinite Material underlying all the natural and spiritual life which it originates, as also the Infinite Form - that which sets this Material in motion. On the one hand, Reason is the substance of the Universe; viz. That by which and in which all reality has its being and subsistence. On the other hand, it is the Infinite Energy of the Universe; since Reason is not so powerless as to be incapable of producing anything but a mere ideal, a mere intention - having its place outside reality, nobody knows where; something separate and abstract in the heads of certain human beings. It is the infinite complex of things, their entire Essence and Truth. It is its own material which it commits to its own Active Energy to work up; not needing, as finite action does, the conditions of an external material of given means from which it may obtain its support, and the objects of its activity. It supplies its own nourishment, and is the object of its own operations. While it is exclusively its own basis of existence, and absolute final aim, it is also the energising power realising this aim; developing it not only in the phenomena of the Natural, but also of the Spiritual Universe - the History of the World. That this 'Idea' or 'Reason' is the True, the Eternal, the absolutely powerful essence; that it reveals itself in the World, and that in that world nothing else is revealed but this and its honour and glory - is the thesis which, as we have said, has been proved in Philosophy, and is here regarded as demonstrated.'

One can only remark in leaving such a statement behind, that when Hegel is proposing an idea which he thinks difficult of comprehension to relatively ordinary mortals, he simply gives his assurance that this has been proved by philosophy and that it can, therefore, be accepted for the rest of the argument. What Hegel thought to be proved in philosophy seems now quite incredible, but we shall return to this in our later criticisms of Hegel. It is at least abundantly clear, however, how Hegel himself regarded the nature of Reason : as a substantive reality interpenetrating the entire world of nature and history.

Hegal then went on to give a detailed account of this dialectical process of Reason in nature and history.

The primary 'thesis' in the creation of the world - in the process of 'becoming of things' in the world - was the World Spirit itself; *THE IDEA* in which all actualisation originated. This spirit was the initial Idea in which all subsequent creation, all subsequent actualizations of truth in the world, was a potentiality. The world spirit, however, encountered the constraints and limitations of its own 'antithesis' : MATTER. The conflicts and contradictions between thesis and antithesis, spirit and matter, were thereafter worked out, giving rise to new syntheses, and thus the process of creation began, continued, and continues. What was originally *IDEA,* a potentiality of spirit, came to be made real in the world; came to be actualised *in* the created world; as the world of objects, creatures, events as we know it. In such a way, Hegel offered an account of the entire development of universal history; the total process of creation of the physical world; but he then went on to claim that this same actualisation of the potentialities of the world spirit continued and could be seen in the events of human history and the development of civilization. The 'intelligibility' of history as well as of nature, could be clarified by unravelling the complexity of its events and tracing the dialectical unfolding of the world spirit in the activities and institutions of society.

In giving the same kind of dialectical account of the processes of history, Hegel conceived the World Spirit, still, as being the initial 'idea' or 'thesis' of history, and its antithesis as being the materially rooted desires and passions of mankind, those impulsive appetites over which mind strives to establish adequate control in order to achieve, for all of them, their richest mutual fulfilment. The ultimate aim and outcome of this dialectical struggle between mind and spirit on the one hand, and materially rooted impulse on the other, was therefore a movement towards order and liberty which, according to Hegel, could only be achieved under the conditions of morality worked out in the form of the state. Hegel wrote as follows:

> 'Two elements, therefore, enter into the object of our investigations; the first the Idea, the second the complex of human passions; the one the warp, the other the woof of the vast arras-web of Universal History. The concrete mean and union of the two is Liberty, under the conditions of morality in a state.'

Hegel also believed that in this struggle towards formal liberty there was not only an actualisation of what was initially potential in spirit, but also that these potentialities of spirit moved from the realm of unconsciousness into the level of human consciousness, so that the ultimate outcome was the full consciousness and enjoyment on the part of the spirit, of its own created freedom.

> 'The History of the World begins with its general aim - the realization of the Idea of Spirit - only in an implicit form in Nature; a hidden, most profoundly hidden, unconscious instinct; and the whole process of History (as already observed), is directed to rendering this unconscious impulse a conscious one.'

And again :

> 'The realisation of freedom is the absolute final aim' of the process of history, and this, he maintained, 'exists for its own sake.'

We must note next how Hegel accounted for this process of historical change in terms of dialectical development. First, it is important to see the way in which he described the idea of development itself, for this was to become a central concept in the work of later sociologists, especially for example, in that of Hobhouse. Hegel wrote:

> 'The principle of Development involves the existence of a latent germ of being - a capacity or potentiality striving to realise itself. This format conception finds actual existence in Spirit; which has the History of the World for its theatre, its possession, and the sphere

of its realisation. It is not of such a nature as to be tossed to and fro amid the superficial play of accidents, but is rather the absolute arbiter of things; entirely unmoved by contingencies, which, indeed, it applies and manages for its own purposes. Development, however, is also a property of organised natural objects. Their existence presents itself, not as an exclusively dependent one, subjected to external changes, but as one which expands itself in virtue of an internal unchangeable principle; a simple essence, whose existence, *i.e.,* as a germ, is primarily simple, but which subsequently develops a variety of parts, that become involved with other objects, and consequently live through a continuous process of changes; a process nevertheless, that results in the very contrary of change, and is even transformed into a *vis conservatrix* of the organic principle, and the form embodying it. Thus, the organized individuum produces itself; it expands itself actually to what it was always potentially. So Spirit is only that which it attains by its own efforts; it makes itself actually what it always was potentially. That development (of natural organism) takes place in a direct, unopposed, unhindered manner. Between the Idea and its realisation the essential constitution of the original germ and the conformity to it of the existence derived from it no disturbing influence can intrude. But in relation to Spirit it is quite otherwise. The realisation of its Idea is mediated by consciousness and will; these very faculties are, in the first instance, sunk in their primary merely natural life; the first objects and goal of their striving is the realisation of their merely natural destiny but which, since it is Spirit that animates it, is possessed of vast attractions and displays great power and (moral) richness. Thus, Spirit is at war with itself; it has to overcome itself as its most formidable obstacle. That development which in the sphere of Nature is a peaceful growth, is in that of Spirit, a severe, a mighty conflict with itself. What Spirit really strives for is the realisation of its Ideal being, but in doing so, it hides that goal from its own vision, and is proud and well satisfied in this alienation from it.'

'Its expansion, therefore, does not prevent the harmless tranquillity of mere growth, as does that of organic life, but a stern reluctant working against itself. It exhibits, moreover, not the mere formal conception of development, but the attainment of a definite result. The goal of attainment we determined at the outset; it is Spirit in its *completeness,* in its essential nature, i.e. Freedom. This is the fundamental object, and therefore also the leading principle of the development - that whereby it receives meaning and importance...'

As to the dialectical nature of this development of spirit in the world, after having written briefly about the complicated contents of world history - 'that vast picture of changes and transactions; of infinitely manifold forms of peoples, states, individuals in unresting succession' - Hegel continued:

> 'The general thought - the category which first presents itself in this restless mutation of individuals and peoples, existing for a time and then vanishing - is that of *change* at large. The sight of the ruins of some ancient sovereignty directly leads us to contemplate this thought of change in its negative aspect. What traveller among the ruins of Carthage, of Palmyra, Persepolis, or Rome, has not been stimulated to reflections on the transiency of kingdoms and men, and to sadness at the thought of a vigorous and rich life now departed - a sadness which does not expend itself on personal losses and the uncertainty of one's own undertakings, but is a disinterested sorrow at the decay of a splendid and highly cultured national life! But the next consideration which allies itself with that of change is, that change while it imports dissolution, involves at the same time the rise of a new life - that while death is the issue of life, life is also the issue of death. This is a grand conception; one which the Oriental thinkers attained, and which is perhaps the highest in their metaphysics. In the idea of Metempsychosis we find it evolved in its relation to individual existence; but a myth more generally known, is that of the Phoenix as a type of life of Nature; eternally preparing for itself its funeral pile, and consuming itself upon it; but so that from its ashes is produced the new, renovated, fresh life. But this image is only Asiatic; oriental not occidental. Spirit - consuming the envelope of its existence - does not merely pass into another envelope, nor rise rejuvenescent from the ashes of its previous form; it comes forth exalted, glorified, a purer spirit. It certainly makes war upon itself - consumes its own existence; but in this very destruction it works up that existence into a new form, and each successive phase becomes in its turn a material, working on which it exalts itself to a new grade.'

The next point in Hegel's system which must be made clear is his teaching that the dialectical processes whereby the World Spirit becomes actualised in history (becomes objectified and then borne in upon human consciousness) takes the form of large scale social movements which assume their patterns of institutionalisation, over and above the heads of individuals and without awareness or foresight. It is the State according to Hegel, which is the vehicle of spiritual advance. It is in the State, not in the minds of individuals, that the achievements of the world spirit, at any particular time, come to be objectified. And by the State, Hegel meant the totality of the inter-connected social institutions of any particular epoch of civilisation. The will and achievement of the world spirit in any period is to be seen in the characteristic institutions of the State, and individuals can only find their fulfilment and historical destiny in so far as they submit themselves to those values and purposes which are manifested in the State of their time. The whole - qualitatively as well as quantitatively - is greater than the parts (including the individuals) of which it consists. The highest objective spiritual truth of any epoch lies in the totality of the state, and individuals realise and fulfil their own nature by virtue of their participation in the whole. It is not the case that the whole, the totality of institutions, is consciously brought about by the efforts of purposive individuals. The whole makes the parts, not the parts the whole. The qualities of the whole are not simply a sum of the independent qualities of the individual parts. Qualities arise in the creative process of the whole itself and these qualities are then engendered and created in individuals (the parts) as they enter, and are appreciated in, their consciousnes.

There are several important elements in this point of view which need special attention.

Firstly, from the point of view of subsequent sociological analysis, it is important to notice that the conception of a society which Hegel found it necessary to use was already a clear idea of the social system: consisting of various institutions which, though existing for specific purposes and having particular functions in relation to some aspect of human nature and human freedom, were nonetheless interdependent in their characteristics, all - together - forming one total society with its own qualitatively distinct ethos. This 'ethos' of the whole society, too, was conceived as having an important determining influence upon the nature and character of the individuals in society. Hegel, in short, had a distinct conception of 'social psychology' in the sense that it was the psychological aspect of the collectivity of society which engendered qualities in individual minds and personalities. But another very interesting point in this connection is that

Hegel believed a society to be a total phenomenon which, in fact, could not, excepting superficially, be said to consist of separable parts at all. A society, a 'totality of institutions', was a qualitatively new and distinct creative process in nature; it was a 'total' historical and cultural phenomenon and could only be properly understood as such.

It is only from our own point of view, and for purposes of analysis that we can 'separate' aspects of the whole into parts. Thus, we can speak of the 'religion' of a society, the 'economic' organisation of a society, the 'political' system in a society, the 'art' of a society, and so on, but this is a matter of analytical necessity only. We find it impossible to understand the whole without some such kind of preliminary analysis and description. Nonethesess, Hegel maintains, a society is, in fact, a totality which does not possess these sharp distinctions. The religious aspects, the economic aspects, the governmental aspects, the artistic aspects, of a society all interpenetrate each other. Together, they all constitute one living creative whole. Hegel wrote, for example, when speaking of the union between the objective manifestation of the world spirit and the subjective will of individual personalities.

> 'The objective existence of this union is the State, which is therefore the basis and centre of the other concrete elements of the life of a people - of art, of law, of morals, of religion, of science.'

And, he went on:

> 'A state is an individual totality of which you cannot select any particular side, even a supremely important one such as its political constitution, and deliberate and decide respecting it in that isolated form.'

It is clear beyond doubt then, that Hegel can be said, quite definitely, to have been a 'sociologist' in his way of regarding society and his proposed way of understanding and explaining it. He was perfectly clear in both his conception and his treatment, that the analysis of society had to be based upon the recognition of this intimate interconnection between social institutions; and that it was a positive error to believe that any one institution in a society could be understood in isolation from the rest. He thought of a social system, a set of social institutions interconnected with each other, almost exactly as we now think of it. This is a very important insight, and later we shall see that it has considerable weight and raises difficult problems, from the point of view of distinguishing between concepts we find useful for describing and analysing the constituent parts of a society, and the concepts we require for the causal explanation of its nature and changes. But this question must be left until the very end of our study, when we have considered the ways in which many sociologists have thought about it and tried to deal with it.

Before leaving this whole question, however, let us see exactly how Hegel thought about the nature of the state as the objectification of the world spirit. First of all, he wrote:

> 'What is the material in which the Idea of Reason is wrought out? The primary answer would be, Personality itself - human desires - Subjectivity generally. In human knowledge and volition, as its material element, Reason attains positive existence. We have considered subjective volition where it has an object which is the truth and essence of a reality, viz. where it constitutes a great world-historical passion. As a subjective will, occupied with limited passions, it is dependent, and can gratify its desires only within the limits of this dependence. But the subjective will has also a substantial life - a reality, in which it moves in the region of essential being, and has the essential itself as the object of its existence. This essential being is the union of the subjective with the rational Will: it is the moral Whole, the State, which is that form of reality in which the individual has and enjoys his freedom, but on the condition of his recognising, believing in, and willing that which is common to the Whole. And this must not be understood as if the subjective will of the social unit attained its gratification and enjoyment through that common Will; as if this were a means provided for its benefit; as if the individual, in his relations to other individuals, thus limited his freedom, in order that this universal limitation - the mutual constraint of all - might secure a small space of liberty for each. Rather, we affirm, are Law, Morality, Government, and they alone, the positive reality and completion of Freedom. Freedom of a low and limited order, is mere caprice; which finds its exercise in the sphere of particular and limited desires.'

> 'In the history of the World, only those peoples can come under our notice which form a state. For it must be understood that this latter is

the realisation of Freedom, *i.e.* of the absolute final aim, and that it exists for its own sake. It must further be understood that all the worth which the human being possesses - and spiritual reality, he possesses only through the State. For his spiritual reality consists in this, that his own essence - Reason - is objectively present to him, that it possesses objective immediate existence for him. Thus, only is he fully conscious; thus only is he a partaker of morality - of a just and moral social and political life. For Truth is the Unity of the universal and subjective Will; and the Universal is to be found in the State, in its laws, universal and rational arrangements. The State is the Divine Idea as it exists on Earth.'

And then:

'Summing up what has been said of the State, we find that we have been led to call its vital principle, as actuating the individuals who compose it, Morality. The State, its laws, its arrangements, constitute the rights of its members; its natural features, its mountains, air, and waters, are their country, their fatherland, their outward material property; the history of this State, their deeds; what their ancestors have produced, belongs to them and lives in their memory. All is their possession, just as they are possessed by it; for it constitutes their existence, their being.'

'Their imagination is occupied with the ideas thus presented, while the adoption of these laws, and of a fatherland so conditioned is the expression of their will. It is this matured totality which thus constitutes one Being, the spirit of one people. To it the individual members belong; each unit is the Son of his Nation, and at the same time - in as far as the State to which he belongs is undergoing development - the Son of his Age. None remains behind it, still less advances beyond it. This Spiritual Being (the Spirit of his Time) is his; he is a representative of it; it is that in which he originated, and in which he lives.'

Hegel then went on to claim that the entire process of history could be divided clearly into certain important epochs of civilisation, each of which was characterised by a newly emergent form of the state (a new 'totality of institutions)', and each of which constituted an advance of the world spirit. In each epoch there was a distinctive quality of perception, thought, and feeling in religious institutions; of moral and philosophical conceptions in political institutions; of perceptions and insight into the nature of things in artistic creation; and similarly in all aspects of social life and organisation. Amongst all these there was an all-pervading consensus, a unified 'ethos', which linked them all together, permeating them with a common quality and character; and all these aspects of this 'totality' of civilised achievement were aspects of that actualization, accomplished in that period, of what was originally potential in the world-spirit. Individuals had the fullest experience of the freedom and fulfilment which their nature allowed, if they were fully aware of this ethos of their own time and dedicated themselves to it.

Hegel then undertook a detailed study of history in order to trace and describe such epochs, and there were, he claimed, three major epochs of human civilisation which could be clearly distinguished.

'The Oriental World' (of the large, highly centralised civilisations of antiquity) was characterised by central despotic authority. *No-one* therefore, was free. Sometimes Hegel wrote as though only one person was free in such a despotism, namely the despot himself; but in his detailed consideration of this he maintained that the despot himself must have been so bound up within the authoritarian network of the 'totality' of institutions that even he himself could not be considered free. The second epoch was that of the *Graeco-Roman* world in which some were free (i.e., the principle of political citizenship had emerged, and some people enjoyed it, but there was still an uncritical assumption that some men were born to slavery and the institutions of society still rested upon an unfree section of the population). Thirdly, there was the *German-European* epoch in which all were free; that is, the conception had emerged in this latter epoch that man as such *(and universally)* was free, and the institutions of society were changing in such a way as effectively to secure this for all citizens.

Fach of these epochs manifested (in the creative 'totality' of the state) a new 'thesis' for the subsequent dialectical development of the world spirit. Each, however, gave rise within its own created institutions to its 'anti-thesis'. The institutions of each gave rise to contradictions, which grew like the seeds of a new birth within the womb of the old society. Dialectical conflict ensued. The old order of the state was gradually disintegrated, giving rise to the new. Hegel sometimes wrote as though he believed that in the German-European epoch of his own time, the world spirit had, in large part, achieved its task, since this represented a full achievement of human freedom, and, as we have seen, the criterion of spiritual advance which Hegel adopted as the ultimate end of the whole process of history, was the progressive achievement of freedom. But this apparent finality must not be taken too seriously, as we shall see.

Before considering the ways in which Hegel's system is open to criticism, there is one other important aspect of his 'theory' which deserves attention and emphasis. This is the role which he attributed in the 'dialectics of history' to 'World Historical Individuals'. And this can best be introduced by thinking of the relation between the 'totality' of the state as Hegel thought of it, and 'totalitarianism' as it has come to exist in modern political thought and action.

If we think of Hegel's system without reference to recent political events, it may seem an exciting, speculative philosophy which is politically harmless; having little to do with fanaticism or dictatorship. When Hegel spoke of the 'totality' of the state, he was obviously referring to the gradual unfolding of a consensus in the thought, feeling and institutions of a civilisation. He referred to the all-pervading ethos of an epoch as a unified spiritual achievement, which emerged gradually and historically. And this seems to have little to do with modern totalitarian dictators. For they - whether Fascist, National Socialist or communist - have, on the contrary, positively imposed the uniformity which they desire upon all the people in society. They have positively created a 'totality' of institutions in society: forcing a whole people to accept the values and the 'historical task' which they themselves dictate; forcing thought into certain channels; dictating certain principles for the creation of works of art; forbidding anything which militates against their own ideology. On the face of it, there seems to be a great gulf between a Hegel and a Hitler.

This gap, however, is not as wide as it appears when we consider what Hegel had to say about the nature and task of great men in history; the men he called 'WORLD

HISTORICAL INDIVIDUALS'. Although Hegel insisted that the World Spirit was manifested in the 'totality' of society and that this occurred over and above the consciousness and efforts of individuals as such, he nonetheless claimed that some men were specially gifted and possessed a greater and more far-reaching vision than the average individuals in society. They possessed an insight into the dialectical processes of history that went beyond that of ordinary men. They could divine in the bewildering changes which were going on about them the next historical step of the 'World Spirit'. They could see the next important advance in human destiny. Their task, then, was always to act as luminaries, as leaders, to the confused people of their day, clarifying their immediate historic task and helping them to achieve it.

When describing such World Historical Individuals, Hegel tended to write with a certain poetic fervour, maintaining that these men could commit deeds which, to others, would seem unjustifiable, and which might indeed, for other men, be thought immoral and punishable. They, if necessary, could ignore the sufferings of their fellows because their task was so noble and of such crucial importance.

Why it is that the World Spirit, after all these massive aggregate dialectical processes, suddenly needs to make use of eminent individuals of this kind, Hegel does not tell us. But it is clear, on considering what Hegel said about them, that he and the Hitlers of this world are not so far apart as one might have thought at first glance. Neither does it seem so clear that there are the two brands of totalitarianism, which we distinguished at the outset. The two seem to fuse into one.

Having said that world historical individuals are those who direct 'those momentous collisions between existing acknowledged duties, laws and rights and those contingencies which are adverse to this fixed system', and having mentioned men like Caesar and Napoleon as examples. Hegel went on to write:

> 'Such are all great historical men, whose own particular aims involve those large issues which are the will of the World-Spirit. They may be called Heroes, inasmuch as they have derived their purposes and their

> vocation, not from the calm, regular course of things, sanctioned by the existing order; but form a concealed fount - one which has not attained to phenomenal, present existence, from that inner Spirit, still hidden beneath the surface, which, impinging on the outer world as on a shell, bursts it in pieces, because it is another kernel than that which belonged to the shell in question. They are men, therefore, who appear to draw the impulse of their life from themselves; and whose deeds have produced a condition of things and a complex of historical relations which appear to be only their interest, and their work.'
>
> 'They are thinking men, who had an insight into the requirements of the time - what was ripe for development. This was the very Truth for their age, for their world; the species next in order, so to speak, and which was already formed in the womb of time. It was theirs to know this nascent principle; the necessary, directly sequent step in progress, which their world was to take; to make this their aim, and to expend their energy in promoting it. World-historical men - the Heroes of an epoch - must, therefore, be recognised as its clear-sighted ones; their deeds, their words are the best of that time.'

And as to what can only be called the ethical privileges of such individuals, Hegel wrote:

> 'A World-historical individual is not so unwise as to indulge a variety of wishes to divide his regards. He is devoted to the One Aim regardless of all else. It is even possible that such men may treat other great, even sacred interests, inconsiderately; conduct which is indeed obnoxious to moral reprehension. But so mighty a form must trample down many an innocent flower - crush to pieces many an object in its path.'
>
> 'The deeds of great men, who are the Individuals of the World's History, thus appear not only justified in view of that intrinsic result of which they were not conscious, but also from the point of view occupied by the secular moralist. But looked at from this point, moral claims that are irrelevant, must not be brought into collision with world-historical deeds and their accomplishment. The Litany of Private virtues - modesty, humility, philanthrophy and forbearance - must not be raised against them.'

One can only hope, when such Individuals are putting Jews in gas ovens, burning heretics, smashing kulaks, and even forcing upon us a 'choice' between fivepenny and fourpenny mail, that the World Spirit will understand us in entertaining a measure of doubt about their authority, and a certain resentment at their privilege.

In what ways can Hegel's philosophy of history be criticised?

In the first place, Hegel had the merit of seeing the world, and the human situation in the world, as a process of ongoing change, and made an awe-inspiring attempt to bring together the earlier absolutism of metaphysics and this new dynamic conception of a changing universe. Those who criticise his grandiose attempt and find his talk of the World Spirit, the Idea and the Real, the Potential and the Actual, the role of World Historical Individuals, confusing should at least stop and reflect whether their own beliefs and assumptions do not imply similar difficulties. The Christian, for example, who believes in a God who created and sustains the world and who is working his purpose out in history, must meet exactly the same kind of difficulties in bringing his notions of God and spiritual reality together with our modern scientific knowledge of the changing universe and the changes of human society. Hegel may have failed - but is there any other philosophy of history basing itself on the primacy of spirit or mind as the fundamental ground of reality, which has succeeded any better than he did? The answer, as far as I am aware, is - no!

I think it is worth saying too, that we should beware of rejecting Hegel's ideas, and his 'metaphysically toned' way of stating them, too easily. We live in a climate of thought so closely dictated by the immediate empiricism of science, and a very technologically orientated science at that, that we are altogether too prone to assume that our own perspective is the right one. There is also a hectic pressure about our academic thinking that well-nigh precludes the kind of searching thought that an assessment of Hegel, or any of the other great philosophers requires. Speaking personally, and although I find some things in him quite unacceptable, I always feel Hegel to be full of a profundity which one cannot leave unconsidered. There is something so telling in his notions of 'creativity' and 'development' and the significance of 'forms' in nature and history; he seems so intriguingly to bring the central ideas of early metaphysics into the context of our modern 'dynamic' conception of nature and history; that I always feel persuaded that he deserves long and careful study. Certainly some of the 'materialist' notions which have followed him are brash in comparison. And, after all, it is a possibility that God exists!

Hegel also had the great merit of introducing perspective into historical knowledge. His was not the first attempt; but it was certainly more clear and more detailed than anything that had been attempted before. Furthermore, his lectures on the philosophy of history are full of fascinating observations as, for example, on the intimate relation between religious perception and experience and artistic perception and experience in the various epochs, and many other similar insights. Hegel's work contains a richness to which this kind of brief account cannot possibly do justice. It is also worth bearing in mind that Hegel was one of the first thinkers to reflect, not only upon the facts of history, but upon the methods of writing history itself, and his observations in the field of historiography are still of the greatest interest.

When all is said in Hegel's favour, however, his system does appear to suffer from some defects and some grave dangers.

In the first place, his notion of reason as a substantive reality in the world (actually existent in the material nature of the world), and his identification of processes of logic with the actual processes of natural and historical events, is not a view which can now be upheld. Now-a-days we think of reasoning, thinking, the procedures of logical inferences, as an activity which men undertake. Reasoning is a matter of men thinking. We can certainly abstract a statement of what constitutes 'rational thought' from the active procedures of men thinking. But reason cannot be said to exist as a substantive fact apart from this. Reason does not exist independently of men reasoning, or clarifying the processes of their reasoning. And though men may make statements about nature and history from which logical inferences may be made, so that their statements may be logically connected, the actual porcesses of nature and history cannot themselves be held necessarily to be logically interconnected. This, if I understand it a right, is one aspect of the fundamental point which Hume makes in his theory of knowledge.

For example, suppose that a man is walking under a cliff when a boulder is dislodged by a violent wind, and, in falling, this crushes and kills him. Or suppose that a volcanic eruption spills lava over a small island in the Atlantic and destroys the people who live on it. In both these cases, we can assemble knowledge about all the processes involved: the force of the wind, the force of gravity, the resistance to pressure of the human body; the power of a volcanic eruption, the effect of lava upon human bodies, and so on. We can then provide a wide body of statements which are themselves logically interconnected and from which further inferences can be made to the effect that if such and such happens, then men will be killed and communities will be destroyed. But it cannot be maintained, surely, that the natural events themselves are logically connected? That they are the manifestation of substantive reason? They are interconnected facts in our experience, but it would surely be very difficult to see such sequences of facts as being rationally meaningful in terms of any substantive reason or spirit? Indeed, if some 'spiritual reality' underlay events of this kind; if it constituted interconnections of this kind, and brought them about deliberately; we should be driven to have a very jaundiced conception of it. Men can reason about the regular connections between rocks, wind, volcanoes, and human death, but the physical interdependencies cannot, surely, be said to be 'substantive reason'? Nature and history, then, cannot be assumed to be the substantive rational processes that Hegel conceived them to be, and his assertion that this assumption is one already proved in philosophy is an assertion that we ourselves cannot possibly accept or adopt.

Secondly, whilst there is merit in Hegel's insistence that reality can only be properly conceived as a process of change; and whilst his conception of 'dialectical' change seems as though it would be useful in analysing the contradictions and conflicting forces in nature and history; it must be said that the points and methods of transition in historical change, as described by Hegel, turn out to be extremely vague. In a sense, of course, it is a simple truism that the assumption of a definite form by social institutions and their values necessarily introduces related constraints. These can give rise to conflict, and this can bring about further change whereby the problems are resolved. But this changed institution will create new constraints, and so on. But Hegel nowhere makes very clear the actual mechanisms of social change which are at work. In this, as we shall see later, Marx sought to improve upon Hegel.

It has been stated as a third criticism, that Hegel's apparent finality is curious, to say the least. The idea that the task of the world spirit was more or less completed in the Europe of his own day seems, now, rather an odd conclusion. To my mind, however, this is a relatively minor criticism, for one or two reasons.

Firstly, because it is a criticism which is applicable to all thinkers of this kind, who are seeking a 'system' of explanation; and can be understood. There seems to be a powerful inclination in men towards the achievement of certainty, conclusiveness, completeness in the statement of their theories. There is a certain aesthetic love of rounding off one's own metaphysical system; making it a complete, finished, harmonious whole; which tends to make all thinkers bring their systems to a conclusion. The world itself, however, is never as final as our speculative systems of thought about it. It goes on and changes, and men find their 'completed' systems of thought no longer satisfactory. This is so much so that one might even conclude that any system of thought or any theory of society which claims finality, which claims to explain everything, demonstrates at once its weakness and inadequacy.

The statement made by A. N. Whitehead in the preface to his book *Process and Reality*—

> 'There remains the final reflection, how shallow, puny, and imperfect are efforts to sound the depths in the nature of things. In philosophical discussion, the merest hint of dogmatic certainty as to finality of statement is an exhibition of folly.'—seems to me altogether salutary.

The second reason, however, why one cannot make this a weighty criticism of Hegel, is that it is altogether doubtful whether he was as final in his conceptions as his work sometimes tends to suggest. The apparent finality is because he confined his analysis entirely to what had already happened in history, and explicitly set aside any consideration of what might happen in future. But in what he had to say about the new world of

America, it is clear that his mind was by no means altogether closed to the probability of future development and advance.In writing of'the new world and the dreams to which it may give rise', he said:

> 'America is therefore the land of the future, where, in the ages that lie before us, the burden of the World's History shall reveal itself - perhaps in a contest between North and South America. It is a land of desire for all those who are weary of the historical lumber-room of old Europe. Napoleon is reported to have said, 'Cette vieille Europe m'ennuie.' It is for America to abandon the ground on which hitherto the History of the World has developed itself. What has taken place in the New World up to the present time is only an echo of the Old World, the expression of a foreign life; and as a Land of the Future, it has no interest for us here, for, as regards History, our concern must be with that which has been and that which is. In regard to Philosophy, on the other hand, we have to do with that which (stricly speaking) is neither past nor future, but with that which is, which has an eternal existence - with Reason; and this is quite sufficient to occupy us.'

It seems obvious that we should not make too much of this particular criticism of Hegel.

A fourth criticism is that his doctrine of 'the Real Will' of the World Spirit, and of the role of 'World Historical Individuals' in serving this will, is dangerous in its totalitarian and authoritarian implications. How are ordinary mortals to judge which of these - among the many power-seeking leaders who seem desirous of setting them about their historical task - are the great men possessing genuine insight into the real will of the world spirit? Which among them is really the servant of the world spirit and which is merely an upstart? This is an especially pressing question when some of the "Leaders' who tramp about the stage of the world do not seem to have the insight into world-history of an average bus-conductor. According to Hegel, obviously, ordinary people can have no ground for judgment. Indeed, it is doubtful whether in his system they can be said to have a right to judge. If one sympathises with 'World Spirits' one might be inclined to respond to the grandeur of Hegel's zeal. But if, on the countrary, one sympathises with ordinary mortals one might be strongly disinclined to agree with Hegel on this matter. From this latter point of view, as soon as a man puts himself forward as a World Historical Individual, claiming a right to trample upon others for the purpose of historical destiny, our principle ought always to be - to trim his down to scale; to put him in prison rather than in government, in an asylum rather than the House of Lords.

Philosophically speaking, however, it is enough to point out that there seem to be no criteria whatever for demonstrating the existence of such a 'real will' independent of the minds of men in society, and for the belief that there are some great individuals who have been given a preferential insight into the nature of it.

Closely linked to this is the fifth criticism - that Hegel's notion of freedom is not easily comprehensible. It has uncomfortable ambiguities. It is certainly intelligible to maintain that a person may find a rich fulfilment of the many aspects of his nature by devoting himself to tasks and values which he finds in the society about him, and even in the values and aims of his social tradition which he feels to be greater than himself. It is also intelligible to speak of the maximisation of freedom being only possible in the conditions of morality secured by certain institutions of the state. But to speak of this in terms of submitting himself to what is 'objectified' in the 'totality' of the state can surely be a complete abnegation of freedom as we know it. Hegel seems to conceive of freedom and complete submission to the objective qualities and values of the state as being identical. And this seems both philosophically unwarranted and politically highly dangerous.

It is quite clear from these brief accounts that these theories selected from the 'philosophy of history' possessed the same characteristics as the theories in myth and religion, and moral and political philosophy, which we considered earlier. Here again, we find that they were based upon the facts of nature and history; attempted a certain moral justification of the forms of society and authority in history; offered an analysis of the many institutions of society in their interdependence within society as a 'whole'; and clearly thought of the nature of the individual and society as being very closely and reciprocally linked. Perhaps more like the 'religious' theories than the theories of moral and political philosophy, these 'philosophies of history' also placed man and society within the wider context of reality at large, and provided an 'intelligible' account of this reality. The same elements of theory were therefore clearly present.

Our discussion of the ideas of Hegel in particular, however, has indicated one or two important points which ought to be emphasised.

Firstly, it is perfectly clear that Hegel was already employing 'sociological' insight in his conception of the nature of society and social change. His analysis of society as a 'whole' in terms of a pattern of interconnected institutions is scarcely different from that of a modern sociologist. He also saw quite clearly, like Condorcet, Montesquieu, and many later writers, that the development of mind and the growth of knowledge is significantly correlated with changes in all the other institutions of society, and that it can therefore be used as a central measure for comparative studies. He saw perfectly clearly too, the close interdependence between the nature of the individual personality and the symbolic content of the social tradition, and that the two should properly be studied in the closest inter relationship. In short, in his pursuit of a satisfactory 'philosophy of history', a satisfactory account of the nature of man and his place in the world, Hegel had found a 'sociological analysis of society in history indispensable.

We have seen, however, that in spite of this conception, Hegel's system and method of interpretation was still strongly rooted in dogmatic metaphysics. Many principle which Hegel seemed to accept uncritically, and certainly many of the large-scale pronouncements which he derived from them, were such as to seem philosophically in error, and dangerous for political practice.

And this leads to the final point which has become quite plain: that the very existence of a philosophy of history like that of Hegel, which can become so influential in political thought and practice, and which possesses so much that is dubious and dangerous, demonstrates, perhaps more forcibly than anything else, the need for a more reliable science of society. It is only possible to criticize such systems of thought adequately if we can show that we have better methods than they have; if we can show that our judgments and hypotheses rest on more accurate criteria than theirs; if we can provide a better and more reliable (more testable) survey of the facts of history and historical change than that which Hegel and similar thinkers put forward.

One can say, in conclusion, that although Hegel's philosophy of history did not constitute a scientific sociology, it had the great merit of making the development of such a science necessary; of making the need for it starkly apparent. And this, in a way, is the kind of dialectical development of knowledge that he himself had in mind. The contribution he made was certainly a telling and a productive one. So much sprang, by way of criticism, from the systematic statement which he accomplished.

D. SCIENCE AND EPISTEMOLOGY

In addition to the later developments of moral and political philosophy and the philosophy of history, there two other developments of thought during the eighteenth century which were especially important in leading to fundamental criticisms of early social theories, and which culminated, at the same time, in the clear need for a science of society. These were, firstly, the development and extension of the natural sciences: their increasing success in producing a testable and useful body of knowledge about various aspects of the nature of the world; and, secondly, the development in the theory of knowledge (epistemology) attendant upon this.

Little need be said about the developments of science. It is enough simply to note that following the exacting criticisms of the methods of attaining knowledge undertaken by philosophers such as Hobbes and Descartes there had been an extension of the methods of science in investigating all aspects of the nature of the physical world - in physics, astronomy, chemistry, and so on. In all these fields science was proving itself increasingly superior to other and earlier methods of study. It was not only extending man's knowledge of the world, but also bringing about an increasing degree of control over the environment with regard to the better satisfaction of human needs and the increase in human welfare. The chief thing to emphasise, for our purposes, is that this development of the natural sciences gave rise to a totally new perspective, concerning the place of man in nature.

Two sciences in particular were responsible for this. The first was the science of geology which, in its new methods of dating the geological strata of the earth, began to give completely new perspectives of time as far as the origin and history of man in the world was concerned. The place of man in the scheme of creation; of the human species within the context of all other species; could now be dated in a much more exact way, so that early theories concerning the special creation of man were at least thrown open to serious question. But the second and probably more important science was that of biology. There had been many doubts about the possibility of applying the scientific method to the study of man, but once biology became established as a science it could no longer be doubted that the study of at least some aspects of man permitted of scientific study. Whatever Man might be besides, he had now to be seen, at least, as one animal species amongst others. This at once gave support to the idea that science could be employed in the study of man and stimulated its further exploration. It also cast severe doubt upon the earlier theories of the origin and development of man and led to a search for a more satisfactory picture. And it led to a growing assumption that the development of human society and human civilisation had also to be understood in historical and developmental terms. Just as man seemed to have evolved from some earlier animal condition, so it seemed necessary and feasible to think that human society had developed from some condition of primitive savagery to the latter-day condition of complex and highly sophisticated civilisation.

All the older theories of man in society had now to come to terms with these new perspectives which the development of science provided.

Apart from establishing their own particular bodies of knowledge, however, the sciences gave rise, in general, to more exacting demands for standards of accuracy in any theories, about anything which claimed to be true. These new standards of rigour in 'explaining' events in nature were scrutinised and clarified very carefully in what has come to be called 'The Theory of Knowledge'. And undoubtedly the two people who contributed most in this direction were David Hume and Immanuel Kant.

The procedures whereby science arrived at testable knowledge were not at all the procedures of inference which had been clarified by logic and metaphysics in the past, and it was Hume more than any other who attempted very carefully to make clear what exactly was meant by 'scientific method' and what exactly was meant by the 'laws of causality' at which it arrived. In doing this he showed the ways in which speculative metaphysics was totally insufficient, when compared with scientific theories, in establishing testable knowledge about the world as we experience it.

David Hume

Hume asked quite directly, in his *Treatise of Human Nature:* What do we understand by causal laws? Or, putting the matter even more simply : when we say that certain factors, in conjunction, cause certain events, and that these cause-and-effect relationships are 'laws of nature', what exactly do we mean? His answer was simply this: that when we speak of certain factors causing subsequent events we mean only (a) that these factors are found in a certain special contiguity with each other when the subsequent event occurs, (b) that they are related to the event in a certain irreversible temporal sequence, and (c) that they are always so conjoined in our experience. It is this fact that they are always conjoined in our experience which leads us to claim that there is a necessary connection between them. In short, causal laws are merely statements of 'uniformities of co-existence' and 'uniformities of succession' which are constant in our experience. They are nothing more than this. They possess no logical certainty whatever - indeed logical certainty does not pertain to them. They are simply regularities among phenomena that we find in our experience.

When we say, for example, that putting a match to a vat of petrol causes an explosion we are saying no more than that a certain source of heat in special contiguity with petrol is constantly found in our experience to be followed by an explosion; and, furthermore, that the temporal sequence is always in the one direction. It is never the case that an explosion is followed by the appearance of a vat of petrol and the subsequent striking of a match. A 'causal law' comes to be stated, of course, not only about a particular match, vat of petrol, and explosion - but generally in terms of the ignition point of petrol. A particular explosion is then 'explained' in relation to this 'law'. But this is all that is involved. Furthermore, it is all that is necessary for the exact observation and measurement of events in nature and the statement of careful predictions about them.

Hume wrote:

> 'We have no other notion of cause and effect, but that of certain objects, which have been always conjoined together, and which in all past instances have been found inseparable. We cannot penetrate into the reason of the conjunction. We only observe the thing itself...
>
> Thus, though causation be a philosophical relation, as implying contiguity, succession, and constant conjunction, yet it is only so far as it is a natural relation, and produces a union among our ideas, that we are able to reason upon it, or draw any inference from it.'

Hume went so far as to say that all knowledge consisted of either deductive logical inference (i.e. the explicit clarification of the entailments of premises) or the statement of testable causal laws of the kind he had described. Nothing else constituted knowledge at all. At one stroke, then, all the metaphysical and religious theories of the past went into the wastepaper basket.

Immanuel Kant

This doctrine of extreme empiricism was, itself, something of an explosion to all those who had not radically and systematically doubted established religious and metaphysical theories, and Immanuel Kant, the German philosopher was among these. Kant was so profoundly disturbed by Hume's analysis as to feel compelled to undertake his own 'critical philosophy' in order to examine his contentions and to see how far they were correct. It is enough for our purposes to say that although, in his elaborate theory of knowledge, he modified very considerably Hume's views concerning the nature of the mind and the categories it brings with it to 'experiencing' the world and 'knowing' it, he did not so much refute Hume on the matter of his empiricism as take it one degree further.

Kant insisted that the human mind is much more than any kind of naive 'reflection' of facts or objects that exist in the external world, and that it brings categories of its own without which the perception of the world would be quite impossible. At the same time his position was in agreement with that of Hume that all our knowledge of the world is, and can only be, a knowledge of 'phenomena' : a knowledge of the world as it appears to us through the media of our human senses and human categories. Beyon this we cannot go. We can never know the world as it may actually exist beyond our experience of it. Kant said that we can have knowledge only of 'phenomena'; never of 'noumena'- by which he meant 'things in themselves.' To put this in another way - it may well be the case that the nature of the world has dimensions that go beyond human perception, but we can never establish knowledge of this reality. We can only establish knowledge in terms of regularities among phenomena: the objects and events of the world as we experience them.

All knowledge, then, is human knowledge, and consists, as Hume maintained, of 'analytical' knowledge (sequences of deductive logical inference) and 'synthetic' knowledge (propositions about the factual nature of the world as we experience it).

The upshot of these developments in science and the theory of knowledge meant quite simply that, henceforth, any theory about the nature of man and society had now to contend with the rigour of these new standards. Metaphysical assertion, which could not prescribe any conditions of test could no longer expect to be accepted whether on the grounds of faith, dogma, or anything else, without justifiable challenge. All theories now had to produce their credentials. They had to demonstrate the grounds of method on which they rested, and this meant that many of the earlier social theories which we have considered were seen to have considerable shortcomings. This was not to by any means, that they were worthless. Only that in many respects they fell short of accuracy, and therefore required improvement.

In addition to the trends of thought in moral philosophy and the philosophy of history, powerful in themselves, there was, therefore, this other movement, that could not be gainsaid, towards the need for some theory of man and society which could lay claim to respectability and exactitude in accordance with these new terms.

3

THE NEED FOR SOCIOLOGY

Revolution and the Reconstruction of Modern Society

We have now discussed our common-sense assumptions about the nature of man and society and the several kinds of early 'theories' which put forward certain 'truths' and speculations about them with sufficient thoroughness to see quite clearly how sociology is rooted in them and grew out of them. Both common-sense and the various theories of religion and philosophy possess a good deal that is of value, and a good deal which, in fact, constitutes the basis of sociology itself. Sociology is not something totally new which imposes itself in total opposition to them; it is something which grows quite consistently out of them, and which remains rooted in them. But it does and has to grow out of them, and beyond them, for the simple reason - which we have seen plainly - that they prove to be insufficient in our experience; they prove to be inadequate for our needs. And I would like to emphasise, as a final note in this first section on the 'Beginnings' of sociology, this element of need. It cannot be too much stressed for a proper understanding of sociology, that the subject emerged as a 'science' at a particular time when it became positively necessary. It was no accident. It was not some new, precious intellectual extravagance dreamed into being at someone's scholarly whim. It was needed by men. And it is still needed.

In all that we have said, it is quite plain, firstly, that the emergence of sociology - as an attempt to achieve a 'science' of society - was a necessary intellectual development. Throughout the eighteenth and in the early nineteenth centuries, there were developments of thought and knowledge in the sciences themselves, in the theory of knowledge, in moral and political philosophy, and in the philosophy of history which were all such as to lead to, and to emphasise the need for, the careful creation and elaboration of a science of society. None of the problems in these fields of thought could be studied at the level of profundity required, unless a scientific study of society as a whole, and of the place of man as an individual within it, was attempted, and, indeed, achieved to that degree of exactitude which proved possible. All these directions of thought were moving towards a point of culmination at which the new standards of scientific rigour were required in order to establish the basis of any new advances, or, indeed, for any satisfactory treatment of problems and questions already encountered.

All this has already been made clear.

Thought, however, does not take place in abstraction from society itself. Men do not theorise excepting in the context of their own life and times. And these changing theories of society were, in fact, part of a rising tide of social change which was to prove probably the most cataclysmic that men have ever experienced in their history, and which, in our own time, is becoming a flood embracing every corner of the world. The widespread commerce which had gradually changed and then disrupted the order of Christendom was now developing into a new industrial capitalism in which science was becoming harnessed to agricultural and industrial technology and in which secular nation states were the established and powerful units of political authority. The old order of institutions - of traditional authority in government; of sacred authority in the Church; of established status and privilege among the 'Estates' - Crown, nobles, commoners; of property and economic organisation appropriate to a still predominantly agrarian society, though much changed by mercantilism . . . all this was proving quite inadequate for the new complexity of activity in society. The 'ancien régime' was doomed, and it was to be broken asunder during the revolutionary decades of the end of the eighteenth century. The French Revolution especially was the symptomatic bursting of these many ill of social change.

The point which is central for our purpose is simply this: since the breakdown of society was a total breakdown, men experienced the need for a total social reconstruction. Since the entire fabric of institutions was falling apart, it was no longer thought feasible to reform society in a bit-and-piece manner. It was not enough to change the family here, education there, the political constitution at this point, economic organisation at that. A total re-making of society was thought to be necessary. And two things followed closely upon this persuasion. With the disruption of traditional authorities and, coupled with this, the disruption of religious belief, men (or at least significant numbers of them) came to believe that they themselves were responsible for the re-making of society. This was a conscious assumption of man's responsibility for the making of his own destiny of a kind and a magnitude quite new in history. And the second fact, attendant upon this, was that, needing responsibility to undertake the total reconstruction of their society, men also felt the need for a body of knowledge about the nature of society as a totality of institution to serve as a firm and reliable basis for their judgment and activities.

A science of society was needed by the politicians and others who were living within the wreck of an outmoded social order, and who had - in the most detailed and practical way : drawing up new laws of property; working out new constitutions; organising a new system of education - to make a new one. A knowledge of society was therefore of the very greatest urgency and importance.

It is worthwhile to press home this point : that this is a factor which has remained at the heart of sociology from that day to this. With the transformation of human society from the relatively simple conditions of traditional agrarian communities to the vast complexity of the conditions of industrial and urban organisation, a new body of knowledge has been, and is, necessary - if men are going to exercise any effective control whatsoever over the social forces which these new conditions have unleashed.

But there is another distinctive fact, implicit in all these intense actualities of social change, which was of vital importance then - in this early revolutionary epoch - and which remains so now. This is the awareness of the international implications of the social changes which were afoot.

From the age of mercantilism on, men had become increasingly aware of the international fabric of their trading relations and the links between political societies which these entailed. This did not mean that they necessarily desired international unity. The mercantilist themselves, with this awareness, had in fact sought separateness and independent nationhood. New ideas of national self-interest, however, were breaking down this simplicity. The free-trade ideas of Adam Smith were pointing to the interdependencies of nations in their trading and manufacturing activities, and, for many reformers, the old orders of power and authority were obstacles in the way of this new international freedom. The thought which accompanied the American and the French Revolutions was certainly already of an international and universal flavour. All the slogans were about the rights of man. Liberty, equality, fraternity - for men everywhere regardless of class, colour, creed - these were the principles on the lips of Tom Paine as well as on those of Jean-Jacques Rousseau. And there was another aspect of this.

Men were becoming aware - not only, now, in terms of ideas, but in terms of the seen and known implications of their economic and political activity - of the inter-linking of all the nations of the world into a global entirety of 'human society'. The unity of mankind was no longer an issue for ethical doubt or conviction; it was something - with all its threats and promises, all its difficulties and potentialities of achievement - which was clearly taking place. Commercial and industrial links, with their correlated political negotiations would come, gradually, to create a unity of interest throughout the world at large. The new conception of the responsible self-direction of man was therefore, at once, a conception of a united world.

The concern which emerged at the turning point of the eighteenth and nineteenth centuries with the role of the advanced societies of Europe and America with regard to the less technologically developed societies of the world, became a central preoccupation; and again, of course, it remains so to this day. We shall see that, at the very outset of the making of sociology proper, Auguste Comte was proposing a Council of European States which, utilising their advanced knowledge and experience in all fields, could aid the underdeveloped societies of the world. In 1970 we are still preoccupied with the consideration, though not, alas, with the possibility, for many realistic reasons, of the same simple expansiveness of altruistic feeling and effort which Comte had envisaged and hoped for. But again, we see here, in the awareness of a growing internationalism and the problems it entailed, a positive need for a scientific body of knowledge about the nature and interconnections of human societies.

In connection with the same point it is also worthwhile and important to note that, from the time of the Renaissance to the time of the French Revolution, the increase and the spread of human knowledge (achieved so much more effectively with the development of printing) had brought about an increased awareness, on the part of Europeans, of other peoples and civilisations. Men's conjectures about human nature and the nature of society had already begun to take into account the apparent diversities of practices between men in different parts of the world; between societies with different patterns of culture. When Montaigne, in his essays, was speculating about the human nature he saw about him in France and about which he read in his classical authors, he was able, rather wryly, to compare this with the practices of men who, apparently did not wear trousers! Anthropology was afoot. The new theories of society were therefore already taking these new comparative studies into account and it was already seen that the newly needed science of society required broad comparative studies in order properly to consider the actualities of human nature in various kinds of society.

It is also necessary to remember that, in the intense and many-sided conflicts which these massive social changes represented and brought in their train; in the radical cleavages between traditionalist and revolutionary; the movements and changes of social theory were far from being a peaceful matter of 'ivory-tower' scholasticism. The intellectuals were in the wars too. Hobbes had to seek refuge in Holland from Royalist and Roundhead alike; as had Spinoza from the spiky fist of orthodox theology. Tom Paine was imprisoned for his humanity, and Condorcet spent time in prison under threat of execution. His book on the development of the human mind which we now read in relative peace was published posthumously. But the chief point in mentioning this battle of ideas is simply-this. The movement towards a 'science of society' was not only not a peaceful thing: it was fought into existence in the teeth of earlier orthodoxies of ideas, and (and this is the crux of the matter) these orthodoxies have never relinquished their claims and their power. They remained when 'sociology' came into being. They remain now.

Theories of human nature and society have been, and are, claims for men's allegiance. Far more is attached to them, and invested in them, than purely intellectual questions as to their truth. All of which means that there are always theories of man and society making competing claims for men's support and loyalty. And it is therefore clear, too, that, in assessing these competing claims - the relative truths and falsities of all these theories - men experience the need for some firm ground of judgment and adjudication between them. In short, the intense dialogue between powerful ideological claims necessarily drives men towards the quest for some criteria of objective knowledge which will provide degrees of resolution.

Of course, though men are powerfully driven in their arguments, it does not follow by any means that they will like, admit, and accept the truth when they find it. And this leads to one final aspect of the felt need for a 'science' of society which deserves a good deal of emphasis.

It is simply that, in the thories of these violent changes, these hot arguments, these pressures towards extremism and fanaticism of all kinds, men came to fear 'idealism' in political affairs in the absence of reason, judgment, and a readiness to be tempered by the realism of considered knowledge. Plato had thought extreme democracy next door to tyranny, and, in this modern period of revolution, many men found that their demagogue of today was their dictator of tomorrow. It was this fear which drove Edmund Burke to criticise in the most searching way every procedure that the French Revolution stood for. He was not opposed to the attainment of justice and excellence in society, but he was passionately persuaded that the hot revolutionary method of transforming society overnight was not the right or the effective way to do it. Again, it is enough that we should simply note that some men, at least, came to see the need for knowledge and balanced judgment in approaching the thorny problems of the social transformations that were taking place about them, and this again led to the positive need for the systematic study of society, as distinct from simply entertaining passionate ideals about its future. We shall see that practically all the major sociologists, from Comte onwards, had at the very heart of their intellectual concerns this awareness of the problems of statesmanship in dealing wisely with the complex political scene of the modern world. They were all aware that man had been overtaken by perhaps the greatest crisis in his history; that the very greatest standards of knowledge, wisdom, and political judgment and action were necessary if he was to survive it; and that 'idealism' alone was not only not enough, but could even be the ground for its own defeat.

Sociology, then, was not only rooted in common-sense and in early social theories in any straightforward way. Its development from them was a matter of intense struggle, within the wider context of the political struggle which attended the transformation of limited traditional societies to a modern technological and industrialised society which seemed likely to encompass the whole world. It was not only in common-sense assumptions or in earlier theories, but also in these many, urgent, cumulative, and essentially interrelated needs, that sociology had its troubled 'beginnings'.

4

THE EARLY AMERICANS: EVOLUTION, KNOWLEDGE AND CONSCIOUS CONTROL

We have seen how, rooted in the insufficiencies of commonsense assumptions and early social theories, the making of sociology took shape in Europe. And we have seen that the intellectual task of creating a new science of society was also essentially rooted in the disruption of the old traditional order of society, marked most conspicuously by the French Revolution, and in the many problems which sprang up with the rapidity of industrial change. The making of sociology was part of the task of making a new society.

It is time now to remember, and indeed to emphasise, that America was as much at the heart of this vital transformation as any part of Europe, and shared this same perspective. The distinction between the 'Old' World and the 'New' was, strictly speaking, a geographical apportionment. In a historical sense, the same sweep of events with the same significances of meaning embraced the revolt in America and the revolt in Paris. America had its revolution as well as France; and Tom Paine, so to speak, attended both. In a real sense, England and France were no longer in Europe alone, but bestrode the Atlantic, and the blood of Europe's history flowed through living veins into these new distances. In America, too, and with a declared political independence based upon the same 'Rights of Man' for which men fought in Europe, men were embarked upon the task of making a new society. For them too, therefore, a knowledge of society, a science of society, became a great and growing need.

It is worthwhile to note, now, that all those elements in the making of sociology which we have seen to be characteristic of Europe, were also characteristic of scholarship in America. The roots of European, British and American sociology were, and are, the same, and the strong, close interdependence of this common tradition has been continuously in evidence throughout the shaping and the development of the subject.

In sociological thought, however, as in politics, it was no straightforward borrowing from Europe that we have to look for here. Certainly the influences of European thought upon the foundation of sociology in America were massive, detailed, and fundamental, but they were influences received into an already existing creative development of certain directions of thought which were themselves strongly rooted in the 'early social theories' we have mentioned, and which were themselves grappling with the new perspectives brought about by the natural sciences: by biology, for example, and the new perspective of 'evolution'. I wish to emphasise, and make abundantly clear, the continuous interdependence of European and American scholarship in the making of sociology, but this must not be done at the expense of belittling, or under-emphasising, the independence of many of the intellectual efforts that were made; and therefore a few careful points are worth making before we look at the ideas of some of those American thinkers who were most responsible for the founding of sociology there. Here, these points will be made very briefly, but they will be developed, and their significance will be seen with full clarity when we come to examine the idea of each man.

The first point of quite basic importance is that the making of sociology in America began under the enormous stimulation of the ideas of Comte and Spencer especially. This influence was powerful and quite fundamental. The 'foundations' of sociology in America were, in this quite direct sense, the same as those in Europe. At the same time, it needs to be emphasised, as we have just noted, that this was no 'passive borrowing', but an active, critical co-operation with ideas from Europe which were already being worked out in what we might call 'native' American thinking. Of course it is only the 'geographical apportionment' we have talked about which leads us to talk like this. Actually, a man like Lester Ward in exactly the same way as Comte, Mill, Spencer, Marx and Engels, inherited the same intellectual tradition. American scholars felt the philosophy and science of Europe at their own roots as much as European scholars did. However, this does need quite strong emphasis in these days when what is thought 'American' is thought to be quite qualitatively distinct from what is 'European'. The fact was that American scholars were, during the nineteenth century, working out their own systems of thought in coming to terms with the new perspectives of knowledge, and their ready acceptance of certain dominant European influences was a constructive and critical activity not at all a bowing before Gods from the old world.

The second point worth special emphasis follows directly from this, and has a dual nature. On the one hand, as one would expect, the early Americans did agree with all the major components of the new science of society which these European scholars had outlined. They accepted the methods of science in place of speculative metaphysics; they accepted the delimited precision of science; they accepted the evolutionary perspective; they accepted the materialist context of scientific thinking - to an extent far greater than is now commonly supposed; they accepted all the major concepts of the nature of sociology: the necessary use of classificatory, comparative, historical methods of study; the distinction between 'statics' and 'dynamics'; the employment of a 'structural-functional' model of analysis combined with 'social - psychological' studies and the understanding of purposeful social action. They accepted all these things and much more besides; but - and this is the important other aspect of this - they introduced their own particular emphasis of theory, and placed their own particular stresses upon certain dimensions of analysis, which were quite distinctively important. Two particular things deserve forthright mention. In the analysis of society they emphasised, and discussed far more extensively than European scholars had done, the psychological dimensions of social processes. And secondly, they moved very definitely away from too metaphysically-toned a preoccupation with the 'hidden causes' of society and its changes (though they were very far from ignoring these), and emphasised much more the conscious, deliberate, purposeful actions of men in society, and the element of conscious control based upon the transmission and advancement of knowledge.

There was, then, both strong similarity and significant difference between the early Americans and their dominant European influences, and these need to be made clear. And from this a third point follows: that the different emphasis of the Americans were not simply a number of slight 'riders' to the European foundations; they constituted a quite definite contribution to the founding of the subject; and this contribution formed a definite and traceable link with the subsequent developments which took place, both in Europe and America, early in our own century. Perhaps the emphasis worth making here is that the ideas of the early Americans had a strong influence upon much of the work in social psychology and sociology which took place in Europe in the early part of the twentieth century. European and American influences were therefore reciprocal in the making of the subject.

This mention of the links between nineteenth and twentieth century work in both Europe and America which we shall note in some detail, and quite deliberately in the next chapter - indicates a fourth point on which some clarification is required. The work we have discussed so far - of Comte, Mill, Spencer, Marx and Engels does, in fact, bring us almost exactly to the end of the nineteenth century, and, as we shall see, a distinctively new departure, a quite conscious attempt of develop sociology from the nineteenth-century foundations which had been laid, began immediately after the death of Spencer. There was, in short, quite a definite 'point of arrival and point of departure' here which we shall later remark, and must not be under-emphasized. At the same time, the making of sociology during the two or three decades at the end of the nineteenth century in America took place in the context of so many developments that any sharp distinction in time, or in the play of ideas, would be misplaced, and such as to falsify our picture of the situation. There are three aspects of this which I would like to mention and stress clearly.

We have, so far, clarified the ideas of the most influential nineteenth century thinkers as constituting the 'Foundations' of sociology. However, it is very important to note that when the early Americans—such as Ward, Giddings, Summer (whom I have specially selected)—were working upon their own statements of the 'foundations' of sociology, and utilizing the ideas of Comte and Spencer especially, the work of some of these 'second generation' scholars in Europe was already becoming known and already being taken into account by the Americans. And again, these 'second generation' ideas were by no means simply borrowed, or accepted; they were critically digested, together with the earlier and more basic ideas of Comte and Spencer, in constructing a clear statement of the nature and elements of sociology. The situation was, in short, very complex, but this, of course, is no problem for us. It is simply that we need to note it, so that we do not over-simplify the picture that arises from our discussion. And, especially, it leads us to give reasons for selecting some early Americans rather than others. This I shall come to in a moment.

The second aspect of this complexity of the American-European interchange and interdependency of ideas from about 1880 onwards, I will mention only briefly here - because it is a question to which we shall return at the end of our entire study. It is simply that we need to be very careful indeed in our estimation of these developments of American and European sociology, if we are going to avoid very considerable error in our perspective of judgment as to what the important developments and contributions of American sociology, in particular, have been. To exaggerate a little, but scarcely too much, there are people who think that light dawned upon the vast darkness of the American continent with the first page of Talcott Parsons' 'Structural of Social Action'. Before this glorious dawn of grand theory, that continent had been hid in nature's dark night of directionless empiricism. Only with the penetrating revelation of this new light did American sociology proper begin. Only after this were sociological studies illuminated by a new theoretical radiance. There are some (young) British sociologists who build their entire courses of instruction in universities on this radiance, and on this perspective. How far this is so in America it is difficult for an outsider to judge; but one can only hope and trust that American sociologists know the development of their subject in their own country much better than this. However, my sole point here is that there has been a detailed interconnection, in sociological theory, between the ideas of European and American scholars from the very earliest foundation of the subject in America. And this intimate interdependency needs much emphasis. But to this, we shall return.

The third aspect of this complex development in America which has infinitely greater importance for the making of sociology than can possibly appear in a brief statement of this kind, is that - in America - almost as soon as the early statements of the subject were achieved; indeed in part concurrently with the writing of them; the subject was involved in what can only be called 'professionalisation'. Sociology was established as a 'subject' in colleges and universities; and courses of instruction, the writing of text-books, the undertaking of research, came to be organised in these terms. Men like Albion Small, Giddings, and others, founded the subject as an academic discipline. Now I do not want to comment on this fact, critically or otherwise, at this stage, but only to note it. Clearly, this development was of the greatest significance for the spreading influence of sociology and was bound to have quite crucial determining constraints on the directions of development of the subject from that point on. I would, at this stage, like only to note two points. Firstly, that none of the thinkers we have discussed so far were 'academics', and none of them devoted themselves to the subject as some thing which could be established as a 'discipline' in the universities. Their central concern was to achieve a science of society for the making of a new society. Secondly, that the 'professionalisation' of a 'subject' as a department in academic institutions; especially in our modern universities with their planned teaching courses, determinate specialisations, and the like; raises problems for the very nature of the subject to an extent, and in profound ways, that we are only just beginning to realise. It is still not sufficiently realised that this academic professionalisation of subjects is something almost entirely new, and something which could as much lead to the death of the intellect as to its stimulation and vitality; which could as much despoil and destroy, inflate and distort, a 'subject' as it could further its progress. Such 'professionalisation' not only brings with it organisational constraints which might force bogus divisions and claims upon a subject; it also gives rise to an altogether new set of motives for study administrative motives, 'power' motives, career motives; all of which may not only be foreign to intellectual pursuits proper, but and this is the supreme danger - such as to lead to a positive denial of the basic *raison d'être* of the subject. Instead of a situation in which men study sociology because of its d irect and deep-rooted connections with man's historical dilemmas, with the important judgments and actions which men now have to take, this 'professionalisation' could produce a situation in which a set of 'academics' positively construe it as their duty to deny any such concern, and, meanwhile, professionally deny scientific status to anyone outside their 'degree-substantiated' boundaries. It was Bernard Shaw, who said somewhere that 'professions' were 'conspiracies against the public' - and how disastrously dangerous this could be if it turned out to be true in this case!

Later, I shall argue that, in our own time, these grave dangers have indeed fallen upon us, and that many of the difficulties and divisions of the subject that bewilder the public and underpin some very high salaries, are contrivances of these professional pressures. Here, however, I am only noting that this professionalisation followed close upon the heels of the earliest statements of the 'foundations' of sociology in America, and that, as soon as it began, some of its attendant difficulties began to make themselves apparent. We shall come back to this point with much vigour later on.

This handful of considerations which preface our study of the early Americans are necessary not only for their own sake i.e., to indicate the complexity of the scene through which we shall stride boldly - but also, and particularly, to explain why, out of all the scholars involved in early American sociology, I have chosen Ward, Giddings and Sumner. The reason is that, as far as I am able to judge, these men were most clearly representative of the ways in which, in American sociology, the great impact and influence of Comte and Spencer were critically worked into a distinctively American perspective. The three men also represent a kind of spectrum of theoretical points of view ranging from an almost entirely conservative and 'laissez faire' point of view in the implications of Sumner's system, to the equally powerful reformist note - and zeal! - to be found in that of Ward. The work of these three men can give a good, clear picture of the laying of the foundations of sociology in America, so long as we remember always that their work was couched within the context of increasingly complicated developments as the turn of the century approached.

A. LESTER F. WARD

Lester Ward, in terms of his personal character, his passionate concern for the radical reform of industrial society as he knew it, and his wide grasp of the subjects within which his attempt at the making of sociology was rooted, was a man akin to, and of similar stature to the men we have considered so far. He was not a professional 'academician' in any orthodox sense. He had little introductory education, and pursued his later education in a part-time way whilst working as a clerk. From the age of about forty, he worked as a palaeontologist with the United States Geological Survey, and though he did a little teaching in sociology in a visiting capacity at one or two colleges, it was not until he was about sixty-five years of age that he became a full-time university teacher. But he had the great distinction of being elected president of the International Institute of Sociology in 1903, and the first president of the American Sociological Society in 1906. He was undoubtedly the central figure in the making of sociology in America.

He was also, in his own person and in his own work, a living embodiment of all the points we have made by way of introduction. His point of departure was the great influence upon him of Comte and Spencer. But his acceptance of their dominant importance was by no means uncritical. He both accepted and rejected elements of each. Indeed, his pages are made all the more interesting in that they contain actual correspondence that he undertook with Spencer, following upon Spencer's criticism of him. But also, Ward's grasp of all the other subjects which went into a full understanding of the new perspective was broad, detailed, profound and admirable. He understood the issues at stake between earlier philosophy, even critical philosophy, and the new procedures of science very well. His discussions, for example, of Bishop Butler in relation to ethics and the nature of ideals, and of Kant in relation to the empirical knowledge of science, showed a very clear grasp of them. His position was by no means a superficial echo of the views of others. His knowledge of the natural sciences, of biology especially, and of the important figures in it - such as Lamarck, Darwin, Romanes, Huxley - was extraordinarily detailed and exact. And his awareness of other scholars of the time - in history, anthropology, law, and other departments of social science - was remarkable. He commented critically and soundly, for example, on various aspects of the work of Lecky, Sir William Hamilton, Sir John Lubbock, John Fiske, Sir Henry Maine, Tylor, Sidgwick, Littré, Lewis Henry Morgan, James Bryce - to mention only a few. He was also critically aware of the work of Gumplowicz, Ratzenhofer, Simmel and Durkheim, and, in his discussion of (these) strictly contemporary issues he introduced the work of men like Sidney Webb, Dr. Henry Maudsley, Grant Allen, and Havelock Ellis. Ward was a scholar of the greatest ability, and his judicious discussion of the many aspects of the making of sociology, including the careful and pleasing style in which he expressed all this, was of the very highest standard of excellence.

There were important ways, too, in which Ward, in accepting and agreeing with some of the major ideas and perspectives of these European thinkers, nonetheless managed to avoid some of their extremes which, as we have seen, were open to criticism. And he managed to adopt mid-way positions which were much sounder. But this we can see clearly as we look at each of the main ideas of his system.

The Scientific Study of Nature, Man, Society: Evolution and Progress

(a) *Science against speculative philosophy as being productive of knowledge*

As much as any of the European scholars we have considered, Ward was forthrightly opposed to the continuity of theological and philosophical speculation, and strongly upheld science alone as being productive of knowledge. And, very powerfully, he argued that this new departure in the approach to the acquisition of knowledge was far from being simply a matter of the quantity of knowledge that was possible by these different methods, but, on the contrary, was a matter of adopting fundamentally different assumptions, of assuming a quite basically different perspective. This was true with regard to the study of nature, and equally true with regard to the study of man.

Nothing could lead man further astray, Ward argued, than speculative or dogmatic reason undisciplined by the need to study facts.

> 'Men must first orient themselves', he wrote, 'before they can expect to go aright. A man lost in a forest, or a pilot at sea in a fog without a compass, is as likely, in obeying his notions of the direction he should go, to go in the opposite direction or at right angles to the true direction as to adopt that only course which can bring him to safety. The chances of going wrong are vastly against him. So is it with ignorant humanity in the fogs and forests of philosophy. Increasing intellectual power often serves to lead men further astray than pure animal instinct could do. False ideas are reached by reasoning from false premises consisting of deceptive appearness.'
>
> 'From this point of view it is extremely interesting to note to what extent the rational faculty of man, instead of serving him as a compass to point out his safe course, has, in fact, guided his hapless bark upon shoals and rocks, and into storms and whirlpools.'

The only orientation towards nature that could yield reliable knowledge was that of disciplined science, and this had two aspects. Man had to approach nature firstly as a student, and secondly as a master. In terms of his needs, his problems, his sufferings, his curiosity, man had to establish knowledge about the world and his own place and nature within it; but this, he held:

> '......can only be done by study. The phenomena that lie on the surface are of little value. They mislead at every turn. Not only must the deep-lying facts, difficult of access, be sought out with great labour and perseverance, but they must be co-ordinated into laws capable of affording safe and reliable guides to human operations. To do this requires a vast amount of patient study.....'
>
> 'In the domain of physical forces and chemical substances he is able to exercise prevision in many ways to secure advantages and avert evils, but in most of the higher fields of vital, mental, moral, and social phenomena, these relations are either utterly ignored of but dimly suspected, so that his knowledge of them avails him nothing. The great work before him, therefore, still is study.'

Only the methods of science could provide such testable laws which could be a reliable basis of prediction and guidance of action, and these methods, demonstrated in the so-called 'natural' sciences should be extended to the study of man. And Ward was especially intent on emphasising that man was a part of nature and as much a subject for scientific study as anything else.

> 'Nature stands to man', he wrote, 'in the relation of the whole to a part. Man is an integral part of the universe, and, in order to be correctly conceived and properly studied, he must be conceived and studied as an objective phenomenon presented by nature. Neither the animal and vegetable forms, nor the rock formations, nor the chemical elements, are more to be regarded as natural objects for scientific study than are individual men or human societies. The laws governing the migrations of birds, or the geographical distribution of plants, or the movement of storms, or the elective affinities of chemicals, are not more the legitimate subjects of scientific investigation than are the individual or collective actions of men or the changes that take place in human opinions and public sentiment. From the scientific point of view, all phenomena are equally legitimate objects of study.'

It was a proper, then, philosophically speaking, to consider a science of man as it was to think of a science of any other aspect of nature, and, indeed, only by the creation of such a science could knowledge about the nature of man be arrived at. We shall see in a moment the conception of man's place in nature which underlay Ward's system, but here, we can simply note what, fór him, were the crucial methods of science.

First of all, he insisted, scientific questions were solved by the painstaking study of facts.

> 'Nothing in concrete science is demonstrated *a priori*. The practical truths of the universe are established a posteriori - by massing the evidence.'

And Ward argued very strongly that this establishing of testable empirical knowledge by science had become so dominant as to sweep even critical philosophy (such as that of Kant) before it. Even the vestiges of teleological explanations of nature - of seeing divine purposes or final ends behind the actual processes of nature - were attacked by Ward as being positive and remaining hindrances to a proper approach to knowledge.

> 'Eternal matter,' he wrote, 'with its eternal activities suffices to account for all the phenomena of the universe, which are as infinite in causation as in duration or extent. All departments of science confirm this truth. Like many other once useful hypotheses, that of theo teleology has outlived its usefulness, and , where still called in, becomes a burden to the advancement of science.'

What has been accomplished in the scientific revolution, he insisted:

> '.....is nothing less than the establishment of the antitheses, or empirical propositions, of Kant's antinomies. They have been removed from the domain of transcendental philosophy, subjected to scientific methods, such as are applied to all other problems, and proved as other propositions are proved by the inductive method. The eternity of matter and motion and the infinitude of space have passed into scientific postulates, while the uninterrupted and unlimited casual dependence of all phenomena in their relation of antecedence and sequence is the fundamental axiom from which all scientific investigation now proceeds. The entire self-sufficiency of the universe is the great truth which advancing intelligence is daily perceiving more clearly.'

It will be seen from this passage that for Ward, as for Comte, Mill and Spencer, scientific knowledge consisted not simply of accumulating quantities of facts, but of discovering and stating laws of the interconnections (of contiguity and sequence) among them. And indeed Ward was very specific in saying that: 'a knowledge of facts is of very little use to us unless by such knowledge we can establish some law'.

Against all the dubious systems of dogma and metaphysics, this discovery of the regularities, or laws, of nature stood firm as a:

> '......consistent philosophy of casual circumstances. The necessity of nature is a rational necessity. Its truths are such, not because they have been willed or decreed, but in and of themselves. By necessity it is only meant that phenomena are uniform and unvarying. The same circumstances must produce the same effect. If truths were not necessary, they could not be relied upon. If they were not unvarying, they could not be traced, discovered, or utilised.'

And it was not only the broad regularities of nature, but also the specific irregularities, or the apparent exceptions to 'laws' which could be explained by science. Ward gave, here, many examples, as in astronomy, where even the apparently unique perturbations in planetary orbits had come to be quite thoroughly known, and in this he was making essentially the same point as Mill: that a science advances towards exactness of prediction as all its 'antecedents' become known. But perhaps Ward's main emphasis when claiming the reliability of science as against earlier philosophy was that it enabled us to lay down a confident programme of work, the results of which - we could be sure - would be the most exact and the most useful for our many purposes that we could possibly obtain.

> 'Truth', he claimed, 'is no longer a privileged commodity; it is the common property of all who want it. The pursuit of knowledge is no longer the pursuit of a phantom. It is a safe investment of time and talent. In learning that all truth is necessary, we have also learned that it is obtainable. For, if whatever exists or happens has and can have but one definite, necessary cause, without which it could not exist or happen, and with which it could not but exist or happen, then it only remains to ascertain that cause. And, since all causes consist of real and tangible circumstances or combinations

of circumstances, they can in most cases be reproduced or prevented in future according as they produce beneficial or injurious results. If we can create the same conditions, we may be sure of the same result; if we can break up those conditions, we can avoid the result. In this way we may in time reach the antecedent causes of the most subtle truths of nature.'

We have noted that a second important aspect of Science which Ward emphasised was that of control; of mastery over nature - but it is best to leave our consideration of this until we have seen fully his conception of the materialistic context of man's place in nature.

(b) *The materialistic basis of Man's place in nature, and of science*

We have said much about Marx's 'materialist' conception of nature and human society, and we have noted that Herbert Spencer might be said to be an even more consistent "Dialectical Materialist' than he. But now it may be a matter of surprise to discover that the first great exponent of sociology in America was as much of a 'Dialectical Materialist' as either of these two thinkers. And this is far from being a rather whimsical, or contrived interpretation of Ward: it is the fundamental basis of his system; and it is in the way in which he treats it that there is a positive advancement of conceptualisation and clarification on his part.

Let us see, first of all, how completely Ward was in agreement with Marx concerning man's place in nature; how completely he agreed with the materialist (as opposed to the 'Idealist') conception of the emergence of life and mind from the material processes of the universe; how completely he agreed with the persuasions of both Marx and Spencer that the forms of nature and society could only be analysed and explained as processes adapting themselves to environmental circumstances; and how important he felt this materialist conception to be - both as a necessary and correct perspective for any reliable study of man and society, and as a perspective which actually required certain specific assumptions and procedures of science.

We have already seen that Ward accepted a philosophical view of the sufficiency of the actualities of nature for any explanations which we required of it - without seeking any kind of transcendent 'purposes' outside or beyond it; a view in which - 'eternal matter with its eternal activities suffices to account for all the phenomena of the universe . . . ' We can now note further that he agreed with the conception that all the 'forms' of nature were the outcome of material processes in continuous relationship with each other, in a continuous process of reciprocal adaptation to each other; that the universe was, in fact, a continuous process of 'transformation' in which 'objects' or 'forms' were different kinds of 'aggregations' of matter. And he thought that the attributes of these qualitatively different forms could be analysed in more-or-less Spencerian terms.

Within this material universe, on the basis of certain kinds of aggregation and process, forms of organic life, and man, had emerged; and the definiteness of the order and perspective of this was of the almost importance for a science of man.

It was not only the case that man was a part of nature, but also that:

> 'Nature presents the relation of progenitor of man. Man is not only a part of nature as a whole, but nature antedated him and has produced him. This, however, is true only in the sense that it is true of every other part of nature, every other object in the universe.
>
> 'Man, too, has been slowly evolved out of materials which have indeed always existed, but have but very recently assumed this form. The particular form, character, structure, and attributes which belong to the creature denominated man are such as they are in virtue of an inexorable necessity involved in the nature of things; they are the result of the interaction of coincident forces, the activities of molecular aggregates, possessing just such degrees and kinds of aggregation, and thrown into just such relations to one another as were adapted to the development of just such a being. The necessity of his existence is, therefore, just equal to the impossibility of his non-existence. Both are absolute. Nature, therefore, occupies the relation to man of cause to effect, of antecedent to consequent.'

The material processes of nature have brought man into being; they are necessary for a causal account of the emergent nature of man. But Ward insisted upon other aspects of this perspective which were of vital importance for the proper appreciation of the relation of the human mind to nature. His emphasis was that, until the emergence of man, the entirety of material nature was devoid of consciousness.

> 'Nature', he wrote, 'must be regarded as unconscious. Throughout all the changes which have resulted in the evolution of man, the process has been purely automatic. No thought, no ideas, no plan, no purpose has entered into the great cosmic movement . . . all the great processes of nature, including the development of organic forms and of man, have been impelled by blind and mindless energies guided by no intelligence or conscious power either from within or from without.'

This entire process was an unconscious coherence of material units into aggregations of varying orders; and the 'forms' which emerged were an outcome of continuous adaptive interaction. This conception of the 'form' of anything in nature being essentially related to its surrounding 'milieu', or 'environment', or 'circumstances', in terms of a continuous play of adaptive adjustments, was absolutely central, Ward insisted, for the explanation of it; and the entirety of nature, up to and including the emergence of man, was a vast, ordered complexity of such adaptive interactions.

> 'The directive law (i.e., in the emergence of forms in nature)' he wrote, 'is that of adaptation. Things are adapted because they have adapted themselves. What we see exists of necessity. It might have been other than it is, had the conditions been other than they were. The conditions being what they were, the results could be no other than they are. A certain degree of adaptation is necessary to the existence of a form. For forms to exist at all, they must be to a certain extent adapted.'

We shall see in a moment that Ward did not mean to insist here that everything in nature was tightly or well-adapted to its circumstances; but, for now, the essential point is that the entire nature of the universe was viewed as an unconscious process of cohering aggregates and energies in continuous, adaptive interaction with each other.

Now the essential point which Ward then made and stressed was that this vast process of nature could not be explained in terms of mind and purpose, but, on the contrary, that mind and purpose had emerged out of it, as a very limited and very recent (as far as we are aware occurrence, and that the emergence of mind could only be explained (up to the emergence of man) in terms of it.

> 'Mind', wrote Ward, 'is found only at the end of the series, and not at the beginning. It is the distinctive attribute of the creature, and not of the creator. It resides in man, and not in nature'.

Mind and purpose gradually come into being as aspects of certain kinds of 'organisation of matter'.

> 'The tendency to organisation which has existed on this planet for a vast period, in connection with the increasing adaptation of the conditions now found upon its surface from the time when it assumed a cooled exterior to the present time, has gradually evolved a class of forms called animals, in which the remarkable quality denominated consciousness is manifested. This quality exhibits all conceivable degrees, from that seen in the monad to that found in enlightened man, and throughout this series the capacity for teleological action has steadily and uniformly kept pace with the degree of intelligence. We are, therefore, forced to conclude that consciousness and intelligence are products of organisation; that organised beings are, as it were, devices for the concentration and intensification of molecular activities; and that mind and thought are among the necessary products of such concentrated and intensified activities - the properties of matter thus organised. The "soul of truth," therefore, in the belief that the universe possesses consciousness, intelligence, and mind, consists in the fact that the primary activities of diffused matter - activities which are never divorced from it - constitute the sole element out of which, by simple focalisation, these qualities are produced.'

The following passage is perhaps one of Ward's best statements of this 'materialist' position.

> 'Intelligence appears rather as a product than as a quality of nature. In vain we look for an intelligent recognition of our human emotions in the galaxies of incandescent worlds above us. In vain we look for an appreciating voice from within the penetralia of the earth. True, it is not the silence of eternal rest; the stars glow and the planets roll, the crystal sparkles and the flower blooms, but not until we reach the animal world is there one token of sympathy, one

evidence of joy, one ray of intelligence. Poets may tell of the smiling landscape, the modest flower, the angry ocean, or the pensive stream; these are but figures of speech, and serve only as associations for the mind. There is beauty, there is grandeur, there is activity, there is even life, but mind there is none. Thought and feeling are not there. The universe is insensible. Nature has no soul, although within her are all the elements of sensibility and all the materials of intelligence. For mind is merely a relation. Though is a mode of material activity. Intellect is a brain-wave. To secure it only requires an appropriate form. One revolution of the wheel of organisation evolved the living vegetable world; another culminated in the creation of sentient beings. Higher and higher has arisen the type, finer and finer has grown the product, till brain has become the ruling force, and man has emerged from that darkness which hitherto had never permitted Nature to contemplate herself. This highest product of evolution, and which may properly be called spirit, has been described as that which "sleeps in the stone, dreams in the animal, awakes in man".'

Having made his conception of the relation of mind to nature perfectly clear, Ward then made equally clear the implications of this for 'scientific explanation' at different levels - and it is in this, and his elaboration of it in 'sociological explanation', that he made a marked advance in clarity.

As far as the study of nature was concerned, scientific explanation must be in terms of efficient causes; the outcome of the analysis of the interdependent processes of nature which were genetic. In all explanations of nature, 'final causes' or 'purposes' were completely misplaced and in error.

'Nature's processes are genetic. The cause not only always precedes the effect, but it immediately precedes it. The effect is in immediate proximity to the cause . . . The word genetic combines better than any other the idea of causation in all its delicate forms with that of continuance, without suggesting either an origin or a purpose . . . Genesis is only another name for causation, and causation is the production of change through impact. A *causa efficiens*, which is the essence of the genetic process, is simply a direct and immediate cause - one in which there is neither interval nor indirection between the cause and the effect.'

So much for the unconscious realms of material nature. With the emergence of mind and consciousness, however, a completely different principle of 'explanation' was introduced. Mind was consciously aware of certain ends of action and therefore any satisfactory explanation must now take into account the understanding of purpose. The explanation of psychical as distinct from physical facts must be teleological as well as being, in part, genetic. And the conscious control of action in terms of purpose meant that there might well be delay and complexities of deliberation in the relationships between cause and effect; ends sought and means employed, etc.

> 'The wholly unconscious and unintelligent character of nature's processes may be safely concluded from their genetic stamp. Intelligence works quite otherwise. The inseparable characteristic of conscious action is that it is teleological. Cause and effect are remote from each other. Means are adapted to distant ends. The chain of causal impulses connecting antecedents with consequents is not direct.'

The great importance of Ward's distinction between genetic and teleological explanation will be seen especially when we come to his system of sociology, but, for the moment, we have seen very clearly the way in which he shared a 'materialist' position with Marx and Spencer and how this conception led him to important distinctions of scientific procedure and 'explanation'. Above all, however, we have seen clearly that, though maintaining this 'materialist perspective', he did not fall into the metaphysical error of thinking that because mind had emerged out of matter it could be satisfactorily explained in the same terms. His sharp distinction here was a very considerable improvement on the 'dialectical materialism' of Marx, and even (though this was not so unqualified) on the materialism of Spencer. Like both these men, however, Ward insisted on an evolutionary as well as a materialist perspective.

(c) *Evolution*

Ward maintained not only that there was a coherence among all the aggregates and forms of nature as a result of 'adaptation', but also that certain sequences and patterns of transformation were demonstrable.

> 'So far as the history of our globe is known, the phenomena taking place upon it have presented a decided preponderance of ascending series from the remotest periods of which science furnishes any account, and such would also seem to be the case throughout the solar system at large, with exceptions only in some of the smallest bodies, as the earth's satellite. There has thus taken place a sort of development, or evolution, which in the inorganic world proceeds from a more homogeneous and less differentiated state towards a more heterogeneous state with greater concentration of parts. In organic nature organisation increases, structure is complicated, and the physiological division of functional labour is combined with the integration of differentiated organs and their subordination to large complex organisms.'
>
> 'As, in passing from cosmic to organic evolution, we see the continued operation of the same uniform law, so, in crossing the boundary which divides organic from super-organic phenomena - the animal from the social world - we are able to trace the same unbroken process.

This was exactly Spencer's conception, and no more need be said about it. We should note a few central points, however, in passing. Like Spencer, for example, Ward did not insist upon a strictly unilinear pattern of evolution; he spoke of 'descending' as well as 'ascending' orders of complexity. Secondly, it is clear that he also analysed the 'transformations' of evolution in the same terms as Spencer - in terms of structural-functional differentiation, integration, heterogeneity and coherence of organisation, and the like. And thirdly, we might note that Ward also thought that evolution was a pattern of change found in all phenomena, and that this was therefore a certain unifying element among all the sciences. He wrote, for example:

> 'We not only discover one great law of evolution applicable to all the fields covered by the several sciences of the series, but we can learn something more about the true method of evolution by observing how it takes place in each of these fields. Even some of the subordinate sciences falling under the great groups that we have been considering, are capable of shedding light upon the method of evolution, and probably any specialist in science, if he would look carefully for such indications, could supplement the knowledge we have relative to the essential nature of evolutionary processes.'

Though it need not be elaborated here, it is clear that Ward conceived of a unity among the sciences, a kind of 'hierarchy' of sciences, essentially the same as that proposed by Spencer and Comte - though he disliked the term 'hierarchy' in this connection.

It is important to note too, that Ward agreed with Spencer in accounting for the 'directions of change' in evolution in terms of the following of the line of least resistance; of adaptation to environmental circumstances; of an equilibrium-disequilibrium balance of forces, and the like. There was a complete agreement here.

The material universe therefore manifested a pattern of developmental, evolutionary change which had moved from the physical to the emergence of the psychical, and then, with the increasing teleological powers of mind, to the complex development of the social - of the 'super-organic'.

Perhaps we can leave this matter with an emphasis upon one point; a point which is as relevant now as it was in Ward's time. He realised well enough that the materialist-evolutionary perspective that he was advocating, with its enormous scale of time, and its enormous range of complex explanation of those things in nature and society which most people simply took for granted, was one which would seem too vast, too remote, perhaps beyond the grasp and beyond the patience of many. But in his view, such a resistance to this perspective was quite mistaken and unfortunate, and any sound judgment concerning the human situation and any sound employment of science positively necessitated the adoption of it.

> 'The human mind', he wrote, 'must learn to accustom itself to contemplate nature in its true relations and magnitude, and the human race can never rise to a just conception of nature or of the reciprocal relations of man and nature until the notion of infinitude, both in time and space as well as in power, has been definitely formed. It is narrow, finite, anthropomorphic conceptions of the universe which have dwarfed the labours of otherwise great minds and kept back the truths which the world now chiefly values, and it is due to the enlargement of men's views respecting the vastness of nature's periods and spaces that all true progress in our acquaintance with the universe has been achieved.'

This is a salutary statement for those in our own time who think that anything that was published more than a fortnight ago is 'out-of-date'!

(d) *Progress: the efficient control of mind, and the application of knowledge to Man's practical advantage*

We come now to one of the most central features of Ward's system: the nature of progress.

It would be putting the matter altogether minimally, and therefore misleadingly, simply to say that, as with earlier writers (such as Spencer and Marx). Ward's ideas of material change, development, and evolution implied the notion of progress. Ward was far more forthright than this. He positively insisted that, in clearly defined ways, the emergence of mind in nature was attended by progress, and, furthermore, that the conscious and extended control which the human mind could exercise over nature by the accumulation of knowledge and techniques was a central fact of progress in the context of evolution. Ward was as forthright as Comte about this, and this point enables us to draw a few threads together. In it, we return to the point mentioned at the outset - that one essential aspect of the scientific attitude towards nature should be that of control, of mastery over nature, as well as that of careful study of it. In it also we can see strong agreements with the earlier thinkers we have mentioned - especially with Comte and Mill in their emphasis upon the centrality of mind and knowledge in society. But - and this is one of the most interesting facts - we can also see in it a very strong agreement with the emphasis of Marx upon the basic importance of men's practical activities in nature and society and the application of knowledge in technology. But it is here too that we can see Ward's superiority to Marx - in that the metaphysical obscurantism is done away with; the false metaphysically dogmatic 'materialism' is done away with; and the emphasis upon the accumulation and transmission of knowledge in relation to men's practical activities is stated with luminous clarity. And, as we shall see, other important principles of analysis and policy are built upon it, and the social evils which Marx raged about are attacked in quite a different way.

There were several distinct and important strands in Ward's conception of progress in nature and society.

Perhaps the best with which of begin is what he referred to as the wastefulness, the unconsidered extravagance of energies and resources, the sheer inefficiency of nature (of the genetic processes of the world); and, by contrast, the superior efficiency of mind - which by a clear awareness of the end desired, and a knowledge of how to attain it, can accomplish that end with a far greater economy of means. The teleological (consciously and purposefully directed) powers of mind are far superior to the genetic processed of nature. It was here that Ward made it very clear that although he conceived of all the elements of nature as being interrelated in 'genetic' processes of adaptation, he was far from thinking that this 'adaptation' of nature was characterised by perfection. On the contrary, he thought that nature was profligate; expending almost countless resources in producing particular results. Nature manifested a kind of rough-and-ready interconnection of things - by no means a perfectly well-adjusted, perfectly articulated order. Man should not be in awe of nature, in the sense of bowing to the superiority of nature. On the contrary, man should realise the inefficiencies of nature, the superiority of the powers of mind and knowledge, and replace his enslavement to nature by his control over her.

> 'Nature acts', wrote Ward, 'on the assumption that her resources are inexhaustible, and, while she never buys a wholly worthless article, she usually pays an extravagant price.'

He gave many examples of this: that 'the octopus, in order to hold its own, must lay 50,000 eggs': that 'the codfish produces 1,000,000 young fish each year that two may survive and the species not become extinct' - and many others of a similar and well-known kind. For our purposes, however, it is more instructive to see that Ward thinks in exactly the same way about the inefficiency of 'genetic' processes even in the development of human societies.

> 'That the same laws have operated', he wrote, 'in the super-organic as in the organic world is quite obvious. Not only the progress out of barbarism into civilisation, but the march of civilisation itself, has been attended with the same incidents that characterise the

development of a species or of an individual. The archaeologist digs the remains of extinct civilisations out of the earth in much the same manner as the paleontologist does those of extinct animals and plants. Besides his wars with the elements and with wild beasts, man has been perpetually afflicted by wars with his own kind; and yet this warfare of men with their surroundings, with other species, and with one another, is the strict analogue of that of the lower forms of organised beings. Even the silent battle for subsistence has its counterpart in the competitive struggles of industry. The same wasteful methods prevail in society as in the animal and vegetable kingdoms. The natural resources of the earth are squandered with a wanton disregard of the future. The forests are cut down to supply temporary wants, or purposely cleared for tillage, until the habitable portions of the earth are transformed into lifeless deserts. The soil is rapidly exhausted by the first occupants, who know only the immediate present. The wild animals useful to man are soon extinguished by the heartless destruction of the fertile females and helpless young. Population distributes itself to great disadvantage. Cities grow up with narrow crooked streets, which must, from time to time, be widened and straightened at large absolute cost. Filth and disease - germs, due to dense, unregulated population, bring pestilence, and sweep away at rhythmic intervals the excess. Famines come to scale down the ranks of such as have forced their way in during years of plenty. Bitter partisanship prevails everywhere throughout society, the nearly successful effort of each party being to undo that the other has done. Labour and capital, whose dependence upon each other is absolute, are constantly found in open hostility, which greatly reduces the productiveness of both. Exchange of products is largely carried on by redundant third parties, who, through no fault of their own, are allowed to absorb the largest share of the wealth produced. Trade consists to a large extent of unnecessary and duplicated transportation. Wealth is not only unequally but inequitably distributed. In short, all the functions of society are performed in a sort of chance way, which is precisely the reverse of economical, but wholly analogous to the natural processes of the lower organic world. Great results, it is true, are accomplished, even in society, by these unregulated forces, but they fall far short of what may be easily seen to be attainable; they are not the best.

All true progress springs from that restless skepticism which dares to question the methods of nature.'

The unconsciously connected processes of nature and society do result in a certain order, but this is not by any means such that it cannot be improved upon by the directing powers of mind, resting upon carefully established knowledge. One very important point we might simply note here is that it is perfectly possible to have a structural-functional analysis of the nature of societies and the ways in which their parts adjust themselves to circumstances of various kinds, without in any sense holding that societies do not experience conflict, and without in any sense holding that societies achieve something called 'functional harmony' or 'functional unity'. As far as Ward was concerned - societies manifested a certain order in their adaptive arrangements, but this not only could be improved upon but ought to be improved, and could only be improved, by the deliberate design and activity of mind in exercising purposeful control. Progress was achieved, then, when the genetic processes of nature and society were increasingly brought under the control of the teleological direction of mind.

> 'Man', Ward wrote, 'has been the servant of Nature too long. All true progress has been measured by his growing mastery over her, which has in turn been strictly proportional to his knowledge of her truths.'

Certain other specific points were rooted in this idea, and were separately emphasised by Ward.

One basic consideration was the fact that since the 'genetic' processes of nature were 'blind' regularities, they could be controlled to man's advantage with relative ease. Knowing the various forces of nature, man could engineer certain alterations of circumstance in such ways as to divert these energies to accomplish desired ends. Control over nature was, in fact, not a mastery over the laws of nature (i.e., in the sense of a power to change them), but - with a knowledge of these - a supervisory manipulation of them in such ways as to utilise their resources and energies.

> 'We must learn', said Ward '. . . the important lesson that nature is really easily controlled. A very little acquaintance with natural laws is sufficient to enable us to achieve stupendous effects.'

In exactly the same way, Ward believed that society could be improved, on the basis of a detailed knowledge of its nature, by the manipulation of its existing energies, institutions, and resources. Such control, Ward called 'attractive legislation', and it must be emphasised that he did not regard this as an 'authoritarian' business of government, but the bringing into proximity of certain improvements with clearly seen individual and group interests by the widest extension of knowledge and deliberation in a democratic society.

> 'If,' he argued, 'in the framing of human laws this principle were always carefully studied it would soon be discovered that man is as easily managed by intelligence as, (earlier) nature was shown to be.'

Two other central elements in Ward's notions are immediately apparent. The first, of course, and this was the most dominant element of all, was that KNOWLEDGE - the attainment, accumulation, advancement and transmission of KNOWLEDGE - was the necessary basis of all control, and therefore all progress.

> 'Knowledge is the chief element of power in enabling the mind to exercise a control over the materials and the forces of nature, and a settled conviction that effects must of necessity follow and correspond to causes, renders all efforts to acquire knowledge profitable, and the possession of any knowledge possible.'

It is because of this central importance of knowledge for control that science, of course, was so important: since the methods of science were the most effective ways of achieving and advancing knowledge. But the importance of knowledge was so dominant a component in Ward's system that we must look at it specially in a moment.

The second element which, in Ward's mind, was essentially connected with this, and with the idea of progress, was that, in most men, it was, in fact, the desire to control nature and society which formed the chief motive in seeking knowledge. And the reason why they sought to know and to control nature and society was - the desire for practical advantage.

> 'The primary end of knowledge is to secure practical advantage', Ward wrote.

And it was in this that his position came very close indeed to that of Marx, because it was, he maintained, in the continual practical activities of men to control nature in pursuit of their ends that the advancement of knowledge and therefore the achievement of progress took place. This we shall see more fully soon; but perhaps it is important to stress here, too, that by 'practical activities', Ward did not mean only something called 'material' activities. He did not only think of 'practical advantage' in purely material terms. He did not think of progress as 'technical' progress in a limited material sense. Man's control over nature - practical and technical and advantageous - also involved moral principle, moral judgment and moral direction. In this again, Ward was in agreement with Comte in placing much emphasis upon the extension of 'altruism' in human society. All to often the 'moral' is, for some reason, abstracted from the 'practical' and the 'technical', and Ward's insistence against this was of very real importance.

Men have suffered in countless ways within the blind forces of nature and society - from disease, poverty, warfare, untimely death in innumerable ways; from degradation, humiliation, tragedy in the clutch of brutal and enigmatic circumstances - and progress, claimed Ward, was a completely clear matter of eliminating these elements of experience as far as possible; of maximizing practical advantage by exercising control in the light of secure knowledge.

> 'Men are still continually dashing blindly against the barriers which the environment presents to their free activities.'

But with greater knowledge and greater control, man's enslavement to the power of circumstances could be diminished, and his freedom extended.

This was a luminously clear idea, and, in it, man's moral aims were rightly seen as being closely enmeshed in his 'practical' ones. In order to see Ward's conjunction of the ideas of evolution and progress more fully, however, it is necessary to look more closely at some of the specific points we have introduced.

(e) *The teleological attributes of mind and their crucial significance: action, purpose, systematic knowledge, invention.*

We have seen that Ward's picture of evolution was one moving from the physical to the psychical, and then to the psycho-social; and we have seen quite clearly, too, the significant distinction which he drew between the 'genetic' processes of the physical (continuing into the psychical and the social) and the quite different 'teleological' abilities of mind. We must now clarify certain other distinctions which he made in this connection.

First of all, Ward took great pains to make it clear that with the emergence of mind, with its distinctive teleological capacities and modes of operation, it was quite imperative to distinguish action from interdependence of fact. These, he insisted were two quite distinguishable categories of empirical occurrences; and they made necessary two quite distinguishable kinds of 'explanation'.

The specific interdependencies of, say, oxygen and hydrogen in producing water, or of the power of exploding dynamite in shattering the rock-face of a quarry, are interconnections of substances in motion, and can be explained in terms of known regularities and 'efficient causation'.

The sequence of experience, behaviour, and events, however, when men, say, taken one trade route to India (through the Suez Canal) rather than another (round the Cape) - is a qualitatively quite different phenomenon. It is a sequence of action; and though physical regularities certainly underlie it, it cannot be explained in these terms alone; it requires also an explanation in terms of the ends the men were seeking, the motives and desires that impelled them to seek these ends, the ways in which they had calculated various means, and had decided to adopt these, rather than others. Here, explanation would rest not only upon sensory (or perceptual) observations, but also upon conceptual and experiential understanding.

A full explanation of the entirety of nature, including the existence and operation of mind, and especially the human mind, within it, must therefore necessarily include both genetic and teleological kinds of explanation. One or other of these kinds of explanation was necessarily insufficient in itself. This was a most important distinction which Ward made perfectly clearly; which is wholly correct; and which is of fundamental importance for any explanation of man and society.

But it is not only the two categories of explanation which War was concerned to distinguish, but, more basically, the two categories of fact, or phenomena, or events in the world. And it was the distinction between the two categories of fact which was central to his account of evolution and progress.

The first category, as we have seen, was that of all the material or physical process of nature, and here 'forms' came into being through 'blind' regularities of adaptation. The second category of events was that appropriate to life and mind, to 'physical' phenomena, and such events were quite different. These events were actions as well as involving attendant material processes, and Ward analysed the elements of actions as distinct from other events.

Actions, he held, had the following attributes:

(1) They stemmed from desires within the organism. (2) These desires were promptings towards certain sequences of behaviour which would lead to the satisfying attainment of certain ends. (3) Such sequences of behaviour involved an employment (whether well-calculated or not) of certain means. (4) Such actions were therefore volitional and motivated. (5) They were marked by consciousness: consciousness in the experience of the desire; consciousness of the end; consciousness in the employment of the means and the appropriateness or inappropriateness of them); and consciousness of satisfaction in the attainment of the end, or of frustration in failure to attain it. (6) Actions therefore involved purpose. (7) The end, and the apprehension of the end, was therefore a necessary component among the 'causes' of actions. (8) Finally, actions were therefore characterised by the making of efforts; they were, said Ward, conative; they involved the element of striving for the ends apprehended, and the satisfaction of desire.

The kind of 'adaptation to their circumstances' in which all forms of organic life, including human beings, were involved was therefore quite different from the 'blind' adaptation of purely physical events, it was an adaptation which necessarily involved all these components of experience and behaviour. It will be readily seen that within this entire 'class' of 'Conative Actions', Ward was able to conceive of a whole 'series' of 'levels' of mind among all organic species: from very simple organisms in which 'action' was very little distinguished from the automatic adaptation of physical processes; through the series of more complex species of organism in which a consciousness of ends and desires and a purposeful direction of behaviour seemed to be more marked; to man in whose conduct conscious and purposeful action was patently apparent. In all this, Ward's discussion was of great interest, and he wrote of 'instinct', for example, among animals and in man, as being a kind of 'link' of conative action - between relatively automatic responses at the level of the most simple organisms and the more conscious 'intelligent' direction of purposeful behaviour in the higher animals, and man. However, given this distinction of 'conative actions' as a class of events quite different from those of purely material interconnection, there were really only two further distinctions which Ward made which are essential for our understanding of his system.

Among all conative actions, he thought that two chief kinds could be clearly distinguished. These were direct and indirect methods of conation; and the terms speak for themselves. Direct conative action was immediate impulsive action, using immediate muscular activity to secure the end desired. But it was indirect conative action which was distinctively human, and this was conscious and deliberately planned action which rested upon the acquisition and retention of systematic knowledge. This, Ward insisted, involved an entirely new principle and produced wholly new, extensive, and effective results. Its crucial characteristic was the development and use of the intellectual capacity of man.

> 'Henceforth,' wrote Ward, 'the possibilities of vital existence are to be multiplied, and the rate of organic progress enormously accelerated. For success in the sentient world is the ability to attain its ends, and the intellectual element is especially adapted to

> augmenting that power. By the direct method, action in this direction is restricted to cases which are within the muscular strength of the organism, and easily accessible without the intervention of obstacles. The utmost possible to be accomplished by it was measured by the energy actually expended. The least obstruction beyond the power of the individual to clear away by muscular force is an effectual bar to its access to the object of desire. By the aid of the new element all this is changed. Interposed barriers are evaded by circuitous routes of approach. Powerful natural forces are by appropriate adjustments made to do the work of overcoming resistance, and what is wholly unattainable in the present, is by the necessary adaptation, secured in the future.'

The intellect, according to Ward, was not similar to the other sources of conative energy in human nature (e.g., the desires, and motives springing from feeling); it was not a 'force' of energy in itself; but rather a mental capacity for knowing and systematically ordering all the elements of experience in such a way as to serve and guide the desires in the use of means to attain their ends.

And it is here that we come to the second important aspect of this distinction which brings us back to a full understanding of Ward's emphasis upon the 'practical activities' of men in achieving progress. For, he claimed, the fundamental way in which the intellect does enable man to harness and utilise natural forces for the better satisfaction of his ends is that of invention. On the basis of his knowledge, man makes artiefacts, and learns to practise arts, which enable him to canalise the forces of nature in such a way as to have them work more effectively for him. And this invention rests upon certain principles. For example, man learns that he can affect both the amount and the direction of natural energies. He can intensify the amount of force in its application (as in the lever and the fulcrum). He can direct forces more usefully (as in irrigation). And he can achieve a commutation of forces in various ways.

The central fact in all this, however, on which Ward places his strongest emphasis, is that progress within the context of evolution rests upon the control of the natural by the artificial, achieved by the intellect as it establishes ever more extensive, systematic, and reliable knowledge. And this progress of both knowledge and control is manifested crucially in inventions in relation to man's desire for 'practical advantage'.

Ward gave an excellent summary statement of these distinct sequences in evolution and progress.

> 'We are able to perceive the several stages of progress,' he wrote, 'in the direction of economy of results. The lowest stage is that of genetic phenomena, in which we saw how great was the waste and how exceedingly small the degree of progress as compared with the amount of energy expended. This is nature's method, pure and simple.
>
> 'The next stage is that of the direct method of conation. Here the phenomena are teleological, and hence far more productive of results in proportion to the force exerted. The immense element of waste is eliminated. Action that is not equi'ibrated by attempting what is beyond the power of the agent results in accomplishing the same amount of work as is represented by the energy put forth, but no more. As in genetic phenomena we were dealing with true natural forces, so in those teleological phenomena which are accomplished by the direct method we are still dealing with true natural forces. The difference is, that while the genetic forces are physical, teleological forces are physical.'
>
> 'Finally, we have as a third stage that in which the indirect method is applied, and here we see the maximum economy and the maximum efficiency in the accomplishment of results. With the development of this mode of action, great and increasing disproportion is secured between the energy expended and the work accomplished; space, time, and intervening obstacles are overcome, and the conditions are at length established for social evolution.'

It will be clearly seen from the end of this statement that Ward thought of sociology as the scientific study of men's collective 'achievements', as societies developed cumulative traditions of knowledge, inventions, and skills, based upon this capacity for 'indirect conative action'. But, in this place, it is enough to have seen very clearly Ward's entire scheme of analysis concerning the nature of evolution and progress; the place of the human mind, knowledge, practical activities, invention, and control over nature, within this entire perspective; and the different levels and kinds of 'explanation' on which he insisted.

(f) *The superiority of the teleological; the efficiency of scientific knowledge and control; its difficulties but its necessity*

Before moving on to outline Ward's construction of Sociology within, and as a necessary part of, this context, a remaining handful of points are worth making.

It is worthwhile to emphasise a little more than we have done so far, that Ward stressed the efficiency of the teleological processes of mind as against the genetic processes of nature. The purposive action of mind, resting upon carefully elaborated knowledge, could achieve its ends with a far greater economy of means by its artificial (i.e., by the practice of arts and inventions) control, than could profligate nature teeming with its blind, if luxurious, forces and resources. This was to become a very important basis of his attitude towards the role of government in society. But there is another aspect of Ward's thinking, connected with this, which must also be noted.

It is - that though he made the very clear distinction between genetic and teleological processes and modes of explanation, insisting that teleological processes were most highly significant in man, even so, he did not believe (a) that only teleological processes and modes of explanation were characteristic of man or (b) that the achievement of the satisfactory blend of genetic and teleological explanation which was necessary for the understanding and knowledge of human society was easy to achieve.

Ward was well aware, and made it very clear, that genetic processes underlay human nature and human society and continued into them, so to speak, even though teleological processes increased in their dominance. Man as a species had, of course, emerged out of the creativity of genetic processes. And these had therefore always to be taken into account. Many basic biological and psychological attributes of man were firmly laid down by nature, were a matter of genetic endowment, and social relationships, arrangements, organisation, rested upon them and sprang from desires and needs rooted in them. And secondly - genetic processes of adaptation continued in the change and development of societies, even though the teleological activities of mind were involved in many specific directions of social organisation. It was only gradually that man could gain knowledge and foresight of the entirety of society, and gain purposeful control at that high level. But this must arise in the context of massive 'genetic' adjustments; the massive creation of certain interdependencies of institutions in 'social systems'; which had already taken shape. Systematic knowledge and intelligent social control would therefore be very difficult to achieve. It would require tremendous efforts of both thought, study, research and social reform. And it was here, of course, that the need for sociology - a systematic science of society - could be clearly seen.

Ward also saw, with great clarity, another major obstacle. Science and its extension into the study of man and society would be a struggle against traditionally founded, and deeply rooted (dogmatic) ideology. Men believed they already knew about man and society in terms of their religious beliefs, their political creeds, their metaphysical dogmas. They had for long governed society (or, at least, certain élites had) on certain accepted assumptions. To introduce unfamiliar perspectives of science into the knowing and making of society would be to place a cat among pigeons indeed: and the pigeons would flurry and squawk no matter how docile the cat appeared. Of course, Ward was perfectly right - and the birds are squawking still. But Ward had an interesting point of view abut this. He was concerned to show that, properly understood, it was the attempt to retain dogmatic ideologies that was likely to be the greater source of social restlessness, discontent and conflict, without in any way constructively resolving social problems, whereas the extension of knowledge to as many people as possible, though it could not automatically dissipate problems, would at least provide the only sound basis for their firm solution. Ward wrote:

> 'Criticism of received beliefs is always sweet to a considerable number who rejoice at the overthrow of the leaders of opinion or the fall of paragons of morality. And this it is which often renders the peace of society insecure. The established code of morals is dimly felt by the lower classes to be, in some respects, radically unsound. The broad contrast between men's nominal beliefs, as

> spoken, and their beliefs, as acted, is apparent even to children. The standard of conduct is so much higher than that which the controllers of conduct can themselves live up to, resulting always in the punishment of the weak and the poor for the same transgressions as are daily committed with impunity by the rich and influential, that the lowest miscreant feels that there is some fundamental wrong underlying the entire social fabric, although he cannot tell what it is. All this must be regarded as the legitimate consequence of the undue supremacy of dogmatic ideas in society. So far from favouring morality, they are the direct cause of the most dangerous form of immorality, viz., a mutinous revolt against too severe and unnatural moral restraints. Rules of conduct based on these conceptions are necessarily arbitrary, while the normal intellect naturally asks a reason for its obedience.'

In this again, Ward had clear similarities with Marx's and Engels' notion that 'ideologies' were in a sense 'false' systems of doctrines, rituals, etc., rooted in social groupings and their interests, which had to be fought and dispelled by scientific knowledge. But Ward had, which Marx and Engels had not, a clear set of criteria in terms of which knowledge could claim to be knowledge as distinct from ideology. His system was not vitiated by an unbounded 'relativism'; nor, as we shall see, were his social proposals themselves (as was the case with Marx and Engels) confined by any metaphysical marriage to one socio-economic-political group rather than others. Ward wanted a radical change of industrial society as passionately as anyone: but he did not relish the idea of any 'advance-guard' telling the rest of the citizens of society what their 'real interests' were. Ward was a genuine democrat, not a metaphysically castrated one.

And the final point we might emphasise here, is that - like all the men we have considered earlier - Ward wanted a sociology because he saw clearly, or believed, that the explosive expansion and complexities of modern industrial society were in great danger of outstripping man's knowledge, foresight and control. Sociology was the science needed in the modern world of science, technology, and attendant social transformations. And again, Ward - though confident in proposing the scientific and reforming effort that was necessary - was by no means untroubled by the difficulties.

> 'The future of the human race,' he wrote, 'must not be too confidently inferred from the past. The difficulties increase at a much greater rate than the density of population. The complexity of civilisation augments at a rate altogether out of proportion to the advance of intelligence. Moreover, in the present state of enlightened societies, the progress being made by the élite of the world in scientific discovery and mechanical application is far beyond the possible power of the masses, under existing methods of instruction to comprehend it. This tends rapidly to increase the disproportion and confusion in society, and threatens to precipitate the grand crisis which wise men cannot but foresee approaching unless a radical change is soon inaugurated in the social constitution of the civilised world. Science must supplant empiricism, and fundamental knowledge be universally diffused.'

Despite the difficulties and obstacles in the way, however, the making of sociology was a necessary task. Ward's faith, it that is the right word to use, was that in sociology, as in the history of other fields of human opinion and knowledge, the most obdurate ideologies would have to yield before the 'march of established facts'.

The Nature and Elements of Sociology

We are now in a position to give a clear outline of the nature of sociology as Ward constructed it - borrowing, as he did, from earlier thinkers and other contemporaries, and couched within the scientific perspective which he had clarified.

(a) *Sociology: the Science of Society: the Study of Social Achievement*

In the context of nature and the evolution of mind which he had elaborated, Ward went on to define Sociology as the scientific study of the interdependent functioning, within and among societies, of cumulative human achievements. Many social sciences provided knowledge of human achievements in specific fields, but these were all brought together by sociology - which was the study of the interdependent functioning of institutional achievements in societies as wholes.

Ward wrote:

'My thesis is that the subject-matter of sociology is human achievement. It is not what men are, but what they do. It is not the structure, but the function. Sociologists are nearly all working in the department of social anatomy, when they should turn their attention to social physiology. Most of them have imbibed the false notion that physiology is dynamic, and is in some way connected with social progress. They scarcely dare inquire what social physiology is, for fear that it may involve them in questions of social reform. But physiology is merely function. It is what structures and organs to, what they were made to do, the only purpose they have. Structures and organs are only means. Function is the end. It is, therefore, easy to see how much more important physiology is than anatomy. The latter is, of course, a necessary study, since functions cannot be performed without organs; but it is in the nature of preparation, and can be relegated to one or other of the special social sciences, which, as I have shown, supply the data for the study of sociology. The principal sources of such data are history, demography, anthropology, psychology, biology, civics and economics; but all the sciences contribute to that highest science, social physiology.'

And because of this, of course, sociology was essentially a historical and developmental subject because social achievement was an active and changing process, and social development (i.e. cumulative achievement) was a demonstrable fact.

'Sociology,' Ward stated again, 'is concerned with social activities. It is a study of action. It is not a descriptive science that describes objects looked upon as finished products. It is rather a study of how the various social products have been created. These products once formed become permanent. They may be slowly modified and perfected, but they constitute the basis for new products, and so on indefinitely. Viewed from the evolutionary standpoint, the highest types of men stand on an elevated platform which man and nature working together have erected in the long course of ages.'

The 'human polyp', he wrote, trying to give a colourful illustration:

'. . .is perpetually building a coral reef, on the upper surface of which the last generation lives and builds. The generations live and die, but they leave behind them the result of all that they accomplished when living. This result is a permanent part of the great ocean bed of human achievement. As time goes on these successive additions, superimposed the one upon the other, form the bed-rock of civilisation. They become lithified, as it were, and constitute the strata of the psychozoic age of the world, through which the true historian, like the geologist, cuts his sections and lays bare in profile the successive stages of human culture.'

And the crucial distinction which differentiated sociology as a science of human achievements from other sciences of nature, and especially from the scientific study of the other animals was that 'whereas the environment transforms the animal', in the case of man 'it is man who transforms the environment.'

Sociology, then, analysed the structural organisation and interdependent functioning of human achievement in societies as wholes (in relation to their environments), and studied the historical, evolutionary and developmental patterns of change which they had manifested; in all this taking fully into account, as a distinguishing feature of its subject-matter, the transforming power of mind, resting on acquired knowledge and seeking improvements of practical advantage.

It is important again to see how close Ward was to Marx here, but how clearly he was an improvement upon him.

He insisted that men's achievements were cumulative alterations of their material civilisation; closely attendant upon their practical activities, and their practical advantage, and he also readily and clearly claimed that the cultural and spiritual life of men was so enmeshed with their material civilisation as to make it a meaningless and unnecessary abstraction to try to separate the two. The directness of the following passage illustrates this very well.

'Material civilisation consists in the utilisation of the materials and forces of nature. It is, however, becoming more and more apparent that the spiritual part of civilisation is at least conditioned upon material civilisation. It does not derogate from its worth to admit that without a material basis it cannot exist. But it is also true that the moment such a basis is supplied, it comes forth in all ages and races of men. It may therefore be regarded as innate in man and potential everywhere, but a flower so delicate that it can only bloom in the rich soil of material prosperity. As such it does not need to be specially fostered. No amount of care devoted to it alone could make it flourish in the absence of suitable conditions, and with such conditions it requires no special attention. It may therefore be dismissed from our considerations, and our interest may be centered in the question of material civilisation, and this will be understood without the use of the adjective.'

But - Ward did not make the error of thinking that, given all this, the basic activities and continued achievements of men were material. Indeed he was superbly clear that these achievements were the institutionalisation of knowledge and ways of doing things. He wrote:

'Achievement does not consist in wealth. Wealth is fleeting and ephemeral. Achievement is permanent and eternal. And mark the paradox. Wealth, the transient, is material; achievement, the enduring, is immaterial. The products of achievement are not material things at all. They are not ends but means. They are methods, ways, principles, devices, arts, systems, institutions. In a word, they are inventions. It is anything and everything that rises above mere imitation or repetition. Every such increment to civilisation is a permanent gain, because it is imitated, repeated, perpetuated, and never lost. It is chiefly mental or physical, but it may be physical in the sense of skill.'

He also went further, and made it clear that to speak of the most simple, direct, manual labour as being something denuded of mental and moral effort and direction was an error. Quoting Professor John Clark (a contemporary), he wrote:

'In view of the constant presence of these three elements in labour, the physical, the mental, and the moral, any effort, in the supposed interest of the working classes, to depreciate mental labour in comparison with physical is unintelligent. All labour is mental. To a large and controlling extent the mental element is present in the simplest operations. With the labourer who shovels in the gravel pit the directing and controlling influence of the mind predominates, to an indefinite extent, over the simple foot-pounds of mechanical force which he exerts.'

And it was on exactly this kind of ground, Ward argued, that human labour and animal activity were generically distinct and therefore required different kinds and levels of explanation. Inventions with their appropriate and attendant arts were the basic elements in the advancement of human control on the basis of knowledge.

> 'In fact,' he said, 'in most of them there is scarcely any line of demarcation between them. They are pre-eminently "teleological", and it is the function that is primarily in the inventor's mind. He knows what he wants done, and merely devises the means of doing it. It is thus that the arts grow up. What the inventor does is to discover the principle by which he can cause the forces of nature, including the properties of the substances that he is acquainted with, to do the work that he wishes to have done and cannot do with his unaided hands. The discovery of this principle and the mode of applying it is what constitutes the achievement. This discovery, and not the resulting material product, is the lasing element in the operation. It can be used thenceforth for all time.'

But then Ward extended his notion of 'inventions' and 'arts' from specific tasks in nature and society to the achievement of forms of social organisation. Men's practical activities and practical advantage involved also the making and improvement of political, judicial, military, industrial institutions, and their over-all organisation in the entire community. It will be seen again how this conception immediately lifted Ward from the Marxian kind of dilemma of having to 'weight' one institutional field against others as being more 'objectively real' or more 'basic' than others. For Ward, man's mental capacities for invention and purposive action were applicable to all institutions. And it was this which led Ward to a beautifully clear, simple and succinct definition of sociology and its distinctive subject-matter. For all cumulative achievements, he argued, could be termed 'institutions'.

> 'The term institution,' he wrote, 'is capable of such expansion as to embrace all human achievement, and in this enlarged sense institutions become the chief study of the sociologist. All achievements are institution, and there is a decided gain to the mind in seeking to determine the true subject-matter of sociology, to regard human institutions and human achievements as synonymous terms, and as constituting, in the broadest sense of both, the field of research of a great science.'

This, it seems to me, was a marvellously clear statement. Sociology is the attempt to study as scientifically as possible all human social institutions: their nature, functions, interconnections and patterns of change in all societies known to us. There is not much that is wrong, it seems to me, in this definition, and there is certainly no lack of clarity whatever.

Ward elaborated this in much more detail, speaking of the institutions of society, the 'social structure', as the 'social heritage' whereby achievements were transmitted from generation to generation and so 'continued' to form a basis for further cumulative development. But all this, I think, is already clear enough.

(b) *Sociology: Pure and applied*

Consistently with his view that the attitude and perspective of science contained the two elements of study and control, and consistently too with his view that human achievement consisted of the application of knowledge in inventions which furthered human advantage, Ward divided Sociology into the 'Pure' and the 'Applied'. This we can simply note, and it need not detain us because it is so clear. Ward believed that, having established knowledge of society by exact methods of study, it was then a legitimate task of sociology to advise on the practical means, the various kinds of 'attractive legislation', whereby the details of social organisation could be improved. As we have seen, this concern for the making of sociology as a basis for guiding the making of society in its modern period of industrial change, has been a perennial preoccupation.

(c) *Sociology: Statics and Dynamics*

Ward also showed his total agreement with Comte, Mill and Spencer, in dividing Sociology into 'Statics' and 'Dynamics', as two aspects of the study of society meriting methodological distinction. In his mind too, this distinction was exactly the same as that proposed by Comte: that is to say, it was not a distinction between the 'stationary' and the 'moving and changing' as many people now think of it; but a distinction between the analytical clarification of the nature and components of society as a subject of study, on the one hand (Statics), and the application of this analysis in detailed empirical studies of the varieties of actual, changing societies (in seeking to establish 'theories' or theoretical 'laws' about them) on the other (Dynamics).

Ward was not only perfectly clear about this distinction, but he took to task those contemporary scholars who had misunderstood it. And this is worth noting very emphatically, because the error Ward castigated has come to be writ large in twentieth century sociology. And it is here too that we can begin to see the intellectual problems of the educational 'professionalisation' of the subject creeping in. The planning of 'courses' in sociology in colleges was already being well established in the last two decades of the nineteenth century in America. And within this context, there was already a tendency for the several aspects of the subject to become 'compartmentalised'. One such tendency was to regard 'Statics', quite literally as a 'stationary' analysis of structures, and to think of the 'functioning' of these stationary structures as the subject-matter of 'Dynamics'. The utter absurdity of this - bearing in mind all we have seen in the making of nineteenth century sociology - makes one gasp; but it is the case, hard though it is to believe, that some people involved in sociology as 'educational professionals' have interpreted the words 'Static' and 'Dynamic' in a completely literal way - with the profundity of discernment to be found in the nursery-cot. Ward hammered at this misconception.

We have already seen how, in his definition of the subject-matter of sociology, Ward made it clear that social institutions were achievements, the outcome of vital human energies and actions, and an interdependent patterning of these.

> 'It is not what men are, but what they do. It is not the structure, but the function. Sociologists are nearly all working in the department of social anatomy, when they should turn their attention to social physiology. Most of them have imbibed the false notion that physiology is dynamic, and is in some way connected with social progress. They scarcely dare inquire what social physiology is, for fear it may involve them in questions of social reform. But physiology is merely function. It is what structures and organs do, what they were made to do, the only purpose they have . . .'

> . . .and so on. But he went on to make this emphasis even more clear.
>
> 'Social structures are the products of the interactions of different social forces, all of which, in and of themselves, are destructive, but whose combined effect, mutually checking, constraining, and equilibrating one another, is to produce structures...
>
> It must not be supposed that social statics deals with stagnant societies. A static condition is to be sharply distinguished from a stationary condition. Failure to make this distinction is due to what I have called the fallacy of the stationary. Social structures are genetic mechanisms for the production of results, and the results cannot be secured without them. They are reservoirs of power.'

Ward's conception is completely clear in the following passage:

> 'Social structures are all the result of some form of struggle among the social forces whereby the centrifugal and destructive character of each force acting alone is neutralised and each is made to contribute to the constructive work of society. In forming these structures the various forces are equilibrated, conserved, commuted, and converted into energy and power. The structures once created become reservoirs of power, and it is through them alone that all the work of society is performed. All these structures are interrelated and the performance of their functions brings them into contact or even conflict with one another. This mild struggle among social structures has the same effect as other struggles, and leads to general social organisation. The final result is the social order, or society itself as an organised whole - a vast magazine of social energy stored for use by human institutions.'

(I) *Social Statics: The Analysis of the Nature of Society*

> 'Social Statics,' wrote Ward, 'is that sub-division of sociology which deals with the social order. The social order is made up of social structures, and is complete in proportion as those structures are integrated, while it is high in proportion as those structures are differentiated and multiplied and still perfectly integrated, or reduced to a completely subordinated and coordinated system. This branch of sociology will therefore deal chiefly with social structures and their functions, with their origin and nature, their relations of subordination and coordination, and with the final product of the entire process which is society itself.'

It is obvious, from what we have said, that, for Ward, the 'order' of institutions found in any society at any time was a structuring of vital energies. A structural-functional analysis of this network of institutions was therefore clearly necessary, but this by no means implied the existence of something called social or functional 'harmony'. The 'order' which prevailed was an intricate accommodation of conflicting and co-operating forces, actions, achievements, pursuits of specific ends, with each other; and it was an order which canalised and directed the collective energies of men in certain determinate ways. Change was therefore of the essence of society. Conflict, as well as co-operative accommodation, was of the essence of society. A vigorous play of energies, knowledge, inventiveness, pursuit of practical advantage in men's actions within the context of institutions was of the essence of society. A continuous surge of disequilibrium-equilibrium forces was of the essence of society.

Without elaborating this at all further, it is clear that the analysis of the nature of society involved at least (a) a structural-functional analysis of institutions, (b) an analysis of the sequences of social action pursued within them, (c) a disequilibrium-equilibrium analysis of the forces of conflict, co-operation, and adaptive accommodation, which made for both order and change. But Ward also insisted that the clear analysis of the regularities of institutional interrelationships in society required a historical and comparative perspective of study. And in emphasising this he showed his full awareness of all who had declared the importance of it before. Sociology, he claimed was essentially a generalising science; it sought to clarify, refine upon, and extend, those regularities which all knowledgeable scholars perceived among all societies of past and present. The clear understanding of the nature of society required, he wrote:

> '. . . the historical perspective. It is the discovery of law in history, whether it be the history of the past or the present, and including under history, social as well as political phenomena. There is nothing very new in this. It is really the oldest of all sociological conceptions. The earliest gropings after a social science consisted in a recognition of law in human affairs. The so-called precursors

WARD'S SYSTEM OF ANALYSIS

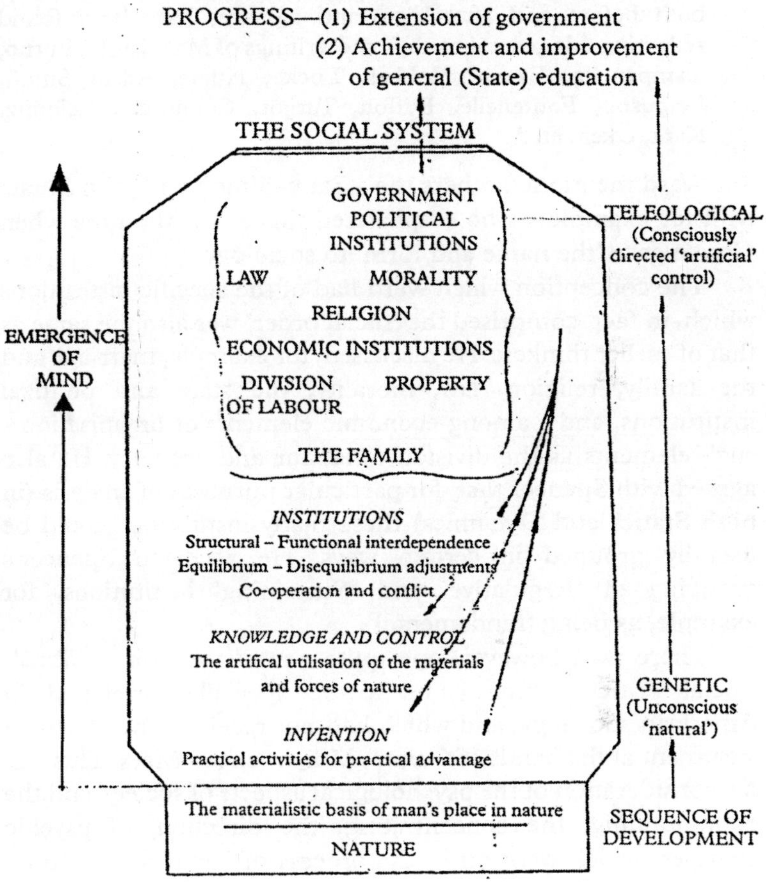

of sociology have been those who have perceived more or less distinctly a method or order in human events. All who have done this, however dimly, have been set down as the heralds of the new science. Such adumbrations of the idea of law in society were frequent in antiquity. They are to be found in the sayings of Socrates and the writings of Aristotle. Lucretius sparkles with them. In medieval times they were more rare, but Ibn Khaldun, a Saracen of Tunis, in the fourteenth century gave clear expression to this conception. His work, however, was lost sight of until recently, and Vico, who worte at the close of the seventeenth and beginning of the eighteenth century, was long regarded as the true forerunner of Montesquieu. Still, there were many others

> both before and after Vico, and passages have been found reflecting this general truth in the writings of Machiavelli, Burno, Campanella, Bacon, Hobbes, Locke, Hume, Adam Smith, Ferguson, Fontenelle, Buffon, Turgot, Condorcet, Leibnitz, Kant, Oken, etc.'

Ward mentioned others too - Saint-Simon and John Stuart Mill for example - who emphasized this about the time when Comte gave 'the name and form' to sociology.

The conception which Ward had of the specific institutions which, in fact, comprised the 'social order' was also the same as that of earlier thinkers. He discussed, for example, marriage and the family, religion, law, morality, the state and political institutions, and - among economic elements of organisation - such elements as the division of labour and property. He also agreed with Spencer that, for particular purposes of analysis (in both Statics and Dynamics) these many institutions could be usefully grouped in certain ways. He accepted Spencer's grouping of 'Regulative' and 'Sustaining' institutions, for example, as being 'fundamental'.

There was, however, one quite new dimension in Ward's 'social statics' which came to be specially developed in American sociology, and which had not received any extensive treatment at the hands of Comte, Mill, Spencer, Marx. This was his consideration of the psychological aspects of society, and the compounding, the concentrating, the direction, of psychic energies, which went on in the process of institutionalization: what Ward called - 'Synergy'. These elements require special mention.

(II) *The Social Forces and Synergy*

It will be remembered that Ward distinguished mind from material processes by its 'teleological' capacities. The conscious operations of mind could issue in actions which deliberately employed certain means to attain certain ends and in order to satisfy desires. Such purposive actions were to be distinguished from blind genetic processes in that they were conative; they were marked by a striving for ends and the intellectual capacities of man were able to guide them by knowledge and control. For Ward, then, the basic springs of human action in the life of a community were the many desires which motivated men in seeking their 'practical advantage', and this led him to offer a certain systematic way of regarding them and taking them into account in sociological analysis. Comte, of course, had written of 'social psychology' as distinct from the bio-psychological needs with which human nature was endowed; Mill had insisted strongly on the place of psychology and social psychology in a general science of society; Marx had claimed that the material conditions of society determined 'man's consciousness'; but no-one had made any steps at all in the direction of attempting any systematic analysis of what these 'basic' an 'social' psychological elements were.

Ward distinguished between (1) those 'desires' which sprang directly from the physiological needs of the body - hunger, thirst, sex and the like (and, coupled with these, the 'desires' which were 'indirectly' connected with them - such as the preference for pleasure and the avoidance of pain, and, in connection with sex, subsequent consanguineal feelings), and (2) those 'desires' which seemed distinctive of the human psycho ('spiritual desires') - such as moral and intellectual desires. The scheme which he proposed was as follows:

The Social Forces are
- Physical Forces (Function bodily)
  - Ontogenetic Forces
    - Positive, attractive (seeking pleasure)
    - Negative, protective (avoiding pain)
  - Phylogenetic Forces
    - Direct, sexual
    - Indirect, consanguineal
- Spiritual Forces (Function psychic)
  - Sociogenetic Forces
    - Moral (seeking the safe and good)
    - Esthetic (seeking the beautiful)
    - Intellectual (seeking the useful and true)

But though men, in their actions, sought the satisfaction of specific desires of all these kinds, the satisfaction of all of them in some sort of total patterning of experience was also an end of human desire.

> '... psychologically,' Ward wrote, 'all motives whatever are desires, and their satisfaction becomes an end of conation. In man, too, the satisfaction of desire in general, which in each particular case is attended with, or rather consists in, pleasure, acquires, in consequence of the highly derivative and greatly varied character of his desires, a distinctive name, not applicable to animals, and is called happiness. So far as the direct purposes of the sociologist are concerned, therefore, the ultimate end of conation is happiness.'

The driving forces of human actions in society, then, were these 'desires'. But Ward then went on to try to conceptualise the way in which all these many conflicting psychic energies in society came, through their very conflict, to necessitate a 'structuring', a kind of balanced accommodation with each other, which provided a stable context - a complex of reciprocal degrees of latitude and constraint - for their action and satisfaction. Each and any one of these human strivings, pursued with total disregard to others, could lead to disruption, chaos, destruction. Some accommodation of reciprocal adaptation and constraining order there must be.

> 'We may qualify Darwin's severe formula of the struggle for existence,' Ward wrote, 'and took upon the whole panorama rather as a struggle for structure.'

But the further important emphasis of Ward here was that 'institutions' in society are not just administrative frameworks; they are, in fact, living modes of the constrained but also creative canalisations of psychic energy. And as such, they are genuinely social psychological phenomena. They are not, that is to say, just 'raw' impulses or desires or motives as such; neither are they just additive summations of these; they are qualitatively new forms and actualities of psychological experience and behaviour which rest upon the necessitous constraining creativity peculiar to association and its demands; peculiar, that is, to society. Now this idea of the psychological creativity of social processes was one which Ward emphasised very plainly, but which was not to receive its fullest and most controversial statement until the work of Emile Durkheim; and there are many who cannot see the nature and importance of this social dimension of the creation of the experience and action of individuals to this day.

It is enough for now, however, to see that Ward introduced this important dimension of the psychological aspects of society, and built it into the 'statical' analysis of the nature of society in a very clear way. This was undoubtedly one enrichment of the making of sociology for which Ward was chiefly responsible. It will be readily seen how this analysis of these 'social forces' and the nature of 'synergy' fitted into the other components - structural-functional analysis, the analysis of social action, disequilibrium - equilibrium analysis, etc. - which Ward outlined.

(III) *Social Dynamics*

Social Dynamics was then, of course, the application of this analysis together with the classification of 'types' of society, to the empirical study of actual societies and the changes which took place within and among them. It is enough to say, on this, that Ward incorporated most of the aspects of change, and factors of change, already used by earlier writers. He discussed social growth, differentiation, and integration; the division of labour, property, and class exploitation; cultural contact and interchange between societies - including conquest and assimilation: invention and innovation; and many other notions which we have already seen in the schemes of other writers. And all this was couched within an overall framework of 'evolutionary' analysis.

Using the analytical methods of 'Statics' and undertaking the empirical studies of 'Dynamics', sociology could therefore deal manageably and systematically with its vast and complex subject-matter, and become an exact science.

> 'It is the function of methodology in social science, 'Ward wrote, 'to classify social phenomena in such a manner that the groups may be brought under uniform laws and treated by exact methods. Sociology then becomes an exact science. In doing this, too, it will be found that we have passed from chaos to cosmos. Human history presents a chaos. The only science that can convert the milky way of history into a definite social universe is sociology, and this can only be done by the use of appropriate methods . . . using the data furnished by all the special social sciences, including the

great scientific trunks of psychology, biology, and cosmology, and generalising and coordinating the facts and groups of facts until unity is attained.'

(d) *Teleology: purposive action: the superiority of the 'artificial', of 'indirect' control*

It is necessary, briefly, to reiterate some of our earlier points, in order to see how in sociology in particular, Ward came to his final and most central emphasis. Here we may simply remind ourselves that Ward maintained that the actions of men in the institutional fabric of society were teleological, and that, utilising indirect (artificial) control resting upon systematic knowledge, men could improve their conditions. Perhaps the one thing we might note here is that to think of man in 'teleological' terms did not send shudders of philosophical horror down Ward's spine. He was quite outrightly of the opinion that mind was, at least in large part, purposive. Later, we shall argue that he was completely right.

(e) *But Society includes BOTH genetic AND teleological processes combined. The analysis of intended and unintended consequences*

We also said earlier, however, that Ward recognised that human nature and society involved genetic as well as teleological causes, and that both had to be taken into account. And it is timely now to make this point again, and in such a way as to show that Ward's analysis, again, came close to that of Marx, but without lapsing into any ambiguity whatever.

Ward saw that there was a genetic process of adaptation and efficient causation in society as a whole, even though the many particular actions of men, within particular institutions, were purposive. This was a matter of unforeseen consequences; or reciprocal adaptation between institutional elements of which men were not conscious. Men acted purposively to achieve practical advantage in particular respects, but that might well be where their interest ceased. But institutional adaptations might take place beyond this. To take technological and economic actions as an example, Ward said :

> 'In transforming the physical environment the entire social system is profoundly affected and society itself is transformed. Although this is accomplished, wholly through teleological activity, still there is a sense in which social evolution thus brought about may be regarded as genetic. What the economists call the law of supply and demand is a natural law . . .This sociologic law is not affected by the fact that social demands are in large part supplied through the sagacious foresight of shrewd businessmen in a manner that is preeminently teleological, although strictly individualistic.
>
> For example, as a modern city grows street railway lines are gradually extended farther and farther out into the suburbs to anticipate the increasing demands, and this will take place although the citizens of those sections make no special demand and take no steps to secure it. The corporations controlling the urban lines are ever on the alert to increase the volume of their business, and by the exercise of a strictly teleological method forestall any such demand on the part of the citizens, who from inherent inertia, natural conservatism, personal indifference, and especially defective organisation, would be extremely slow to move in such matters and could scarcely be brought to the point of raising the funds necessary to construct such lines. Now although every step in social development of this is teleological, still the development itself is genetic, and only goes on as fast as or a trifle faster than is necessary fully to supply the demand . . .Thus is social genesis secured through individual telesis.
>
> If we look over the whole field of human achievement and social evolution we shall see that by far the greater part of it belongs to the class just described. The initiative is almost exclusively individual and the ends sought are egocentric in the widest sense, which must include the satisfaction of intellectual, moral, and even transcendental interests as well as those so-called physical wants that have to do with the functions of nutrition and reproduction. The social consequences. . .are unintended, and social evolution, however large the teleological factor in it may be, is to all intents and purposes unconscious.'

In sociological analysis both genetic and teleological processes had to be taken into account.

(f) *Progress: Knowledge, control, 'socialisation'*

Consistently, however, Ward maintained that with the advancement in our knowledge of the processes of society, the unconscious and unforeseen 'genetic' aspects could be brought ever more consciously, clearly, and effectively into control. With knowledge, and the conscious creation of improved institutions, the conditions of men's life could be brought more closely into accord with their practical advantage and happiness. And to provide the way of doing this was the task of applied sociology. The one central point we need to make here is that Ward was quite insistent that this meant an extension of what he called 'socialisation'. For Ward, however, this word simply meant the extension of the role of the State in purposefully controlling (improving) the institutions of society. Two aspects of this point are important.

The first is that Ward poured scorn upon the idea of 'Laissez-Faire' in government. All the evidence we had, he insisted, of the 'natural' processes of adaptation in nature and society was to the effect that, though arriving at a rough-and-ready equilibrium, these processes were profligate, wasteful, inefficient, and no respecters of persons or of human values. 'Laissez-Faire' notions of government were no less than a misguided leaving of the adaptations of society to processes which were insufficient and which could be improved on in many ways. Knowledge made possible control and improvement, and this could only be accomplished in society by extending the supervisory power of government. Of 'Laissez-Faire' notions. Ward wrote:

> 'Nothing could be more false or more pernicious. Scientists of this school, from the weight which their opinions must have, are really doing more to counteract the true tendencies of social progress than those who openly oppose them. All social progress is artificial. It is the consequence of teleological foresight, design, and intellectual labour, which are processes diametrically opposed in principle to the processes of nature. If in learning the law of evolution we must apply it to society, it would have been better to have remained ignorant of that law. In passing from the policy of inaction due to the belief that Providence is alone able to act, to the policy of inaction due to the belief that Nature is alone able to act, we have gained nothing. As well worship the old god as the new one. But, rightly interpreted, science teaches no such thing. It teaches the universal dependence of all phenomena upon antecedents, and it is this law that forms the basis of all successful

action in transforming rude nature into useful shapes and guiding wild forces into advantageous channels.'

The second aspect of this point was that Ward's treatment of the nature and development of institutions has led him to a much better, and much less negative, account of the functions of the 'State' in society than that which had been provided by Marx. Reinforcing his own conclusions by reference to the views of Comte, and also of contemporaries such as Simmel, Gumplowicz, and Ratzenhofer, Ward outlined the functions of the State as, amongst other things, those of resolving the conflicting interests of factions in society by accomplishing a 'mutual process of constraint and liberation'.

We see, he said:

'that the state, though genetic in its origin, is teleological in its method; that it has but one purpose, function, or mission, that of securing the welfare of society; that its mode of operation is that of preventing the anti-social actions of individuals; that in doing this it increases the freedom of human action so long as it is not anti-social; that the state is therefore essentially moral or ethical; that its own acts must necessarily be ethical; that being a natural product it must in a large sense be representative; that in point of fact it always is as good as society will permit it to be; that while thus far in the history of society the state has rarely performed acts that tend to advance mankind, it has been the condition to all achievement, making possible all the social, industrial, artistic, literary, and scientific activities that go on within the state and under its protection. There is no other human institution with which the state can be compared, and yet, in view of all this, it is the most important of all human institutions.'

The state itself, then, could be improved as a vehicle for extending knowledge and effective control in society. 'Progress' could become an increasingly conscious and deliberate matter in human society.

(g) *The Supreme Importance of Education*

It was in this way that Ward came to the central upshot of his sociological analysis and his teaching; namely the absolutely central and crucial importance of Education in society for the fullest accomplishment of progress. And this was a persuasion arising from his sociology both 'pure' and 'applied'. In all societies it was the system (institution) of instruction and education which secured the continuity of the 'achievements' of society from one generation to the next, and which thus provided the basis for further cumulative advancements in knowledge and inventions. But also, the fullest progress in the extension of accurate knowledge about nature and society, and its best applications to human advantage, could only be accomplished if education was improved. And Ward argued strongly that education should be compulsory, and provided for all citizens by the State. Ward was so concerned to press home the importance of this, that he set his conclusions out almost in the form of a formula, or, as he put it, as a 'set of theorems'. First, he gave a clear list of six definitions.

A. *Happiness* - Excess of pleasure, or enjoyment, over pain, or discomfort.

B. *Profess* - Success in harmonising natural phenomena with human advantage.

C. *Dynamic Action* - Employment of the intellectual, inventive, or indirect method of conation.

D. *Dynamic Opinion* - Correct views of the relations of man to the universe.

E. *Knowledge* - Acquaintance with the environment.

F. *Education* - Universal distribution of extant knowledge.'

And then he stated six corresponding 'theorems of dynamic sociology' as follows:

'A. Happiness is the ultimate end of conation.

B. Progress is the direct means to Happiness; it is, therefore, the first proximate end of conation, or primary means to the ultimate end.

C. Dynamic Action is the direct means to Progress; it is, therefore, the second proximate end of conation, or secondary means to the ultimate end.

D. Dynamic Opinion is the direct means to Dynamic Action; it is, therefore, the third proximate end of conation, or tertiary means to the ultimate end.

E. Knowledge is the direct means to Dynamic Opinion; it is,

therefore, the fourth proximate end of conation, or fourth means to the ultimate end.

F. Education is the direct means to knowledge; it is, therefore, the fifth proximate end of conation, and is the fifth and initial means to the ultimate end.

Using the mathematical sign of equivalence (≎), which, he said, should be read as — 'will result in'–his formula was then:

F ≎ E ≎ D ≎ C ≎ B ≎ A

And this scheme, Ward argued, simple though it seemed, could be elaborately defended, and was complete. The first term - A - was the ultimate end of society, he claimed, and the final term - F - was the initial means of moving towards its attainment.

Ward's analysis of education in society, and especially his proposals for the reform of education, were perhaps the most impressive part of his entire system, and it is highly significant that State education - since his time - has, in almost all modern countries, approximated to the characteristics of education which he claimed to be necessary.

Having distinguished between five chief kinds of education: education by experience, discipline, culture, research, and information, it was the last which he supported most strongly. Education should chiefly be, he argued:

> '. . .a system of extending to all the members of society such of the extant knowledge of the world as may be deemed most important.'

It should devote itself to the contents of the mind rather than its capacity; it should be provided by the State; it should be compulsory; and it should be universal. Only if all the members of a society had the opportunity of acquiring the stock of knowledge available, could there be the best possible basis of the fullest application of knowledge in all activities; the best basis for research and the advancement of knowledge; and the best basis for the formation of opinion, for deliberation and judgment; and, following from this, the best basis for government itself.

> 'Education,' wrote Ward, 'is not only the science of sciences, but the art of the arts.'

Ward put forward the most detailed and persuasive arguments in support of these ideas, and lest it should be thought that his proposals were 'light-weight' reformist ideas when compared with the 'revolutionary' proposals of a Marx or an Engels, let it be noticed that his insistence throughout was the effective removal of inequalities of opportunity and unwarranted class difference.

> 'The knowledge,' he wrote, 'which enables one class of men to enslave another class brings misery to thousands and enjoyment to but few. The greater part of the evils of society, which are usually and correctly ascribed to ignorance, might with almost equal propriety be ascribed to intelligence. The ignorance which causes them is only relative ignorance. The power that enacts them is the power of relatively greater intelligence. . .
>
> Some will wonder why so little is said in this work of the great social economic problems; why the distribution of wealth, rather than of education, is not insisted upon, since happiness depends greatly upon the possession of the objects of desire; why the contrast between civilisation and barbarism, intelligence and ignorance, has been so strongly drawn, while that between wealth and indigence, "progress and poverty," has been neglected. The answer must be that the sole object of this treatise is to arrive at the initial means . . . .And it is high time for socialists to perceive that, as a rule, they are working at the roof instead of at the foundation of the structure which they desire to erect.'
>
> 'The distribution of knowledge,' he went on, 'underlies all social reform. So long as capital and labour are the respective symbols of intelligence and ignorance, the present inequity in the distribution of wealth must continue...
>
> The differences in native capacity, though admittedly great, are small compared to the differences of information. The supposed intellectual inequality is greatly exaggerated. The large fund of good sense which is always found among the lower, uneducated classes is an obtrusive fact to every observing mind. The ability with which ignorant people employ their small fund of knowledge has surprised many learned men. While there may doubtless be found all grades of intellect, from the highest philosophic to the lowest idiotic, the number who fall below a certain average standard is insignificant, and so, too, is the number who rise above it. The great bulk of humanity are fully witted, and amply capable of taking care of themselves if afforded an opportunity.'

Ward's passionate condemnation of the inequity of the 'unequal distribution of knowledge' among classes in society may be seen, finally, in the following passage.

'The present enormous chasm between the ignorant and the intelligent, caused by the unequal distribution of knowledge, is the worst evil under which society labours. This is because it places it in the power of a small number, having no greater natural capacity, and no natural right or title, to seek their happiness at the expense of a large number. The large number, deprived of the means of intelligence, though born with the capacity for it, are really compelled by the small number, through the exercise of a superior intelligence, to serve them without compensation. This is the result of the ultimate analysis of the problem of the present unequal distribution of wealth. For it is not the idler, but the toiler, the real producer of wealth, who has none; while the man who has wealth is usually a man of leisure – at least he has rarely or never acquired it through labour in creating it. The former occupies his position solely in consequence of his relative ignorance, the latter occupies his solely in consequence of his relative intelligence. Knowledge is power, and power has ever been wielded for self - aggrandisement, and must ever be so wielded. To prevent inequality of advantages there must be equality of power, i.e., equality of knowledge.' 'A system of education,' he concluded, 'to be worthy the name, must be framed for the great proletariat. Most systems of education seem designed exclusively for the sons of wealthy gentry, who are supposed to have nothing else to do in life but seek the highest culture in the most approved and fashionable ways. But the great mass, too, need educating.'

It can only be emphasised, in leaving this point, that Ward's case for making education the crucial lever for social reform and social progress was far more strongly argued, and in far more detail, than can possibly be stated in an exposition of this kind. To my mind, his arguments are convincing and of the utmost importance for our problems even now.

'The problem of education is,' he insisted, 'reduced to this: . . . whether the social system shall always be left to nature, always be genetic and spontaneous, and be allowed to drift listlessly on, intrusted to the by no means always progressive influences which have developed it and brought it to its present condition, or whether it shall be regarded as a proper subject of art, treated as other natural products have been treated by human intelligence, and made as much superior to nature, in this only proper sense of the word, as other artificial productions are superior to natural ones.'

This, then, in outline, was Lester Ward's contribution to the making of sociology. Many other elements of his system have not been mentioned: – the important place he attributed to the creation of moral and social 'ideals' in the pursuit of social purpose; the distinction he drew between anthropology and sociology; his rejection of many aspects of social administration and social work as spurious pretenders to sociology; his rejection of 'mathematical' sociology; and others of considerable interest. But the main components of the nature of sociology as the new and necessary science of society as he conceived it have been touched upon, and we have seen with sufficient clarity for our purposes, the important similarities and the interesting and worthwhile differences between his work and the work of Comte, Mill, Spencer and Marx.

B. WILLIAM GRAHAM SUMNER

Somewhere, I remember reading that G. K. Chesterton, exasperated at being unable to find a fitting description, referred to Walt Whitman as a 'great big something or other'. This seems a peculiarly apt description of William Graham Sumner. He seems to have been a large, dogmatic, challenging, many-sided man. He was once a clergyman: a fiery, militant preacher by all accounts. His wide studies (some of them undertaken in Europe) covered theology and philosophy as well as anthropology and economics (which he taught). He came to despise theology and philosophy especially. 'Philosophy,' he is reported to have said at a college meeting, 'is in every way as bad as astrology. It is a complete fake!' It is obvious at once, then, that he was fully agreed with all the men we have studied, that science should replace these more speculative subjects in any attempt to establish a knowledge of man and society. On the strength of this persuasion, he moved quite boldly into the making of sociology; he saw the need for a science of society; but – even here (bearing in mind what we have already said about the tendencies towards the rapid, the superficial, and the contrived, in the academic 'professionalisation' of the subject) – it is said that he 'detested with fury most of the work done under the name of Sociology, most of its tendencies, and nearly all those who taught it'. He must have been a forceful and impressive teacher, and was undoubtedly one of the most important American scholars contributing to the making of sociology towards the end of the nineteenth century.

His most influential book - *Folkways* - was, in fact, published in 1906, but it is correct to include him as a late nineteenth century figure since he was formulating his conceptions of society and the scientific study of it at the same time as Lester Ward. And, indeed, it is fitting that we should consider him now because he has come to be placed, in much current judgment, at the opposite end of the spectrum from Ward. Greatly influenced by Spencer's analysis of social systems and the part played by 'custom' in the 'simple societies', Sumner was also close to Spencer's 'laissez-faire' convictions concerning the role of government and legislation in society. So that whereas Ward advocated the extension of 'collectivism' and the supervision by the State of the acquisition, transmission, and application of knowledge, Sumner was much more chary of rationally based 'enactments'. Also, whereas Ward believed in the reality of 'progress', Sumner has been judged a 'relativist'. He has therefore seemed to stand in complete opposition to Ward. In what follows, however, we shall see that this is too strong, too sharp, a distinction. Sumner was, in fact, not sufficiently exacting in the philosophical clarification of his points and his distinctions, and the ambiguities which result tend to cloud his position. When these are removed, it can be seen that his differences with the 'progressive' position put forward by Ward were really differences of degree and emphasis, not at all basic differences of kind.

In general, Sumner was never specific, clear and detailed about methodological matters, and there is not a lot to be gained from him in this direction. However, in his study of *Folkways* he offered a very clear analysis of the nature, processes and components of society, and of certain tendencies of social change. To use our earlier terms: he put forward a very clear 'social statics' and 'social dynamics', and brought together an enormous range of comparative and historical data to substantiate the analysis he proposed. *Folkways* is in fact, a work of massive scholarship, and has been, and is, one of the most 'seminal' books in sociology.

In this account of his 'system', I want, above all, to show clearly his agreement with the thinkers we have considered so far as to the nature and elements of a science of society. This is our major concern. But there were distinctive elements in Sumner's work, which were both developments of dimensions stressed by earlier thinkers and introductions of new components of analysis and theory which were going to receive considerable emphasis and development at the hands of others. Sumner is a kind of 'bridge' figure in certain ways, between the conspectus of the science as it was established by the end of the nineteenth century, and the development of specific elements of analysis within this conspectus which has taken place during the twentieth. It is worthwhile to indicate some of these points at the outset.

One central emphasis in Sumner's study was upon the psychological aspects of society; upon the ways in which the experience and actions of men come to give rise to a 'societal' network of usages, rituals, values, beliefs, regulations which go beyond individuals but are, at the same time, creative of individual qualities; a network which is distinctively a societal process and which is, at one and the same time, both constraining and creative. In this, he developed very considerably that element of sociological analysis which Mill called 'Ethology'. But this was also the special emphasis of the work of Durkheim, which we shall consider later, and certain American scholars too, especially Mead and Cooley, were to develop the study of this 'middle-range' element of sociological analysis - the psychological aspects of social processes - particularly. As a part of this emphasis, Sumner also introduced the distinction between 'In-Groups' and 'Out-Groups', and this, too, has led to the whole development of group analysis for the understanding of attitude and sentiment formation. Similarly, in his analysis of the way in which the 'folkways and mores' in simpler societies give way to the more rationally based 'institutions and laws' of more complex societies, Sumner provided one of the earliest formulations of what has become perhaps the most central theory of social change in the whole of sociology - one which, as we shall see, has come to be attributed particularly to Ferdinand Tonnies. In the work of Sumner, then, we are coming not only to the point of seeing the agreed formulation of the subject at the end of the nineteenth century, but also the strong germinal force of new ideas which were like seeds planted implicitly within it. But we must restrain ourselves, and deal here, still, with a clear outline of the foundations themselves.

Society

Sumner put forward a very clear 'model' of society: of its chief components and processes; and here we will outline each element systematically in order to bring out the similarities between these and the ideas of Comte, Mill, Spencer, Marx and Ward.

(a) *Necessity, Action and the Struggle for Existence*

As the basis of his conception of society, Sumner adopted a materialist standpoint just as emphatically as did Spencer or Marx.

> 'The first task of life,' he wrote, 'is to live. Men begin with acts, not with thoughts. Every moment brings necessities which must be satisfied at once.'

Men have basic needs which must, of necessity, be satisfied if they are to survive, and in this, action, not contemplation, is of primary urgency. This, inescapably, gives rise to a struggle for sheer existence, and this is intensified by the fact that, in large part, it must be competitive, and must take place in relation to the available conditions and resources of the environment: what Sumner called the 'life conditions'

> 'The struggle for existence must be carried on under life conditions and in connection with the competition of life. The life conditions consist in variable elements of the environment, the supply of materials necessary to support life, the difficulty of exploiting them, the state of the arts, and the circumstances of physiography, climate, meteorology, etc., which favour life or the contrary. The struggle for existence is a process in which an

> individual and nature are the parties. The individual is engaged in a process by which he wins from his environment what he needs to support his existence. In the competition of life the parties are men and other organisms. The men strive with each other, or with the flora and fauna with which they are associated. The competition of life is the rivalry, antagonism, and mutual displacement in which the individual is involved with other organisms by his efforts to carry on the struggle for existence for himself. It is, therefore, the competition of life which is the societal element, and which produces societal organisation.'

Society is grounded in this basic material and human struggle.

(I) *Size of Population: An Important Factor*

One factor of central importance in the struggle for existence and for the determination of the kind of social life which springs from it, is, claimed Sumner, the size of the population who share the struggle.

> 'The number present and in competition is another of the life conditions. At a time and place the life conditions are the same for a number of human beings who are present, and the problem of life policy are the same. This is another reason why the attempts to satisfy interest become mass phenomena and result in folkways. The individual and social elements are always in interplay with each other if there are a number present. If one is trying to carry on the struggle for existence with nature, the fact that others are doing the same in the same environment is an essential condition for him.'

This point is worth noting separately as it was also made by Spencer, and came to be emphasised by Durkheim as one of the most important factors underlying the division of labour in society.

(II) *Conflict and Co-operation*

In this struggle for existence, men are confronted with two alternatives. They can compete individually, and risk failure, or:

> '. . .they may combine, and by co-operation raise their efforts against nature to a higher power. This latter method is industrial organisation. The crisis which produces it is constantly renewed,

> and men are forced to raise the organisation to greater complexity and more comprehensive power, without limit. Interests are the relations of action and reaction between the individual and the life conditions, through which relations the evolution of the individual is produced. That evolution, so long as it goes on prosperously, is well living, and it results in the self-realisation of the individual, for we may think of each one as capable of fulfilling some career and attaining to some character and state of power by the developing of predispositions which he possesses. It would be an error, however, to suppose that all nature is a chaos of warfare and competition. Combination and co-operation are fundamentally necessary.'

As a matter of fact, Sumner argued, there is always a tension of competition and co-operation between the members of a society; a condition of what he called 'antagonistic co-operation'. A society is always a kind of tensile order, binding together both similar and divergent, both harmonious and conflicting, interests.

It will be seen, in this basic materialist position, how close Sumner was to Marx; and it is also worthwhile to notice that - as with Marx and others – Sumner held that though this was a competitive-co-operative struggle among men; a matter of necessity and constraint; it was also creative of the conditions for the self-realization of the individual.

(b) *Basic motives, instincts and interests*

The struggle for existence is not, however, without shape or direction: or, indeed (among human groups) without uniformity. Though the desires of men may become very complex, there are, Sumner maintained 'four great motives of human action,' which are universal in human nature and human society. These are hunger, sexual passion, vanity, and fear. And under the heading of 'fear' Sumner included the fear of ghosts, spirits, and the dead, as well as of more ordinary dangers. These four basic motives gave rise to powerful interests which always drove men to action. But, though he did not wish to be precise about this, Sumner also thought it probable that man possessed a certain set of 'instinctual' responses connected with these four basic motives. He wrote, for example:

> 'It is generally taken for granted that men inherited some guiding instincts from their beast ancestry, and it may be true, although it has never been proved. If there were such inheritances, they controlled and aided the first efforts to satisfy needs.'

And also:

> 'It is now the accepted opinion, and it may be correct, that men inherited from their beast ancestors psychophysical traits, instincts and dexterities, or at least predispositions, which give them aid in solving the problems of food supply, sex commerce, and vanity. The result is mass phenomena; currents of similarity, concurrence, and mutual contribution; and these produce folkways. The folkways are unconscious, spontaneous, uncoordinated. It is never known who led in devising them...'

Sumner never explored this 'instinctual' element, and did not make it an essential part of his system, but it is important to see that he did think that any such pattern of experience and behaviour that might have a hereditary basis in man could provide an element in explaining the universality of the folkways in human societies; the basic pattern of motives which lay at the roots of them in all communities.

At any rate, we can see that Sumner's initial steps of analysis rested upon the systematically related conception of four basic needs and motives, with a possible basis of instinct, which give rise to specific interests, which underlie men's competitive and co-operative action in the struggle for existence.

Bearing in mind Ward, Marx, and others, we can also see here the element of purpose in men's material and social activities; and, indeed, Sumner held that, in all such activity:

> 'However great the errors and misconceptions may be which are included in the efforts, the purpose always is advantage and expediency.'

Sumner tempered the word 'expediency' in certain ways.

This collective, competitive and co-operative activity of the members of a population who share the struggle for existence in certain life conditions, gives rise to the 'folkways'. And first of all we must concern ourselves with definitions.

(c) *The Folkways: A Socio-psychological Process of Creativity: A Societal Environment*

As primitive groups of men first came to grips with their many-sided struggle for survival, they were in a condition of ignorance; or, as Sumner put it, of 'primeval stupidity'. He put the matter as strongly as this in order to stress that men were not only without knowledge, but also that they made great errors in the formulation of their folkways owing to irrational fears and superstitions. Men's early efforts in material and social activities must have been of a 'trial-and-error' nature; they must have been attended by error, accident, and luck. There was nothing necessarily well guided about them. However, in terms of seen advantage, and balance of pleasure over pain with regard to individual and group welfare, some ways of doing things were preferred to others, and came to be adopted and established.

> '. . .ways of doing things were selected which were expedient. They answered the purpose better than other ways, or with less toil and pain. Along the course on which efforts were compelled to go, habit, routine, and skill were developed. . .
>
> Each profited by the other's experience; hence there was concurrence towards that which proved to be most expedient. All at last adopted the same way for the same purpose; hence the ways turned into customs and became mass phenomena.
>
> In this way folkways arise.'

Those activities which most satisfactorily fulfilled interests became habitual among individuals and customs throughout the group. And Sumner conceived of the folkways as the very gradual creation of an entire network of customary practices which regulated every important activity in the community. At any given time, in a community, the folkways: 'provide for all the needs of life then and there.' But let us look more closely at the attributes which, according to Sumner, they possess.

> Though, in their emergence they are 'unconscious, spontaneous, unco-ordinated,' they come to be, he argued, 'uniform, universal in the group, imperative, and invariable.'

All these qualities are important, but perhaps the chief one to emphasise here is that the folkways are not only usages, but sanctioned and obligatory usages throughout the community, binding upon its members. In this sense, the folkways, when they have assumed this force of custom, have become a societal force, going beyond individuals, and imposing upon individuals the regulatory framework within which all their energies and experience can be expressed.

> 'The body of the 'folkways,' Sumner wrote, 'constitutes a societal environment. Every one born into it must enter into relations of give and take with it. He is subjected to influences from it, and it is one of the life conditions under which he must work out his career of self-realisation.'
>
> 'By habit and custom it exerts a strain on every individual within its range; therefore it rises to a societal force to which great classes of societal phenomena are due. . .We have to recognise it as one of the chief forces by which a society is made to be what it is.'

What Sumner claimed, then, was not simply that a network of folkways emerged and took definite shape out of the shared communal activities of a people, but that this close mesh of constraining and authoritative tradition was creative of the later formal structures of society as, or if, it developed. Custom was a creative social-psychological force of the most fundamental importance in the making of societies.

Before we see the process of social development which Sumner traced, however, certain other points need separate statement and emphasis.

(I) *The Authority of the Folkways*

Sumner stressed very powerfully the strength and peculiarity of the authority possessed by the folkways, and his position on this point must be noticed very carefully, because it is an insight which, later on, I wish to consider as one possessing the most central importance for sociological analysis; one at the very root of all the major statements of sociological theory.

The folkways are both 'true' and 'right' within the community, Sumner showed, and yet the authority which they possess is of a very specific kind. They tend to be 'true', by and large, in that they accord with common-sense experience, expediency, and common advantage - so that, in a sense, they may be said to be borne out by experience. But firstly - this is not always so. Sometimes the folkways have been founded upon erroneous superstition, or accidental coincidence, and can be positively disadvantageous to the community - at least in some respects. So that they are not always 'true' in this sense. And secondly – even when they are 'true', it is not their truth which vests them with authority. Their authority resides in their 'rightness', and they are 'right' by the simple fact of their existence as sanctified immemorial usage. Custom carries a basic authority in its own irreducible right.

> 'The folkways are the "right" ways to satisfy all interests, because they are traditional, and exist in fact. They extend over the whole of life. There is a right way to catch game, to win a wife, to make one's self appear, to cure disease, to honour ghosts, to treat comrades or strangers, to behave when a child is born, on the warpath, in council, and so on in all cases which can arise. The ways are defined on the negative side, that is, by taboos. The "right" way is the way which the ancestors used and which has been handed down. The tradition is its own warrant. It is not hold subject to verification by experience. The notion of right is in the folkways. It is not outside of them, or independent origin, and brought to them to test them. In the folkways, whatever is, is right. This is because they are traditional, and therefore contain in themselves the authority of the ancestral ghosts. When we come to the folkways we are at the end of our analysis.'

It will be seen in this passage that the sanctity of the folkways is supported by the feeling that they have been the ways of the ancestors; they are the ancestral traditions of the community; and it is in this sense that Sumner argued that they tended, universally in human societies, to be supported by 'ghost fear'; by the sense of awe surrounding the dead; by religion.

The further point here is that the authority does not reside in the known origins of the folkways, because no-one knows what these origins were. 'They arise no-one knows whence or how.' Indeed, said Sumner: 'It is only by analysis and inference that we can form any conception of the "beginning" which we are always so eager to find.'

The point which is of the greatest importance here, however, is this. The basic regulatory order of a society, beyond which societal analysis can scarcely probe (indeed, beyond which it can only probe by conjecture); which embraces the material technical, organisational structuring of men's relationships; is essentially a moral order. There is no societal fabric of technical and social procedures and relationships which is not at once an order interpenetrated by morality. The importance of this point cannot here be sufficiently brought out, but it is enough just to note and to insist upon Sumner's teaching - that morality is not, and is never, an abstract, intuitive thing of philosophical ethics alone, but is a part and parcel of men's practical efforts to live well, to accomplish welfare in society, and - what is crucial - is not one aspect of society, but an all-pervading, interpenetrating core of all social relationships.

> 'The morality of a group at a time', wrote Sumner, 'is the sum of the taboos and prescriptions in the folkways by which right conduct is defined. Therefore, morals can never be intuitive. They are historical, institutional and empirical.
>
> World philosophy, life policy, right, rights and morality are all products of the folkways. They are reflections on, and generalisations from, the experience of pleasure and pain which is won in efforts to carry on the struggle for existence under actual life conditions. The generalisations are very crude and vague in their germinal forms. They are all embodied in folklore, and all our philosophy and science have been developed out of them.'

This point must be left now, for the moment (reluctantly!), but its importance cannot be over-emphasised.

(II) *The Folkways: A Long Historical Tradition*

It follows, of course, that the established folkways of a community, in Sumner's view, were always the outcome of an extremely long historical past, and embodied the cumulative experience of countless generations of men, and countless accommodations to particular, and perhaps changing, life conditions. It was in this sense - almost in the sense of an Edmund Burke – that Sumner could be said to be 'relativist.' His point was only that the system of folkways in any community was valid for the life conditions of that community – no matter how strange they might appear to others. But we have already seen that because of the basic motives, needs, and interests in all societies, Sumner's position was not entirely 'relativist', in the sense that there was, for him, a core of uniformity, of similarity, of universality, at the roots of the folkways of all societies no matter how widely their specific forms varied. And we shall come to other elements of Sumner's analysis, too, which will demonstrate the error of regarding him as being committed to an extreme 'relativity' of values.

(III) *The Folkways: A Continuous Creation*

It is also important to note, however, that - though they stemmed from a long ancestral past - the folkways were never final in Sumner's conception. They possessed flexibility and could be changed as 'life-conditions' changed. Their essence was that they were a continuous process of creative accommodation to conditions. In this sense, Sumner gave illustrations of contemporary folkways that were taking shape in relation to new techniques and instruments – such as the telephone, and mass-communications, for example.

(IV) *The Folkways: The Outcome of Unintended Consequences: The Unconscious, Cumulative Laying Down of a Social Order*

One other essential aspect of Sumner's conception was that although he believed that men acted purposely - as individuals - with motives pressing them, with interests in mind, seeking their own advantage, he did not believe that the creation of the folkways was a conscious purposeful process. We have already seen that he thought of the emergence of the folkways as being 'unconscious, spontaneous, unco-ordinated'. He wrote very clearly and definitely in this way:

> 'It is of the first importance to notice that, from the first acts by which men try to satisfy needs, each act stands by itself, and looks no further than the immediate satisfaction. From recurrent needs arise habits for the individual and customs for the group, but these results are consequences which were never conscious, and never foreseen or intended. They are not noticed until they have long

existed, and it is still longer before they are appreciated. Another long time must pass, and a higher stage of mental development must be reached, before they can be used as a basis from which to deduce rules for meeting, in the future, problems whose pressure can be foreseen. The folkways, therefore, are not creations of human purpose and wit. They are like products of natural forces which men unconsciously set in operation, which are developed out of experience, which reach a final form of maximum adaptation to an interest, which are handed down by tradition and admit of no exception or variation, yet change to meet new conditions, still within the same limited methods, and without rational reflection or purpose. From this it results that all the life of human beings, in all ages and stages of culture, is primarily controlled by a vast mass of folkways handed down from the earliest existence of the race, only the topmost layers of which are subject to change and control, and have been somewhat modified by human philosophy, ethics, and religion, or by other acts of intelligent reflection.'

Here, yet again, we have the emphasis upon the importance of 'unintended consequences' in the creation of societies; but perhaps the chief point to isolate for clarity here is that, in this way, an interconnected social order, integrated to some degree, fitted to the environmental and social conditions of the community, is laid down without over-all conscious and rational planning, and before men become aware of it, let alone desirous of reforming it. And it is out of this order, that later and more formal differentiations of structure may arise, and that conscious control (to some extent) may take place. But the order is laid down before this, and, indeed, it is always the case that no man can ever possibly see, grasp, or understand the entirely of it. This, again, is a point of the most basic importance.

Before leaving this, we might pause to note that, on the face of his treatment, Sumner seemed to lay much greater weight than did Ward upon what Ward called the genetic rather than the teleological aspects of the making of society; and we shall see later that this impression seems to be reinforced by Sumner's apparently greater reluctance to concede a role of any great extent to social legislation and reform. It might be said that Sumner placed more emphasis upon the worth and wisdom of the genetic processes of society than did Ward. But such a judgment would be, it seems to me, a mistake. We have already seen that Sumner thought the folkways could rest upon error, accident, and superstition, and we shall see, increasingly, that, in fact, he was quite as definite and committed as Ward on the matter of reform and progress - it is only that he was clouded by ambiguities, or perhaps one should say an insufficiency of care in making himself clear. We can see some of the evidence for this point of view in the next point.

(V) *The Folkways: The Strain Towards Improvement and Consistency*

The picture given by the emphasis upon the 'unconscious' and 'unintended' growth of the folkways was qualified by Sumner's insistence that there was a strain towards improvement, and a strain towards consistency among them. Sumner made these points as an outcome of the fact that the folkways came into being to satisfy needs, to serve powerful motives, and were adopted because of a balance of pleasure over pain, and of practical advantage. If this was so, then if they were only imperfectly adapted to the 'life conditions' of the community, there must always be a strain towards the improvement of them; and, since they would be more efficient if well articulated with each other, there must always also be a strain towards consistency among all of them. In short, there was a tendency towards progress in the light of extended knowledge and experience, and a tendency towards the making of a coherent system of all the elements of custom.

> 'The folkways', Sumner wrote, 'are, therefore, (1) subject to a strain of improvement towards better adaptation of means to ends, as long as the adaptation is so imperfect that pain is produced. They are also (2) subject to a strain of consistency with each other, because they all answer their several purposes with less friction and antagonism when they co-operate and support each other. The forms of industry, the forms of the family, the notions of property, the constructions of rights, and the types of religion show the strain of consistency with each other through the whole history of civilisation.'

Furthermore, the extent to which conscious reason and reflection could, and should, enter into men's judgments about the nature and quality of the folkways can be seen in what Sumner had to say about 'suggestion' and 'suggestibility' which, together with constraining pressures and imitation, he thought were the psychological processes whereby the folkways were communally established. Criticism, he maintained, was the only way in which individuals could protect themselves against credulity, emotional bias and fallacy.

> 'The power of criticism', he wrote, 'is the one which education should chiefly train...Our judicial institutions are devised to hold suggestion aloof until the evidence is examined. An educated man ought to be beyond the reach of suggestions from advertisements, newspapers, speeches and stories. If he is wise, just when a crowd is filled with enthusiasm and emotion, he will leave it and will go off by himself to form his judgment. In short, individuality and personality of character are the opposites of suggestibility. . .A highly trained judgment is required to correct or select one's own ideas and to resist fixed ideas. The supreme criticism is criticism of one's self.'

It is quite clear that, if this argument was to be followed, critical reason could enter into the reform of the folkways in good measure; and we shall see later that Sumner really did advocate this. It was only - again like Burke - that he threw all his weight in the scales against brash, careless, uninformed, and irresponsible efforts of reform, of which, of course, there are plenty in this world.

So much, however, for the nature of the primary folkways in Sumner's system: the first, basic societal order.

(d) *Mystical Regulatory Doctrines*

The next major element in Sumner's 'model' of society was the 'Mores' which grew distinctively out of the primary stuff of the 'Folkways', but this growth was mediated, he claimed, by the development of 'mystical doctrines' - myths - which provided a kind of over-all 'rationale' for the folkways. It was here that Sumner stressed the element of 'ghost fear' and religion as an important support of the folkways. There was a kind of blending of the fear of the dead ancestors and the awe in which they were held, and the practical provisions both for them and the needs of the living.

> 'With great unanimity', Sumner wrote, 'all over the globe primitive men followed the same line of thought. The dead were believed to live on as ghosts in another world just like this one. The ghosts had just the same needs, tastes, passions, etc., as the living men had had. These transcendental notions were the beginning of the mental outfit of mankind. They are articles of faith, not rational convictions. The living had duties to the ghosts, and the ghosts had rights; they also had power to enforce their rights. It behaved the living therefore to learn how to deal with ghosts. Here we have a complete world philosophy and a life policy deduced from it. When pain, loss, and ill were experienced, and the question was provoked, Who did this to us? the world philosophy furnished the answer. When the painful experience forced the question, Why are the ghosts angry and what must we do to appease them? the "right" answer was the one which fitted into the philosophy of ghost fear. All acts were therefore constrained and trained into the forms of the world philosophy by ghost fear, ancestral authority, taboos, and habit. The habits and customs created a practical philosophy of welfare, and they confirmed and developed the religious theories. . . '

These 'myths' were therefore theoretical and regulatory justifications of the folkways, but their important characteristic was that they introduced new, and general, ideas and concerns for welfare. They included judgments about welfare, and this, Sumner held, lifted some of the folkways to a new and qualitatively distinct level: it gave rise to the 'Mores'. Here again, we must be very careful about definitions.

(e) *The Mores*

Sumner defined the 'mores' in this way:

> 'When the elements of truth and right are developed into doctrines of welfare, the folkways are raised to another plane. They then become capable of producing inferences, developing into new forms, and extending their constructive influence over men and society. Then we call them the mores. The mores are the folkways, including the philosophical and ethical generalisations as to societal welfare which are suggested by them, and inherent in them, as they grow.'

Now it is very clear from this that the folkways and the mores, in Sumner's analysis, are not different entities; they are qualitatively different levels of development of the same social -

psychological processes. The mores are the folkways - but now with the additionally developed qualities of more explicit, general, ethical conceptions and judgments of welfare. It is most important to see that this very conception is a theory of social development; and it cannot be understood otherwise. Sumner's model of society was therefore, clearly, a developmental model. Let us look again at a very careful definition of the 'mores' which Sumner gave:

> 'They are the ways of doing things which are current in a society to satisfy human needs and desires, together with the faiths, notions, codes, and standards of well living which inhere in those ways, having a genetic connection with them. By virtue of the latter element the mores are traits in the specific character (ethos) of a society or a period. They pervade and control the ways of thinking in all the exigencies of life, returning from the world of abstractions to the world of action, to give guidance and to win revivification.'

(I) *Taboos and Myths*

The mores consisted in large part, Sumner held, of behavioural 'taboos' which directly regulated conduct, and the 'myths' which provided colourful, dramatic and symbolic notions of destiny and welfare. They were not 'rational philosophies', but they encapsulated ideas and judgments in their imagery.

> 'The myths, fables, proverbs and maxims of primitive men,' Sumner wrote, 'show that the subtler relations of things did not escape them, and that reflection was not wanting, but the method of it was very different from ours. The notion of societal welfare was not wanting, although it was never consciously put before themselves as their purpose. . .'

(II) *Ritual*

One other vital process in the development, establishment and continuity of the 'mores' which Sumner emphasised was that of ritual. Ritual is a repetitive regularity of observance consisting of elements, such as words, gestures, symbols, signs, and is very much more powerful in the sustaining and transmission of values and ideas than the apprehension of the ideas themselves.

> 'In primitive society', wrote Sumner, 'it is the prevailing method of activity and primitive religion is entirely a matter of ritual. . . Primitive religion is ritualistic not because religion makes ritual, but because ritual makes religion. . .
>
> Ritual is not easy compliance with usage; it is strict compliance with detailed and punctilious rule. It admits of no exception of deviation.
>
> Ritual may embody an idea. . .but it always tends to become perfunctory, and the idea is only subconscious. . .
>
> Ritual operates a constant suggestion and the suggestion is at once put in operation in acts. Ritual therefore suggests sentiments, but it never inculcates doctrines.'

The power of ritual in impressing and upholding the continuous 'suggestion' which perpetuates the 'mores' in society was made a matter of the utmost emphasis by Sumner, and it must be understood that he was not only referring to the markedly conspicuous ritual attending religious ceremonial and the like, but also to every element and facet of established regularity of practice in all the ways of behaviour of a people – in their eating, drinking, family life, recreation, work, and in the entire fabric of their conduct. Sumner wrote, for example:

'The mores are social ritual in which we all participate unconsciously. The current habits as to hours of labour, meal hours, family life, the social intercourse of the sexes, propriety, amusements, travel, holidays, education, the use of periodicals and libraries, and innumerable other details of life fall under this ritual. Each does as everybody does. For the great mass of mankind as to all things, and for all of us for a great many things, the rule to do as all do suffices. We are led by suggestion and association to believe that there must be wisdom and utility in what all do. The great mass of the folkways give us discipline and the support of routine and habit.'

In this sense, the entire patterning of life in a community is sustained and transmitted by a vast and intricate play of ritual of which the members of the community may be scarcely aware.

(III) *Status*

One other important aspect of the entire network of the mores in a society upon which Sumner placed great emphasis, was that this, in fact, was a vast system of conferring statuses upon all the members of society in relation to their membership of groups, their tasks, their relationships with each other. And this vast network of statuses held and 'grasped' people; was a determinate patterning influence upon their nature and conduct; and could not easily be altered. From the apparently inter-personal relationships of marriage and the membership of the family, through the whole gamut of ordered relationships, to the most massive authorities of the state, people were vested with appropriate statuses; all the intricacies of human relationships were governed by their appropriate context of rights, duties, expectations. Later, we shall see that Sumner was disturbed by the extent to which this fabric of 'status' in society was upset, disrupted, and indeed not even understood, in the great expansion of 'contract' and legislation in more complex societies. Here again, we can see more than the germ of another central generalisation which has emerged in sociology, and which has been specifically attributed to Sir Henry Maine – namely the movement from 'Status' to 'Contract' in the development of society.

(IV) *Groups, Group Interests and Force in the Mores*

It is necessary to mention too, but only briefly for the sake of completeness, that Sumner did not by any means give a picture of a smooth development of the mores from the folkways accomplished by the community as a whole. He especially noted that particular groups and classes in society pursued their own interests as against the interests of others and used all kinds of force in doing so. These specific elements of interests and force were often woven into the pattern of the folkways and mores, and characterised the 'ethics' of a society; and they, too, came to be built into the taboos, myths, rituals and network of statuses. The mores included accommodation to the conflicts of specific factions in society as well as embodying many interests and practices of the people 'as a whole'.

(V) *Imagination and Knowledge*

It also deserves to be mentioned that Sumner discussed the ways in which imagination and the growth of increasingly accurate knowledge entered into the 'myths' and the 'world philosophies' which they presented. And this will serve to illustrate very well the kind of ambiguity in which his writing, appears to result. That imagination and knowledge did enter actively into the shaping of the mores, Sumner had no doubts.

> 'The correct apprehension of facts and events by the mind', he wrote, 'and the correct inferences as to the relations between them, constitute knowledge, and it is chiefly by knowledge that men have become better able to live well on earth. Therefore, the alternation between experience or observation and the intellectual processes by which the sense, sequence, inter-dependence, and rational consequences of facts are ascertained, is undoubtedly the most important process of sinning increased power to live well.'

It is obvious that if this point was pursued to its logical conclusion (which Sumner did indicate elsewhere), it would give a clear basis for the analysis, critical assessment, judgment, and conscious reform of the mores; and Sumner did believe that this was possible. Yet - having clarified the worth of knowledge, he wrote:

> 'Yet we find that this process has been liable to the most pernicious errors...'

and he went on to show how the 'knowledge' of particular societies in particular periods had been woven, in the form of great errors and fallacies, into mores and myths, and in such a way as to accommodate themselves to the 'life-conditions' prevailing. And it was this that led him to insist upon a 'cultural relativism'.

> 'The logic of one age' he wrote, 'is not that of another. It is one of the chief useful purposes of a study of the mores to learn to discern in them the operation of traditional error, prevailing dogmas, logical fallacy, delusion, and current false estimates of goods worth striving for.'

Actually there is no necessary connection between the diversity of cultures (and the difference of 'truths', 'values', 'logics', relative to them) and relativity in epistemology or ethics. This we shall come to much later; but it is worth noting that even Sumner himself believed this - even though his writing appears to suggest the contrary.

(VI) *The 'Ethos' of a Society*

A final particular emphasis which Sumner made was this. The folkways and mores are not a set of societal 'entities' totally distinct from the people who live within them - like a set of clothes they can wear or discard as they wish. They are, in fact, the collective character of the people; they are the ways of feeling, thinking, acting, doing, organising, deciding, speaking, dressing, gesturing. . .and so on almost indefinitely, of the people in that community. The folkways and mores constitute a distinctive 'ethos' of that people, and Sumner made it clear that he would, indeed, have much liked to used a word derived from the Greek word 'ethos' to indicate very specifically what he had in mind. He considered the words 'Ethica' and 'Ethology', but felt that these had been spoiled. Especially, he thought that the term 'Ethics' had come to be so attached to the philosophical study of the presuppositions of moral assumptions, and so divorced from the study of morals as they existed among men in societies, that he did not wish to entertain the possibility of confusion.

> 'These methods of discussion', he wrote, (i.e. of philosophical ethics), 'are most employed in treating of social topics, and they are disastrous to sound study of facts. . .They help to hold the social sciences under the dominion of metaphysics.'

Sumner therefore abandoned such terminology and used the Romans' word – 'mores' – instead. It is important for our purposes, however, to see that Sumner had in mind this conception of a societal se of tregulated usages which were simultaneously (in terms of both social and individual psychology) the character of a people. This, it will be seen, is completely in keeping with Comte's 'social psychology' notions, Mill's 'Ethology', Marx's 'social consciousness', and other ideas we have considered.

So much, then, for the nature of the 'mores' as a major element in Sumner's 'model' of society. Before we leave this however, let us note again the all-embracing role that he gave them, the all-embracing nature which, in his conception, they had.

> 'We must conceive of the mores as a vast system of usages, covering the whole of life, and serving all its interests; also containing in themselves their own justification by tradition and use and wont, and approved by mystic sanctions until, by rational reflection, they develop their own philosophical and ethical generalisations, which are elevated into "principles" of truth and right.
>
> The mores come down to us from the past. Each individual is born into them as he is born into the atmosphere, and he does not reflect on them, or criticise them any more than a baby analyses the atmosphere before he begins to breathe it. Each one is subjected to the influence of the mores, and formed by them, before he is capable of reasoning about them.
>
> We learn the mores as unconsciously as we learn to walk and eat and breathe. The masses never learn how we walk, and eat, and breathe, and they never know any reason why the mores are what they are. The justification of them is that when we wake to consciousness of life we find them facts which already hold us in the bonds of tradition, custom, and habit.'

(f) *The Folkways and the Science of Society: A Summary*

Of all the components we have dealt with so far, Sumner himself gave an excellent summary, and it is of importance that we should note this as it states with great clarity the relations between the folkways and the structuring of groups, the nature of the entire 'societal process' as he conceived it, and the way in which Sumner conceived the science of society as a study of them.

> 'Men in groups,' he wrote, 'are under life conditions; they have needs which are similar under the state of the life conditions; the relations of the needs to the conditions are interests under the heads of hunger, love, vanity, and fear; efforts of numbers at the same time to satisfy interests produce mass phenomena which are folkways by virtue of uniformity, repetition, and wide concurrence. The folkways are attended by pleasure or pain according as they are well fitted for the purpose. Pain forces reflection and

observation of some relation between acts and welfare. At this point the prevailing world philosophy (beginning with goblinism) suggests explanations and inferences, which become entangled with judgments of expediency. However, the folkways take on a philosophy of right living and a life policy for welfare. Then they become mores, and they may be developed by inferences from the philosophy or the rules in the endeavour to satisfy needs without pain. Hence, they undergo improvement and are made consistent with each other.'

Then: on the emergence of groups and social organisation in the struggle for existence:

'The relations of men to each other, when they are carrying on the struggle for existence near each other, consist in mutual reactions (antagonisms, rivalries, alliances, coercions and co-operations), from which result societal concatenations and concretions, that is, more or less fixed positions of individuals and subgroups towards each other, and more or less established sequences and methods of interaction between them, by which the interests of all members of the group are served.'

On the relations between these elements of grouping and social organisation and the folkways:

'The societal concretions are due to the folkways in this way - that the men, each struggling to carry on existence, unconsciously co-operate to build up associations, organisation, customs, and institutions which, after a time, appear full grown and actual, although no one intended, or planned, or understood them in advance. They stand there as produced by "ancestors". These concretions of relation and act in war, labour, religion, amusement, family life, and civil institutions are attended by faiths, doctrines of philosophy (myths, folklore), and by precepts of right conduct and duty (taboos).'

And on the part of individuals in the folkways and their unique 'societal' nature:

'Every act of each man fixes an atom in a structure, both fulfilling a duty derived from what preceded and conditioning what is to come afterwards by the authority of traditional custom. The structure thus built up is not physical, but societal and institutional, that is to say, it belongs to a category which must be defined and studied by itself. It is a category in which custom produces continuity,

> coherence, and consistency, so that the word "structure" may properly be applied to the fabric of relations and prescribed positions with which societal functions are permanently connected. The process of making folkways is never superseded or changed. It goes on now just as it did at the beginning of civilization. "Use and wont" exert their force on all men always.'

Elsewhere, too, Sumner insisted that the nature of 'societal' phenomena formed a category of facts distinct from material and organic facts, and, as such, required a new science.

> The folkways, he wrote: '. . .are not organic or material. They belong to a super-organic system of relations, conventions, and institutional arrangements. The study of them is called for by their social character, by virtue of which they are leading factors in the science of society.'
>
> 'The life of society consists in making folkways and applying them. The science of society might be construed as the study of them.'

Sumner's systematic exploration of the nature of society was admirably clear. On this basis, he then went on to consider and analyse the ways in which the established order of folkways and mores in a society changed, giving rise to more formal elements of social structure. It is these ideas of change and development which round out and complete Sumner's system.

(g) *Social Change and 'Types' of Society*

From what has been said about Sumner's conception of the folkways and mores as a process of creative accommodation to 'life conditions' it is obvious that, though he emphasised their controlling, constraining, conserving power, he did not think of them as being 'static' in any sense. He thought, as we have seen, that they were developments over a historical period so long as to be unrecorded in its early beginnings, and the 'strain' towards improvement and consistency clearly provided grounds for analysing the directions of change. But Sumner's basic teaching here was that since the folkways are accommodations to 'life conditions', the primary reasons why they change must be changes in the 'life conditions'. It is here that the causes of societal change must be sought. This, again, will be seen to be a position completely in accord with the ideas of Marx and Ward, but without entailing any metaphysic of 'determinism'.

> 'Changes in history,' wrote Sumner, 'are primarily due to changes in life conditions. Then the folkways change. Then new philosophies and ethical rules are invented to try to justify the new ways. The whole vast body of modern mores has thus been developed out of the philosophy and ethics of the Middle Ages. So the mores which have been developed to suit the system of great secular states, world commerce, credit institutions, contract wages and rent, emigration to outlying continents, etc., have become the norm for the whole body of usages, manners, ideas, faiths, customs, and institutions which embrace the whole life of a society and characterize an historical epoch.'

It will be noted that the mores are not thought to 'reflect' the 'life conditions' and the social regularities of a period, they are thought to be part of the social activity of men which 'suits' their grappling with their new problems: they are an essential part of the creative societal activity itself. Though there is no 'metaphysic' of 'material determinism' here, therefore, there is nonetheless a view about the close interdependency of all social phenomena in relation to the changing life conditions which points to a very systematic method of analyzing and explaining social change. Sumner's conception of this is worth noting both because of its accordance with earlier thinkers and because of its similarity to the ideas of important theorists - such as Durkheim - which we shall come to consider later.

When seeking an understanding of the reasons for the existence and form of any particular element of social structure, it must be looked for by tracing its relation to the mores of the society in that period. 'The real reason' for the existence and nature of any element of social structure, said Sumner, 'is that it conforms to the mores of the time and place.'

When seeking an understanding of the reasons for changes in the structures of societies, it must be sought by: 'showing their connection with changes in the life conditions, or with the readjustments of the mores to changes in those conditions.'

What is more, Sumner argued that this perspective of the interdependency of institutions with each other and with relation to the life conditions was the only perspective within which social change could be understood.

> 'Historians,' he wrote, 'have always recognized incidentally the operation of such a determining force. What is now maintained is that it is not incidental or subordinate. It is supreme and controlling.'

Nothing can be understood excepting in this context of social interdependency in coming to terms with changing life conditions.

Bearing in mind Sumner's conception of the validity of a particular system of folkways for a particular people in coming to terms with their own particular life conditions, and thus creating an 'ethos' distinctively their own, it follows that Sumner also thought that historical change and development gave rise to 'types' of society. Social systems were entireties with distinctive total characteristics. 'A society is a whole made up of parts. All the parts have a share in the acts and sufferings of the society. All the parts contribute to the life and work of the society.' And 'types' of society arose in so far as their life conditions were similar. (It may be noted, by the way, that to think of 'types' of society in no way denies the uniqueness of each society: it only postulates significant similarities among some of them which makes it worthwhile to group them together for study.)

> 'India, Chaldea, Assyria, Egypt, Greece, Rome, the Middle Ages, Modern Times,' wrote Sumner, 'are cases in which the integration of the mores upon different life conditions produced societal states of complete and distinct individuality (ethos).'

It is clear from this that Sumner's position is very similar to that of Marx: in classifying societies according to the basic characteristics of the 'life conditions' with which they are having to deal.

(h) *Social Change: Complexity, Elites, Hierarchical Organisation and Institutions*

So far, we have seen how Sumner's 'model' of society depicted the activities of men, based upon motives and interests in relation to life conditions, giving rise to the folkways and mores with their collective 'sentiments' and their over-all 'ethos'. With the consideration of the factors involved in social change, and the growth of types of society from simple communities governed by the folkways to large complex civilizations with massive structures of social organization, Sumner introduced additional elements in his 'model' of a very interesting kind. Though we can deal with these elements only briefly, it is essential to see them clearly because they are all ideas of importance.

(I) *'In-groups' and 'Out-groups'*

First of all, Sumner tried to give a clear analysis of the processes which led to the formation and intensification of the folkways and mores in the simplest groups and most simple (primitive) societies. This was important for itself, but also to explain the great dominance which the folkways and their attendant myths had upon the minds of men in societies, and the ways in which they frequently stood in the way (as powerful obstacles) of any wider co-operation between groups and societies; of the ways, in short, in which they operated to cement human differences and distinctions. Sumner put the matter very clearly like this:

> 'The conception of "primitive society" which we ought to form is that of small groups scattered over a territory. The size of the groups is determined by the conditions of the struggle for existence. The internal organisation of each group corresponds to its size. A group of groups may have some relation to each other (kin, neighbourhood, alliance, connubium and commercium) which draws them together and differentiates them from others. Thus, a differentiation arises between ourselves, the we-group, or in-group, and everybody else, or the others-groups, out-groups. The insiders in a we-group are in a relation of peace, order, law, government, and industry, to each other. Their relation to all outsiders, or others-groups, is one of war and plunder, except so far as agreements have modified it.'

Beyond this, however, said Sumner, the intensification of the sentiments among the members of the 'In-Group' is directly connected with the sentiments of hostility which they share towards the 'Out-Group'.

> 'The relation of comradeship and peace in the we-group and that of hostility and war towards others-groups are correlative to each

other. The exigencies of war with outsiders are what make peace inside, lest internal discord should weaken the we-group for war. These exigencies also make government and law in the in-group, in order to prevent quarrels and enforce discipline. Thus, war and peace have reacted on each other and developed each other, one within the group, the other in the intergroup relation. The closer the neighbours, and the stronger they are, the intenser is the warfare, and then the intenser is the internal organisation and discipline of each. Sentiments are produced to correspond. Loyalty to the group, sacrifice for it, hatred and contempt for outsiders, brotherhood within, warlikeness without - all grow together, common products of the same situation. These relations and sentiments constitute a social philosophy. It is sanctified by connection with religion. Men of an others-group are outsiders with whose ancestors the ancestors of the we-group waged war. The ghosts of the latter will see with pleasure their descendants keep up the fight, and will help them. Virtue consists in killing, plundering, and enslaving outsiders.'

This process of reciprocal intensification gives rise, Sumner claimed, to 'Ethnocentrism'.

'Each group nourishes its own pride and vanity, boasts itself superior, exalts its own divinities, and looks with contempt on outsiders. Each group thinks its own folkways the only right ones, and if it observes that other groups have other folkways, these excite its scorn. Opprobrious epithets are derived from these differences. "Pig-eater", "cow-eater", "uncircumcised", "jabberers", are epithets of contempt and abomination. Ethnocentrism leads a people to exaggerate and intensify everything in their own folkways which is peculiar and which differentiates them from others. It strengthens the folkways.'

It will readily be seen that this analysis of sentiment formation in the context of group-relations can be extended to the study of groups, both large and small, within communities as well as between them, and this has in fact become one of the basic components of sociological analysis - commonly referred to now as 'Reference Group Theory'. But it is enough for us to see that, by this means, Sumner explained the cohesion of simpler societies in history; the laying down of the systems of folkways in the world; which really were the foundation of all subsequent patterns of conflict and co-operation as culture-contact between the peoples of the world came to be extended.

(II) *Some Grounds of Social Change*

This early and relatively simple and intense cohesion between relatively unified communities obviously came to be changed, splintered, disrupted, made more complex, brought into various kinds of international connection, and it is only necessary here to note that Sumner did offer a discussion of the many factors involved. He discussed for example, the kinds of 'criticism' and change of the folkways brought about by the differing experience of 'generations' - even within the same society; by 'social mobility' (of movement of individuals between social classes), and 'travel', which leads people to consider their folkways more objectively and to reflect upon them; by 'missionary' activity of various kinds between societies; and by 'agitation' of various kinds resulting from changes of fortune of particular sections of a community. Most important, perhaps, was his discussion of kinds of contact between groups and societies, and what he called 'syncretism'. Sumner wrote in this way:

> 'When groups are compounded by intermarriage, intercourse, conquest, immigration, or slavery, syncretism of the folkways takes place. One of the component groups takes precedence and sets the standards. The inferior groups or classes imitate the ways of the dominant group, and eradicate from their children the traditions of their own ancestors. . .
>
> Contiguity, neighbourhood, or even literature may suffice to bring about syncretism of the mores. One group learns that the people of another group regard some one of its ways or notions as base. This knowledge may produce shame and an effort to breed out the custom. Thus, whenever two groups are brought into contact and contagion, there is, by syncretism, a selection of the folkways which is destructive to some of them. This is the process by which folkways are rendered obsolete.'

As a result of these, and other factors, then, societies become larger, interrelated with other societies, and more complex in their organisation. There was one other fact about society, however, on which Sumner placed special stress in his analysis of change: this was the existence in any total population of certain classes; but his treatment of this was extremely interesting and quite different from that of Marx.

(III) *Classes in a Society's Population*

By the 'classes' of a population, Sumner did not mean at all what almost every other sociologist has meant: some form of 'stratification' according to socio-economic position. He based his analysis on the work of Galton, and argued that each population consisted of classes of people of differing ranges of ability. To put the matter simply here, Sumner argued that there was always a small proportion of the population possessing very high ability; an equally small proportion possessing very low ability; and a very large middle range possessing mediocre ability (graded between low and high). Though we shall not consider this in detail, it might be clearest to give the diagram which he used - drawn from Ammon's development of Galton's ideas. It was as follows.

It is enough for us to see that one essential component of Sumner's 'model' of society, and a component continuously employed in the analysis of changing folkways and changing social structures, was this conception of 'elitism'. In many ways - large and small and variously effective - there was a continuous interplay of influence between the able and active

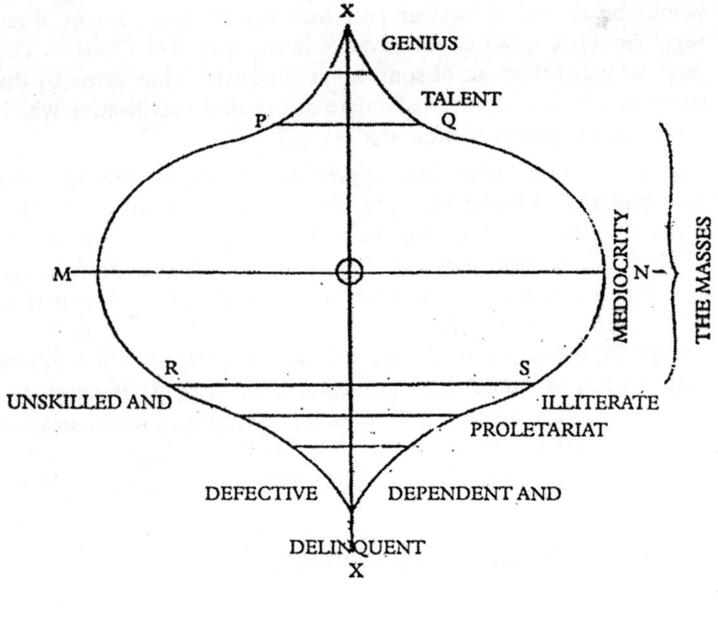

élite in society and the less able and more conservative 'masses'; and the changing folkways included accommodations between 'classes' of this kind. It is interesting to notice that, in Sumner's conception, it was always 'the masses' who were the most conservative element (and thus a massive constraint in another sense) as far as the persistence of the folkways was concerned. It is also worth noting that Sumner thought that every society had to carry a 'lower' proportion which was always a 'weight' of subnormal and defective ability prone to delinquency and social 'diseconomies' of various kinds.

The major point which Sumner drew from this analysis of 'classes', however, was the necessity for 'hierarchical organisation' in society.

(IV) *Hierarchical Organization and its Social Benefits*

Sumner was refreshingly forthright on this subject.

> 'Masses of men,' he wrote, 'who are on a substantial equality with each other never can be anything but hopeless savages. The eighteenth-century notion that men in a state of nature were all equal is wrong-side up. Men who were equal would be in a state of nature such as was imagined. They could not form a society. They would be forced to scatter and wander, at most two or three together. They never could advance in the arts of civilization. The popular belief that out of some such horde there has come by the spontaneous development of innate forces all the civilisation which we possess is entirely unfounded. . .
>
> Masses of men who are approximately equal are in time exterminated or enslaved. Only when enslaved or subjugated are some of them carried up with their conquerors by organisation and discipline. . .A horde in which the only differences are those of age and sex is not capable of maintaining existence. . .When it is subjugated and disciplined it consists of workers to be labour the ground for others, or tax payers to fill a treasury from which others may spend, or food for gunpowder, or voting material for demagogues. It is an object of exploitation. At one moment, in spite of its aggregate muscle, it is helpless and imbecile; the next moment it is swept away into folly and mischief by a suggestion or an impulse.'

Very definitely, Sumner concluded:

> 'Organisation, leadership, and discipline are indispensable to any beneficial action by masses of men.'

Furthermore, Sumner was very positive in his view that this kind of organisation required the creation of regulating institutions, and that these were produced never by the masses, but by those leading men and 'classes' who gained control over the collective power and resources of society and, out of the mores, created the kinds of arrangement they judged important in dealing with societies' problems. This, in short, was a process of 'élitist' creation of institutions within the context of the folkways and mores - again a very clear and firm plank of analysis. For the creation of these institutions, Sumner wrote:

> 'The increase of power is the primary condition. The classes strive with each other for the new power. Peace is necessary, for without peace none of them can enjoy power. Compromise, adjustment of interest, antagonistic co-operation, harmony, are produced, and institutions are the regulative processes and apparatus by which warfare is replaced by system.'

Sumner was therefore quite definite in his 'elitism' in this growth of institutional organisation. Indeed, he went so far as to deny the efficacy of 'educating' the masses with regard to accomplishing their 'enlightened' participation in the making of institutions. This, he thought, was absurdly unrealistic.

> 'Every impulse given to the masses', he wrote, 'is, in its nature, spasmodic and transitory. No systematic enterprise to enlighten the masses ever can be carried out. Campaigns of education contain a fallacy. Education takes time. It cannot be treated as subsidiary for a lifetime and then be made the chief business for six months with the desired result.'

This, however, did not mean, as we shall see, a lack of concern for education in a general sense - only an impatience with the idea of a kind of 'egalitarian participation' in the making of institutions produced by an appropriate 'education of the masses'. This, he thought, was a pipe-dream.

(V) *Institutions and Laws*

It is here that we come to the final component in Sumner's 'model' of society. We have seen how he portrayed the two distinctive societal levels of the folkways and - developing out of these - the mores. Now we can see how, within this same context, he distinguished the third level: the development of institutions. And again, we must be very clear about Sumner's definitions.

> 'Institutions and laws', he wrote, 'are produced out of mores.
>
> 'An institution consists of a concept (idea, notion, doctrine, interest) and a structure. The structure is a framework, or apparatus, or perhaps only a number of functionaries set to co-operate in prescribed ways at a certain conjuncture. The structure holds the concept and furnishes instrumentalities for bringing it into the world of facts and action in a way to serve the interests of men in society.'

Let us notice very clearly, here, the components of 'institutions' as distinct from the nature of the folkways and mores. They are specific structures of procedure, embodying specific concepts, a specific apparatus, specific functionaries and instrumentalities to pursue specific interests. Later, we shall see how similar this conception is to that of Malinowski, for example. Institutions, then, are specific differentiations of structure and function crystallizing (whether by conscious device or not) out of the folkways and mores. But Sumner then thought it important to distinguish between two kinds of institutions.

> 'Institutions', he wrote, 'are either crescive or enacted'.
>
> 'They are crescive when they take shape in the mores, growing by the instinctive efforts by which the mores are produced. Then the efforts, through long use, become definite and specific. Property, marriage, and religion are the most primary institutions. They began in folkways. They became customs. They developed into mores by the addition of some philosophy of welfare, however crude. Then they were made more definite and specific as regards the rules, the prescribed acts, and the apparatus to be employed. This produced a structure and the institution was complete.'

They are enacted when they are:

> '. . .products of rational invention and intention. They belong to high civilisation. Banks are institutions of credit founded on usages which can be traced back to barbarism. There came a time when, guided by rational reflection on experience, men systematised and

regulated the usages which had become current, and thus created positive institutions of credit, defined by law and sanctioned by the force of the state. Pure enacted institutions which are strong and prosperous are hard to find. It is too difficult to invent and create an institution, for a purpose, out of nothing. All institutions have come out of mores, although the rational element in them is sometimes so large that their origin in the mores is not to be ascertained, except by an historical investigation (legislatures, courts, juries, joint stock companies, the stock exchange).'

Enacted institutions, of course, are closely connected with legislation, and in this, too, Sumner gave a clear picture of the growth of rationally directed law from the earlier 'custom' and 'common law' of the folkways. Enactments and the institutions they created were specific, and were provided with specific sanctions, and thus were rather more rigid than the process of the folkways; they entailed a certain measure of 'sacrifice of the elasticity and automatic self-adaptation of custom', but their creation could be understood when 'conscious purposes' were formed. Again, we see the emergence of the 'teleological' out of the 'genetic' which Ward had described.

Sumner emphasised especially the differences of 'sentiment' and 'reason', the differences of diffuseness and specificity, which distinguished 'institutions and laws' from the folkways and mores. For example:

'The element of sentiment and faith inheres in the mores. Laws and institutions have a rational and practical character, and are more mechanical and utilitarian. The great difference is that institutions and laws have a positive character, while mores are unformulated and undefined. . .Acts under the laws and institutions are conscious and voluntary; under the folkways they are always unconscious and involuntary, so that they have the character of natural necessity. . .The laws, being positive prescriptions, supersede the mores so far as they are adopted. It follows that the mores come into operation where laws and tribunals fail. The mores cover the great field of common life where there are no laws. . .They cover an immense and undefined domain, and they break the way in new domains, not yet controlled at all. The mores, therefore, build up new laws. . .in time.'

It will be seen in this 'model' of society and this analysis of change, that Sumner was stating a very large-scale theory of social development: that human societies, in coming to terms with their life conditions, developed from a relatively simple condition in which the societal order consisted of the folkways, through a rather more complex and reflective creation of the mores, to conditions of considerable complexity in which there was a differentiation of specific institutions and laws consciously articulated for specific purposes. The earlier condition was characterised by 'sentiment' and sanctioned usage, the later condition by conscious reflection and purpose and 'rational' calculation. As we shall see, this generalization was to become one of the most centrally agreed ideas in sociological analysis, and one of central (theoretical) utility for the understanding of the changes in society brought about by science and its application in industrial technology. But its similarity to all that had been said by Comte, Mill, Spencer, Marx and Ward is also patently clear.

This component of the 'institutions and laws' of society rounded off Sumner's 'model' for the analysis of social order and social change. All that remains is that we should be clear about his apparent 'ambiguities' with regard to 'relativity' and 'progressive reform' and that we should see, too, the particular nature of his concern about the dilemmas of modern industrial society: for here, too, we shall find him in close agreement with the major scholars who both preceded and followed him.

(i) *The Limitations of Reform; Progress; Social Science and the Art of Administration; the Problems of Modern Industrial Society*

There is no doubt that Sumner not only appeared ambiguous, but was ambiguous, in many of his statements about the 'rightness' and 'sufficiency' of the folkways and mores for a society at any one time; about their validity for particular societies relative to their life-conditions; and about the extent to which 'reflection, reason, and conscious purpose' was disruptive of them, and of no avail with regard to them. It would be too long a task to document every aspect of this; but a few examples will be enough.

SUMNER'S SYSTEM OF ANALYSIS

THE SOCIAL SYSTEM

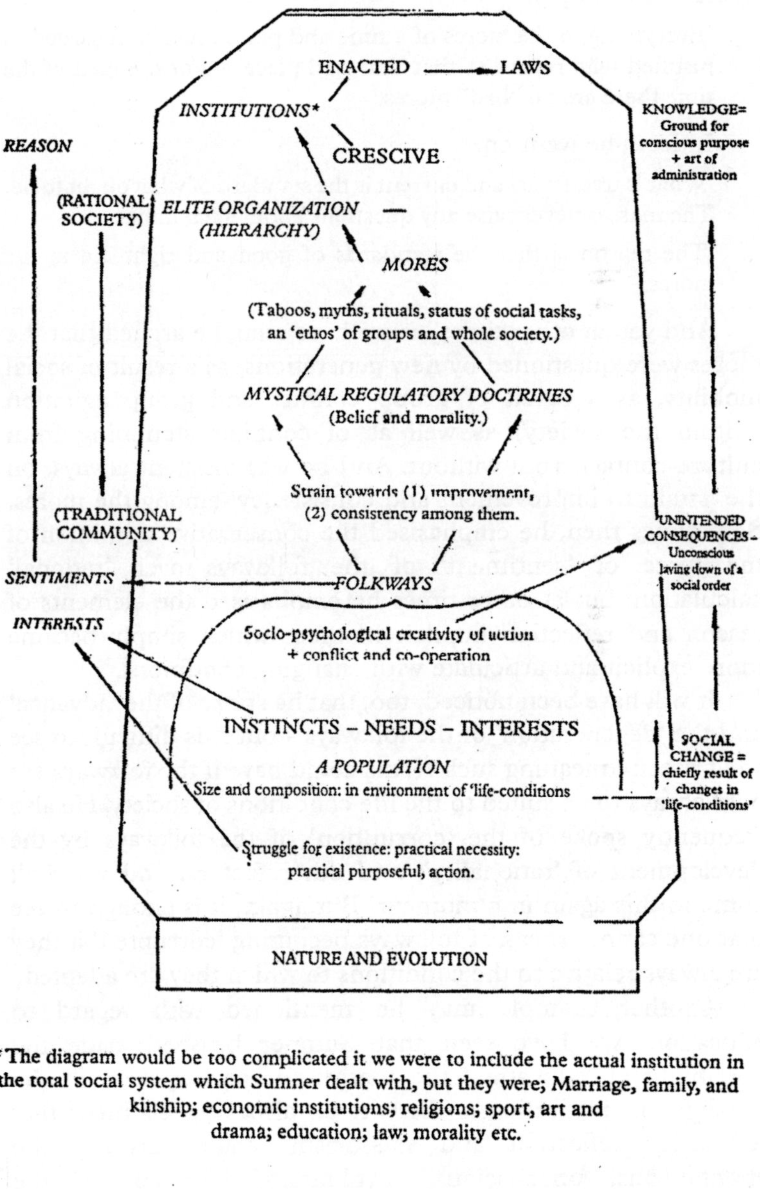

*The diagram would be too complicated it we were to include the actual institution in the total social system which Sumner dealt with, but they were; Marriage, family, and kinship; economic institutions; religions; sport, art and drama; education; law; morality etc.

In some of his statements, Sumner was emphatic about the definiteness, the all-sufficiency, the rightness, of the mores. He wrote, for example:

> 'Everything in the mores of a time and place must be regarded as justified with regard to that time and place. . .For the men of the time there are no "bad" mores.'

Indeed, he went on:

> 'What is traditional and current is the standard of what ought to be. The masses never raise any questions about such things. . .
>
> 'The reason is that the standards of good and right are in the mores.'

And yet, at other times, as we have seen, he argued that the mores were questioned by new generations, as a result of social mobility, as a result of group conflict and group agitation (within the society) as well as of conflicts stemming from culture-contact from without. And he was insistent always, on the 'strain to improvement and consistency' among the mores. Sometimes then, he emphasised the conservative dominion of the force of 'sentiment' of the folkways over 'rational' calculation; but at other times he emphasised the elements of reason and reflection implicit in them which simply became more explicit and articulate with changing conditions.

It will have been noticed, too, that he spoke of the 'advance' and the 'degeneration' of the folkways - but it is difficult to see what precise meaning such terms could have if the folkways are held always to be suited to the life conditions of society. He also frequently spoke of the 'corruption' of the folkways by the development of 'rationality', and other factors, and we shall come to this again in a moment. But again, it is enough to see that one cannot speak of folkways becoming 'corrupted' if they are always relative to the conditions to which they are adapted.

Another example may be mentioned with regard to education. We have seen that Sumner brushed aside the possibility of 'educating' the masses for participation in the making of institutions. Elsewhere, also, he claimed that 'educative reflection and skepticism' could 'disturb' the spontaneous, unconscious, involuntary operation of the folkways. And yet - in his discussion of 'Ethnocentrism'– we find that he distinguished between genuine and false 'patriotism', and insisted that education should be a guide enabling men to judge soundly between them. Patriotism, he argued, may degenerate into a vice, as:

> '. . . is shown by the invention of a name for the vice: chauvinism. It is a name for boastful and truculent group self-assertion. It overrules personal judgment and character, and puts the whole group at the mercy of the clique which is ruling at the moment. It produces the dominance of watch-words and phrases which take the place of reason and conscience in determining conduct. The patriotic bias is a recognized perversion of thought and judgment against which our education should guard us.'

Not only were there distinctions, then, between genuine folkways and 'degenerations' or 'vices' - but only reason could clarify the criteria by which we should judge, and only education could secure the persistence of sound judgment. There are obviously quite definite elements of ambiguity here.

Furthermore, Sumner positively advocated free and rational criticism for the 'health' of the mores.

> 'Since it appears', he wrote, 'that the old mores are mischievous if they last beyond the duration of the conditions and needs to which they were adapted, and that constant, gradual, smooth, and easy readjustment is the course of things which is conducive to healthful life, it follows that free and rational criticism of traditional mores is essential to societal welfare. We have seen that the inherited mores exert a coercion on every one born in the group. It follows that only greatest and best can react against the mores so as to modify them. . .The trained reason and conscience never have heavier tasks laid upon them than where questions of conformity to, or dissent from, the mores are raised. It is by the dissent and free judgment of the best reason and conscience that the mores win flexibility and automatic readjustment.'

One other example (an important one) will be enough.

In some of his emphases, Sumner was very far-reaching in the claim that he made for the dominion of the mores over man's thought. Indeed, he argued, men could not liberate themselves from this domination.

> 'It is vain', he insisted, 'to imagine that any man can lift himself out of these characteristic features in the mores of the group to which he belongs...It is vain to imagine that a "scientific man" can divest himself of prejudice or previous opinion, and put himself in an attitude of neutral independence towards the mores. He might as well try to get out of gravity or the pressure of the atmosphere. The most learned scholar reveals all the philistinism and prejudice of the man-on-the-curbstone when mores are in discussion. The most elaborate discussion only consists in revolving on one's own axis. One only finds again the prepossessions which he brought to the consideration of the subject, returned to him with a little more intense faith.'

And it is upon this kind of ground, as well as upon his persuasion concerning the dominating force and conservatism of the mores, that he argued strongly that the possibilities of legislative reform in society were so limited. And yet, knowing how mistaken the mores can be – we find him writing like this:

> 'Stoll boldly declares that if one of us had been a judge in the times of the witch trials he would have reasoned as the witch judges did, and would have tortured like them. If that is so, then it behooves us by education and will, with intelligent purpose, to criticise and judge even the most established ways of our time, and to put courage and labour into resistance to the current mores where we judge them wrong.'

But if this is so - then we must have confidence that, in our thinking, we can indeed liberate ourselves from the mores which are so constraining upon us; go beyond them; and - what is more - find criteria of truth which are not 'relative' with regard to them, and provide procedures of education which instil these criteria, and these qualities of mind, as a basis of critical judgment against the folkways. In a way which was genuinely inconsistent and ambiguous, Sumner seemed to see a close relation between reason and feeling when speaking of their interconnections in the folkways themselves, but to insist on a flat conflict between them when the folkways came to be subjected to rational criticism. And - hating philosophy as he did - he seems not to have made sufficient use of the clarification which it can offer!

However, having noted (and given due weight to) these elements of ambiguity in Sumner's system, we can resolve them quite satisfactorily for our own purposes. For a completely fair statement of Sumner's position is this. He was not, in any fundamental sense, opposed to the conscious application of reason, critical reflection, legislative reform, and education in efforts to improve the social order. Indeed, as we have seen, his entire theory is one in which the folkways, mores, and created institutions, 'strain towards' improvement. What he was opposed to - and very powerfully - was the brash, uninformed, superficial, irresponsible attitudes of mind of those politicians and others who thought they could create institutions anew without any knowledge of the deeply-rooted fabric of the folkways, and without taking them fully into account. And he was opposed to this not only because it could fail disastrously as such, but also that it could spill over - beyond all wise bounds - into areas of social life in which it was misplaced, and in so doing, it could indeed despoil and wreck the folkways - putting nothing in their place but emptiness and confusion. Legislation, too irresponsibly expanded, could destroy the communal ways of a people, and leave only a tragic and dangerous vacuum in their place.

Once this emphasis is clearly understood it can be seen that no fundamental gulf or difference separates Sumner from Ward or any of the other theorists we have studied. He is as much concerned with the reasonable improvement of the life of society as they; it is only that he wants the nature of society to be fully appreciated by those responsible for legislative reform, and he wants to see legislation very carefully done. He was, of course, quite right in this emphasis, and we can see how reminiscent his whole stand was of that of earlier men such as Montesquieu and Burke.

That this is a correct, and not just a personal interpretation of his standpoint may be seen from his own words, and we can see here again the perennial and all-pervading desire of all the men concerned with the making of sociology - namely, that such a science should be the basis for a wise and satisfactory art of achieving a new, enriched order of human society out of the chaos of modern industrial change.

Having emphasized in many ways the difficulties of changing the folkways, and the care which should be exercised in trying to improve them, Sumner wrote:

> 'It is not to be inferred that reform and correction are hopeless...
>
> The statesman and social philosopher can act with such influences, sum up the forces which make them, and greatly help the result. The inference is that intelligent art can be introduced here as elsewhere, but that it is necessary to understand the mores and to be able to discern the elements in them, just as it is always necessary for good art to understand the facts of nature with which it will have to deal. It belongs to the work of publicists and statesmen to gauge the forces in the mores and to perceive their tendencies...
>
> Great crises come when great new forces are at work changing fundamental conditions, while powerful institutions and traditions still hold old systems intact...It is in such crises that great men find their opportunity. The man and the age react on each other...
>
> 'The interaction defies our analysis, but it does not discourage our reason and conscience from their play on the situation, if we are content to know that their function must be humble...'

This, surely, was a very wise statement of conclusion.

> 'It would be a mighty achievement of the science of society', Sumner said, 'if it could lead up to an art of societal administration which should be intelligent, effective and scientific.'

Clearly, there was no divergence between Ward and Sumner here. They were spokesmen of the same excellent and humane objectives: of the achievement of the most reliable knowledge, and the attempt at the most responsible control: the objectives which underlay the aspirations not only of the early Americans, but united all the sociologists of Europe and America from Comte onwards.

It is worth our while, in bringing our study of Sumner to a close, to see clearly how similar his worries were about the nature and dangers of nineteenth-century industrial capitalism to those of the other men we have considered.

> 'The history of the nineteenth century', he wrote, 'plainly showed the power of capital in the modern state. Special legislation, charters, and franchises proved to be easy legislative means of

using the powers of the state for the pecuniary benefit of the few. . .The history is disgraceful, and it is a permanent degradation of popular government that power could not be found, or did not exist, in the system to subjugate this abuse and repress this corruption of state power. . .The corrupt use of legislation and political power has affected the mores. Every one must have his little sphere of plunder and special advantage. This conviction and taste becomes so current that it affects all new legislation. The legislators do not doubt that it is reasonable and right to enact laws which provide favour for special interests. . .They laugh at remonstrance as out of date and "unpractical". They think that that is only common-sense. "What else are we here for?". . .'

And in his judgment of this rapid and savage development of industrial capitalism, we can see that Sumner believed that this actually and actively led to a moral deterioration, a moral vacuum in society. Later, we shall see how completely this is in agreement with almost all the major sociologists and especially with Emile Durkheim's notion of the development of 'Anomie' (normlessness) in the complexities of modern industrial society.

'It is the supreme test of a system of government', Sumner wrote, 'whether its machinery is adequate for repressing the selfish undertakings of cliques formed on special interests and saving the public from raids of plunderers. The modern democratic states fail under this test. There is not a great state in the world which was not democratised in the nineteenth century. There is not one of them which did not have great financial scandals before the century closed. Financial scandal is the curse of all the modern parliamentary states with a wide suffrage. They give liberty and security, with open chances for individual enterprise, from which results great individual satisfaction and happiness, but the political machinery offers opportunities for manipulation and corrupt abuse. They educate their citizens to seek advantages in the industrial organisation by legislative devices, and to use them to the uttermost. The effect is seen in the mores. We hear of plutocracy and tainted money, of the power of wealth, and the wickedness of corporations. The disease is less specific. It is constitutional. The critics are as subject to it as the criticised. A disease of the mores is a disease of public opinion as to standards, codes, ideas of truth and right, and of things worth working for and means of success. Such a disease affects everybody. It penetrates and spoils every institution. It spreads from generation to generation, and at last it destroys in the masses the power of ethical judgment.'

For Sumner then, as for all the others, the pressing need for the making of sociology was the same to provide reliable knowledge of society so that such matters could be put right.

C. FRANKLIN H. GIDDINGS

A third scholar who contributed much to the making of sociology in America was Franklin Giddings. It might be argued by some that Giddings made no contribution of note distinctively beyond the work of Ward and Sumner, but accomplished, rather, a more systematic statement than they of all that was already agreed and accepted. To some extent this was true. Giddings devoted a good deal of effort to clear teaching. He was convinced (like Ward) of the importance of education as such; but he was also convinced of the great importance of sociology as a subject for education in the modern world. By 1898, he had not only written a large-scale *Principles of Sociology* and a book on *The Theory of Socialisation,* but also a text-book for colleges and schools on *The Elements of Sociology.*

This sheer effort at clear statement for educational purposes was itself worthwhile from our own point of view. It showed, with perfect clarity, how the contributions of Comte and Spencer had been accepted (to a very large extent) by the Americans, and used to form the foundations for an entire scheme of sociological analysis. It displayed the clear and systematic method which sociological analysis could bring to the study of man and society, and demonstrated the utility of such studies for educating young people in the tasks and duties of citizenship. It was a good example of how, by the end of the nineteenth century, sociology had not only been founded as a science, but had also come to be conceived as a subject which could and should play an important part in higher education. Giddings text-book gave a clear picture of how the subject was then designed for teaching purposes. There is no doubt, then, of the truth of the statement that Giddings' contribution was in large part that of a 'teacher'; a 'systematizer' - if that is not too ugly a word. But to leave the judgment there would be an error. There are several reasons why we should take the work of

Giddings into account - in addition to that of Ward and Sumner - if we are to provide ourselves with a reasonably complete picture of the foundation of sociology as it was conceived by the early Americans.

Giddings, like Ward and Sumner, was a man of very considerable breadth of learning who brought together many other subjects in his formulation of sociology. He was not simply a kind of systematic regurgitation of Comte, Spencer, etc. He drew on men as diverse as Aristotle, Tacltus, Burke, Lecky, Bagehot, Buckle in discussing aspects of the development of institutions. He considered the views of Blackstone, Wundt and Maine in his discussion of the nature of 'custom', its relation to law, and its place in various kinds of societies. He was well aware of the analyses of Adam Smith and Gabriel Tarde when discussing the growth of group sentiments and social values. But besides being well informed in this general scholarly sense, Giddings was acutely aware of the developments of his own time. Like Sumner, for example, he knew the work of Galton, and tried to incorporate it into his analysis of populations. He knew Sidney Webb's *History of Trade Unions* and took it into account in discussing the complexities of 'conflict and co-operations' in modern industrial societies. Two things, however, are perhaps particularly important.

The first was that Giddings did not only draw together, in systematic form, the earlier contributions of Comte and Spencer. He drew these together in relation, also, to the contemporary work of Ward and other American influences. Giddings, in short, accomplished a contemporaneous systematization; a bringing together of many of the current contributions towards the end of the nineteenth century. And the second fact of considerable importance was really a part of this, but deserves special emphasis.

This was that Giddings, like Ward, was very clearly aware of the intimate relationship between psychology and sociology, and, in pursuing his study of this, brought the work of men like William James, Titchener and Wundt into the context of his analysis of social processes. In his conception of a science of man and society (as had been the case with Mill), psychology and sociology were closely conjoined.

In matters concerning the analysis of the nature and components of societies (i.e., in terms of elements of social structure or organisation); in the classification and comparative study of types of society; and in theories of social change, development, evolution and progress; Giddings was almost entirely in agreement with Comte and Spencer and had little to add to them. On all these elements of analysis - important though they are - our discussion can only be relatively brief and confined chiefly to seeing clearly the nature of Giddings' agreement about them. Even here, however, we shall see that Giddings had something very interesting to say about the study of 'social action' and the way in which this was related to 'social structures' and 'types' of society.

It was in the systematic analysis of the psychological processes accompanying association, however, (the 'middle' field which Mill had called 'Ethology') that Giddings, like Ward, went beyond these European thinkers. Too much must not be claimed even here; but some aspects of Giddings' treatment do deserve special note. Ward had made much of the psychological aspects of social processes but Giddings, though not, perhaps, more profound than Ward, might be said to have been more systematic in laying out an analysis of all the components involved in the relations between the 'self' and 'society', and this, though far from being definitive, was a foundation of what was to be perhaps the most distinctive contribution of the Americans: the development of 'social psychology'. We have seen that, apart from John Stuart Mill's methodological discussion of the importance of these 'middle principles' of personality and social psychology, the European scholars had so far left this are a relatively unexplored. Ward had made much of it. Sumner was emphasising its importance in analysing the formation of the 'folkways'. But Giddings set the entire matter out with great conceptual clarity and with a clear system of analysis, and it was within this kind of context that the work of C.H. Cooley and G.H. Mead was to develop. When we come to twentieth-century developments I shall argue that this has been probably the major distinctive contribution of American sociology, and has culminated in much of what has come to be called 'role theory', and some of the most central work of Robert Merton, for example, in his considerable emphasis upon 'Reference Group Theory'.

What this amounts to, then, is that Giddings, as one of those who contributed to the making of sociology in America was another scholar who not only drew together existing contributions in a critically digested and systematic form, but also contributed a conceptual and analytical formulation which possessed originality and was a basis for much future development.

There are one or two other points which I will bring in at this stage - though I want to make them much more forcefully later. They are very important. We have already seen that, among all the thinkers we have discussed so far, but perhaps most explicitly and articulately in Ward, the study of 'social action' in terms of the ends which men seek and the means which they employ, was clearly thought to be a necessary element in any satisfactory 'causal' account of society and its processes. It was quite clearly conceived as a kind of 'teleological' causality, different from 'efficient' or 'genetic' causality, which distinguished the subject-matter of sociology from all other fields of 'phenomena' in nature. There was not the slightest lack of clarity about this. And yet it has come to be a firm persuasion among present-day scholars (even Americans) that this dimension of sociological analysis and theory-construction was absent from sociology until it was stated with a flash of originality out of the depths of a philosophical fog in continental Europe (in this case - Germany). Here I want only to note this, and to point out (and this will be much more clear very soon) that Giddings too had very significant things to say in this direction. But - and it is this consideration which leads me to introduce these points here - it is also thought that the introduction of the conception of 'social' psychological facts; of psychological facts which were the outcome of processes of association, of collective processes; the introduction of the 'perspective' that the understanding of individual personality required the analysis of social processes; was an original contribution stemming from France. And again, I want only to note that this is not true. Ward and Giddings (and other Americans we shall consider later) had already built this with complete conceptual clarity into the entire nature of sociological analysis by the end of the nineteenth century.

Though I do not wish to develop these points here, I think it is important to make it clear that they are raised not at all simply as a matter of claiming 'who said what first'. My much more important underlying concern is this. It seems to me that many of the elements and dimensions of analysis developed by Marx Weber and Emile Durkheim - Durkheim especially - have brought with them a kind of 'philosophical mystique' (different in each case) which is altogether avoided in the formulations of the early Americans. In short, that in some ways, the distinctive 'teleological' dimensions of human society and sociology were better formulated by the Americans than by Max Weber. (They were not weighed down by having to struggle out of the same philosophical fog.) And the relations between 'individual' and 'social' psychological facts were in some ways better formulated by Ward, Giddings, Cooley and Mead than by Emile Durkheim. This must not, by any means, be taken to be a derogatory statement about the contributions of Weber and Drukheim. Later, we shall, in fact, come to consider their very great importance. It is only (a) to note that the elements of analysis on which they placed much emphasis were already taken into account in American sociology, and (b) that in some respects the formulation of the American scholars was, by contrast with some later formulations, to be upheld for its care and lucidity. However, these points will be fully pursued later.

For the moment, and bearing these issues in mind, let us complete our picture of the 'early Americans' by a brief outline of Giddings' 'system'. Perhaps it should be noted that here we shall deal only with the work Giddings had produced before the end of the nineteenth century. Later, for example, he contributed much in exploring and emphasising the employment of statistics in sociological investigation; but this will not enter into our consideration here.

Science and Knowledge

Like all the other men we have considered, Giddings agreed that only the methods of science produced testable knowledge and that if we desire reliable knowledge about man and society these were the methods which we should employ - to such degree of exactitude as was possible. To a large extent, Giddings wrote of 'science' as a process of meticulous and accurate 'description'. Each science clarified its 'unit of investigation', its distinctive subject-matter, and then tried to achieve a thorough 'description' of its nature, its components and the relations between them, and the 'processes' of order and change which were peculiar to it. Giddings used the term 'description' to emphasise the empirical, factual, testable grounding of scientific methods, but he included within this 'causal' theories and the statement of 'laws', which were: 'certain uniformities of order, sequence, proportion, and so on, among the facts that have been described'.

Indeed, this matter of the discovery and clear statement of 'uniformities' was quite a central emphasis in Giddings' treatment. Quite fundamentally, science followed upon our perception of 'resemblances' among all the elements of our experience. It was, initially, a grouping of things together in terms of the resemblances and differences which we felt to be significant among them; it was a formation of 'classes' or 'categories'.

'Endless progress in knowledge is possible only because we observe resemblance as well as differences. As rapidly as we discover that things are alike, we put them together in our thought as a group, or class, or kind ...

> 'Classification, then, is the foundation of all scientific knowledge; and classification consists simply in putting together in our thought those things that are truly and essentially alike.'

This was then followed by careful analysis and the formulation of 'causal' theories which were subjected to test. All this, then, was simple and clear. Like Comte and Spencer, Giddings was also quite clear about the limitations of science, and kept well away from the 'metaphysical' dimensions which crept into the implicit assumptions of a man like Marx. Disclaiming any kind of ultimate 'monistic materialism' or 'idealism', Giddings wrote quite clearly:

> 'It is not any part of the business of science to deal with these ultimate problems of philosophy. Science stops short at the point where the possibility of verification ends and knowledge passes into speculation. Verification is a confirmation by the senses of conclusions reached by reasoning.'

Science, in short, was confined by the testability of hypotheses.

The Concept of Evolution and the Relations between the Sciences

Giddings also accepted the new perspective provided by the concept of 'evolution'. Like all the men we have mentioned, he saw nature as a complex process of interrelated and interdependent 'forms' which existed always in an environmental context, and were continually undergoing processes of 'transformation' - both in presisting in a certain order, and being modified by patterns and sequences of change. The scientific study of all aspects of nature must therefore essentially take account of this continuous interrelated process of order and change, and each science had its defined place in that it concerned itself with the study of one distinctive and determinate aspect of it. In this way, Giddings had the same conception of the interconnected order of the sciences, and the relation between the sciences, as had Comte, Spencer, Ward and others, and he did not feel it necessary to comment on this further. He simply accepted it. Like the others, too, whilst holding that all the sciences should be seen in relation to each other, he did not hold that the 'laws' or 'hypotheses' of any one science could be 'reduced' to the concepts and hypotheses of another.

For Giddings then, as for others, the 'evolutionary perspective' was one in which all aspects of nature could be consistently seen for the systematic exploration of science. Human societies, as well as biological organisms and purely physical systems, were a part of this vast process of order and transformation, and all could be analysed usefully in the similar terms of growth, differentiation of parts and functions, segregation, integration, adaptation to changing circumstances of the environment, and the like. It can be seen from this how solidly Giddings accepted Spencer's perspective and system of analysis.

The Study of Society : Populations in their Environments

Before moving to Giddings' clear definition of the distinctive subject-matter of sociology, it is interesting to note two relatively preliminary points which followed from his conception of science and evolution, and which remained permanent elements and emphases in his system.

Obviously, in some sense or other, sociology was concerned with aggregations of human beings; with human populations. And obviously, in keeping with the classificatory procedure of science, it must 'distinguish' populations, and 'group' them together in some way according to the 'resemblances' to be observed among them. But here, at once, Giddings argued, we come to some qualitative distinctions between sociology and its subject-matter and other sciences which are of quite a fundamental nature; and there ware two considerations especially which Giddings emphasised. The first was that in 'distinguishing', 'grouping', or 'classifying' human populations for purposes of study, sociologist were not in the ordinary position of scientists who could rest their criteria upon the 'resemblances' which they themselves perceived in their subject-matter. A botanist, for example, could 'group' certain trees in accordance with whether or not they shed their leaves with certain seasonal changes; or certain plants in accordance with whether they were characterised by 'bulbs' or 'corms' or 'roots', etc. The sociologist, however, found that some of the criteria of 'resemblance' and 'difference' which he had to take into account in classifying and describing populations, were conceptions of 'resemblance' or 'difference' which the members of the populations themselves subjectively perceived and adopted in their own selective associations. Among human populations there always existed some subjectively held 'consciousness of kind' in relation to which, alone, certain groupings and conflicts and regulations could be understood and explained. So that some of the 'objective' criteria of the procedures of description and classification of the sociologist were the 'subjective' criteria of 'resemblance' held by the populations themselves. This was, immediately, a qualitative difference of methodology which distinguished sociology from other 'natural' sciences, and it involved clearly a dimension of 'subjective understanding' in 'objective procedures' from which other sciences were free.

The second important aspect of this point, however, which was a fundamental consideration at the very roots of Giddings' systematic development of the 'social psychological' aspects of social processes, was the actual existence of this 'consciousness of kind' in all populations as a basic principle of (or concomitant of) human grouping. Clearly the 'resemblances' which men saw between themselves and others, and which led them to associate with these men rather that those, varied very considerably. Men might sympathetically identify themselves with each other as a result of the similar colour of their skins, their membership of the same kinship grouping, the fact that they were born in the same locality, spoke the same language, shared the same occupation, and so on. But the fact was that all forms of association entailed some kind of 'consciousness of kind'; indeed the process of association established, cultivated, and consolidated it; this was an objective characteristic of human populations; and therefore the study of it (and of its various kinds and sources) must form a basic part of sociological analysis. The study of 'forms of association' must necessarily include study of those distinctive varieties of 'consciousness of kind' in relation to which these associations persisted. The very ground of sociological understanding was therefore, in large part, a social psychological ground.

The grouping of human populations on the basis of some 'resemblances' which were significant for classification, analysis, description, and the exploration of theories, therefore led Giddings to this very fundamental starting-point; the recognition of subjectively held 'consciousnesses of kind' among people (a) as objective facts interpenetrating the observable 'forms' of association and 'society', and (b) as necessary components of investigation, method, and theory-construction in sociology.

Bearing this in mind Giddings then simply noted that, no matter how complicated the analysis of 'societies' might become, sociology was still basically concerned with the study of aggregate populations which were living in the context of the characteristics and resources of determinate physical environments.

In sociology, then, ecological studies (of the life of populations in relation to their environments) and studies of the size and composition of populations must always be important. It is not necessary to elaborate on these two points, excepting to note that Giddings did propose a systematic method of studying populations - distinguishing changes in size due to 'Genetic Aggregation' (natural balance of births against deaths) from those due to various kinds of 'Congregation' (internal and external migration, etc.), and establishing clear knowledge of the 'composition' of populations (the numbers and distribution of ethnic groups, national groups, immigrants, etc.). Though we shall not dwell upon them here, ecological and demographic studies were therefore seen as being of basic importance by Giddings, and his studies of 'consciousness of kind' were always in relation to the understanding of varying degrees of cohesion, unity, variation, conflict and change among the various groupings within a population.

Society and the Science of Society

It is significant, bearing in mind this 'psychological' emphasis that underlay Giddings' whole approach, that, when he came to define 'society', he began with the 'verbal' sense of the word: treating it as an activity of association, and only finally concluded with the world as a 'noun' : referring to some kind of collectivity of associational forms. It is significant, too, that his basic and distinctive 'unit of investigation' for sociology was the individual as a 'socius' (i.e., as an associating person); the individual in his associational aspects.

> 'The word "society", he wrote, 'is derived from the Latin word socius, meaning a companion or associate ...
>
> 'Society, then, as a mode of activity of intelligent individuals is the cultivation of both acquaintance and like-mindedness.

> 'Its product is a group of like-minded persons who enjoy and keep up this mode of activity. Such a group or product is called a society.'

The passage from 'verb' to 'noun' is very clear here. He rounded out his definition with one more element - the working for common ends.

> 'A society is a group of like-minded individuals ("socii") who know and enjoy their like-mindedness, and are therefore able to work together for common ends.'

This, however, was only the most general of definitions, and Giddings extended and elaborated it by describing different 'kinds' of society. He distinguished, for example, a 'Natural Society, which was a population sharing a mode of life in a particular area and working together for common ends. An 'Integral Society' was a natural society large enough to carry on all the known kinds of associational activity, and which was able, independently, to govern its own destiny within the area it occupied. It was a total society - incorporating all the major forms of social structure:family, economic system, government, law, religion, education, etc.Within the Integral (total) Society, two further kinds of society were distinguished : 'Component Societies' - which were smaller communal groups which were capable, if necessary, of maintaining a complete social life of their own (for example - 'states' within federal totalities; village and town communities; or even neighbourhood communities of family group), and 'Constituent Societies' which were purposefully and rationally devised associations, with definite forms of organisation, established for the pursuit of specific ends. These were, in fact, specific associational groups, but, Giddings argued, they were always interrelated and interconnected in any total society, so that, taken together, they constituted the 'complete social organisation of the integral society.'

From the 'unit of investigation' as the 'associating individual', Giddings thus moved from the activity of society to the clear analysis of various kinds of societies : and his analysis of any total social system - of any 'Integral Society' - into its organizational structure of 'constitutent societies '(specific associations); and its composition of 'components societies' (communities) and 'natural societies' (populations sharing the particular environmental conditions of a territory), was perfectly clear.

It must be emphasized, too, that Giddings was very meticulous when defining the 'unit of investigation' of sociology in terms of the 'individual'. He was well aware that the individual as such; as an organic and psychic totality; was not the distinctive focus of sociology. Biology included within its province the study of the organic attributes of the human individual, and psychology properly focused upon the psychic attributes of the individual. It was all those attributes of the individual which were relevant to the study of his associational activities and experiences that Giddings marked out as the distinctive province of sociology. This, he claimed was a clear and distinct field of study; a field which it was necessary to distinguish if we were to achieve reliable and testable knowledge about it; and a field which contained elements other than those of biology and psychology. Furthermore, Giddings argued, the associational and cultural fabric of human relationships is a cumulative societal context which has its continuous influence upon psychological and biological elements of human nature. The understanding of man the individual personality could therefore only be accomplished by establishing knowledge about the associational context of his life - and for this, the distinctive science of sociology was necessary.

Here again, we can see how perfectly clear and valid Giddings' position was, and how completely in keeping it was with that of Comte and others. Later, we shall see that this was the position also elaborated by Durkheim, so that, far from being an innovation of twentieth-century thought, a clear continuity of this distinguishing feature of sociology can be traced from the earliest statement of the subject to the present day.

However, it is enough for the present to see that, following upon these considerations of the 'distinctive subject-matter', Giddings' definition of sociology was also perfectly clear.

> 'The facts that we have been describing', he wrote, 'are social facts or facts of society.
>
> 'Scientific description results in the discovery of . . .causes and laws, which are . . . certain uniformities of order, sequence, proportion, and so on, among the facts that have been described.
>
> Using the word "description" in this sense, we may say that Sociology is the scientific description of society.'

The Practical Activities of Men in Society

Giddings' agreement with the other thinkers we have considered was also shown clearly by the emphasis which he placed upon the 'practical activities' of men in working upon, and accommodating themselves to, their environment, as the basis for all the forms of association, of social structure, which developed among them. His direct similarity to Spencer, Marx, Ward, Sumner, was quite evident. Even so, with his social psychological emphasis, he outlined the elements of these 'practical activities' in the form of a systematic analysis based upon the ways in which all individuals had to come to terms with the physical and social environment with which they were confronted.

There were, Giddings claimed, four necessary components in all forms of human social action, and these he called the *Simple Modes of Activity.* First of all, there was the activity of Appreciation. Individuals had to learn effectively about all the characteristics of the environment with which they had to come to terms. Secondly, there was the activity of Utilisation. Individuals, having established effective knowledge about the elements of their environment, had to learn how to manipulate and utilise these elements in the satisfaction of their wants and the pursuit of their interests. Thirdly, in this complex process of learning about the environment and learning how to act in relation to it in order to use it, indivduals were forced to the realisation that effective and successful action rested upon the achievement, in themselves, of certain qualities of character. There was the activity of Characterisation. Courage, persistence, endurance, initiative, independence, and many other qualities were called for, and, of course, the relative weighting of these, and the emphasis placed upon all kinds of secondary qualities would vary in accordance with the nature of the society of which the individuals were members. 'Character-Formation' would therefore have variations from society to society. And fourthly, there was the activity of 'Socialisation'. In knowing and using elements of their environment in accordance with certain required qualities of personality and character, individuals found that they were involved in relationships of conflict and co-operation with other individuals, and therefore had to come to terms with the institutions and associational groupings of society. They had to develop effective behaviour in the context of social relationships, and, indeed, learn how to initiate and cultivate social relationships in relation to their interests.

Before leaving this analysis of 'simple practical activities' which Giddings thought necessary and fundamental in all forms of human action, we must note that Giddings also outlined these activities as a sequential order which was followed by the child in growing up to become an effective adult member of a society. It was, in fact, an order and process of individual maturation in society, as well as merely a set of activities. And this must be borne in mind because Giddings' whole conception of the relationship between 'society' and the formation of the 'self' can be seen in it.

Giddings also systematically analysed the 'motives' and the 'methods' which were appropriate to each of these four basic activities. These need not be elaboratesd here, but it is important to notice that Giddings did in fact provide an entire and systematic analysis of the whole process of the growth of the individual to adulthood in society. This was an analysis which connected, in the most detailed and systematic way, the knowledge of the entire structure of a society on the one hand with the components of social action and the growth of the individual personality within this context, on the other. It was an entire fabric of sociological and social-psychlogical analysis.

Following this, however, Giddings then went on to clarify the various 'forms' of social action in which these four 'simple activities' came to be embodied by an analysis of 'complex' activities, and by these he meant the major forms of institutionalization which took shape in all societies; the chief elements of social structure. Those on which he placed most emphasis were Economic Activity, Legal Activity and Political Activity, and he dealt with the development of attendant and additional values, beliefs, ideals, etc., under the heading of Cultural Activity - in which artistic, religious, and educational institutions were included. Again, we need not elaborate this: it was an account of those elements of social structure which comprise a total society such as the other theorists had made clear: but again, it is worthwhile to note that Giddings was very systematic in this: showing, in each case, how the 'simple' modes of human action - appreciation, utilisation, characterisation, and socialisation - were characteristically embodied in economic, legal, political, religious, educational (etc.) institutions in turn. The methodical elaboration of a complete system of analysis was very impressively carried out in all Giddings' work.

For our own purposes, however, it is clear enough how, on the basis of the analysis of 'practical activities', Giddings moved towards a systematic account of all the elements of social structure in a society as a whole. It was, in short, a 'structural-functional' model of the entire organisational framework of society, within which all the activities and experiences of men and the formation of their individual personalities could be systematically studied.

Perhaps the one remaining point which deserves emphasis before leaving this aspect of Giddings' work is that, in this whole analysis, the element on which he placed most stress was that of 'socialisation'. He did not stress this unduly, or conspicuously, but he did deal with it at rather greater length and with more elaboration than with the other components of his system. He analysed the kinds of resemblance which led men into various concerns with 'socialisation', and emphasised, for example, the importance of family and kinship ties, the mental and moral resemblances which led men into activity resting upon common values, beliefs and purposes, and the perception of 'potentialities' of similarities between individuals and groups which led men to seek to cultivate certain kinds of activity and association rather than others. He also analysed the psychological factors involved in this 'consciousness' of the various kinds of resemblance : various kinds of reflective sympathy, affection and affinity, desire for recognition, and so on. And he discussed too the important aspects of the processes of association and communication (as objective factors) which led to the consolidation, extension and cultivation of these subjectively - felt ties of resemblance. This emphasis upon the central importance of the characteristics of the system of communications in a society for the establishment of a sense of community and the closely related formation of individual character, was an especially important insight of Giddings, and we shall see later how this was also made a central consideration in the work of C. H. Cooley.

'Socialisation', then, was one of the most important strands in Giddings' analysis of the entire social system, and it is clear that this stemmed from his central persuasion that varieties of 'consciousness of kind' lay at the heart of the forms of association in a society and his concern to understand the factors that gave rise to these and sustained them.

The Continuous Interplay of Conflict and Co-operation

In clarifying his 'structural-functional' analysis of the nature of a society and its parts: of a fabric of associations which was the persisting resultant of the accommodation to each other of many social activities - and all in relation to an environment and its resources, Giddings did not think of this for a moment as a process of accomplished harmony. On the contrary, he argued that in all societies, the manifold practical activities of men must always give rise to both conflict and co-operation. The very accommodation of groups and organizations and individuals to each other; the very business of modifying and restraining and compromising and deliberating upon, different interests, different policies, different purposes, but often with common concerns, principles, and widely agreed objectives; was evidence of the continuous give-and-take, stress-and-strain, of conflict and co-operation. And, indeed - Giddings held - one of the important ingredients of social progress was the growing recognition by men of the benefits of diversity in society; of the tolerance of differences as well as the enjoyment of resemblances.

The important thing, again, for us to notice is only that a 'structural-functional' way of analysing the nature of a society was not by any means identical with a static or harmonious conception of society. On the contrary, the structure of society was conceived as an order of institutions which persistently accommodated both conflict and co-operation and made possible the tolerance of conflict and the acceptance of change. Here again, Giddings was completely in agreement with all the other thinkers we have considered. Like them he thought that societies were essentially historical processes, in which order was commensurate with conflict and change. And indeed, like Spencer, Marx, Ward and Sumner, he saw this as an inescapable aspect of the continuous transforming processes of the material universe; it was an enduring characteristic of nature. Conflict and change were the very stuff of the 'forms' produced in the evolution of societies, just as they were in the evolution of other forms of nature.

Furthermore, Giddings believed that - no matter what the 'equilibrium' of institutional structure a society had developed - there were always factors which made for radical conflict, and potential disruption. These were, he wrote :

> '. . .the instincts of conquest which are kept alive the necessity of destroying life to maintain life, and the instincts of aggression that are kept alive by the opposition always met with by those individuals and populations that develop more rapidly than others. Wherever civilisation finds itself face to face with savagery, or a young and growing civilisation finds itself opposed to one old and decaying, the antagonism is too serious to expend itself in the lesser forms of secondary conflict.'

There were also radical differences between new sections of populations (e.g., immigrants) which were insufficiently 'assimilated' in the larger society; and occasional disruptions caused by disasters of natural fortune : such as a massive failure of crops, the unexpected spread of a plague, the destructiveness of floods, and the like.

There was then - once again - nothing approaching a 'static' conception of society, or a conception of 'functional harmony', in Giddings' 'structural-functional' system of analysis. This conception of the interdependent fabric of institutions especially rested upon a basic conception of a continuous interplay of conflict and co-operation, of order as an accommodation to elements of difference and change. The network of institutions in a society was in part an embodiment of the toleration of diversity; which could be attended, in more complex societies, by a subjective appreciation (among their members) of the positive value of tolerance in society.

The one other aspect of this recognition of continuous conflict and co-operation in the conception of Giddings which we can simply note, was the element, in his system, of 'equilibrium-disequilibrium' analysis: another point of clear agreement with the earlier writers.

The Psychological Aspects of 'Society'

It was in his careful analysis of the psychological aspects of all the processes of 'society', or 'association', that Giddings went distinctively beyond the earlier writers (with the possible exception of Ward). We have already seen the elements of the systematic way in which he examined the growth of the 'self' in the context of 'society', and it would be too elaborate a task to undertake a detailed exposition of his system here. It will be enough, however, if we see very carefully the way in which Giddings' 'sociological' perspective led him to understand the 'psychology' of the individual personality - for this is a fundamental position of sociology which must be made clear; and if we then go on to see clearly what Giddings had to say about the basic 'modes' of the 'social mind' and 'social nature' which had developed in different types of society.

(a) *The insufficiency of a purely individual psychology for the understanding of the individual*

This is a point of the most fundamental importance. It is very simple; yet few people seem able clearly to comprehend it. It is as though people have a kind of mental 'blockage' against conceiving the 'individual' as being anything other than an entity bounded by his skin. By contrast, 'society' seems to them something vague and nebulous. It therefore goes without saying, for them, that 'society' can be explained in terms of 'individuals'; but that 'individual psychology' cannot possibly be derived from 'society'. Such a conception is an absolutely fundamental error, and one of the great merits of Giddings' writing was that it made this matter perfectly clear.

The qualities and characteristics which distinguish an individual human person from individual animals of other species are the elements of a social nature, and the qualities of mind resulting from social influence and social experiences, which he, or she, has come to possess. The very conception of 'self' and of his own 'self' which a person comes to have is an outcome of communication with others, and results from the observations and judgments which they make and which the person experiences from earliest childhood. The very awareness of self is a concomitant of social intercourse. But also all the elements of judgment, value, belief, qualities of character, truth, taste, and the awareness of the language, symbols, gestures and art in which these are all expressed elements established in the individual's mind and feelings as a result of his social experiences. A large part of an individual's personal nature is socially engendered.

It follows from this that society is a collective associational process possessing psychological aspects within the context of which individual persons come to be what they are. And it also follows from this that to study the individual alone, in terms of something called 'individual psychology' alone, cannot possibly provide a satisfactory knowledge of the individual. It must leave out all those dimensions of the person's nature which are attendant upon social processes. An analysis of society, a social psychology, is the only possible way in which we can come to an understanding of the nature of the individual.

Giddings wrote like this :

> 'There was a time when the human mind was studied as if it were an independent thing. The various states of mind were analysed and classified. No one thought of asking whether they had been

> produced by the interplay of the mind with other minds and with physical nature. In short, the mind was studied as if it had either existed from all time without change, or had instantly come into existence complete and fully prepared for the experiences of life.'

However, he continued, the study of the individual mind could now be undertaken within the context of the changing, historical society in which it existed, and :

> 'In studying the mind from this evolutionary or genetic point of view, it is discovered that in almost every experience and in every stage of growth, the social intercourse of an individual with his fellow-beings is one of the chief influences at work upon his own processes of thought, affection and will.'

The sociological perspective is therefore necessary for a full understanding of the nature of the individual. Giddings, of course, went on to provide an analysis of this socio-psychological process, but it is enough for our purposes to have noted clearly this emphasis.

In exactly the same way, Giddings was perfectly clear in guarding against possible misconceptions of this point, and it is here that his position, or rather his statement of this position, may be favourably compared with that of Durkheim - to whom we shall come later.

One of the commonest misconceptions of this position, and indeed one of the commonest dangers to which it is prone, is the idea that it is claiming that there exists in society a 'consciousness' or a 'collective psychology'additional to all the conscious individual minds and independent of them : hanging like some great metaphysical ceiling over their heads, and determining them. But, of course, this conception suggests nothing of the kind. It merely insists that human minds in association with each other have a collective, creative outcome which is different from what each individual mind could possibly be in isolation. The association of minds is a creative process. It brings into being an accumulative fabric of institutions, symbols, languages, regulated modes of conduct, stocks of knowledge, proverbs, customs, shared judgments, all of which persist as a traditional heritage which influences subsequent minds, and none of which could be said to exist in any one individual mind before it experienced association with others. There exists in society no 'conscious mind' independent of individual minds, but yet the 'associational activity of intercommunicating minds' is a level of creative psychological experience on which these individual minds could not, and would not operate, excepting in this associational activity. This is such an important matter that we should note exactly how Giddings expressed it.

> 'There is no reason', he wrote, 'to suppose that society is a great being which is conscious of itself through some mysterious process of thinking, separate and distinct from the thinking that goes on in the brains of individual men. At any rate, there is no possible way yet known to man of proving that there is any such supreme social consciousness.
>
> Nevertheless, there is a group of facts of great interest to the sociologist and to the man of affairs for which the name "the social mind" can, with entire propriety and with great convenience, be used... We have shown that the most essential fact in society is like-mindedness, meaning by this terms a close resemblance between the ideas, emotions and preferences of any given individual and those of other individuals who live in the same social group with him. It has been shown also that such like-minded individuals usually discover their mental and moral resemblançes, think about them, take pleasure in them, and turn them to good account in many useful ways.
>
> When, then, two or more individuals at the same moment are receiving like sensations, perceiving the same relations, experiencing the same kind of emotion, thinking the same thoughts, arriving in their judgments at the same conclusion - a state of facts exists in the population which evidently must be classed among facts of mind, and yet must be distinguished from the mental activity of an individual who, absolutely alone, completely cut off from communication with his fellow-men, thinks solely about himself and his immediate material surroundings. In the one case there exists a concert of the emotions and thoughts of two or more individuals; in the other case, thought of the individual is peculiar to himself and his isolated condition.
>
> 'To the group of facts that may be described as the simultaneous like-mental-activity of two or more individuals, in communication

> with one another, or as a concert of the emotion, thought, and will of two or more communicating individuals, we give the name, the social mind. This name, accordingly, should be regarded as meaning just this group of facts and nothing more. It does not mean that there is any other consciousness than that of individual minds. It does mean that individual minds act simultaneously in like ways and continually influence one another; and that certain mental products result from such combined mental action which could not result from the thinking of an individual who had no communication with fellow-beings.'

If that is not perfectly clear, then heaven help us all!

Giddings then went on to analyse the nature of these 'social-mental' processes. At the simplest level of all, he described the awareness among people of a sheer simultaneous similarity of response which, with the awareness, came to have a 'concerted' power: as, for example, when people became suddenly aware of a common terror and panicked into an explosion of blind action. Secondly he discussed the consolidation of social feelings, conceptions and ties which came as a reciprocal consciousness of kind developed among people. Thirdly, he analysed the way in which 'symbols' came to be created as part of the collective culture of a people and served to focus and canalise their feelings, conceptions and energies. That Giddings did not think that these were necessarily wisely based was reflected in the fact that he referred to them as 'Shibboleths' as well as 'Emblems'. Fourthly, he described the integration and consolidation of a people's shared values, judgments and orientations of ideas and actions which came about with the developed consciousness of a shared historical tradition : when the collective culture of a people linked the living with the past, and possessed a powerful authority over new generations. And finally, he distinguished the formation of shared public opinion which came with the opportunity and practice of critical, rational deliberation and the dissemination of knowledge in society. This again was all redolent of the ways in which Ward and Sumner were thinking, but the aspects of Giddings' analysis here which it is most important to select for special emphasis is what he called the 'Modes of Social Action'.

(b) *The Models of Social Action*

The entire analysis of the elements and processes at work in the emergence of various types of 'consciousness of kind', and the development of 'socal aspects of mind' was of basic importance in Giddings' mind for one central reason: because it provided the necessary basis for understanding the social action which men pursued. These elements of 'Social mind' resulted, he argued, in 'common purposes and concerted acts', and one important and necessary part of sociology was the explanation of social action. Here, the 'teleological' emphasis of Ward was clearly evident, and agreed upon, but Giddings provided an excellent analysis of 'types of social action' which possessed originality and, to my mind, is of the greatest interest for us because of its important prospective reference to the later work of Max Weber.

Giddings distinguished three types of social action : Impulsive, Traditional and Rational, and each of these rested upon a distinctively different kind of 'Like-mindedness'. The similarity between Giddings' treatment and the later notions of Weber is so staggering (it is almost an *identical* typology) that we simply must see in more than cursory fashion what he said about each 'type'.

(i) *Sympathetic Like-mindedness and Impulsive Social Action*

Impulsive social action was that which sprang from immediate impulse and the simplest kind of 'contagious' sympathetic feeling of which men were aware. It issued in action without intervening reasons or deliberation, and tended to be, therefore, a 'blind' response to feeling. The simplest examples of this were those rooted in 'panic' conditions or 'crowd' situations, but Giddings also saw this kind of social action as playing a very important part in the ongoing events and affairs of historical societies, since it could spring from conditions of ignorance, and could therefore be played upon by leaders and *élites*, as well as being aggravated by unexpected social conditions - such as chronic unemployment, poverty, mass-deprivation, and the like.

'The simplest combination of the feelings and ideas of a number of individuals', Giddings wrote, 'is that which occurs sympathetically and imitatively without the intervention of any process of critical thinking. The panic of a terrified crowd was mentioned as one of the lamentable forms that sympathetic mental activity may assume. That the like-mindedness which is purely sympathetic, imitative, or emotional should be impulsive and hasty in action, is inevitable . . . This action takes place without any thought process or critical reasoning . . .

A good chess player does not move his piece until he has thought out all the possible moves that he can make, and has decided which one is, all things considered, the best. A poor player sees, at the most, only two or three of the possible moves; and seeing so little to think about, he moves much sooner than a superior antagonist. These conditions are not changed when men act together in large numbers. On the contrary, if they have natures that are sensitive to every impression that is made upon their senses, if they are sympathetic and quick to imitate, if they have but little power of patient deliberation - they are quick to act, and their action is impulsive, emotional, lacking in coolness of judgment, and perhaps disastrous to themselves and others. Especially is this true if they are by nature or circumstance subject to . . .suggestion; if they respond unconsciously to an idea.'

This 'suggestibility' made possible the influencing of some men by others to 'impulsive action'. In the most subtle ways, Giddings wrote:

'. . .thoughts and courses of action are often suggested to men in crowds. A skilful public speaker can work a crowd to a great pitch of excitement by artfully insinuating the truth of that which he wishes them to believe, or the wisdom of that which he wishes them to do, while apparently directing his argument upon some quite different question.'

Giddings' conception of the extensiveness of this kind of social action in society may be seen in the following passage.

'A large part of all the social action in which many individuals take a concerted part is impulsive rather than deliberate; and therefore many of the dramatic events of history have been impulsive social actions . . .

Sometimes these events are violent in character, taking the form of riots, lynchings, and turbulent conduct in connection with strikes or lockouts. Sometimes they are entirely peaceful and lawful, but nonetheless hasty and inconsiderate - as when a legislative body; moved by a wave of popular feeling enacts a law without deliberation, simply assuming that the popular belief or demand is tc be accepted at its face value without opposition or criticism. Sometimes an entire nation is thus wrought up to impulsive action which carries it onward to frightful disaster.'

Giddings then went on to analyse the conditions which gave rise to impulsive social action : discussing in turn the physical, geographical and climatic conditions of a people; their 'mental conditions' - as, for example, the conditions of fear, ignorance and subjection in which they might be held in a society; 'crowd' conditions; and the like. Following upon this, he stated certain 'law' of the relationship between the incidence of impulsive social action and these conditions : laws which, he thought, could be useful in controlling such action. We have seen clearly, however, how Giddings characterised this 'type' of social action and the part it played in society.

(II) *Formal Like-mindedness : Traditional Social Action*

Traditional social action was still chiefly based upon the 'sympathetic emotional, imitative' modes of mental activity - as distinct from rational and deliberative thought; but, unlike impulsive social action, it did not spring from ungoverned impulse, but from feeling governed by the acceptance of the traditional, customary beliefs, values, ideas of the community. Traditional social action was action in conformity with the 'authority' of customary usage, and it rested upon the 'formal like-mindedness' of the people of the community whose feelings were all similarly governed; whose traditional values and beliefs were shared. It will be seen that this kind of social action rested distinctively upon 'belief', and the 'authority of traditional belief', as against critically assessed, rationally demonstrable knowledge.

The great body of ideas, values, precepts inherited by a community could be collectively called its 'Tradition'. And, Giddings wrote :

'The popular acceptance of tradition - of beliefs that have been handed down from past generations - and obedience to the rules and precepts that are embodied in the various traditions, are modes of like-mindedness. But, unlike those described in the preceding chapter, they are not spontaneous or impulsive; they are rather to be described as formal like-mindedness. They are analogous to habit in the individual mind.'

This 'formal like-mindedness', and its strength and authority, was produced, Giddings held, by two factors in particular : firstly, the reinforcing power of the knowledge that beliefs were shared by others - in both the present and the past - in whom people have confidence, and secondly, the power of education, including habitual discipline.

On the first of these, Giddings wrote:

'The tendency of the mind to accept as true whatever is vividly imagined or ardently desired, if no critical activity of the reason intervenes, is enormously strengthened when the thing believed ... is already believed by other persons in whom the individual has personal confidence . . . In short the consciousness of kind is a powerful element in the growth of pupular belief.

Yet further is the tendency to believe strengthened by the knowledge that not only one's contemporaries believe, but that preceding generations for ages past also have believed. The presumption in favour of the truth of the belief has become enormous, not only because its antiquity is an impressive fact appealing to imagination, but because, if the critical intelligence begins to question, it is likely to be easily satisfied by the reflection that if the belief were untrue, its falsity must long ago have been discovered and exposed.

Tradition thus acquired in human society all the tremendous force of authority. Authority is a moral power that constrains man's will without his knowing or being able to find out why. It is born of emotion and belief rather than of reason, which is ever asking the wherefore and the why. Nevertheless, since reason and rational self-control are of slow growth, the authority of tradition serves a useful end in helping to maintain social order.'

And on the second - the factor of direct teaching, discipline and habituation - he wrote as follows:

'Tradition is imposed upon the child by his parents and elder acquaintances. He is directly taught that the traditional beliefs are true, and that it is even wrong to doubt their truth and authority.

Disbelief is often punished; and disobedience of traditional precept is punished usually. Not only so, but through the intimate association between tradition and the everyday activities of life, the child insensibly associates the practical activity with its traditional background. In his economic life, in his legal relations and political activities, he can take no single step without practically accepting most of the traditional system. Daily life thus becomes a ceaseless discipline and drill in activities which openly or tacitly assume the truth and sufficiency of tradition . . .'

'The routine of habitual activity, the teaching and the discipline of life, continually tend to produce formal like-mindedness, including conformity to established customs.'

As we might suppose, Giddings believed that 'traditional' social action played a very large part indeed in the ordered patterns of action in all societies. We can see how similar his conception was to Sumner's analysis of the formation of the 'folkways and mores' and Ward's analysis of the 'genetic' building up of a social order. In his discussion of the kinds and sequences of traditional social action, however, his great similarity to all the other men we have considered was clearly apparent.

Basing his analysis upon his earlier account of men's 'simple' and 'complex' kinds of 'practical activities', Giddings distinguished three orders of tradition : primary, secondary and tertiary. The primary tradition in any society was the accumulated body of ideas, values, symbols, precepts and procedures which had become the embodiment of its economic, legal and political activities. These three were directly and intimately related to each other; indeed, in his conception of the sequence of these, Giddings was very close to the teaching of Marx. The economic tradition, he claimed, was 'probably the first to grow out of human experience'. The juristic tradition '. . .grows out of the relations of antagonistic equals', and was second in importance, and : 'the political tradition is developed out of the economic and juridical traditions, and in its evolution is closely interwoven with them.' This similarity is also clearly seen in the fact that Giddings classified the 'ideological' traditions of men - their religions, poetry, art, etc., - as the 'secondary' order of traditions.

However, too close a parallel must not be drawn. Giddings, point of distinction was really that the primary order of traditions dealt with human experience of, and relations with, the tangible world, whereas the secondary order of traditions dealt with men's impressions of the intangible elements of their experience of the world.

The third order was that of 'tertiary' traditions, and these were the traditions forming and governing systems of conceptual thought. These constituted a record of 'reasoning and speculative thinking rather than of mere impression and belief', said Giddings, and he then went on to describe the three chief tertiary traditions (systems of conceptual thought) which were distinguishable in a comparative and historical study of societies. And here again, we must look at his own words, because in them we can see how completely he drew into his system the generalisations of Comte. Here - quite plainly and deliberately - Giddings utilized Comte's law 'of the three stages'; his conception of the three 'types of social order' resting on three distinctive systems of 'knowledge'.

> 'The oldest of the tertiary traditions', wrote Giddings, 'is the theological tradition, which was created by an elaborate process of reasoning and speculation upon the materials furnished by popular religious beliefs. It is the sum and record of attempts to demonstrate by reason the existence of a personal God, to explain his nature and purposes, and to prove that he created and providentially governs the world and man.
>
> The second of the tertiary traditions is the metaphysical. It has been derived from the theological. It refines the theological explanation of the universe by interposing "secondary causes", laws, and principles between phenomena and their ultimate cause - the fiat of God.
>
> The third of the tertiary traditions is the scientific. The scientific tradition is the sum of our actual knowledge of the world and of man as distinguished from our conjectures abut them. It is the sifted record of observations, experiments and classifications. Making no attempt to penetrate the final mystery of existence, the scientific tradition explains the constitution of the world only to the extent of showing how one thing is related to other things in sequence and in coexistence.'

It is abundantly clear in Giddings' treatment of the types of social action how practically all the conceptions we have considered earlier were brought together, and found their place, within a systematic whole. The making of sociology was clearly being undertaken as a critically creative, a systematising process of knitting together the various contirbutions as they arose. But it was not being done conspicuously or dramatically : it was assumed to be part and parcel of the continuous, deliberative effort which was directed to the satifactory creation of the new science. In the work of Giddings this was very marked, and it is worthwhile to notice, too, that he made no attempt whatever to appear original in all this. On the contrary, he openly utilised the contributions and conceptions of others as the 'building blocks' of the science which all scholars concerned were trying to fit together. It was assumed to be an argumentative cooperative, creative inter-communication of scholarship throughout.

So much, however, for Giddings' clarification of 'traditional' social action.

(III) *Rational Social Action: The Formation of Public Opinion and Social Values*

The third 'type' of social action was that characterised by 'rationality' and resting crucially on critical judgment and knowledge. Giddings distinguished sharply between 'public belief' (still resting upon emotion and traditional authority) and 'public opinion' - which was the formation of considered judgments following a process of critical reflection and involving, therefore, clearly defined rational criteria.

> 'Public opinion', he wrote, 'comes into existence only when a sympathetic like-mindedness or an agreement in belief is subjected to criticism, started by some sceptical individual who doubts the truth of the belief or the wisdom of the agreement; and an opinion is then thought out to which many communicating minds can yield their rational assent.'

The very possibility of rational deliberation and rational social action necessitated certain conditions. Public opinion developed in any community, Giddings maintained:

> '. . .just to the extent that men are in the habit of asking searching questions and compelling one another to prove their assertions.

> Public opinion, therefore, can exist only where men are in continual communication, and where they are free to express their real minds, without fear or restraint. Wherever men are forbidden by governmental or other authority to assemble, to hold meetings, to speak or write freely, or wherever they stand in fear of losing social position, or employment, or property, if they freely speak their minds, there is no true public opinion; there is only a mass of traditional beliefs or outbursts of popular feeling.
>
> The essential condition of deliberate social decision is the alternation of meeting and discussion with separation.'

Rational social action always grew out of critical reflection upon impulsive and traditional social action, and Giddings went on to show how - in each sphere of practical and social activity - new rational elements came to be blended with earlier traditional elements. Thus, traditional economic methods of technique and exchange came to be modified by rational calculation of production for complex market situations. Custom came to be amended and replaced by legal reforms and legal codes. Traditional political authority came to be changed by new rationally devised political constitutions and public 'policies' of all kinds. And in the same way, science itself grew out of the questioning and challenging of previously uncritically accepted beliefs.

Rationality also brought with it the considered clarification of new personal and social values, and these - related to every aspect of personal and social life in more complex societies - were different from earlier traditional values in that their basis of authority no longer lay simply in the fact of immemorial usage and emotional acceptance, but in the reasons that could be given for holding them. This was an extremely important change, because, with the emergence, development and extension of rationality, the clarification of the rational values on which the entire process of rational deliberation and rational social action rested became supremely necessary. Without this clarification, the disruption of traditional values by rational criticism might leave - only a vacuum! Here again, we see in the American writers this strong awareness of the central importance of values in society; this vision of values as the very mesh of social institutions – as the thread of regulation that fastens together the entire fabric of the social order; and this is a central insight which we shall come to focus on with very powerful insistence a little later.

Giddings, like Ward, emphasised the growing importance of rational, self-direction in society and wished to point to the continuous efforts which it entailed. He was well aware that many denied and decried the efforts of reason in society; but this was his answer :

> 'Social values are the grounds of rational social choice, and of all action of the social will that is deliberate rather than impulsive.
>
> There have been writers on Sociology who have denied that masses of men ever act rationally. They have argued that as men differ less in feeling than in intelligence and as men in crowds are peculiarly susceptible to emotion and suggestion, the intellectual processes have, under such circumstances, very little opportunity to manifest themselves.
>
> Nevertheless, there is abundant historical proof that communities do oftentimes arrive at rational decisions, after many years of persistent discussion of the merits of the question. Among excellent examples have been most of the amendments to the constitution of the United States, and to the constitutions of the several commonwealth'.

Giddings did however, as we have seen before think that some (more able) men could influence others of lesser ability and greater ignorance, and it is necessary just to note that he undoubtedly adopted an 'élitist' view in this matter.

The 'Classes' of Society

In almost exactly the same way as Sumner, Giddings drew upon the work of Galton and conceived of every total population (in an entire society) as consisting of various proportions of people possessing differing ranges of intelligence and ability. His notion of 'classes' in society was therefore of this kind, rather than of the nature of 'socio-economic strata' as we now tend to think of them. We need not here elaborate Giddings' treatment of this aspect of his analysis – it was so similar to that of Sumner; but it is worthwhile to note how strongly he conceived the role of the intellectual, moral, social élite to be. It was this proportion of any society, in his view, which was responsible for the extent and effectiveness of such rational progress as it achieved; and - in our very egalitarian age - Giddings seemed uncomfortably definite and direct about this.

> 'Men and women; he wrote, 'who have health, originality, and that unselfish love of mankind which moves them to devote their efforts to promoting the social welfare, certainly deserve to be recognised as, in the truest sense of the word, superior to their fellow-beings.
>
> 'This superior section of the social class is the most efficient class in the community. Small as it is in numbers, it accomplishes the greater part of those undertakings which, in their totality, we call progress. It gives to society the new inventions, the improvements in law, industry, art, religion and morals which make life richer in its achievements and larger in its possibilities. It is this class alone that deserves to be called an élite or an aristocracy'.

This pre-eminent social class, Giddings maintained, 'does most of the original thinking for society' it 'does most of the leading directing, and organising'; and, in the long-run, 'the unwritten laws of society' are made by it.

All we need notice here, however, is that in the changing nature of the 'consciousness of kind' in the various associations of society; in the changing, cumulative social systems of traditions, symbols, and rational procedures; and in the sequences of change from one 'mode' of social action to another; Giddings takes into account the differential part played by various sections of the population - from the few of markedly high ability to the masses whose ability and condition of knowledge is relatively low.

In these ways, then, Giddings gave a systematic account of the 'psychological aspects of society' and the several 'types of social action' and it will have been seen that this account included, quite clearly, both the 'genetic' and the 'teleological' components distinguished and insisted upon by Ward. All this, however, Giddings framed within the context of a strictly organisational analysis of the structure of society, and a theory of the evolution and progress of 'types' of society, and to round out his entire system we must glance quickly at this 'societal' account.

Before doing this, however, let us pause again just to reiterate deliberately and emphatically this central and continuing point. We have seen - clearly, and with not a vestige of doubt - that in the system of sociological analysis offered by Giddings all the following components : a structural-functional account of the nature of societies; an essentially historical account of social change involving both conflict and co-operation; a psychological account of the relations between individual and society and of the 'psychological aspects' of all the elements of social structure and forms of association; a subjective understanding of several 'types' of social action; an analysis of populations in the context of their environments; and a theory of social evolution and progress - were combined, and seen as being essential parts and dimensions of a satisfactory way of conceiving, studying and producing testable knowledge about societies as whole social systems. All these elements were interrelated parts of Giddings' system - just as they had been in the work of all the other men we have studied. Here we will simply note this - with a kind of dogged insistence, and later its full significance will be seen.

To conclude our study of Giddings, however, let us look briefly at his analysis of 'social organisation' and his picture of 'social evolution' because it is important to see how the 'types of social action' were seen to be correlated with, and seen in the context of, specific changes of social organization and 'types of society'.

Elements of Social Organization

Giddings' analysis of the components of the organisational structure of society has already been indicated briefly in section (iv) above, but it is worthwhile to note this a little more fully now. Very much like Ward and Sumner, Giddings thought of the formation of the established structure of society as being the outcome of a two-fold process. In the thronging practical activities of men, in the context of conflict and co-operation, certain spontaneous ways of doing things and regulating relationships emerged, and those which were most advantageous in shared experience came to be supported and became habitual and 'customary'. These came also to be connected in unforeseen and unintended ways (i.e., had unintended consequences) so that they came to assume, to some degree, the nature of an interconnected 'system'. This way Ward's 'genetic' order and Sumner's network of 'folkways'. At some point, however, and for some reasons, men came to be consciously aware of these established elements of order and came to reflect upon them, to challenge them, to deliberate about them and to change them or reinforce them. In short, a formal conscious, purposeful 're-making' of the social order took place and a conscious furthering or creation of new forms of social organisation was undertaken in the light of new knowledge and new pruposes. This was Ward's 'teleological' development, and Sumner's development of the 'mores' and subsequent 'law-making' which grew out of reflection upon the 'folkways'. The conception was the same; but the elements of social structure which Giddings specified were these.

First of all he distinguished 'institutions' from the less formal and reflective relationships in society.

> 'An institution', he wrote, 'is a social relation that is established by adequate and rightful authority. The ultimate source of authority in society is the social mind. Consequently, those forms of organisation, those relations and arrangements which the social mind has reflected upon, which it has accepted, allowed, or commanded - and those only - are institutions'.

Secondly, the structure of society could in part be analysed in terms of its 'Social Composition' which consisted of various 'component societies'(each with its own particular 'consciousness of kind'). And thirdly, in part it could be analysed in terms of its 'Social Constitution' which was the entire network of social organization formed by its 'constituent societies' (again, each with its own appropriate 'consciousness of kind').

The component societies which made up the entire composition of society were wholly or partly aggregations of kindred: wholly, for example, in the case of facilities, and perhaps some villages; partly, in the case of cities and distinctive territorial regional communities. In the latter cases, various factors making for kinds of 'congregation' existed in addition to the purely 'genetic' (i.e. in this sense - blood-kinship) social bond. Under this heading of 'component societies', Giddings discussed families, tribal societies, ethnic groups, and groupings of a non-kinship nature. As 'ethnic societies,' he analysed hordes, tribes, confederations of tribes, and distinguished groups based upon matriarchal and patriarchal principles.

Under the heading of constituent societies, Giddings dealt with all organized forms of association - from those which were actually a part of the simpler 'component societies' : such as the 'household', the 'clan', and other 'tribal' associations, to those large-scale associations of complex societies such as the highly organised components in the constitutions of 'civil societies' up to the organisation of the 'State' itself. Here, his picture was one of an increasing differentiation of specialised associations, as society became larger and more complicated, and as rational social action increased over earlier traditional forms. Here, it is worthwhile to note in detail his own conception of such a specialised 'association' because it is useful to compare it with the picture of institutional development put forward by Ward and Sumner.

> 'Every purposive association', Giddings wrote, 'has not only a function but also a composition and a constitution which are adapted to the performance of the function.
>
> In the composition of purposive association, individuals are combined as persons and by categories; for example, the categories of employer and employee, in the composition of an industrial group. The composition of associations must be studied with reference to the common trait or interest that unites their members.
>
> The constitution of a purposive association is the plan of organisation of its membership. The categories of individuals which compose it are combined in accordance with some principle of subordination or coordination; and the entire membership may be divided into sub-societies, bureaus, or committees.'

Later, this may also be compared with Malinowski's conception of an 'institution', but we might note here the several important elements into which an 'association' can be broken down by analysis. It has a 'composition' and a 'constitution' specifically related to the pursuit or performance of a 'function'. It has also a definite 'personnel', the members of which are organised in certain 'categories' or roles and in certain relationships of authority, and certain operational 'groups' (such as committees). The members are also related to each other in terms of some 'consciousness of kind'; some 'traits' of 'interests' which unite them.

It will be seen at once that Giddings' analysis of the entire organisation of a society dissected every element of association - from the most massive structure of the 'state', through all the large-scale elements of the 'legal system', the 'economic system', the 'religious system', the 'educational system', right down to the specific specialist association, even the 'household'; and, furthermore, that his analysis of association dissected social structure right down to the specific roles which individual persons fulfilled. This was therefore a satisfactory 'schema' of analysis - embracing every detail from social structure at the most large-scale and general level, to the formal tasks of individuals, the complexes of roles which they had to fulfil.

Giddings also elaborated his analysis further to take into account public and private organisations, incorporated and unincorporated organisations, and voluntary organisations in all fields of social activity : political, legal, economic, cultural, etc.; but these we need only mention. Here again, there was a strong similarity between Giddings' treatment and the distinction which Sumner made between 'crescive' and 'enacted' institutions.

One final aspect of Giddings account of the elements of social organization which must be stressed, is the fact that he saw all these elements as being interrelated in a close way - in the sense of interdependence and interaction - in the 'system' of society as a whole. His way of formulating this conception made it clear that there was an 'order' of authority and subordination among them as well as within each of them, and also that he did not - despite his emphasis upon 'practical activities' and their primacy - hold any kind of 'material determinism', but agreed closely with Ward that men, in furthering their knowledge and deliberation, acted purposively to shape the structure of society towards the attainment of their ends. It is clear, too, that Giddings saw the proliferation of 'associations' of 'constituent societies', as part and parcel not of social disorder, but the gradual achievement of a more flexible social order in which rational action and the pursuit of a diversity of purposes was both possible and tolerated. It was, in short, a process of enriching society and the creation of a kind of order which made continuous progress possible. Again, we see Comte's dictum of 'order' and 'progress' writ large. Giddings put the matter simply like this :

> 'The various organisations of society are not only correlated, but are also subordinated, some to other organisations, and all to a general end. The supreme end of society in general is the protection and perfecting of sentient life. The end of human society is the development of the rational and spiritual personality of its members. Only the cultural associations are immediately concerned in this function. Educational institutions, religious, scientific, ethical, and aesthetic organisations, and polite society act for good or ill directly upon the individual. To these the economic, the legal, and the political organisation are, in a functional sense, subordinate. In a functional sense, they exist for the sake of cultural organisation and activity. The social mind has always perceived this truth, and by means of its sanctions has endeavoured to mould the social constitution into accordance with it. Associations and relationships are fostered or abolished with a view to cultural no less than to protective ends.
>
> For both ends specialisation and a division of labour are necessary. Therefore, while society maintains the homogeneity of its composition, it is obliged to tolerate and to promote differentiation in its constitution. Psychologically, therefore, the social constitution is the precise opposite of the social composition. It is an alliance, in each simple association, of individuals who, in respect to the purpose of the association, must be mentally and morally alike, but who in all other respects may be unlike; supplemented in the relations of associations to one another and to integral society by toleration and coordination of the unlike. . .

GIDDINGS' SYSTEM OF ANALYSIS

THE SOCIAL SYSTEM

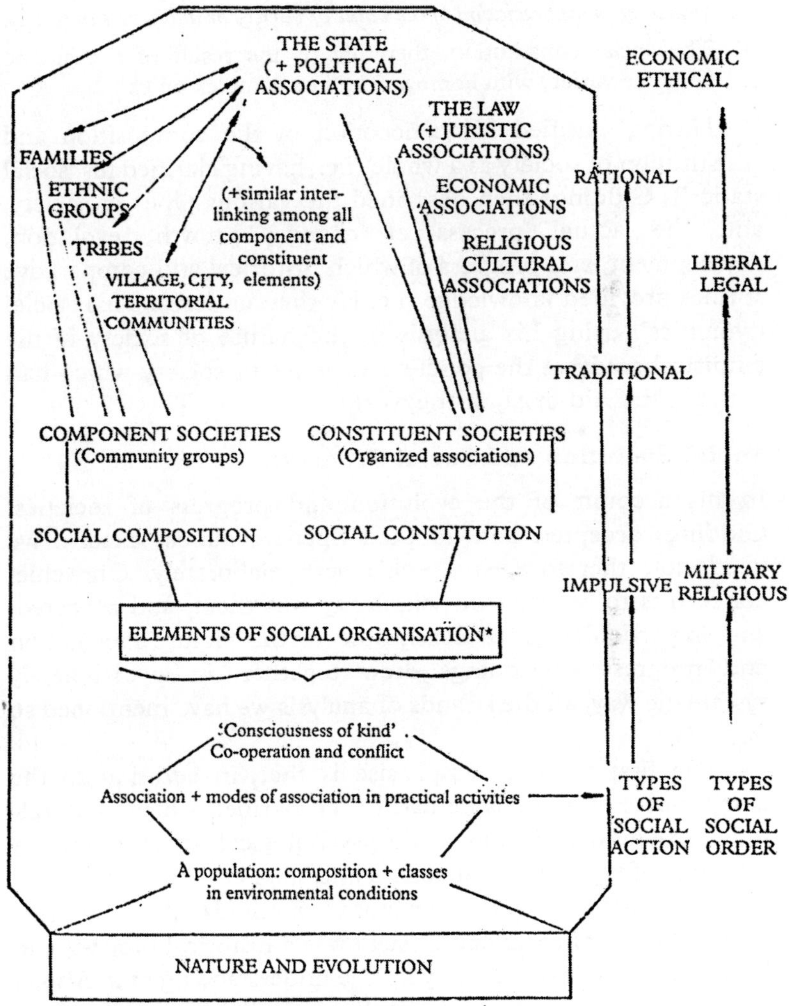

* Again, it would be too complicated to depict all the elements of social organisation Giddings included and the complex interlinkings between all component and constituent elements. These diagrams can only be indicative.

> We may state the law of development of the social constitution as follows: *The development of the social constitution depends upon the growth of an appreciation of the value of variety or unlikeness in society.* The social constitution, therefore, is the result of a desire to combine variety with homogeneity in a complex unity.'

Having clarified his conception of the composition and constitution of society as a whole (i.e., having clarified his 'social statics'), Giddings then described the various types of society, and the actual precess of change, growth, evolution, development, and progress of which historical and comparative studies provided knowledge (i.e. He then undertook his 'social dynamics': using his analysis of the nature of society in the empirical study of the concrete varieties of society which had existed, and did exist, in the world.)

Social Evolution and Social Progress

In his account of the evolution and progress of societies, Giddings accepted and adopted Spencer almost exactly. We need not, therefore, study this very elaborately. Our chief concern is to see that this similarity was there, and accepted, and, in particular, to see clearly how - in this picture of evolution and progress - Giddings drew together, in a completely systematic way, all the strands of analysis we have mentioned so far.

The first thing to emphasise is that, in addition to the components of analysis he had so far clarified - his structural-functional model, his study of the psychological aspects of society, his study of types of social action, and the like - he now insisted that the historical and comparative methods of study were essential parts of sociology. Society was a historical process, and historical study was necessary for the understanding of it. Also, it was impossible to judge and test the generalisations arising from sociological analysis without empirical, comparative studies. Historical and comparative studies were necessary for the straightforward descriptive awareness of the nature of diverse societies, and for the sharper testing of theories.

Giddings' account of social evolution, and his description of 'types of society', followed Spencer even in using the two methods of classification: clarification of the nature of societies in accordance with their 'degree of composition' or 'aggregation', and by the method of constructing 'types' which selectively emphasised the main characteristics in which one was hypothetically interested - i.e., the construction of models.

On the basis of the 'degree of composition', Giddings traced the development of societies in a large-scale manner. He discussed the 'sub-human', 'sub-social' animal ancestry of man and analysed what, in terms of our knowledge, appeared to be the earliest growths of social traditions. Then, from a description of various kinds of 'Tribal Society', he traced the several factors of amalgamation, growth, conquest, which led to 'Tribal Feudalism' and the emergence of the 'Ethnic Nation'. From this, he described the processes of trading and migration which, again, had led to the extension of civilisation over greater areas, and had given rise to 'Developed Feudalism', and, with commercial complexity especially and the growth of towns and great cities, the 'Civic Nation,' and the larger civilisations which had resulted from the various kinds of inter-connections between these. In all this, whilst accepting Spencer, Giddings did not simply reiterate Spencer. This picture of the various forms of societies and the pattern of social evolution which could be discerned among them was put forward on the basis of a very rich historical knowledge. Much detail was produced in its clear elaboration.

It is also important to note that - like Spencer - Giddings did not maintain that all societies experienced *all* these 'stages'; or that the process of evolution, once begun, was inevitable. He discussed societies in the contexts of their environmental situations, and readily saw that some societies remained relatively unchanged over long periods, whilst the environmental conditions remained unchanged. But also, and more important, he analysed the several components of social organisation involved in the nature of a society in changing from one 'type' to another, and claimed, quite clearly, that some societies remained in a certain condition as an outcome of deliberate policy. He analysed, for example, the role of military organisation, religious and ecclesiastical hierarchies, detailed administrative bureaucracies, and - to give but one example - he argued that, when a certain large-scale power and sufficiency had been reached, some societies deliberately 'isolated' themselves from others: with a resulting traditional continuity lasting for millennia. He wrote, for example:

> 'When national unity and power have fairly been achieved and the nation is in no immediate danger of overthrow by more powerful enemies a further policy often carried out is that of isolation. Feeling the superiority of its culture and institutions to those of other peoples, the nation endeavours in a measure to cut itself off from intercourse with them, lest foreign laws and manners shall corrupt, contaminate, and disintegrate the national life. This policy may perhaps have its justification under exceptional circumstances; but usually it has been a step towards national decay. It has been a chief factor in producing what are called "arrested civilisations", like those of China and Persia.'

There was, therefore, nothing 'inevitable' or 'unilinear' about Giddings' account of social evolution. It was a portrayal of the kinds of amalgamation, confederation, assimilation, growth, increasing complexity of social organisation which had taken place in many societies; a 'schema' of 'degree of composition' which could be clarified by bringing together such knowledge as we possessed of all societies; but it was a causal analysis within this schema which could explain how societies became unstable as well as stable; how they diminished as well as grew; declined and dissolved as well as developed into greater complexities; or even became relatively 'arrested' in continuing conditions. As we saw with Spencer, it made possible a kind of 'If . . . then . . .' analysis which was perfectly clear and could examine any kinds or directions of change.

In order to be exactly clear about the framework of Giddings' description of the emergence of 'Civilization' - i.e., the social and cultural system of the 'Civic Nations' - and to see perfectly clearly its complete agreement with Ward, let us see how he summarised this. It is necessary to note, in the following passage, that Giddings used the word 'demogenic' to mean social processes stemming from a 'people', a 'demos', with a shared awareness of each other, and of their social unity, going beyond 'kinship' membership (which is termed 'ethnogenic' association).

> 'Civilisation', wrote Giddings, 'is the first stage of demogenic association. As zoogenic association was that earliest social intercourse which developed the forms of animal life; as anthropogenic association was that more varied intercourse which created the human mind; as ethnogenic association was that organised intercourse which created a folk; so demogenic association is that intercourse, both varied and organised, which develops great civic peoples, ever increasing in wealth and in population, and ever growing more democratic in mind.
>
> Civilisation cannot be defined in a phrase, because it includes many things, all of which are essential. It consists in the adoption of a permanent territorial home and of habits of settled life; in the supremacy of the state and, therefore, of the social constitution over the entire social composition; in the substitution of mental and moral resemblance for kinship, as a basis of social organisation; in the assimilation of various population elements in a new and larger ethnic unity; in an integration of the social composition; and in an increasing homogeneity in politics, religion, manners, and habits. Chief among these elements of civilisation, however, is that sympathetic and traditional like-mindedness which is unlimited by ties of kinship and which, manifesting itself in a passion for homogeneity in the nation, creates those policies of military discipline, religious conformity, and moral requirement that result in national and social unity.
>
> The homogeneity of the civic nation has had two consequences without which those further developments of society and of human life to be described under the head of Progress could not have appeared. . .Liberty depends upon homogeneity in the population. In its earliest stages, civilisation allowed little freedom to the individual. It permitted no growth of the voluntary forms of organisation in the social constitution. But by hastening the processes of assimilation, by eliminating irreconcilable differences from the social population, by creating homogeneity, sympathetic and traditional like-mindedness, it did prepare populations for liberty later on. It made men fit for the self-government and the voluntary enterprise of a second stage of demogenic association.'

This passage is particularly useful for our understanding of Giddings, because it is in considering this 'second stage of demogenic association' that he developed Spencer's second method of classification – the construction of 'types' to highlight certain major considerations, and also linked his conception of progress to the ideas of development and evolution. There is also a striking accordance here, though it is expressed in very different terms, with Marx's idea that the entire development of human society so far has been the 'pre-history' of man, and that only with the emergence of reason, and technological control, and the creation of a humane society can man commence his conscious making of history, free from earlier bonds of subjection, alienation, and the constraining tyranny of dogmatic traditions and ideas.

The facts already set out in this schema of social evolution, Giddings wrote :

> '. . .Whether they appeared in the history of the world before the Christian era, or whether they appear now, are facts of the first stage only of civic national life.
>
> A second stage of demogenic evolution begins whenever the nation learns to appreciate the value of unlike-mindedness in the population; the value of doubt, scepticism, and denial in the social mind; the value of individual initiative and voluntary organisation; the value, in short, of variation and criticism, as causes of progress. In other words, while civilisation is established by sympathetic and traditional like-mindedness, a social organization that is no longer fixed, unyielding, hardening into a rigid system that must presently decay, but is becoming ever more variable, flexible, adaptable, in a word, progressive, is a product of unlike-mindedness, discussion, and agreement, and of the resulting rational like-mindedness.
>
> On the side of the social mind, then, the second stage of civic evolution is the gradual subordination of traditional to rational like-mindedness. On the side of social organisation, it is the growth of the free or voluntary forms of purposive association, replacing the arbitrary coercive forms of a military system; and in the relation of the individual to social organisation, it is the substitution of liberty for authority and coercion.'

Giddings then arranged the 'evolutionary scheme' of societies in a new way, by constructing 'types' of social order, or 'stages', which threw the clearest light upon the nature and possibility of social progress.

Types of Social Order and 'Character-types'

The first massive stage of the building up of the 'traditional' societies of the world, he termed the 'Military-Religious' type of social order, and that which was growing out of these traditional societies in the modern world of scientific knowledge and industrial technology, he termed the 'Liberal-Legal' type of social order. Again we may note the complete identity of this typology with the later formulation of Max Weber of the two basic types of social authority : the 'Traditional' type and the 'Rational–Legal' type. For Giddings, the 'Liberal-Legal' type was that form of civilisation in which : 'the forms of constitutional law and of free contract have replaced those of despotic authority and of "divine right"'. The great and distinctive difference between the 'Liberal-Legal' and the 'Military-Religious' types, as Giddings described them, can be seen in the following passage, and again this might be noted very carefully with our later study of Max Weber in mind.

> 'When a people has consciously entered upon the progressive stage of civic evolution, it usually attempts to perfects its liberal-legal civilisation by a conscious policy, as people in the military-religious civilisation endeavour by definite policies to perfect and maintain that.
>
> The policies by which the liberal-legal civilisation is perfected are naturally quite the opposite of those by which a military-religious civilisation is established. In many respects rational like-mindedness is different from the traditional like-mindedness whose chief component is belief, rather than the opinion that is created by free discussion.
>
> *World Intercourse.* - First, then, among the policies by which the liberal-legal civilization is perfected is the encouragement of the widest and freest world intercourse. The contact with other peoples, customs, manners, and thought is recognised as the indispensable condition for catholicity of view and alertness of mind. Progressive peoples invariably distrust any policy that tends towards isolation.
>
> *Free Thought* - Secondly, progress is assured by encouraging the fullest investigation and the freest discussion of every subject. Instead of trying to compel all men to accept the same beliefs

> taught by authority, the progressive nation encourages every man to think for himself, to develop his own mental powers, to take an independent position upon every question and interest, knowing full well that reason is not a chaotic or lawless power, but is one that invariably brings men to agreement upon the basis of real knowledge and demonstrated truth.
>
> *Legality* – Thirdly, the progressive nation tries to perfect its liberal-legal civilization by a continued study of law and development of legality, which it is ever striving to substitute for arbitrary authority, not only in government, but in all social relations. Only that nation which succeeds in perfecting the constitutional, that is to say the legal and rational, method of government and procedure, can preserve both individual liberty and public order.[3]

Again we must note that Giddings did not think there was anything inevitable about this progress. Many nations, he said, which have entered upon the 'Liberal-Legal' stage of social evolution 'have been unable to complete it'. But we can also notice, again, that the movement towards the 'Liberal-Legal' type of society necessarily involves a change of social values, and necessarily entails a rational clarification of these values. Again, we have this clear sight of the centrality of values in the social system, and for the distinctive differences between social systems. Values actually are the fabric of society. At the end of our entire study we shall see what a fundamental insight this is.

Growing out of the 'Liberal-Legal' type of social order, however, there was, Giddings maintained, a third 'type' of society, and it was in the throes of this that we found ourselves in the contemporary world.

> 'There is a third stage of civic evolution', he wrote, 'upon which nations enter when they have so far perfected the liberal-legal civilisation that they have a strong constitutional government to maintain social order and, at the same time, practically unlimited freedom of individual enterprise and voluntary organisation.
>
> When, in such a nation, the most urgent problems of constitutional government have been solved, men turn their attention seriously to the task of improving their material condition, and give themselves earnestly to industrial affairs. Then is witnessed a marvellous development of invention, of mechanical progress and industrial organisation, and an enormously rapid gorwth of wealth.

> Consequent upon this economic progress, there is an astonishing growth of population, which brings with it new and complicated social problems, especially those that grow out of the relations of employers and employed and the aspirations of the working classes. The final outcome is a development of democracy, and coincident with it a marked development of ethical interest. This third stage of civic evolution may, therefore, be called an "economic-ethical" civilisation, or it may, with equal propriety, be called a democratic civilisation.'

It will be seen how closely Giddings' three 'types' of social order approximated to the 'Militant', 'Industrial', and 'Ethical' types of Spencer. In the rest of his discussion, Giddings analysed the problems of the 'Economic-Ethical' type of society (i.e., in our terms: the 'Welfare State') and exposed the 'perils' as well as the benefits of democracy; and some of his judgments have a remarkable aptness for the problems we are perplexed about in the twentieth century. He also deployed the Spencerian 'explanations' of evolution in systematically analysing this entire schema of evolution and progress. For us, however, it is enough to concentrate on two further points: the first, a note on one aspect of Giddings' 'social psychology' in the context of this elaborate sociological analysis, and second, a clear indication of how the several strands of his system were related to each other.

We have noted throughout that Giddings emphasised the close relation between 'self' and 'society', between individual character and the characteristics and values of the 'associations' in which he was behaviourally involved. Almost as though he was following Mill's emphasis on the importance of 'Ethology' to the letter, Giddings was always careful to examine the psychological attributes correlated with the requirements and constraining influences of 'association'. This was well marked (as in other dimensions of his system) in his attempt to clarify the relationships between 'character and social-structure', and this is important to note because here again we see the preoccupation with an area of analysis in which American scholars have made special contributions, and in which there has been a strong continuity of interest. Giddings gave clear descriptions of the 'character-types' which were correlated with the different kinds of social control and authority which he outlined, and these, it must be agreed, provided a remarkably systematic account in relation to his entire picture of 'social evolution'. The chief types he specified were these:

(i) The Sympathetic Type - Developed in a community of kinsfolk where the chief social bond was that of sympathy.

(ii) The Congenial Type - Developed in a community which was based upon the affinity of ideas and interest; for example - amongst groups which shared particular political persuasions or religious beliefs and ideals.

(iii) The Approbational Type - Developed where the social bond rested simply upon the approbation of particular qualities or modes of conduct; as for example, in groups of warrior - companions, or in gangs.

(iv) The Despotic Type - Developed in a community where the social bond was that of tyrannical power, together with a demand for obedience based completely upon fear.

(v) The Authoritative Type - Developed in communities where the pattern of authority had become powerfully established in tradition and where the social bond rested upon a reverence for this authority.

(vi) The Conspiratorial Type - Developed in situations where the bond of association, and the 'like-mindedness', rested upon intrigue.

(vii) The Contractual Type - Developed where the social bond was based upon mutually undertaken covenant or contract, and an acceptance of reciprocal responsibility.

(viii) The Idealistic Type - Developed where all the members of the community were consciously concerned for social values and responded to the appeal of great ideals; where the social bond was that of mutual faithfulness to these ideals and qualities; where a powerfully shared altruism and idealism was felt and where the members of the community had full confidence in the commitment and the shared qualities of others.

We are now in a position to see how some of the chief strands of Giddings' system were correlated with each other.

Nothing elaborate is required, and I think the relationships can be made clear enough in a simple Table 4.1.

Of course, the 'Character-Types' especially do not link up in the kind of exact order which such a diagrammatic presentation portrays; but I have included them to try to indicate the way in which all the elements of Giddings' analysis did form part of a very impressively worked out system. Here, at least, we can see the relatedness in Giddings' mind between his analysis of the organisational nature of societies, the systems of conceptual thought in them, the systems of social action appropriate to them, the overall 'types' of social order into which they could be grouped, and the 'social-psychological' correlation's between kinds of associational relationship and kinds of individual personality and character which could be uncovered within them.

Table 4.1

SOCIAL EVOLUTION AND PROGRESS

Social Evolution	Types of Social Action	Types of Conceptual Thought	Types of Character	Types of Social Order and Progress
Simple Traditions		Simple	Sympathetic	
		Traditional		
Tribal Societies	Impulsive	Beliefs		
	Social	(Not Conceptual)		Military-
Tribal Feudalism	Action	Thought		Religious
			Congenial	Type
Ethnic Nations	Traditional	Theological	Approbational	
	Social		Despotic	
Developed Feudalism	Action		Authoritative	
		Metaphysical		
Civic Nations	Rational		Conspiratorial	
	Social			Liberal-
Complex Federations	Action	Scientific	Contractual	Legal
and Civilisations			Idealistic	Type
				Economic-
				Ethical Type

It is perfectly clear, too, in this presentation, how Giddings conceived the distinctive changes and qualities which characterized the nature and problems of human society in the modern world. His aim was to throw the rapid changes of modern industrial society into clear perspective; to produce an awareness of the juncture of civilisation at which men had arrived; and - by the making of sociology - to provide a body of knowledge on the basis of which sound judgments could be made and enlightened policies and efforts could be sustained in grappling with these dilemmas. It was in this sense that Giddings thought of sociology not as a 'professional academic expertise', but as a fundamentally important educative subject which could provide a necessary and excellent basis for citizenship: for the wisest approach to both social commitments and personal fulfilment. He was, of course, perfectly right: and again, in his work, we can see the humane commitment and the anxiety to become clear about the plight of mankind in the modern scientific and industrial age, which lay at the heart and the intellectual effort of all the men we have considered. Indeed, the wisdom and profundity of Giddings' commitment both to the making of sociology for the sake of education, and to the clarification of the political perspectives and tasks of our time can be seen in the preface to his textbook. He foresaw very clearly the intensification of these dilemmas that lay ahead for America and for all societies as the social changes which were then afoot extended throughout the world during the twentieth century.

In 1898 he wrote, with regard to Sociological Theory as a subject, as follows:

> 'No other subject calls for such serious attention from teachers and students of educational philosophy at the present times as that of the best preparation for an intelligent and responsible citizenship. Marvellous as the development of the united States has been during the century that is now closing, greater destinies are yet to be realised. Our task in furthering the civilisation of the world is to be a large and responsible one; no other nation can assume it for us or perform it if we fail. Delicate as our international relations have been during our attempt to establish a secure republic in a world of monarchies, they are to be more delicate and more difficult in the near future when the European powers attempt to rectify their colonial boundaries. Complicated as our financial problems have already been, they will hereafter call for greater wisdom than has been bestowed upon them hitherto.

> Difficult as has been the attempt to organize efficient, economical, and honest municipal government for cities numbering millions of inhabitants, the difficult will continue to increase as population grows and wealth accumulates. Neither good luck nor any mere intuition of common-sense will enable us to maintain the reality of republican freedom unless we have other resources to draw upon. Besides common-sense and energy, we must have knowledge, training, and an unselfish devotion to the cause of human progress.
>
> It is certain, however, that schools and colleges cannot furnish detailed courses in all branches of economic, legal, and political science. The field is too vast and the years of study are too brief. To a majority of teachers the alternative seems to be to give either a thorough course in some one subject - Political Economy, for example - or a superficial course in many subjects, including "Civics" (or Elementary Constitutional Law), Inernational Law and Political Ethics.
>
> In the judgment of the present writer, it would be wise to devote a large part of the time available for such disciplines to a careful study of the nature and laws of human society. This study would familiarise the pupil with the principal forms of social organisation; with the thoughts, the sympathies, the purposes, and the virtues that make society possible; with the benefits that society confers; and with the conduct that worthy membership of society requires. These are the facts and principles that underlie all details of law and politics, all sound political economy, and all public morality. Well instructed in these matters, the student is fitted to continue his study of society and public policy throughout life. Without this foundation, no acquaintance with legal or historical detail can give him a comprehensive grasp of social relations.'

This view seems to me, still in 1970, totally correct, and it will be a marvellous day when 'progressive' educationalists not only catch up with this seventy-years-old opinion, but also take the trouble to acquaint themselves with the sociological perspectives on which it was based.

Giddings, then, was one of the early Americans who contributed clearly and substantially to the making of sociology. In his work could be clearly seen the critical digestion of the ideas of the European scholars in the ongoing effort to lay the firm foundations of the subject. And in his work could be clearly seen, also, the strong, consistent, and very clearly stated perspective of 'Evolution, Knowledge and Conscious Control' which was basic in, and common to, other American writers. Our discussion of the work of Ward, Summer and Giddings has, I believe, been sufficient to make this shared position clear beyond any kind of doubt of ambiguity. We have seen, too, the firm beginnings of the concern for the study of the psychological aspects of society which was to be continued by American scholars, and developed more exactingly later; and we have seen too, the clear insight as to the central importance of values in society: a theme which I shall press again and again. A final point we might note in the supreme clarity of the American writers. They escaped all the befogged ambiguities of writers like Marx and Engels; they eschewed all metaphysical assertiveness; but they were no less forthright in stating their intellectual persuasions and humane commitments. We shall see later that this was a quality in which they compared very favourably with some European scholars; but, alas, it is almost as though some recent American sociologists have made their chief objective the transportation of European fogs back into America. The light has been obscured - to say the least.

D. SUMMARY OF THE EARLY AMERICANS

Despite their independence of mind, their differential treatment of certain aspects of the subject, their introduction of different concepts and terms, the great unity of conception of the early American sociologists has become convincingly clear in these brief studies of them. This is especially so when it is borne in mind that we have considered both the 'right' and the 'left' wing of the subject, so to speak. Lester Ward was forthright in his advocacy of 'collectivisation'; the improvement of the administrative processes of the modern state, and, supremely, the state provision of education as the basic means of democratic progress. Sumner was very much, by contrast, of a 'laissez faire' persuasion. However, we have seen that common conception and a common concern underlay these apparent differences. On all fundamentals of both sociological analysis and the criteria of 'progress', they were agreed. We have seen, too, how these American scholars drew upon the work of the Europeans, critically assessing these basic contributions, and building them constructively into their own systems of thought and analysis. The cumulative, co-operative task of the making of sociology was well exemplified in their work.

It has also become quite apparent how, within the context of their agreement with the over-all perspectives of the Europeans, the Americans made quite distinctive contributions. Their perfect clarity concerning distinctions which men like Marx left clouded in ambiguity - such as that between 'genetic' and 'teleological' kinds of causation; their detailed and systematic analysis of the nature and types of 'social action' and of the 'psychological aspects of the society', their fundamental clarity of understanding that the 'social order' of men's practical activities and social relationships was essentially a moral order, an order of values; and their efforts to organize and present sociology as a 'subject' of crucial importance in education: all these have been seen quite clearly. And we may perhaps remark, too, that it has become quite plain how, with this great clarity of important distinctions, the Americans were able to adopt just as radical a position as any of the European scholars with regard to social reform and social action whilst avoiding the extremes into which some of these fell, and which held so much of intellectual and social error and danger. The early Americans embraced the earlier and contemporary nineteenth century contributions to the making of sociology, and then took the subject distinctively further - both in rounding it out as a whole system of analysis, and in deepening it by adding more detailed explorations of particular dimensions within it.

Again, for our own particular purposes of clarifying the foundations of the subject, and seeing the wide and cumulative agreement of all these nineteenth-century scholars, let us attempt a clear summary statement of the ideas of the Americans which we have traced.

Scientific Knowledge: A Clear Delimitation

Ward, Sumner and Giddings obviously agreed completely, both with each other and with the Europeans we have mentioned, that theological and metaphysical speculation had had their day in the pursuit of testable knowledge about our experience of the world, and that only the methods of science were productive of such knowledge. Again, this was not a claim of arrogance, but a claim of modesty: that we could only lay claim to knowledge within clearly delimited bounds. They were just as definite as the varying kinds of European 'positivism' in this; insisting, indeed, that science required a fundamental reorientation in men's attitudes of mind towards acquiring knowledge about nature and society, and considerable effort in coming to the adoption of new and unfamiliar perspective (e.g., as in the enormous time-scale of evolution). They agreed, too, that the adoption of scientific method was a matter of necessity as well as of intellectual interest, in that science alone could provide a reliable basis for prediction and action. The following were some of the characteristics of science on which their agreement was unquestionably clear and firm.

(a) *The Detailed Study of Facts*

Science was, first of all, essentially empirical. It required a detailed and painstaking description and analysis of the facts. Knowledge was not to be had easily, in 'a priori' fashion, but had to be gained by careful empirical study.

(b) *The Elucidation of Laws*

Science was not confined to a bit-and-piece amassing of facts, however. It focused upon the resemblances and differences among things, and sought to establish generalisation, or laws: which were uniformities or regularities of contiguity, order, sequence, in the relations among things.

(c) *The Delimitation of Theories: Verification*

Science also proposed theories to 'explain' these regularities; but these theories differed from other philosophical speculations in that they were deliberately submitted to procedures and criteria of testability. This was their one ground of reliability. They did not seek to go beyond it.

(d) *Each Science: a Distinctive Subject-matter*

Each particular science was defined by its distinctive subject-matter; its 'unit of investigation' which was distinguished from the concerns of other sciences. Having clarified its unit of investigation, each science sought to describe and analyse its appropriate field of 'facts', and to state and explain generalisations about them.

(e) *Prediction and Control*

Theories about generalizations about facts, of this kind, formed the most reliable basis of prediction which could be achieved, and therefore the most reliable basis of guidance for action. And, as we have seen, the Americans made much of the control of the natural by the artificial which knowledge made possible. Any science, then, had its pure and applied aspects.

(f) *A Science of Man and Society*

With all these points in mind, the Americans were agreed that anything that could be called a reliable knowledge of the nature of man and society could only be achieved by applying these methods in the study of man and society to as exacting a degree as was possible. They were all agreed therefore on the necessity and value of trying to create a reliable science of society: Sociology.

It will be readily seen that all these points were in agreement in every respect with those outlined and adopted by the Europeans.

Nature, Man, Society: Evolution and Progress: Over-all Perspectives

The early Americans were also agreed in accepting the over-all perspective of 'evolution' as the correct context in which to couch all scientific studies. Again, it is important to see that this was far from being just an acceptance of the biological theory of evolution. It was, exactly as with Spencer, a much broader cosmological view of the emergence and transformation of all the 'forms' of nature. It saw all 'forms' as particular patterns of growth, adaptation, transformation within specific environmental contexts: so that it was, at once, a way of comprehending and explaining both 'order' and 'change': indeed, kinds of order were kinds of change, which could themselves change in accordance with changes in internal or external conditions. All so-called 'objects' or 'entities' in nature were thus seen essentially as processes. Again, the similarity with Marx's 'Dialectical Materialism' is readily apparent. The following were important aspects of this over-all perspective accepted by the Americans.

(a) *The Context of Evolution: Nature and Man*

Man was esstentially seen as a being who had emerged out of the complexities of an earlier and almost immeasurably long process of physical and biological evolution. A 'casual explanation' of the emergence of man had, therefore, to be sought in these earlier processes of evolution. Such an account was necessary for any accurate understanding of those biological and psychological characteristics of man which underlay, and necessitated, his own particular kinds of social activity. The origins of society were therefore also seen within this evolutionary context, and, furthermore, the ongoing nature of society was thought to be essentially historical and developmental: a process of cumulative achievement, of adaptation and transformation in meeting changing conditions. The time-scale of human and social development was therefore seen to be very large, involving far greater periods of groping, trial-and-error attempts to deal with the world, and far greater details and complexities of social development than had been assumed in earlier doctrines of human nature. Man and society could only properly be understood within this larger context of 'nature' - which was, itself, a vast interwoven fabric of order, change and transformation. This was the new and true perspective.

(b) *Evolution: The Relations Between the Sciences*

As with the earlier thinkers, so the Americans held that all the sciences could be classified, or be seen to fall into a systematic arrangement, in that each of them was devoted to one defined area of subject-matter within the entirety of evolution. The sciences were therefore not arbitrary, but each came into existence to study a distinctive range of facts within this entirety, so that all of them together provided an entire schema of knowledge.

(c) *The Material Basis of Human Society: Men's Practical Activities*

The Americans also accepted in a very real and down-to-earth sense, that man - emerging as one species among others in the physical context of nature - had to make his society by working upon the material resources of the world. Everything that man had to do - from winning his livelihood to organizing armies and governments and religions - necessitiated practical acticities in relation to other men and to nature. Furthermore, all these activities were undertaken for practical advantage. The evolutionary perspective therefore entailed a materialist basis for the social activities of man, and this was a continuous accompaniment of all social evolution, development and progress.

(d) *The Distinction Between Nature and Man: The Genetia and the Telelogical: The Implications for Kinds of 'Casual Explanation'*

Even so, the American sociologists escaped the 'reductionist' error of a 'materialist' explanation of human society (of a meta-physical kind) such as Engels and Marx had put forward. The distinction was clearly drawn between 'genetic' or 'efficient' causation among factors which were blindly involved in material processes (and which interacted unconsciously with each other), and 'teleological causation - when men consciously apprehended certain ends, and in the light of many considerations, deliberately employed a certain set of means to achieve them. Human activity (actions as distinct from the occurrences of events) was predominantly 'teleological' - and therefore 'casual explanations' of human society were different from those of 'nature'. A science of man and society had to incorporate conception, elements, methods, criteria of observation, interpretation, etc., which were different from those of the 'natural' sciences.

Within the over-all evolutionary perspective, therefore, important distinctions of level (of both fact and methods of study and explanation) were clearly and carefully made.

Sociology: the Science of Society

The Americans' conception of the nature and elements of Sociology can, perhaps best be summarised by tracing them from the way in which they saw human activities as being rooted in this larger evolutionary order of the nature of things.

(a) *Necessity: Practical Activities and Practical Advantage*

Men's activities were, primarily, necessitous in the sense of having to grapple with the life-conditions which nature set in such a way as to ensure survival. A rigorous necessity lay at the heart of the origins of human society. The needs which men had as well as the conditions which they confronted were implanted by nature; and the drive of necessity made the success of practical activities imperative.

These activities aimed essentially at practical advantage, and included men's accommodation to each other, as well as to the forces and resources of nature. Material necessity and practical activity therefore lay at the basis of human society. Even at this very basic level, however, the Americans saw that this was a new level of mental and purposive activity in nature, and that in pursuing advantage, it contained, essentially and implicitly, right at the outset, the drive towards 'progress'.

(b) *Populations in their Environments: Ecology*

Human activities were never those of individuals isolated in nature: they were always activities of groups or populations, the members of which, experiencing conflict and co-operation, were unified with a certain 'consciousness of kind', and were thus involved in an interconnected 'whole' of relationships in meeting their collective destiny. Two basic facts which underlay any human society, therefore, were the population and the environment in relation to which it had to build its life. The scientific study of society necessarily involved demographic and ecological aspects. Societies should always be seen within their environmental conditions.

(c) *Population: Size and Quality*

The study of a population should include both its quantitative and qualitative characteristics. The size of population in relation to its environmental resources had important bearings upon its division of labour and other institutional arrangements. But also, a total population might be 'composed' or groups possessing qualitative differences. This qualitative 'composition' should be studies. And, over-all, the population would contain different 'classes' - in terms of ability and potential capacities of different kinds - which had relevance to the emergence of élites and many other aspects of social organisation.

In all societies, questions of population and ecology were of fundamental importance and the study of them was therefore a basic part of sociological analysis.

(d) *The 'GENETIC' Development of Social Systems: the Laying Down of a Social Order*

Although human activities were distinctively purposive, the American sociologists were far from believing that the making of human societies was a matter of purely rational construction. They held that over the greater part of human history, the knowledge of men was slight, erroneous, fragmentary, clouded with many kinds of ideological misconception and that human activities were necessarily of a slow, groping, trial-and-error kind. Nonetheless, the many practical activities of men, resting on their rudimentary knowledge, gave rise to interdependent systems of 'folkways' and 'mores' which possessed credence and authority. In this process of social accommodation, it was also the case that though the many activities of men - each in its own way - were 'teleological' aiming at practical advantage, the interests of men terminated in their attainment of particular advantages, whereas their many achievements would have unintended consequences upon others, on themselves, and on the nature of social relationships, going beyond this. Because of the necessary degrees of interdependence of social relationships, there would also be - in the adjustments of these unintended consequences - a strain towards consistency; so that an over-all system of relationships, a social order as a whole, with its own 'ethos', would arise. In this way there had been and there was always likely to be, a complex process of genetic development, and genetic causation, in the laying down of the order of social systems, even though human activity was distinctively teleological.

In the study of this changing order (the factors making for innovation, change, conflict and the factors making for accommodation interdependency, and social consistency) an 'equilibrium-disequilibrium' analysis was necessary. And it was important to bear in mind that, permeating this entire genetic development, there was this strain towards practical advantage; the 'strain towards improvement'. In short, there was still a progressive, teleological strand within the many-dimensioned genetic process.

(e) *Teleological Developments within the Genetic Social Order: Reconstruction and Progress in the Light of Knowledge and Criticism*

Within the onging complexity of any social order, the Americans held that 'teleological' direction, always implicit, could become increasingly explicit, effective, and dominant as knowledge grew and the criticism of traditional ways of doing things developed accordingly. In the light of more exact knowledge, nature could be more successfully controlled by artifice, and greater practical advantage could be achieved. Progress could be deliberately planned and made.

Out of an earlier genetically created social order in which adaptation to necessitous conditions was predominant, grew an increasingly teleological social order, consciously directed, in which the active transformation of both the natural and social environment was predominant. The evolution of society grew from a predominantly genetic to an increasingly teleological condition—and the acquisition and dissemination of knowledge was the central factor in this process, coupled with the application of this knowledge of the form of inventions. This embraced not only the purely technical activities of men, but also their improvement of social institutions, so that this continued improvement by the artificial control of the natural, was an activitiy of re-making the whole social order. Throughout, then, sociology was a study of the interdependent achievements of human activity. Social evolution was essentially a process of interconnected development (i.e., a cumulative advance upon earlier achievements) and it rested upon a progressive drive and intention.

(f) *Social Statics: The Analysis of Society*

In addition to the study of population and their environments, and this conception of the evolution of society in this entire evolutionary context, the Americans provided a very clear analysis of the nature and elements of Social Systems. Societies were seen as entire systems of interconnected activities, relationships, values, ideas, etc. , and the following components were thought to be essential for a full description and analysis of them, and as a basis for possible theories about them.

(I) *A Structural Functional Analysis*

The patterned relationships to be observed in a society could be analysed in terms of their structure (i.e., the form, regularity or pattern of organisation which they assumed) and the functions which they performed (i.e., in seeking to fulfil certain purposes, satisfy certain needs, operate interdependently with other institutions, etc.). The entire network of society could thus be analysed in terms of family and kinship groups, the division of labour and property relations, law, government, religion, education and the like. Again, we might remind ourselves of Ward's castigation of the 'error of the stationary'. This analysis did not at all imply a static view of society; it was simply a way of analysing the order of society which was essentially a process of activities.

(II) *Order and Change*

Social institutions were developed achievements, and therefore continuity and change were essential characteristics of them. The study of order and of change were therefore parts of the same study, and the structural-functional analysis of institutions was part of a historical analysis. This perspective of process, order, change, development was a necessary accompaniment of structural-functional analysis. There was not, in the slightest degree, any opposition between them.

(III) *Conflict and Co-operation*

Similarly the order of society, though manifesting systematic interconnection, interdependency, and even possessing an over-all 'ethos' did not at all imply a satisfactory order, or a harmonious order in the sense of possessing no characteristics of conflict and pressure for change. On the contrary, the order of a whole society was the outcome of a necessary blend of continuing elements of both conflict and co-operation. In all their many-sided activities and diverse interests, men were bound to experience both; and the order of society was an outcome of reciprocal accommodation among many groups élites, and masses, and many conflicting interests. The structural-functional analysis, and the historical analysis of order and change, assumed, therefore, a continuous experience in societies of conflict and co-operation, and were designed to provide a description and possible explanation of them. Like order and change, conflict and co-operation, properly understood, were two sides of the same coin.

(IV) *From 'Folkways' and 'Mores' to Institutions, Associations and Law*

This analysis of structure-function, order-change, conflict-co-operation, was able to encompass and fully take into account the complex 'genetic' development of social regularities (the systems of 'folkways' and 'mores'), and the more deliberately 'teleological' forms of social regularity (specific institutions and the consciously contrived constitutions and laws that accompanied them). We need not elaborate on this but might only note that this had its importance both for fullness of analysis of any particular society (i.e., in ensuring that all kinds and levels of social regularity were taken into account), and for developmental perspective (i.e., in that 'teleological' institutions could be seen within their earlier 'genetic' contexts, etc.). We may note, too, that this distinction was, of course, not so starkly simple as this summary form of statement implies. Distinctions were also drawn even among institutions - e.g., the 'crescive' and 'enacted' institutions of Sumner, which took the same emphasis of analysis further.

(V) *The Organizational Analysis of Institutions*

In connection with the emergence of more formal 'institutions' or 'associations' it is worth our while to note that the Americans deepended, and made more specific, their 'structural-functional' analysis by making very clear indeed how they would analyse these more complicated forms of social organisation. Sumner, for example, analysed institutions in terms of their concepts (purposes, doctrines, etc.) their structural apparatus, their defined set of functionaries, their prescribed rules, and their organised instrumentalities for achieving the interests of their members. Giddings analysed them in terms of their purposes or functions, their constitutions (for the performance of the functions), their compositions of members in terms of categories and appropriate qualities, the plan of organisation and authority, including any sub-groups, committees, etc.

This was an agreed system of analysis completely clear, and we shall later see how it cropped up in the literature of the twentieth century.

(VI) *Social Action and Types of Social Action*

Since 'action' was of a teleological nature, and quite different from a simple 'occurrence of events', it was necessary, however, to go beyond the structural-functional and historical description of social regularities, and to seek a casual explanation in terms of the understanding of the ends which men sought and the means which they employed to attain them. In short Sociology had to include the understanding and explanation of social action as a special and distinctive component of anlaysis if it was to achieve a full and satisfactory account of its distinctive subject-matter. Distinctive - in that this 'teleological' level of mind in deliberate action which was characteristic of man, did not apply to any other 'phenomena' of nature.

The study of social action was therefore, according to the Americans, an essential and distinctive component of sociology additional to the structural-functional and historical analysis of institutions. As we know, they elaborated this in much detail and clarified certain 'types' of social action - the Impulsive, the Traditional, the Rational - which, again, were 'models' for the interpretation of observed historical changes and tendencies.

(VII) *The Psychological Aspects of Society*

Closely related to this concern for the understanding of purposive social action was also, of course, the importance which the Americans attached to the study of the psychological dimensions of society, and here they laid the foundations for several clear and interesting directions of enquiry. Here, we need only note what these were, but again it is worthwhile to remind ourselves that the early Americans saw no gulf whatever between psychology and sociology; between the study of the individual and the study of society. On the contrary, they saw the study of man and society as a science which necessarily embraced both psychological and societal elements; and furthermore they saw perfectly plainly, as the theorists from Comte to Marx had done, that it was impossible to study man the individual excepting in the context of his social influences: or, to put it differently, that the very dichotomy between individual and society was highly dubious. For the moment, however, we can simply note that the Americans distinguished at least five clear ways in which psychological considerations should form a part of sociological analysis.

PSYCHOLOGICAL FORCES: FROM INDIVIDUAL MOTIVES TO SOCIAL 'CONATION'

Firstly, they saw clearly that psychology was necessary for a knowledge of some of the basic motives which were characteristic of human nature and which underlay much social action. Sumner had spoken, for example, of certain instincts and basic motives of hunger, sex, vanity, and fear, and

Ward and Giddings held similar positions. But also, they were aware that in the many collective influences of social life, conative 'drives', public urges, demands and currents of feeling could be engendered which might, or might not, be connected with basic individual motives, but which certainly possessed powers and qualities going beyond them. Society, in short, was creative of group psychological qualities and purposes which required study.

PSYCHOLOGY AND SOCIAL ACTION

The Americans were also very clear that human psychology, just as human sociology, could never satisfactorily be framed in terms of 'genetic' or 'efficient' causation. Human beings acted (deliberately, exercising choices with ends in mind) and therefore the psychological as well as the societal dimensions of human activities needed to be couched in terms of 'teleological' understanding. For the Americans, then the understanding of social action and psychological explanations were very closely allied.

THE PSYCHOLOGICAL ASPECTS OF INSTITUTIONAL MEMBERSHIP AND SOCIAL RELATIONSHIPS

The Americans also saw clearly that some psychological qualities (of experience and conduct) among individuals, which were of importance for the understanding of their social action, were actually brought about by the structures of group relationships and the requirements of the membership and tasks of institutions. Giddings, for example, showed how different groups and institutions actually engendered, as well as drew upon, differing kinds of 'like-mindedness' or 'consciousness of kind'; and showed also how important these were for explaining the nature and solidarity and boundaries of groups. Sumner, too, in his analysis of 'In-Group' and 'Out-Group' tendencies, showed how group conditions could create collective (and thus individual) psychological qualities. Indeed, Sumner discussed the ways in which a collective 'Ethos' arose in a society as a whole, and which then formed a part of every individual person's private experience.

SOCIETY AND 'SELF'

This leads us directly to the fourth point: that the Americans (and especially, here, in the work of Giddings) saw and explored more clearly and deeply than those before them, the intricate relations between social (or associational) influences and the actual formation of the individual personality and character.

CHARACTER AND SOCIAL STRUCTURE

Similarly, the Americans produced a more detailed analysis than others of the relationships between character and exposure to particular kinds of social structure that John Stuart Mill had in mind in his insistence upon the importance of 'Ethology'.

All these 'psychological aspects' of society, of course, were closely connected in the thinking of the American sociologists, but they are sufficiently important to distinguish, and it is at least sufficiently clear for our purpose that the Americans did much to emphasise, elaborate, and show the worth of these psychological dimensions of sociological anlysis, and began a direction of work for which American sociology has been distinguished ever since.

(VIII) *'Classes' and Elites*

We should note briefly, too, that in their analysis of social systems as wholes, the Americans not only did not neglect to take into account conflict as well as co-operation, they also did not fail to take into account the analysis of 'classes' of ability in the population of a society and the attendant analysis of élites. This included the more ordinary examination of hierarchical organisation in society, the formation of socio-economic classes', etc.; but it also dealt with the difficult questions of ranges of ability in society and what this entailed for issues of government, democracy, education. The impassioned concern of all of them for education - especially of Ward and Giddings - is enough to show that this concern for 'differentials' of ability by no means entailed any 'reactionary' attitudes of mind towards social inequalities.

(IX) *The Central Importance of 'Values' in Society: The Social Order Essentially a Moral Order*

A final component of sociological analysis on which all laid emphasis was this insistence that values lay at the heart of the institutional fabric of society. Though insisting quite firmly upon the basic importance of practical activities for pratical advantage in society, the Americans never lost sight of the fact that these activities were nonetheless purposive, that they gave rise to reciprocal accommodations of interest and the accompanying development of obligations in the regulation of relationships, and furthermore, that they carried with them certain standards and qualities of human character. The fabric of society was in large part a fabric of material and practical activity, but, at one and the same time, it was a moral order. In this realm of the values at the heart of the folkways and institutions, as in all other kinds of activity, the Americans saw a rationally clarified, and consciously sought, moral order of society arising out of the 'genetic', rule-of-thumb values which had been established earlier. Moral progress as well as technical progress found its clear place in their analysis of social systems.

These, then, were the major components in their analysis of the nature of society.

(g) *Social Dynamic: Evolution, Development, Progress*

We have said enough of the way in which, using this system of analysis, the American sociologists went about their comparative and historical study of actual societies and attempted to frame theories and interpretations of social change. For the sake of summary completeness, however, the following clear points ought to be noted.

(I) *Evolution: A Casual Historical Analysis*

Firstly, like Spencer, the Americans did not employ the concept of 'evolution' as a naive, all-embracing descriptive term which was vacuous as far as explanatory worth was concerned; or simple-minded in postulating anything like 'unilinear', 'inevitable' sequences and the like. They analysed the processes of evolutionary change in terms of the factors which came into play when societies met the changing challenges of their environments. They gave casual accounts of kinds and directions of growth; process of differentiation and integration; specific developments in the division of labour, property, class exploitation, education, etc.; processes of invention and innovation; and kinds of influences operating between societies - conquest, trade, assimilation, syncretism, and so on. Evolution was not a simple-minded 'blanket-term' by any means, but a conception of a complex process which yielded a detailed causal and historical analysis.

(II) *Classification and Comparative Studies*

As with the European scholars, the American sociologists saw clearly, and employed fully, the necessary method - in generalising about social change - of classifying 'types' of society in accordance with certain criteria, and undertaking, in the light of such a classification, detailed comparative and historical studies.

(III) *Typologies : of Social Action; of Social Orders*

Similarly, we have seen how the Americans constructed 'models' or 'types' of society in the light of which they were able to interpret and understand observed regularities of change. The 'Impulsive, Traditional and Rational' types of social action were, as we shall see, almost exactly those later constructed by Max Weber. The 'Theological, Metaphysical and Scientific' types of tradition were clearly the three types ('stages') of social order proposed by Comte. The 'Military-Religious', the 'Liberal-Legal' and the 'Economic-Ethical' types of society were almost exactly the same as Spencer's 'Militant, Industrial and Ethical' types. And these 'typologies' were used in exactly the same interpretive way in illuminating sequences of change in 'Social Dynamics'.

(IV) *A Perspective for Action*

Finally, it is perfectly clear how the Americans found, in classifying these sociological perspectives, a clear perspective for judgment and action in their own time, in relation to their own problems. But this leads to a concluding emphasis.

(h) ***Sociology for use***

The early Americans, just as directly and forthrightly as their European counterparts, had crucially in mind the perspective of the modern world which we emphasised at the outset and from which the work of Comte sprang at the beginning. They too were clear-sightedly concerned with the modern disruption of all the traditional orders of societies of the past, and the complex problems born of rapid scientific, technological, industrial and urban change. They were equally aware that these problems would not be resloved without political effort, and without the achievement of a reliable body of knowledge on which the making of social policies could rest. Again, then, we see the making of sociology at the heart of a concern for the re-making of society. The making of sociology was for human use.

In this, the Americans pressed, if anything, further than the Europeans who had influenced them, though their effort was exactly of the same kind. They advocated a new approach to the provision of an informed art of administration, resting on the scientific study of society. They advocated a positive approach to the provision of education for all by the State. And they were foremost in trying to introduce sociology as a subject at various levels of education, and in trying to 'organise' it effectively and persuasively for these teaching purposes.

The early American, then, of great stature and interest in their own right, stood four-square with the European scholars in laying the foundations of sociology, and our study of them demonstrates to the hilt the great cumulative agreement which characterised the efforts to create the subject during the nineteenth century. Their work demonstrated that, by the end of the century, the clear construction of an entire conspectus of the subject had indeed been successfully accomplished.

E. THE PERSPECTIVE OF PROGRESS : A FINAL NOTE

Before leaving this study of the early Americans, there is one further comment I would like to make, which, to me, is of considerable interest and possibly of the very greatest importance in connection with their quite central insistence on the idea of 'progress'. We have already noted their rejection of the 'error of the stationary' when insisting on the necessity of 'structural-functional' analysis; and we have seen, too, that their awareness of the 'teleological' characteristics of human 'action' led them wisely to avoid what we might call the 'error of psychology' : the error of assuming that human experience and behaviour in society could be exhaustively explained in terms of 'efficient' causation. Though concerning themselves very much with the psychological aspects of men's individual and social behaviour, they clearly and carefully introduced, in addition, the teleological 'understanding of social action'. But as well as all this, I would like to suggest that they also exposed with great clarity what I want to call later, the 'error of social anthropology'.

This is what I have in mind, though here I will make the point only briefly.

We have seen that all the nineteenth-century sociologists we have considered - from Comte to Giddings - adopted the evolutionary context for understanding the emergence and development of societies, and, more than this, that they insisted upon the centrality, within this context, of the drive towards progress. Of them all, the American writers, with their distinction between the 'genetic' and the teleological', were perhaps most clear. And certain aspects of the central place attributed to 'progress' within sociological analysis deserve to be made absolutely clear; indeed must be made clear if we are going to have correct perspectives later.

This idea of progress' went far beyond the simple notion of evaluating certain social changes in the light of adopted ethical principles - in the sense that Spencer, for example, held that a laissezfaire' or 'liberal' industrial society was 'better' than a militant society, or that Marx held that a 'collectivised' society was an 'improvement' upon industrial capitalism. It was far more that this. It really stemmed from the insistence that, even in the most simple social conditions known to us, human action was 'purposive'; deliberately undertaking consciously directed actions to achieve clearly apprehended ends; and that, as such, it was a category quite distinct from other events of nature, and even other animal behaviour. This meant that all the practical activities of men aimed at practical advantage, and that, therefore, even in the earliest groping through experience towards more accurate knowledge, the selection of those activities which yielded the greater advantage, clearly implied a drive towards progress (a 'strain towards improvement' as Sumner put it).

The 'functions' of the inventions, folkways, mores, institutions which men developed were therefore nothing mysterious. They were the fulfilments of human intentions and purposes. Now the Americans (and all others) certainly held that a great part of the development of human societies, a very long period of the laying down of established social order, had its genetic aspects; but, even here, there was nothing mysterious (or hidden, in any obscure way) in mind. The fundamental conception here was - among all the theorists - that of unintended consequences. Men sought their own interests teleologically; but (a) their interests frequently only went as far as the successful attainment of their own purposes (they were not necessarily concerned with all the effects of their activities upon others), and (b) they did not foresee all the consequences of their actions - whether upon others, upon themselves, or upon existing relationships and institutions. In short, even the 'genetic' processes of society were pervaded by 'teleological' activities - conscious, purposive, social creativity; in was only that knowledge, foresight and degrees of conscious control over nature and society were limited.

Sociology, as all these nineteenth century scholars conceived it, took the 'simpler' or 'primitive' societies into account, as we have seen, but saw them as 'limited' terms of knowledge and its application; in terms of the control over the natural by the artificial. The 'historical' civilisations, in which literacy, numeracy, the systematic acquisition, dissemination, and application of knowledge, enormously improved men's control over nature and their practical advantage, were seen as developments from the primitive, over the primitive, and as 'progressive' in their successful extension of control. The extension of knowledge and reason were thus central in achieving a progress which had always been implicit in the purposive activity and endeavour of men from the beginning. This perspective was perfectly plain.

Now what I wish to argue here is this. Throughout its creation during the nineteenth century, Sociology was conceived as the scientific study of social systems, among which were included the 'simpler' or 'primitive' societies. These societies, as all others, were seen as manifestations of the purposive activities of populations in seeking practical advantages within their environments. They were held to be 'primitive' or 'limited', not in that their social and psychological processes were entirely different in kind from those of other societies, but only in that their knowledge was such as to give them such limited control over nature by artifice and invention that they were relatively 'arrested' in a certain condition of adaptation to their environments, and did not manifest the more complex patterns of growth, change, development, differentiation such as were manifested in the cumulative historical societies. In this sense, they remained predominantly in the 'genetic' condition, and all the more complex patterns of increasingly exercised 'teleological' social change and development were to be found in the historical civilisations. The 'simpler' societies therefore formed a limited part of sociology, and exemplified these simpler 'genetic' levels of adaptation. The greater part of sociology was concerned with the more complex patterns of society once mind, knowledge and its purposive power had risen above, and grown beyond, these simpler levels.

In this sense, Ward - especially - saw the simpler societies as being a very limited part of Sociology; thinking indeed, that they really formed a part of 'Anthropology' (i.e., then - physical and cultural anthropology; not - social anthropology) as constituting examples of human groups who had grappled with the task of establishing their 'place in nature' only to a limited extent. They constituted social systems resting upon limited achievements of knowledge and technical and institutional kinds of control. The study of them could not be expected to contribute beyond a certain point to the understanding and explanation of the more complex, historical societies, in which the 'teleological' powers of men were so greatly extended. Sociology was predominantly faced, then, with the study of this far larger and more complex fabric of men's societal achievements.

One other point needs great emphasis. All these founders of sociology - seeing the study of the simpler societies within their entire conspectus; readily insisting upon the great importance of the long 'genetic' periods in the gradual making of societies and social traditions; readily seeing that social systems came to assume a shape appropriate to functional adaptation by means of 'hidden consequences' and institutional adjustments as well as by conscious intention - nonetheless not only insisted that the activities of men in the simpler societies were pervaded by teleological dimensions, but also that the pattern of social custom which had come to exist in them could certainly not be taken to be harmonious social patterns (possessing no sources or kinds of conflict); functionally satisfactory social patterns; or even correct social pattern (possessing no possible grounds for social change). On the contrary, these social patterns were seen as the continuing fabric of traditional ways of dealing with conflict as well as co-operation, and as seeking practical advantage - prone to change continuously as 'life conditions' changed. In short, then, the 'simpler' societies were a process of development at their own level. It was simply a limited level. But the fact that they accomplished a certain adaptation to any given life-conditions did not at all mean that they were completely articulated, functionally integrated, systems containing no inadequacies, no conflicts, no rough edges or loose ends, no room for or potentialities for change.

I hope my insistence on this one point will be forgiven; but my concern is this. I want to insist upon the argument as fully and consistently as I can : (a) that the evolutionary and 'progressive' perspective of the founders of sociology was perfectly clear, (b) that it was correct, and did not suffer the supposed errors of false ethical evaluation with which it has been charged, and (c) that the introduction of a supposedly new subject - 'Social' Anthropology' in the early twentieth century has been such as to create grave error and to intrude (or re-intrude) false conceptions, false perspectives, and new mystifications - both philosophical and factual, which have filled the study of society with unnecessary and misleading confusions. Later, I shall argue that 'Social Anthropology' was no more than the discovery and use by physical and cultural anthropologists of Sociology; but that, in applying sociological analysis to the study of the simpler, non-literate societies, the earlier well worked out perspective of sociology was lost sight of; the distinction between 'genetic' and 'teleological' was ignored; the limited degree of application of 'structural-functional' analysis was ignored (indeed its assumptions became absurdly inflated); the fact that societies were essentially processes of development was to an astonishing degree overlooked; and the proper perspective of the study of these societies within the wider comparative studies of other types of society was simply no considered or taken into account. The distinctive kinds of explanation and understanding in terms of men's conscious purposes, which the Americans especially (but others also) had made so scrupulously clear, were abandoned in a new fog of purely 'genetic' explanations in terms of 'efficient' causes, and something called 'functional' explanation - which, fantastic though it seems - was thought to be new. What I am saying is that the supposed novelty of Social Anthropology in the early twentieth century was bogus. And it was not only bogus, but misleading in its errors of omission (in not seeing certain fundamental philosophical distinctions which had already been made clear) and of over-emphasis (i.e., on 'genetic' rather than 'teleological' explanations.) Rather like some psycho-analysts who, burrowing into the dark night of unconscious motives, derogated altogether the rational deliberations and conscious choices of men; so some Social Anthropologists burrowed into a dark night of hidden functions, latent functions, underlying functions, derogating almost entirely the conscious pursuit of ends. A new, retrogressive, 'genetic' metaphysics fell upon us, resting upon a revived notion of 'determinism' - long ago exploded by John Stuart Mill.

With one isolated bit of sociological analysis in their pockets (i.e., structural-functional analysis), made up into a little guidebook for research by Malinowski, the Social Anthropologists ceased to read - whether in the British Museum or at the London School of Economics - and, instead, rode out on bicycles in their white duck suits, to look at men in huts. Now looking at men in huts can certainly be exciting, and it can certainly provide testable knowledge about men in huts; but the persuasion that, excepting within the context of comparative and historical sociology, it can provide more than a limited knowledge of the nature of societies and social processes is an illusion. This fog of error has become so thick that, now-a-days, people have come to speak about the distinction between the 'anthropological' approach and the 'sociological' approach, and about the 'relations between' social anthropology and sociology, whereas, in fact, there is nothing to talk about here at all - except confusion; a confusion inflated by professionals, and misunderstood by ill-informed editors of popular social-science journals and television production.

I have taken this point a little further than I had intended at this stage, but I think it is right to do so. To note it clearly, forcefully, now, will help much more than now seems apparent when we come to disentangle the various 'developments' of sociology in our next section. However, for the moment, we must leave it. It is enough to have seen very clearly that - in addition to the 'consensus' of agreement among the Americans, and between them and the European scholars - there was this quite central dimension of the 'progressive' within the evolutionary and developmental perspective of the changing nature of societies; that this position was very clearly stated and there was much to be said for it; and that much interesting controversy ensued when this perspective came to be forgotten, ignored, or, too brashly, overlooked. But these fireworks of controversy - we must come back to later: and with relish!

Meanwhile, we are now able to move to our conclusions about the nineteenth century 'foundations' in the making of sociology.

5

THE FOUNDATIONS OF SOCIOLOGY: A SUMMARY STATEMENT OF NINETEENTH CENTURY AGREEMENTS

We have now surveyed the major contributions to the making of sociology during the nineteenth century. We have studied the chief theoretical systems produced by scholars in Continental Europe, Britain and the United States and, by this time, their wide-ranging agreement about the nature and elements of the subject, and its importance for both understanding and dealing with the problems which men faced in the period of modern science and industrialisation, must be clear beyond doubt.

Our practice of summarizing the work of each man, or group of men, at the end of our study of them, must have been cumulative evidence of this agreement, and, indeed, must have demonstrated the large extent to which there was cumulative argument and collective achievement among them all. From Comte to the Americans, it has become clear that the basic elements of the new science were conceived to be the same. This is so clear that it would be unduly tedious to go over the entire range of agreements again in an attempt to dovetail them too closely.

At the same time, because I want the conspectus of the nature and elements of sociology which had been clarified by the end of the nineteenth century to be undeniably clear; because I want this study to be definitive, and completely firm for an accurate assessment of subsequent twentieth century developments; I want, at the end of these studies, simply to collect and emphasise in a systematic way, the agreements which had been reached: to draw up a kind of 'end-of-nineteenth-century' statement of agreements. I want to do this, too, in such a way as to show (without reiterating all the intricate details) that the ideas of all the writers we have considered can so be drawn together. Each had his own conception; each had his own emphasis; but the major agreements among all of them were perfectly plain.

If I seem unduly tenacious in this task I can only ask the reader to bear with me, and to remember (a) that I wish to be clear beyond any degree of doubt or equivocation, (b) that I have in mind the condition of knowledge of the critics of sociology, and, in view of this, want to demonstrate the nature of the subject up to the hilt. If your opponent has a skin like the hide of an elephant, and an intellectual awareness of appropriate proportions, you are strongly disposed to drive your sword in deep. Even them, I am well aware that the brute is likely to turn away in silence, giving no sign of admitting anything, but my hope is that, when he does so this time, he will be dead, and (c) I have in mind also the perspectives placed upon the subject by certain twentieth century sociologists; and for the assessment of these, too, we need now to build very firm foundations.

Let us proceed, then, methodically.

A. SCIENCE AND KNOWLEDGE

As to the nature and necessity of science for the acquisition of reliable knowledge, all the thinkers we have studied were agreed:

(a) That only the methods of science were productive of testable knowledge as distinct from conjectural opinion.

(b) That science stemmed from careful reflection on common-sense and common practical experience, and that, though it went beyond this, it could continue to gain help from its shrewd insights and should always meet any questions or objections which it might raise.

(c) That the methods of science produced accurate knowledge in relation to their prescribed limitations.

(d) That science prescribed a limitation of subject-matter: (i) in that each science studied a distinctive, clearly defined 'unit of investigation' or 'range of facts', and (ii) in that it concerned itself only with this defined range of phenomena: qualities, objects, and relations in the worlds as we experience and observe them. Questions concerning the 'ultimate' nature of 'reality' were not the province of science. On these questions, science had to adopt a position of carefully delineated agnosticism.

(e) That science also prescribed, accordingly, a limitation of method in that - though including many methods: of observation, analysis, description, generalization, classification, comparison, experimentation, etc. - its crucial characteristic was that of always submitting its theories to conditions of test in relation to the facts they sought to explain.

(f) That, accordingly, science abandoned the conjectural methods of theology and speculative (or entirely 'a priori' and deductive) metaphysics. This was not to say that these subjects were totally devoid of value; or that they could not give rise to imaginative insight and hypothesis; only that they overstepped the boundaries of testability beyond which science could not go.

(g) That science was not a directionless empiricism: simply collecting and amassing 'facts'; but was a systematic study of the resemblances and differences of things, and of the relations between them, and was centrally concerned to establish laws. Science produced 'empirical generalisations' (descriptive statements of regularities) and 'theories' (hypothetical explanations) about them: all of which were always subjected to conditions of test. The role of 'hypothesis' in the establishing of scientific 'theories' as carefully stated 'conjectures' couched within specified conditions of 'verification' or 'refutation' - was clearly understood and acknowledged. Theory was central in guiding the observation and manipulation (in classification, comparison, experimentation, etc.) of facts.

(h) That science, whilst abandoning speculations about 'ultimate' reality, could nonetheless, by the pursuit of its methods, uncover 'hidden laws' which were beyond the range of common-sense, and which might (1) give hitherto unsuspected explanations of familiar facts, or (2) even reveal realms of facts which were themselves beyond the range of common perception. In such ways science extended knowledge.

(i) That each science concerned itself with its own distinctive subject-matter; and that all the sciences could be arranged or classified in such a way as, together, to provide a systematic compendium of knowledge of all aspects of experience. Though no man could encompass it all, knowledge could be so arranged, and could be transmitted in the many branches of education.

(j) That each science consisted of 'statics' and 'dynamics': the first producing 'laws (uniformities) of coexistence' (about the interdependence of parts in the distinctive 'consensus' of the subject-matter - the 'organism in biology, the 'social system' in sociology, etc.); and the second producing 'laws of succession' - i.e., about the actual changing forms of the subject-matter existing in the world. Statics and Dynamics, however, were not two distinctive kinds of subject-matter within each science, only two (and these very intimately related) different aspects of method and theory.

(k) That science, resting crucially upon testability, provided the most exact basis possible for prediction, action, and control. Each science had, therefore, its pure and applied aspects, which could not be dissociated from each other. The two attitudes of the scientist - to understand and to control - were necessarily connected. To understand nature as a student was inescapably related to the capacity to control nature as a master. Experimentation and practice were closely connected. To control was to manipulate nature in accordance with predictable knowledge. To see was to foresee. The degree of control depended upon things other than knowledge - the nature and magnitude of the facts and forces concerned, the state of accomplished technology, etc. - but the possibility of reliable, calculated control rested upon knowledge.

(l) That scientific knowledge was never final knowledge, but - always exposed to test - was always capable of change and extension. Scientific knowledge provided, within its prescriptions, the most secure grounds for its own continuous testing and probable expansion. Scientific knowledge, furthermore, was always relative to the many conditions of the human situation in which it was, at any time, being pursued; but it was not arbitrary: it was the most accurate knowledge possible by employing scientific method in that time and in these conditions.

(m) That the essential attitudes of mind required by science were those of humility before the facts; rigorous care with regard to prescribed limitations; integrity with regard to purposeful exposure to conditions of test; and readiness to change explanations in the light of evidence. This point deserves emphasis: that in claiming to set the standards of knowledge according to the limitations of human experience and the clearest procedures of the human mind - science was not arrogating to itself a totality of knowledge; it was accurately delimiting the claims of knowledge in accordance with a recognition of human limitations; and, in so doing, it had to deny these degrees of exactitude to those subjects whose conjectures went beyond these bounds.

(n) That, in the application of scientific knowledge for the attainment of certain human ends, the exercise of critical judgment (including a consideration of ethical principles) and an assessment of practical possibilities, and appropriate 'arts' had to enter - which went beyond scientific expertise as such.

(o) That, following upon these considerations, such knowledge as could be established about man and society could only be discovered by employing these methods of science to such a degree of exactitude as proved possible.

B. THE SCIENCES AND THE STUDY OF NATURE, MAN AND SOCIETY: PERSPECTIVES OF KNOWLEDGE

As to their conception of nature, of the place of man and society within it, and the proper conception of the sciences in the study of this entirety of man's experience of things, all the thinkers we have studied were agreed:

(a) That nature consisted of a vast, interconnected multiplicity of finite living forms in a continuous process of order and transformation, and that all these forms were the manifestation of definite regularities and definite relationships with the elements of the environments in the context of which they came into existence, grew, developed, and went out of existence. Any 'order' in nature, any perpetuated 'form', was itself a process. Both order and change in all these forms was a re-ordering of elements in a process of adjustment to specific constraining and sustaining environmental conditions.

(b) That, accordingly, any 'forms' ('object, 'species', etc.) in nature had essentially to be understood as a process within environmental conditions, and could only satisfactorily be explained in these terms.

(c) That nature was not only an interdependent entirety of 'forms', but that all its processes of order and transformation assumed a certain pattern: the pattern of 'evolution'. From simple elements of material substance and energy which were similar to each other, possessing relatively little definiteness of organisation, emerged varieties of definite forms possessing a differentiation of internal parts which were coherently organised. The nature of these forms was intimately connected with their accommodation to their environmental conditions, and followed a definite sequence of origination, growth, development, dissolution, and sometimes reproduction.

Changes in these distinctive forms were closely related to changes in their environmental conditions. Nature's vast mesh of transformations thus possessed an 'evolutionary' pattern.

(d) That the recognition, analysis and study of these processes of 'evolution' therefore provided grounds for the explanation of all the 'forms' of nature. For example: The initial condition of homogeneous elements was seen to be an unstable conditions; once differentiation of particular forms had begun - a multiplicity of effects could be traced; factors making for the specialisation and segregation of parts could be analysed; reciprocal accommodations and adjustments of parts to secure stability, equilibrium, and effectiveness in dealing with environmental circumstances could be analysed and described, as could factors making for decline, disintegration, destruction and dissolution; the ways in which quantitative processes among material substances gave rise to qualitatively new forms could be analysed and explored. The recognition of the processes of evolution provided, then, not simply a descriptive 'word' or 'concept' which - like a magic talisman - was thought to explain everything in nature; but provided a set of concepts, and an awareness of a multiplicity of factors, in accordance with which the complex processes of nature might be explained in detailed ways.

(e) That the 'normal' characteristics of any form in nature, the 'normal' functioning of its parts, and its relations with its environmental conditions, could sometimes be greatly illuminated by the careful study of 'pathological' conditions.

(f) That this conception of nature and all its interdependency of forms opened up vast perspectives - of time, of space, of complex contiguities of things - with which men had been hitherto unfamiliar; and that therefore a great effort of mind and judgment was necessary in approaching the task of knowledge anew.

(g) That, within this entire study of nature and its evolutionary processes, each science concerned itself with the study of one distinctive 'level' of 'forms' (one clearly defined 'level' of subject-matter). The emergence of the sciences was not arbitrary: new sciences emerged to study 'levels' of phenomena of which men were newly aware, and which could not be satisfactorily explored and explained by existing sciences. And again, all the sciences, taken and arranged together, could provide a compendium of knowledge of all 'forms' and all 'levels' of phenomena in nature.

(h) That, accordingly, though all the sciences employed 'scientific methods': observation, analysis, the submission of hypotheses to conditions of test, etc. - there was no such thing as one, uniform, set of 'scientific' concepts or procedures. The concepts, techniques, procedures, used: the degrees of controlled experiment and exactitude it was possible to achieve; would necessarily vary from science to science in accordance with the nature and complexity of its subject-matter. The insistence upon 'positive' science was, in no sense, then, an insistence that all sciences should ape one particular kind of science (say, the 'natural' sciences).

(i) That the one most crucial distinction of 'levels' - both with regard to the qualitative distinction of subject-matter, and with regard to the necessity of distinctively different concepts of 'scientific explanation' - which was to be recognized and clarified within the entire perspective of 'nature' and 'evolution', was that of the emergence of man and of human society. The evolutionary context entailed a new appraisal of man's place in nature.

   (i) One important element of this perspective was that man had emerged out of the material processes of nature, as one animal species among others in the process of biological evolution. A full knowledge of man's nature required, therefore, an understanding of these material and biological roots.

(ii) Human societies were systems of group activities which were also (like other 'forms' in nature) intricately involved in struggles of adaptation within contexts of environmental conditions. They also had origins in a distant past it was difficult to uncover; and they also seemed to assume their over-all shape in relation to factors going beyond 'individual intentions' alone. They were a qualitatively new 'level' of fact of which man had become aware - a 'super-organic level of phenomena'-which required distinctive concepts and a new, distinctive science.

(iii) The nature of 'man the individual' was so much a correlate of the conditions and developments of his social life, that it was at least necessary to study the nature, development and cumulative achievements of society, in order to have a sufficient basis of knowledge for an adequate exploration and understanding of the individual as a person.

(iv) At the same time, men - as individuals or as groups alike - had to make their societies, and win the basis for their livelihood and security, from practical activities in relation to the material resources and conditions of nature. This practical and material basis of human activities had therefore to be borne firmly in mind. The attainments of the human mind and spirit, and glories of culture and civilisation, had been won by man's struggles in nature - not simply dropped like ready-made 'Manna' from some transcendental heaven.

(v) Even so - one absolutely important distinction between man and all else in nature had to be recognised: that the human mind was capable of knowledge, choice, and conscious, deliberate action. Even in his material and practical activities, man was 'purposive'. Human action was categorically distinct, therefore, from inanimate occurrences of events, or sequences of animal behaviour, and therefore required a 'teleological' as distinct from a purely 'genetic' kind of casual explanation. These 'choices' and 'deliberate pursuits of ends' were still determining causes of sequences of human action - but they were causes of a different kind, and they could not be couched in terms of a 'necessitarian determinism'. Knowledge, choice, deliberation, will, and character (as distinct from conditioned 'personality') entered into human individual and social life, and any science of man and society had therefore to take these qualitatively different 'levels' of facts thoroughly into account.

Here, then, was a very special case in which a qualitatively distinctive 'level' of subject-matter necessitated not only a new science, but a new science with distinctively different concepts, methods, and principles of 'explanation'.

(vi) This distinction had one other important corollary. Knowledge brought with it control, and therefore man was also distinctive within nature in that he was able not only to adapt himself to the vicissitudes of nature, but to transform them in accordance with his own ends. Knowledge made possible the control of nature by artifice. Human societies were therefore cumulative developing processes: they were the embodiment of human achievements, and formed a social heritage which transmitted these achievements to new generations.

(j) That the science of man and society, should therefore form one part of the scientific study of nature - and, indeed, since all the sciences were themselves social achievements, sociology should provide a new perspective for the systematic arrangement or classification of the sciences. The science of society was like the other sciences, in trying to pursue the same rigorous methods, but also unlike them (as they, among themselves, were unlike each other) in that it had to include qualitatively distinct dimensions.

(k) That, finally, the sciences could be systematically arranged in accordance with the degree of complexity of their subject-matter, the degree of exactitude that was possible, and the connected degree of modifiability of the subject-matter. The science of society dealt with a subject-matter more complex than that of other sciences; the degree of precision it could expect to accomplish was therefore less; but, nonetheless, such knowledge as it could provide would be of very considerable importance since its subject-matter was more modifiable than that of other sciences and therefore more could be accomplished by control to achieve desired ends.

In these ways, then, the methods of science could establish appropriately exact knowledge about all the processes of transformation of nature - including the nature of man and society. And these were the only methods by which such knowledge could be achieved. The entire scientific enterprise on which man was embarked and which he was seeking to round out and systematise completely in the modern period, was therefore of basic importance for man's understanding and control of all aspects of his situation.

C. SOCIOLOGY: THE SCIENCE OF SOCIETY

As to the nature of Sociology - the new science of society which they were at such great pains to create - all the thinkers we have studied were agreed:

Sociology: A Science

That sociology was, indeed, one science among others in accordance with all the elements of definition clarified above. It had become necessary because a specific 'level' of facts had become recognised in human experience (and in the context of pressing problems) which existing sciences could not sufficiently explore or explain.

The Existence of 'Social Systems': The Distinctive Subject-matter of Sociology

That the groups which men formed, the institutional procedures by which their conduct and relationships were ordered - in short, all the 'associational' aspects of human life - existed in some relationships of interdependence in societies as wholes, and that they could only be properly understood within this perspective. The organisational entirety of societies included elements other than physical processes, other than biological processes, and other than the psychological qualities and intentions of individuals. Sociology was necessary therefore, as the scientific study of 'social systems' - and this was the distinctive definition of it.

The Necessity of the Methods of Science

That testable knowledge (as distinct from untested opinion, speculation, conjecture) about the nature of 'social systems', as about any other 'level' of facts in our experience, could only be achieved by using the methods of science. Sociology should pursue its studies with the same rigorous methods, and the same crucial insistence upon the empirical testing of theories, as the other sciences. This did not mean, however, that it should confine itself to the concepts, techniques and procedures of the other sciences - since every science had (necessarily) distinctive concepts in relation to its own 'level' of subject-matter, and 'social systems' certainly possessed distinctive dimensions which required special concepts. The degree of exactitude which could be achieved in the study of 'social systems' remained to be seen; but it could only be seen by employing the methods of science as far and as carefully as possible.

The Abandonment of 'Metaphysical' Kinds of Explanation

That, accordingly, Sociology should abandon all explanations of 'social systems' in terms of 'final ends' or 'ultimate realities or purposes', or even 'ultimate causes' in the sense of dogmatic reductionism to some ultimate level of fact where supposed causal efficacy was not susceptible to test. 'Casual Laws' were not to be conceived as iron bands inevitably determining the nature of society, but as statements of regularities of our experience and observation of society which were testable; about which testable theories could be stated; and which could be used to explain and predict specific events and relationships.

Especially, too, Sociology should abandon the attitude of mind that a knowledge of man and 'social systems' could be gained in 'a priori' fashion, from solely intuitive sources, and elaborated purely by procedures of deduction. It should adopt the scientific attitude of mind that any knowledge of a specific range of facts could only be accomplished by observing, analysing, describing, classifying, and attempting theoretical explanations of these facts which could be tested. It should adopt the empirical orientation of science, and proceed on the assumption that any reliable knowledge about the nature of 'social systems' could only result from a careful, searching, empirical study of them. We should study social facts with the same orientation towards objectivity that we employ in our study of other facts in our experience.

This did not Mean the Assumption of 'Necessitarian Determinism'

That this adoption of the methods of science did not mean the adoption of any new metaphysic of 'necessitarian determinism'. 'Social Systems' were not physical, or mechanical, or organic phenomena, they were systems of associational forms in which men exercised conscious choice, and pursued deliberate sequences of social action in accordance with interests and to accomplish ends. The nature of 'causality' among the regularities of 'social systems' was therefore complex and contained distinctive qualities. Though always within a context of delimiting constraints, 'men made their own history'. Even so, careful empirical procedures of study were necessary to provide reliable knowledge about them - but this did not at all mean treating 'social systems' and the people who lived and acted within them as if they were sticks or stones. Sociology as a science did not deny, or fail to recognise, the human capacities for calculated knowledge, deliberate choice, and conscious purpose: on the contrary, it shaped its concepts and methods to take these distinctive qualities of its subject-matter satisfactorily into account. This was so both in its recognition of character-formation within societies, as distinct from the conditioning influences of a cultural 'ethos' upon attributes of personality; and in its recognition of the explanation of social action in terms of 'teleological' causation, as a category distinct from the explanation of physical or organic events, or sequences of animal behaviour, which was possible in terms of 'genetic' or 'efficient' causation.

The Delimitation of Sociology

That Sociology, by this kind of careful definition in relation to a distinctive subject-matter was properly delimited to a range of study, a 'universe of discourse', within which it could pursue appropriate kinds and degrees of exactitude. Sociology deliberately confined itself to discovering and stating regularities about the nature of 'social systems': the interconnections between their parts in whole societies; the psychological aspects of these social relationships; the sequences of social action pursued within them; and the relations between such whole societies themselves. Total 'social systems' were related to each other to some extent and in certain ways within 'human society' as a whole throughout the world, and had come to be what they were within the cumulative processes of history. Sociology was concerned to establish knowledge about the many aspects of this entire fabric of 'associational' interdepender :y. It goes without saying that this was the defined 'conspectus' of sociology as a distinctive field of study. No scholar was so megalomaniac as ever to propose that any one man could encompass the whole of it. Within this agreed conspectus, and with all its perspectives in mind, each scholar could pursue his own dimension of interest; his own theoretical concern and persuasion

Sociological 'Laws'

That sociology, in common with other sciences, should not pursue a 'directionless empiricism'; a mere bit-and-piece 'sociography'; an amassing of descriptive studies; but that it should be - according to the character of science properly understood - a generalising, theoretically orientated study of the resemblances and differences of the aspects of social systems, and should seek the clear statement of testable 'laws'. These 'laws' concerning social regularities would be of at least two kinds: (a) 'uniformities of co-existence' (about the nature of the 'social system' as a distinctive subject-matter; the kind of 'consensus' of facts a 'social systems' was; the kinds of relationship which existed between the parts of a 'social system' within the whole, etc.), and (b) 'uniformities of succession' (about the changing nature of the actual varieties of 'social system' in history).

Social Statics and Social Dynamics

That, in Sociology, as in other sciences, it was useful to distinguish two aspects (though closely connected aspects) of method and theory: statics and dynamics. Social Statics was the necessary conceptual analysis of the nature of 'social systems', their components, their functions, their interrelations, their psychological aspects, the patterns of social action which they comprised, etc. Social Dynamics was the application of this analysis to achieve an understanding and explanation of the varieties of social systems in the world. Statics was the analysis of the distinctive nature of social systems; Dynamics, guided by this analysis, was the detailed study of societies (empirical, comparative, historical) in relation to specific theories. Statics and Dynamics did not have separate subject-matters, they were two different aspects of method and theory; and, of course, they were intimately connected, in that the specific studies and theories of Dynamics could well lead to fresh formulations of the analysis of Statics - which itself could then lead to new theoretical insights and new specific studies in Dynamics.

Social Statics: The Analysis of the Distinctive Nature of Society - 'The Social System'

That the nature of a 'society' of 'social system' comprised the following important components and could be analysed exhaustively in terms of them:

(a) *A Population and its Environmental Conditions*

Any society consisted of a population sustaining itself, and creating and perpetuating its social life, by working upon and adjusting itself to a specific set of environmental conditions. The study of the population and of the environmental conditions therefore formed a necessary part of sociological analysis; and both involved quantitative and qualitative aspects. As far as the population was concerned, the qualitative composition and the quantitative size, rate and pattern of change, distribution throughout the territory, etc., were all important factors. But the unity and solidarity of populations - which bound them together as communities, sharing continued traditions - rested upon various types of 'consciousness of kind' in accordance with which men identified themselves with each other and marked themselves off from each other. These too, therefore, were necessary factors of analysis and necessitated the study of societal and psychological components.

(b) *A Consensus of Associational Forms: Structural-Functional Analysis*

In any society, the activities of the population in relation to their life-conditions and to each other were not arbitrary, but assumed certain regularities. In their associations in family life and kinship relationships; working life and property-relations; in their activities of instruction, training and education; in their religious observances of belief and ritual practices; in their procedures of government and law; in all their associations, certain regularities prevailed. These were specific, regular, associational forms of social action. Furthermore, all these specific forms were found to be interconnected and interrelated in a complex and intimate fashion. Marriage, for example, was an institution of the family, of religion, of government, of law, and had many attendant customs; so that all these associational forms were interlinked in a quite definite manner. Similarly, objective conditions and subjective identifications of 'Social Classes' arose from occupations, property-relations, family membership, relationships to law and government, etc. The associational forms in a society were, in short, interconnected in a certain kind of 'consensus' which even came to possess an attendant 'ethos'. There was a 'social system', a system of interdependent institutions, within which many kinds of regular and well-defined groups of the population conducted their activities.

This entire, interlinked network of social relationships with all its elements of social procedure and organization could most clearly be studied by a 'Structural-Functional Analysis'. This had certain clear components.

(I) *The Clear Analysis of Functional Requisites and Appropriate Organizational Forms*

There were certain functional requisites - stemming from the universal psychological characteristics of man and certain determinate problems, which were necessarily encountered where men were collectively involved in working upon the same life-conditions and seeking to satisfy their many needs - which had to be provided for, in appropriate organizational forms, in every society.

Such institutions, rooted in functional requisites, were universally necessary. The following were specified:

DOMESTIC INSTITUTIONS AND ATTENDANT KINSHIP RELATIONSHIP

Some form of marriage and family relationships to regulate sexual behaviour in relation to the responsible upbringing of the young were necessary; and, in relation to any specific form of marriage, there would necessarily be a determinate network of kinship relationships.

ECONOMIC INSTITUTIONS: PRODUCTION, DISTRIBUTION AND PROPERTY

The working activities of the members of a society had to be regulated in such a way as to produce adequate sustenance from the material resources of the environment. This entailed some division of labour - some allocation of tasks to those who were thought most fitted and appropriately trained to do them. Both the material resources, and the products of collective work, had also to be distributed according to some principle and procedure among the population. And the principles and procedures for establishing legitimate degrees of control over material resources and products were institutions of property and gave rise to determinate property-relations.

REGULATORY INSTITUTIONS: CUSTOM, LAW, GOVERNMENT, RELIGION

Some institutions were also necessary to provide stable methods for resolving disputes, and for taking or interpreting these decisions which were binding upon all the members of society. Such institutions had to possess 'authority' and power, and would have to include some consensus of beliefs and values as well as regulated practices. Bodies of custom, more formal systems of law, constitutions of government, and religions with their systems of doctrines and ritual-practices were institutions of this kind.

MILITARY INSTITUTIONS

The members of a society needed to be protected from external threats and attacks as well as from internal disorder and insecurities, so that some form of military organisation, as part and parcel of the 'regulatory institutions' was also necessary.

EDUCATIONAL INSTITUTIONS

If the security, stability and desired qualities of a society were to be preserved, the accumulated knowledge, skills, beliefs and values of the social order would have to be effectively transmitted from generation to generation, so that institutions of instruction, training and education were necessary.

RANKS, CLASSES AND ELITES

This institutional ordering of human relationships in all forms of association necessarily involved differentiations of function and ability; allocation of responsibility; the designation of authority and kinds of subordination; and necessarily led to the distinction of élites, of variously graded 'ranks', and the emergence of 'classes' of the community who experienced differing sets of conditions.

This is by no means an exhaustive statement of this component of 'functional requisites' and their appropriate organisational forms. It is simply a mention of this one basic element of structural-functional analysis: that basic functional requisites could be postulated which were universal in society and gave rise to basic types of institutions - each serving these functions and possessing attributes of form and organisation appropriate to them. This was clearly stated, and the institutions we have mentioned were among those clarified by the nineteenth century thinkers. This analysis itself formed a clear basis for comparative studies, and it may be remembered that Mill was so impressed by the confirming evidence of comparative studies that he was ready to claim that these analytical propositions themselves were of the nature of 'scientific truths'.

(II) *The Proliferation of Interests, Functions and Specialised Associational Forms*

About these basic functional requisites, massive networks of folkways, mores, and then formally regulated and consciously amended institutions and laws developed, and could be analysed in the same structural-functional terms. However, in more complex societies with considerable degrees of differentiation, freedom, and knowledge many consciously devised associations were created to seek quite specific ends. These specialised associations could also be carefully analysed in terms of the purposes they sought, and the structures of organisation - their 'apparatus', their arrangement of 'functionaries', their kinds of 'instrumental means', their pattern of authority, subordination, committee-arrangements, etc. - which they established to seek these ends.

Two points were important here: (a) no matter how complex the number and nature of associations in a society, the method of structural-functional analysis remained applicable and satisfactory, and (b) it was clear that elements of social structure - from the most massive (such as governments, armies, ecclesiastical organizations) to the most small and specialised (such as a society to prevent cruelty to animals) could, by this method, be broken down into all the specific units-of-action of 'functionaries' which were requirement of behaviour for individuals. In short, structural-functional analysis provided a detailed picture of the structure of society within which the units of behaviour of individuals could be clearly seen and understood.

(III) *Functional Interconnection*

Besides the clarification of basic functional requisites of large-scale institutions and the specific purposes of specialised associations, structural-functional analysis also clarified the functional interdependency of all elements of social structure in the 'consensus' of society as a whole. It clarified the ways in which institutions were linked in their connected operation in society as a whole.

(IV) The Process of Society: Order, Change, Development

The structural-functional analysis of institutions was proposed and used with the insistent awareness that society was essentially a historical process of achievements, and the transmission of achievements, as succeeding generations of men grappled with their environmental conditions. It especially warned against the error of the stationary. Structural-functional analysis was part of the study of society necessary for a satisfactory explanation of process: and this included the understanding of both order and change - since both are essentially processes. Indeed, these men who put forward the earliest 'structural-functional' models of social systems were the men who have provided the most impressive and influential theories of social change. It is worth remarking, in addition, that the transmission of achievements in both order and change entailed the recognition of the fact of social development: namely a process of the cumulative furtherance of achievement resting upon earlier achievement.

(V) Conflict and Co-operation in Society: Order not Necessarily Harmony

The structural-functional analysis of institutions was also proposed and used with the insistent awareness that society contained continuous sources of conflict as well as tendencies of co-operation. Social order was not at all construed as something called functional harmony. The order of institutions was a pattern of procedures which had been shaped in order to deal with conflicts of interests, conflicts of classes; its very nature was that of an institutional 'modus vivendi' within which men and groups with manifold interests could pursue these interests and resolve their differences. Sometimes conflict was radical and disruptive; sometimes it was not; but structural-functional analysis took it thoroughly into account.

(VI) *Functional Interconnection not Functional Integration*

Similarly, structural-functional analysis did not at all entail the assumption or reach the conclusion that all the institutions of society were 'integrated' in some sense of being so perfectly articulated that there was no possible source of internal social change. The institutions of a social system were interlinked, but they could be institutionalisations of power and control which might well be disrupted and overthrown, and, in any case, they were in many ways imperfect, resting on limited knowledge which was prone to change. There was always a drive to progress, to a furtherance of practical advantage, within them, as well as a 'strain to consistency' among them, and the activities and interests of men were never smoothly tamed within their bounds.

(VII) *Equilibrium-Disequilibrium Analysis*

Quite apart from any specific theory of social change, then, the structural-functional analysis of society rested upon a firm recognition that the very nature of society was that of a process always prone to change, alive with manifold interests and sources of conflict, and never nicely confined and controlled, so that, as a part of itself, it employed an 'equilibrium-disequilibrium analysis' which could explore the transformation of society from one 'structural-functional' pattern to another.

(VIII) *The Normal and the Pathological*

A final element, most clearly introduced by Comte, was that the understanding of the 'normal' functioning of a social institution within a certain type of social system might well be more clearly illuminated by careful studies of particular 'pathological' situations in which the normal condition of the society had, for some reason, broken down.

A clear analysis of a social system could be achieved, then, by this method of 'structural-functional analysis'; the clear analysis and description of each institution, its own specific functions, and the functional interconnectedness of them all within the system as a whole. It can be seen that this kind of analysis of social systems readily lent itself to a systematic clarification of 'types' of social system and made manageable clearly conceived comparative studies.

(c) *Human Activities: Social Institutions not 'Entities' Self-sufficient for Explanation*

Though structural-functional analysis could provide a clear knowledge of all the associational forms in a society and the nature of their articulation with each other in the entire social system, and though such a picture could provide a clear basis for tracing 'cause and effect' relationships, it was nonetheless still at the level of analysis and description, and not sufficient in itself to explain order and change in society. The order of social institutions had come into being to regulate and serve many kinds of human activities, and therefore the further study of these activities was necessary for causal explanation.

The point of crucial importance emphasise here was that social institutions were not self-subsistent 'entities' which could be held to have cause-and-effect relationships with each other. They were associational regularities: but regularities of what? They were ways of ordering the feeling, thinking, and acting of groups of men pursuing certain interests. Comte, Mill, Spencer, and the Americans alike warned against the basic error of regarding institutions with a misplaced concreteness - as social entities in their own right.

The clear knowledge of social regularities and the interconnections (whether of continuity or change) among them was not therefore in itself sufficient, and had to be supplemented by a study of the many aspects of human activities for any satisfactory causal explanation. We need no elaborate again here the way in which all the nineteenth century thinkers emphasised men's practical activities and their many-sided pursuit of practical advantages within the entire framework of the institutions of society.

One centrally important aspect of this point is that a causal account of changes in society could not take the form of 'weighting' one institution or a group of institutions as being the determinants of others. Any statement that one institution caused changes in others was an error.

The societal level of 'associational forms' or 'regularities' about which it was so important to establish knowledge was still not to be mistaken as a level of self-subsistent entities.

(d) *The Psychological Aspects of Society*

Since the activities of men had to be studied, and since these activities were sequences of feeling, motivation, thinking, choice, deliberation and action, the study of the psychological aspects of social regularities formed a necessary part of sociological analysis. Again, we need not elaborate all that was contributed in clarifying this area of study, but the important points made, and the important dimensions of enquiry distinguished and quite extensively analysed, can be stated in a summary way.

(i) There was no doubt that sociology needed to draw upon biology and psychology for such knowledge as they could provide about the basic bio-psychological endowment of human nature, and that these two sciences were themselves experimental sciences. Basic questions and qualifications were made, however, about the nature of psychology - which we shall come to in a moment.

(ii) Knowledge was also necessary of the 'motives' in human nature - and the motives at all levels. Some of these were at the level of physiology needs and even 'instincts', and these underlay broad ranges of social action: the quest for food, sexual gratification, the protecting of children, security, shelter, etc. Others, however, were engendered by social experience, by tradition, by social constraints themselves: so that the study of collective kinds of 'social conation' was also required.

(iii) Membership of groups, the fulfilling of tasks as 'functionaries' of associations, the experience of the rules, values constraints, and ideals of institutions also had their psychological aspects. Social regularities obviously had their influences upon the experience and behaviour of individuals. This had many dimensions: the existence of many kinds of 'consciousness of kind' in group identification and group demarcation; the creation of a societal 'ethos'; the institutional engendering of specific interests, habits, and characteristic in individuals, etc. And these, of course, might well form part of, or be caught up in, the thick of massive historical movements and intense conflicts, as well as in the more ordinary accommodation to patterns of social life. Groups themselves might entail psychological processes which were formative of constellations of individual perception and feeling: and the analysis of such processes was not only suggested, but substantially begun in the study of 'In-groups' and 'Out-groups'.

(iv) As part of this, but going more deeply, it was also necessary to understand the relationship between the emergent nature of the 'Self'; of the personality and character of the individual; and the cultural context of society. The very study of the 'individual' could, it seemed, only be satisfactorily undertaken within the societal context.

(v) As a corollary of this, too, it was assumed that certain kinds of 'social structure' would be likely, within the constraints and influences of their requirements, to engender appropriate kinds of 'character', and so the exploration of 'types' of 'character and social structure' was begun in comparative studies.

The field of 'social psychology' was therefore not only indicated but quite clearly and substantially defined, and certain very important points were involved in this which deserve clear statement and emphasis.

Firstly: no conflict was seen whatever between psychology and sociology. On the contrary, the study of man and society was seen essentially as a unified science in which the societal and the psychological aspects played their necessarily interconnected parts.

Secondly: these social-psychological dimensions were seen as necessary 'middle-principles' of sociological explanation. This, it will be clearly seen, was by no means, and in no intelligible sense, to 'reduce' sociology to psychology. Causal explanations in terms of 'institutions' as 'entities' were an error. Clearly the 'institutional regularities' of society were also inexplicable in terms of 'individual' psychology; involving many elements which went beyond this. The study of men's 'social activities' was an additional necessity, and part of this was the study of the psychological aspects of life within institutions and groups. No reductionism was involved: this was simply a recognition of the several levels necessarily involved in an entire and satisfactory explanation of the distinctive characteristics of social systems.

The third point which can follow this is that this position clearly demonstrated (far from a 'reductionism' to individual psychology) the necessary sociological perspective of psychology. Just as the study of society was insufficient without the consideration of the psychological dimensions of it, so the study of man the individual was completely impossible excepting by seeing the 'person' within his social context.

And the fourth point which springs out of this is that the extent to which psychology can be an experimental, 'natural' science, was held to be extremely dubious. The comments of Marx here were perhaps the most telling. If man the individual, if the very qualities of distinctively human nature, are the products of long cultural processes of cumulative social creativity, how is it possible to rest a science on the study of human 'experience and behaviour' abstracted from all this? This, in itself, might well be a fundamental error of the most fatal kind, and of the most simple-minded kind, and might lead to a distortion of our views about human nature rather than to a deeper knowledge of it. At any rate, practically all the nineteenth century scholar adopted this direction of view: as Comte put it, that all human psychology was social psychology, and that a sociological perspective was necessary for the understanding of man the individual. Mill was most ready to recognise an experimental science of psychology, but, as we have seen, even he insisted fully on the 'middle principles' of social psychology in addition to this.

A fifth and final point which is of interest and importance is that this exploration of the psychological aspects of society made possible the linking of the study of society and of all the individual members of it. Or - to put this in a better way - it presented a clear perspective of the entirety of society in such a way as not to conceive only of abstract categories of social regularities ('elements of social structure', 'institutions', etc.) but also to see in clear and rich detail the individual 'units' of action, and the individual 'personalities' pursuing their purposes within it. Just as the very detailed way of analysing 'institutions' in such a way as to make clear all the particular tasks of 'functionaries' (put forward by Sumner and Giddings especially) made it possible to see 'individual actions' within the many forms of social structure - no matter how massive they might be; so this study of the psychological aspects of society could explore all the patterns of experience and behaviour within this entirety of social structure - from the largest level of 'collective' motives, constraints, enthusiasms, etc., when the population faced and shared 'collective' conditions, down to the most detailed level of the influence upon the individual of the requirements and performance of particular tasks (e.g., as husband, father, workman, property-owner, political citizen, member of a trade union, member of a religious community, etc.) and the development of the individual's own personality and character within the context of them.

This mention of 'character', however, as distinct from the notion of purely conditioned 'personality' leads to the next distinctive and additional component of sociological analysis.

(e) *The Understanding and Explanation of Social Action: Teleological Dimensions of Facts and Analysis*

Because the human mind was distinguished by its capacity for the conscious apprehension of ends; the acquisition of knowledge; deliberation, judgment and choice; and the deliberate direction of action and critical employment of means to achieve these ends: neither the structural-functional analysis and description of the institutions and groups within which men lived and acted, nor the study of the psychological aspects of experience and behaviour within this framework; nor the two combined - in terms of efficient causation - could possibly be enough. These were two necessary components of sociological analysis, but they were not in themselves enough. Men were distinctively purposive and capable of choice and conscious calculation in formulating and carrying out their activities, and therefore an additional component of analysis was necessary: the teleological explanation of social action in terms of the ends men sought, and their ways of pursuing them.

This was a very important distinction of both fact and method. It insisted that the facts studied by sociology were qualitatively different from the facts studied by other sciences, and it also insisted, accordingly, that the methods and theories of sociology must be qualitatively different in order to deal satisfactorily with them. Kind of social action had to be understood in terms of different kinds of ends and different kinds of means employed for attaining them. These we need not elaborate again here, but we can simply note that certain models for this purpose were provided: Impulsive, Traditional and Rational social action; and these were linked with the analysis of social structures and of psychological processes to provide a full analysis of all the dimensions of society.

From the 'types' of social order elaborated by Comte - the three kinds of ordering of feeling, thought and action; through Mill's insistence upon the human capacity of choice; to the teaching of Ward, Sumner and Giddings at the close of the century on the importance of recognising these dimensions of 'purpose' and 'teleology'; there had been, in the making of sociology, this clear recognition of the need, in the science of society, for a dimension of explanation different from that existing in the so-called 'natural' sciences. And it is important to reiterate: that all these men were, at one and the same time, insistent upon the necessity of using the methods of positive science in the study of society and that these methods would have additional and distinctive components because of the different qualities, the different level of subject-matter with which they had to deal. Sociology was a 'positive science' which incorporated 'teleological' as well as 'genetic' explanations.

(f) *Society MORE than Human Purposes: Hidden Laws: Unintended Consequences*

A systematic and testable knowledge of any society could be provided then, by:

(i) the study of the qualitative and quantitative aspects of the population within,

(ii) its environmental conditions,

(iii) the structural-functional analysis of its 'Consensus' of institutions and groups,

(iv) the study of the psychological aspects of these associational forms and their influences upon individuals, and

(v) the study, in 'teleological' terms, of the sequences of social action which men pursued within this framework.

Even this, however, was not sufficient without taking one other basic and perennial fact into account.

Though men were purposive, the order of society resulted from more than their purposes. Though they pursued activities in the service of interests and to attain ends; the detailed interconnections of social events and actions always went beyond these conscious purposes, in ways, whether advantageous or not, which were unforeseen. For example, though acting consciously to achieve ends, men may be conscious of these ends in varying degrees, not necessarily fully; nor did it follow that other ends may not be pulling them of which they were not conscious. Also, though acting consciously to satisfy interests and achieve ends, men's interests and purposes were limited, terminating at certain points. The consequences of their actions, however, might always go far beyond their intentions - and in many ways. They might have effects upon other people, other institutions, and even upon themselves, in ways which were not looked for, and were not even a matter of conscious interest. There might, in short, be influences working upon their minds shaping the 'ends' for which they struggled, of which they were unaware, or only partially aware. The results of their actions might be altogether or partially different from what they had intended, and might have consequences going far beyond their awareness. And also, institutional adjustments, kinds of reciprocal articulation between associational forms, might well take place as an outcome of the entirety of complex social activity in the community without being consciously sought, or planned, as an over-all pattern of organisation at all, or by anyone.

This recognition of the complex interconnections of social processes - insisted upon repeatedly by all the men we have studied - emphasised, in yet another way, quite basic and important points. It emphasized especially that though components of sociological analysis could be methodologically distinguished and clarified, no one of them was sufficient for satisfactory analysis, description and explanation. Men were purposive, and the teleological understanding of their purposive action was necessary - but it was not of itself, enough. The psychological aspects of men's social activities and their complex 'membership' of institutions and groups, formed a necessary element in any satisfactory knowledge of social processes - but in itself it was not enough. The entire framework of associational forms in which men lived and acted could be clarified by a structural-functional analysis which was necessary - but not of itself, enough. All these elements of fact and components of method were necessary in close conjunction with each other for a satisfactory analysis of the vast 'consensus' of facts which comprised 'the social system': the distinctive subject-matter of sociology. Sociological analysis was not, therefore, one or other of these components, or separate components used here and there, but was distinctly and distinctively all these components together in one entire system of analysis.

This point re-emphasised, and made perfectly clear, too, the way in which sociology - whilst properly rejecting the metaphysical notions of 'ultimates' behind phenomena (whether 'ideal' or 'material'), could, nonetheless, still properly investigate elements and dimensions of the actuality of social and psychological processes which might not be evident in the overt expressions of men's conduct, and might not even exist in their consciousness. And this was nothing mysterious. It was not replacing a 'metaphysical' with a 'scientific' mystique. It was simply a recognition that men's consciousness in society did not, and could not, embrace everything, and that elements of society nor evident, not intended, not foreseen, could be brought to light by careful study. This was a careful insistence, again, that sociology embraced, necessarily, both genetic (in terms of 'efficient' causes of events) and teleological (in terms of 'ends' deliberately sought in action) components and principles of explanation.

And this point re-emphasised, too, the fundamental persuasion of sociology, that social systems existed as complex interdependencies of associational facts. The actual nature of society, though containing individuals and their purposes, was an empirically found interconnectedness of associational facts possessing qualities and including processes which were other than them, and went beyond them.

All the nineteenth century founders of the subject were agreed, then, on this final component in the analysis of the nature of society: the inclusion of the study of the unintended consequences of men's social activities.

To summarise, then:

It was held that a satisfactory analysis of the nature of society, of the 'social system' - which was the distinctive subject-matter of sociology - necessarily included:

(i) the study of the qualitative and quantitative aspects of the population,
(ii) its environmental conditions,
(iii) the structural-functional analysis of its 'consensus' of institutions and groups,
(iv) the study of the psychological aspects of these associational forms and their influences upon individuals,
(v) the study, in 'teleological' terms, of the sequences of social action which men pursued within this framework, and of their 'character' as well as 'personality' formation, and
(vi) the study of the unintended consequences of men's social activities.

Sociological analysis was not one or other of these components, but (though they could be distinguished for purposes of clarity and accuracy of understanding), the incorporation of all of them in a system of analysis which sufficiently took into account the empirical existence of social systems which were actual societal interdependencies of facts of which all these components and dimensions were aspects closely interwoven and conjoint. Any persuasion that part of this societal interdependency of facts could be sufficiently explained in isolation from its context; without being seen within this perspective of interconnection; was, it was insisted, an error.

Social Dynamics: The Application of this Analysis to the Study of Actual Societies in History: Theories of Order and Change, Similarity and Diversity

That this analysis of social systems - derived from the clarification of the distinctive qualities of which we were aware in our existing experience and observation of them - could then be systematically applied to the empirical study of actual societies, of both the past and the present, in an attempt to establish testable knowledge about them; to discover and state generalisations about them; and to achieve theories about the kinds of 'consensus' found among them: theories about their similarities and diversities; about their processes of both order and change.

Social Statics was a systematic analysis of the distinctive subject-matter of sociology: the nature of the 'social system'. Social Dynamics was the application of this analysis in the empirical study of actual societies and the careful elaboration of specific theories about them.

The subject-matter of 'Statics' and 'Dynamics' was the same: the scientific study of social systems; they were only useful distinctions of method and theory - and, as such, they were, clearly, in the closest relationship with each other. The formulation of 'Statics' was derived from our existing experience and observation of the nature of society; and, once clearly formulated, it guided our empirical studies and underlay the hypothetical assumptions of our 'theories' in 'Dynamics'.

But also, conversely, our systematic empirical studies and the detailed consideration of 'theories' might well lead us to alter - perhaps slightly, perhaps considerably - our formulations in 'Static' analysis, to take into account dimensions of fact, or kinds of interconnection, of which we had been unaware and which our empirical studies had revealed. There was, therefore, continuous interchange between the two; they were both parts of the ongoing enterprise of achieving the greatest scientific accuracy possible.

The application of the system of analysis, as outlined, to the empirical study of actual societies and the construction of specific theories, necessitated the recognition, clarification, and employment of the following additional components of fact and method:

(a) ***The Classification and Comparative Study of Societies***

The attempt to establish generalizations about social systems necessitated (indeed entailed!) the gathering together and arrangement of knowledge about them in some systematic and manageable form. To generalize at once meant the clarification of resemblances and differences between societies: it immediately entailed a classification of facts. To generalise also meant, at once, not an arbitrary selection and comparison of facts, but a systematic comparative study so that their empirical truth (the fact that they really were descriptive generalisations) could be demonstrated and checked. Generalisation, classification, systematic comparison, were all of a piece: none could exist without the other. There was, then, no one kind of sociology called 'comparative sociology': sociology was essentially comparative as a scientific study of societies, attempting to establish testable generalisations about them.

But a further point was important here: namely, that generalization, classification, and systematic comparison were inseparable from (were, strictly speaking, part and parcel of) the statement of specific theories. The criteria adopted for the classification of societies (e.g., Property-Relations in the case of Marx, States of Knowledge in the case of Comte, etc.) would themselves be indicative of a hypothetical persuasion that these were the factors most significant for understanding and explaining the various kinds of society and their processes of order and change. This can be put simply in this way: that the procedures of generalisations, classification and systematic comparison were intimately connected with the formulation and satisfactory statement of specific theories; they were the procedural embodiment of hypothetical persuasions - whether implicit or explicit. Bearing this in mind, it can further be said that the procedures of generalisation, classification, and systematic comparison were necessary: (a) for the systematic arrangement of descriptive knowledge - which might yield hypothetical persuasions previously unlooked for, even though it might rest on certain hypothetical persuasions already implicitly held, and (b) for the testing of theoretical generalisations at various levels when they were explicitly made.

The theorists we have studied took these matters into account in both implicit and explicit ways, and it is here that we can see very clearly the theoretical point of 'weighting' some component of the analysis of 'statics' more than other for the construction of theoretical models which embody hypothetical persuasions. It is impossible to be exhaustive on this - but it is sufficient to note clearly that the classification of societies was proposed, and accomplished, in two ways.

On the one hand, societies were classified in accordance with some kind of observable regularity, some empirical fact, which was distinctive. Thus, though some were more specific than others, all the theorists accepted that human societies could be classified in accordance with what Spencer called their 'degree of aggregation': whether they were groups of families, clans, tribes, confederations of tribes, civic nations, empires, confederations of nations. This was one procedure of classification and comparison which made possible much more elaborate study of the kinds of 'consensus' which characterised each 'level of composition', each distinctive 'type' of society: and it could be expected to provide a useful basis for further theories and the advancement of knowledge. Even here, it must be said that this classification entailed the implicit hypothesis of a process of 'social evolution', but, as we have seen, this was not a blanket-like concept of inevitability, as commonly supposed, but provided for a causal analysis of the many factors involved in evolution (and dissolution!) But here it is enough to say that the distinctive degrees of aggregation were empirically there, whatever the details of the evolutionary hypothesis. A 'tribe' was clearly distinguishable from a 'City-State' founded by the union of a number of tribes, and both were distinguishable from, say, the modern 'Nation'. This was a firm empirical basis for classification which stood firm whatever the hypothesis that might be entertained to explain this variety of forms.

However, in addition to this, a second method of classifying societies was also proposed explicitly for a parallel theoretical interpretation of these various forms and 'levels' of social organisation. Thus, Comte's 'Law of the Three Stages' was a construction of three models of social order which also embodied a theoretical understanding of the chief historical changes which were observable among all the societies in the world. They were models of society, incorporating all the components upon which the analysis of 'Statics' insisted, but 'weighting' the component of mind and knowledge, and specific cumulative developments in them and in their powers of control, as being especially significant in bringing about social changes. Similarly, Spencer's classification of three 'types' of society - the Militant, Industrial and Ethical, parallel to the classification in terms of 'degrees of aggregation' - was a construction of three 'models' for analyzing, interpreting, and explaining the patterns of change which the first classification described. And these models - again, including all the components insisted upon by the analysis of 'statics' - were constructed by the significant 'grouping' of institutions (the Regulatory, the Sustaining, the Distributive), and the 'weighting' of one or other of these to explain particular kinds of social change. Marx's classification - though his models were not so clearly worked out - rested similarly upon 'weighting' the economic and property relations, which, in his view, were hypothetically significant. And we have seen how Ward, Sumner and Giddings, too, employed the same practices of classification and comparison: Giddings, especially, managing to incorporate practically all the earlier ideas.

Classification, then, rested upon (1) the designation of observable degrees of social aggregation or social composition: which arranged knowledge systematically for further detailed study, and (2) the construction of 'types' or 'models' which, much more explicitly, incorporated a 'theory'.

A final aspect of this was that the Comparative Method in sociology was accordingly seen in two (though clearly connected) ways: (1) as the systematic descriptive study of societies, accomplishing an arrangement of knowledge resting upon generalisations, but making the explorations for further, and more detailed, generalisations possible, and (2) as the only alternative which sociology had to the method of artificially controlled experiment. In this sense, the careful employment of comparative studies was the only way of testing theories.

(b) *The Construction of Theoretical Models*

Enough has been said on the construction of 'models', appropriately 'weighted', for the careful elaboration of theories, but one or two specific aspects of this method need to be stated clearly. The first is that this method was of more detailed application than that we have mentioned - the construction of 'types of society'. In Giddings most clearly, it was also employed to construct 'models' or 'types' of social action which were used to explain 'teleologically' various kinds of social process -whether large-scale or small. The three types he elucidated: the Impulsive, Traditional and Rational types of social action were applicable to small groups and various institutions as well as to the types of action which paralleled changes in society as a whole (i.e., which involved large-scale historical movements.)

And this leads to the connected point that, because of the distinctive qualities of human societies, theories could not simply be statements of interconnection (whether of institutions or of their psychological aspects) in terms of efficient causation, but had also to incorporate the necessary elements of conscious, deliberate 'teleology'. The interdependencies of institutions and of the psychological aspects of social relationships - all such regularities or uniformities - had also to be accompanied by a teleological explanation in terms of the understanding of social action. What this amounts to is that theories in sociology seemed only possible (seemed only adequate in taking all these interdependencies into account) by the construction of such models.

This, it must be clearly seen, was not in any sense a denial of the methods of empirical science, it was, on the contrary, the proper construction of concepts and methods to make the science of society sufficient for engaging accurately with the actual distinctive complexities of its subject-matter.

(c) *Historical Study: Conceptions of Persistence and Change. Change Evolution, Development and Progress.*

The attempt to achieve testable description, generalization, and explanation, requiring the necessary procedures of classification, comparative study, and the interpretive understanding of social action, was conducted on the completely firm and agreed recognition that societies were essentially cumulative historical phenomena. Certain aspects of this require clear statement.

Social systems - even the most simple societies of all - were essentially accumulations and transmissions of the achievements of men in their many social activities. To adopt a non-historical, or a - historical view of any society (no matter how simple) was therefore an error. Even a simply society which manifested no change now, was, in fact, the outcome of an untold period of accommodation to the life-conditions of the group; so that to regard it as a non-historical system was no more than to lose sight of the true evolutionary perspective of human and social development.

The study of persisting order and of change were therefore both aspects of the recognition that societies were processes of cumulative transmission. It is important to see here that persisting order was as much a historical matter, requiring understanding and explanation, as was change. But both order and change came to be studied within the context of other conceptions.

CHANGE

Firstly, it is worth emphasising that all earlier theories of an eternal order of things, and all 'cyclical' theories of change, were abandoned. Change was simply thought of as something different from that which had existed previously; and it was agreed that human society had undergone ongoing change in this sense.

EVOLUTION

Secondly, however, the changes of societies were held to be not arbitrary, but explicable in terms of the activities of men in meeting their environmental conditions - first in adapting successfully to them, then, increasingly, in achieving the knowledge and power to transform them. But unintended consequences, as well as conscious purposes, entered into the shaping of societies, so that the analysis and explanation of social systems in the contexts of their environments was required, and this was provided by the concept of evolution. Again, this need not be elaborated, but we must note for completeness of statement that this was not a blanket-term description, but the provision of a set of explanatory components. Without being exhaustive, these included at least:

- (i) the grounds of the instability of the homogeneous,
- (ii) the reasons for the multiplication of effects once differentiation has begun,
- (iii) the factors making for the specialisation and segregation of parts,
- (iv) the 'equilibrium-disequilibrium' adjustments to changing conditions,
- (v) the factors making for disintegration and dissolution, and
- (vi) (to bring in Marx) the possibility that changing quantitative conditions may produce qualitatively different modes of social life, etc.

It was clear, in all this, that evolution, was not one theory of change, of a 'mono-causal' theory, but provided within its perspective for many patterns of causal explanation; and it is clear, too, that it entailed an 'equilibrium-disequilibrium' analysis of accommodations to the stresses of changing conditions - which could, of course, result in disequilibrium as well as equilibrium, and which, if extreme, could lead to dissolution as well as integrated development.

DEVELOPMENT

A third essential concept was that of Development. Societies did not simply become different, nor did they only manifest certain patterns of 'adaptation' to their environments. They were characterised by cumulative development. Men achieved certain skills, techniques, bodies of knowledge, judgments of value, in their activities. These were transmitted as the 'heritage' of the society and new achievements were possible on the basis of them. Social development - in the changing nature of technical skills and of social institutions - was recognised as an essential fact of human society and was therefore a necessary element to take into account in theories of social change.

PROGRESS

It is impossible to conceive of development, however (as cumulative achievement), without acknowledging an element of improvement; and this leads to the fourth important element in considering theories of social change: the concept of progress. For the moment, we need not enter into the ethical questions surrounding the idea of 'progress', because the central agreements of the nineteenth century theorists can be made clear without them. Their contention was simply this: that men in their practical activities sought practical advantage; that the folkways, mores, institutions and laws of all societies embodied the ways of doing things which had been selected, largely on a basis of trial and error, over long periods of social development; that men established ever more accurate knowledge that gave them better powers of control over nature and improved their capacities to act purposively in transforming their environments (rather than being a prey to them) so that there was certainly a drive towards progress in society. There was a 'strain towards improvement' in skills and institutions even in their simplest forms in the most traditional societies, and this was consciously and purposively pursued as greater knowledge and control was achieved. The nineteenth century theorists also believed, of course, that moral progress was a possible concomitant of these changes, but none of them held that such progress was inevitable; on the contrary, their very effort in the making of sociology was based upon their conviction as to the conscious and deliberate effort which men would have to make if the massive problems of industrial society were to be satisfactorily met and overcome. The essential point, however, was that - for them - the very nature of society was such as to include a drive for progress, as well as elements of evolutionary adaptation, cumulative development and ongoing difference. The concepts of change, evolution, development, and progress were therefore all necessary concepts in the study of the historical dimensions of societies.

(d) *The Centrality of Mind and Knowledge in the 'Models' of Society and the Theories of Social Change*

A quite basic point of agreement among all the nineteenth century theorists we have studied was their conviction that it was the capacity of the human mind to establish knowledge and control over both nature and society, which was of central importance in explaining the major sequences of social change, evolution, and development in history. The only theorist who might, at first glance, seem to be an exception to this was Marx, but we have seen that once his 'materialism' is thoroughly examined, it, too, is a theory resting upon the extension of knowledge and control in men's practical activities, and the hidden adjustments of society are no more than the 'unintended consequences' which we have seen plainly in all the other theorists. All of them, without exception then, emphasise the central importance of the purposive powers of mind and the cumulative achievement of ever more accurate knowledge on the basis of which prediction could be more reliable and social action more effective in attaining its ends.

Two particular points are worth clear emphasis here.

The first is that it was this persuasion concerning the powers of the human mind and the crucial importance of the acquisition, dissemination, and transmission of knowledge in society which underlay the importance which all these men attributed to 'progress' in social change. These powers of mind, these accumulations of knowledge and control, were the central distinguishing facts in the nature of societies and their processes of change; and no theory of order and change could properly ignore them. This persuasion too, of course, underlay the concern felt by these men for education and democracy in society.

The second point, however, is of even greater interest, and is that - though expressed in various ways - all these men agreed that the entire processes of natural and social change, evolution, development and progress in the entirety of the history of the world before the emergence of the modern scientific epoch was no more than the pre-history of man. Hitherto, through all the long ages of history, through all the complex processes of man's struggle in the world and in society, genetic constraints and limitations had been predominant. Men had groped their way through their many struggles aiming at immediate and necessitous objectives; a social order, culminating from many unintended and unforeseen consequences, had come to be laid down. But only now - with modern science and much improved technological control was man able to comprehend this entire situation, to see and assess it clearly, and, with conscious responsibility, to begin the period of his own purposive creation: to make his own history; to make himself. Again, we see the centrality of sociology (in the minds of these men) in this awareness of the crucial situation of human action. For better, for worse: men now had to be responsible for their own nature and destiny; and for this, a firm knowledge of society, as of nature, was indispensable.

It is, to my mind, of convincing importance that, coming from so many apparently different roots and persuasions, the theories of social change, offered by all these men focused upon this central feature of the modern human situation: man's self-responsibility in knowledge, morality and creative social action.

This it was which had been at the roots of the insufficiency of earlier social theories, and the awareness of the need for a science of society, at the beginning of the nineteenth century. This it was which provided the central focus, the central agreement, of all these theoretical studies which had, by the end of the century, laid the foundations of this science.

An entire conspectus of sociology had therefore been achieved in both 'Statics' and 'Dynamics'. Agreement had been clearly found in the necessary components for the analysis of the distinctive nature of society, of the 'social system'; and agreement had also been found in the necessary components for specific theories in applying this analysis to the study of particular kinds of societies, kinds of social change, etc. And agreement was still clear about the central focus: of the necessity of the science of society for grappling with the qualitatively new and challenging situation in which man found himself.

A simple indication of these similarities of conclusion, despite apparently different concepts and starting-points, may be seen in the accompanying diagram.

Some Distinctive Methods of Sociology

It was agreed, too, that sociology required certain distinctive methods, as a science in accordance with its distinctive subject-matter.

Many of the methods of sociology were, of course, exactly the same as those of other sciences. There was the same insistence upon careful observation, description, analysis, classification, comparative study, in order to arrive at testable generalisations and theories. Where appropriate, there was the same concern for both qualitative and quantitative (i.e. measurable, statistical) methods. We have seen, too, the many specific methods outlined for the study of 'social systems': structural-functional analysis, equilibrium-disequilibrium analysis, the analysis of group processes - including their psychological aspects, and so on - and there is no point in reiterating these. It is worthwhile, however, simply to note clearly those methods which, according to the nineteenth century theorists, were distinctive of sociology, and we might note the agreements about the rejection as well as the acceptance of certain methods.

(a) *The Historical Method*

Social systems were essentially historical processes, and therefore the historical method was essential to sociology. We have seen what went into this, but we may just emphasise again that this was distinctive from anything found in the sciences of 'nature' because social systems were essentially cumulative traditions compounded of human achievements, and these historical processes were different from anything else found in nature.

(b) *The Comparative Method*

Distinctive emphasis was placed upon the Comparative Method not because it was not important in other sciences, but because it was of crucial importance in sociology as the only alternative to artificial experimentation. Only by careful comparative studies could generalisations and theories be subjected to conditions of test.

(c) *The Inverse-Deductive Method*

Since the greater number of the social events which have impressed us, about which we have knowledge, and which lead us to desire theories about them are already of the past, and cannot be artificially re-created for prospective experimental tests, the employment of the historical and comparative methods must entail a certain large measure of 'inverse-deductive' procedure. We are, more often than not, trying to find adequate explanations of empirical generalisations and concrete instances which we already know. This does not preclude all possibility of prediction of existing or forthcoming events for the purpose of submitting a theory to conditions of test; but it does mean that, at any given time, the bulk of our knowledge is of the past; in any ordinary sense unrepeatable; and we are necessarily in the position of seeking, retrospectively, adequate explanations, and can only manipulate the available data to the best advantage possible.

It is a point worth making here, that the greater part of the empirical data of sociology must be of a documentary kind. Much hangs on this. It could be said with much truth that many sociologists have neglected the importance of this. On the other hand men like Comte, Marx, Spencer did not find a lot of worthwhile history to hand when they looked for it. The truth is that sociology and historiography are intimately connected, and the theoretical preoccupations of both have been very similar, if not identical, from the early nineteenth century to row.

(d) *The Multiplicity of Factors and the Compounding of Causes and Effects*

The study of society necessitated the consideration of several essential aspects, always closely related in any social actuality: as, for example, the structure of social organisation, the analysis of functions, the analysis of groups, the study of the psychological aspects of the situation, and the study of the 'teleological' elements of the sequences of social action. Also, the actuality of society was always very complex, so that any simple-minded postulation of one cause explaining one event was of very dubious value, if it was not always doomed to failure. The essential thing in satisfactory sociological analysis was that all these components should be taken into account in relation to each other, and that care should be taken to try to trace the many kinds of causes-and-effect relationship and compound them into a satisfactory explanation.

(e) *Teleological Explanation and the Construction of 'Types' of 'Action'*

The most distinctive method of sociology, however, was attendant upon the persuasion that human action was different from all other events and elements of behaviour in nature, and necessitated a qualitatively different kind of causal explanation in terms of the understanding of the ends which men pursued and the choices, deliberation, calculation, and use of means which went into their conscious activities. All these theorists employed this conception of action: from Comte to Ward and Giddings; and, again, even in Marx there was a forthright recognition of it. This 'teleological' kind of explanation was, then, quite distinctive, and it led to the construction of 'types' or 'models' of societies and of sequences of social action which attempted interpretive explanations in addition to (and parallel to) the 'genetic' kinds of explanation of social and psychological regularities.

(f) ***Agreed REJECTIONS of Method***

It almost goes without saying that all these theorists were agreed in rejecting, as not being distinctive of sociology, (a) the idea of scientific empiricism as a bit-and-piece collection of 'facts' quite unguided by theory, and (b) pure deduction from 'a priori' premises.

The Limitations of Sociology: But its Use for the Central Perspective of Social Action

On the relations between sociology and philosophical ethics there was a good deal of confusion among the nineteenth century theorists, but two or three points were fairly widely and firmly agreed, and all were important. These were:

(a) ***Sociological Knowledge never Final: RELATIVE but not ARBITRARY***

That, in addition to being unable to reach any 'ultimates' in explanation, sociology could never claim to reach final knowledge. The knowledge of sociology; the theories which it proposed and tested; would always, necessarily, be limited to the mental and perceptual equipment of man and relative to the many details of his social situation. At the same time, such knowledge was not arbitrary. It would be the most accurate knowledge possible from the use of the scientific method at the time and in these conditions. But the 'truths' and 'laws' of sociology would always be 'theories' open to test.

(b) ***The Most Reliable Basis for Prediction and Social Practice***

That, if the methods of sociology were carefully pursued, the knowledge provided would be - if not exact (since it could not hope for the degree of exactitude of other sciences) - at least the most exact that was humanly possible. As such, it could provide the best basis for prediction and social action. Even here, however, care had to be exercised. For sociological knowledge (or the knowledge of any other social science) was not in itself enough. Ideally, it was best considered in relation to ethical principles as clarified by the moral philosopher, and the practical assessments and judgments of men who had much experience in the 'arts' of society: the judge, the lawyer, the doctor, the statesman, etc. With all these three combined that basis for action could be arrived at which would be the most reliable that was possible.

The other aspect of this point which was most important was the recognition that the subject-matter which yielded a lesser degree of exactitude of knowledge, was also the subject-matter which was most modifiable by deliberate action. Mill's insistence, then, that: 'a degree of knowledge altogether insufficient for prediction, is nonetheless of the utmost value for guidance. . .' was of very considerable importance. Indeed, when all the theories of the nineteenth century are drawn together, it is the composed, balanced wisdom of Mill which seems of greatest worth in qualifying extremes and leading to properly modest and satisfactory conclusions.

(c) *The Sociological Perspective the Only Perspective for Social Study and Social Action*

The final point on which all were agreed was the conviction that - whatever the difficulties attending the subject - the sociological perspective: the study of societal facts and sequences of social action as parts and aspects of social systems undergoing historical processes of order and change, was the only correct perspective. Any other approach had been shown to be superficial, insufficient and discredited. For better, for worse - sociology was the only valid approach in the quest for testable knowledge about the complex institutional life of men in society: all trends of intellectual thought had led to it; all urgent social needs cried out for it. To try to create such a science, as satisfactorily as possible, was all we could do. If there were those who denied and rejected it: then the onus lay upon them to produce something better.

All the theorists were completely agreed with the perspective which has guided us from the start: namely that a science of society had become necessary as an objective of endeavour in the modern world, because of the disruption of the old traditional order of society and the situation which now confronted mankind - qualitatively new in scale and complexity, in knowledge and power - of taking upon himself, with a full consciousness of his responsibility, the deliberate reconstruction of society; the making of his own destiny. The making of sociology was a necessary part of the making of a new society.

This, then, is a summary statement of the entire conspectus of the new science of sociology as it had been founded by the end of the nineteenth century.

Such a summary could not possibly be exhaustive in its detail; it could not possibly include all the detailed points and nuances provided by each theorist; but I hope that it is reasonably comprehensive as an outline; that it makes clear, at least, all the essential components of the subject; and that it can be seen how the many ideas of the various theorists could be fitted into the entire schema.

Let us now stop for a moment; remind ourselves that all this was accomplished by the end of the nineteenth century; and make one or two comments in retrospect.

It is interesting, first of all, to see that this conspectus of sociology, after all the detailed thought and study that had gone into its foundation throughout the nineteenth century, was, in its achieved form, still entirely in accordance with all the assumptions of common-sense as we outlined them earlier. It is worthwhile at this stage to glance back to our summary statement of our common-sense assumptions and to see how all the persuasions outlined were embodied in the newly defined science of society. The foundations of sociology were, then, well laid in this respect: they clearly constituted a searching reflection upon common-sense assumptions and were a clear advance upon them. They were not foreign to them in any respect.

Similarly, it is also worthwhile at this stage to note that these foundations of sociology were a clear advance upon the earlier social theories - of religion, political philosophy, the philosophy of history, etc. - which we summarised at the outset. A glance at our summary statement of the components of religious theories, for example, will show that sociological theory dealt with the same elements - but with immeasurably improved, more searching, and more reliable methods. At the same time the central humane concern was not diminished by one iota. Indeed the struggle against earlier religious theories for the achievement of sociology and a more reliable understanding of the social predicaments of man was undertaken entirely because of a deep humane concern. It was part of a profound commitment on the part of these men to the struggle to create a new social order which, though rooted in massive disruptions and holdings grave dangers of dehumanisation, could be the basis for the achievement, throughout the world, of those high qualities of life, culture, social justice and personal character which, hitherto, had been only known as elements of 'vision'. Sociology was foreign to these early social theories only in that it sought to be an improvement upon them.

Even in these first foundations, then, sociology had accomplished a clear advance upon both common-sense assumptions and earlier social theories: growing out of them, and growing beyond them. It had already produced specific theories which were rich in the detail of systematic comparative studies, provided new perspectives, and had set out clear principles of analysis and methods of study in the light of which theories could be tested and knowledge could cumulatively advance.

A third comment, worth a simple note, is that the foundations of sociology were perfectly clear. All the elements of the new systematic science of society were stated with perfect clarity. There was nothing whatever that was obscure; nothing difficult; nothing misleading by any kind of purposeful obscurantism; nothing outrageous by way of invalid or unfounded intellectual claims. The nineteenth century theorists struggled towards clarity, and they achieved it. If there are those who do not find these matters clear, we have no alternative but to conclude that there is something defective in their mental equipment. There are only two other possibilities: (a) that they have not sufficiently read and studied that which they criticise, or (b) that they have entrenched academic interests of their own which lead them to preserve and promulgate this endless, tedious, and silly myth about sociology's obscurantism.

The foundations of sociology provided an entire system of analysis very clearly worked out, and accomplished after very thorough argument. Obviously, it was possible to disagree with aspects of this system of analysis and the kinds of theory which it made possible, and the whole emphasis of sociology was that such continuous criticism should take place. Science consists of continuous criticism, and sociology explicitly provided for this in its methods. But in no sense could it be charged with a lack of clarity.

There is, of course, the third possibility that sociology has been not only misconstrued by those who have never studied it, but also attacked by those committed to other subjects which were, and are, endangered by it. At the very end of this book we can come back to this question; but here it is enough to note again the peculiarity of sociology: that it was not founded by 'academics' and was not a 'university subject' (or 'discipline', as the critics like to say). The making of sociology was part of the task of making a new society, and the founding of the new science was accomplished by men who were at the heart of political thought and political action; who were engaged in the fullest sense with public affairs; and involved in continuous critical discussion and writing about them. All the men we have considered were men of powerful human concern; admirable in the depth of their commitment and the scale of their efforts in seeking a basis of knowledge sufficient for the task of reconstruction which they saw before them. All of them had emphasised importance of the sociological perspective in education, from Comte onwards, but it was only among the Americans, at the end of the century, that direct steps were taken to introduce the science as a 'subject' at the several levels of schools, colleges and universities. In Giddings especially, there was the direct concern for teaching, and the writing of a text-book setting out the elements of sociological analysis.

Here we need only note that the practical roots of the intellectual effort that went into the making of sociology; the common-sense roots, too; were also borne out by this fact: that sociology was not a creation of the universities. But the introduction of it into education was just beginning when its foundations had been firmly laid by the end of the century. From this point on, quite new issues of the educational 'professionalisation' of the subject, and the struggles between its proponents and opponents in the universities, began to arise. And these we shall be able to trace when we come to the developments of the subject during our own century.

A final group of points remain.

What are we to make of those people who believe that sociology is a 'new' subject, which has been created in the universities since the last war? Surely only one thing: they are ignorant of it. They can know nothing about it.

What are we to make of those people who believe that sociology is the 'newest' of the social sciences? - having been developed only recently, and long after the consolidation of economics, political science, and the like? Surely, again, only that they are ignorant of these matters.

The foundations of sociology were already firmly and clearly laid by the end of the nineteenth century - and that, after a century of detailed argument and study. And this course of argument and study paralleled the development of economics and political science; being just as long-lived as they, are rooted in exactly the same nexus of intellectual ferment and social disorder.

Such critics simply do not know what they are talking about. They are teaching a perspective which is totally false.

What also are we to say of those people who claim that sociology is a 'rag-bag' of bit-and-piece studies of social life, and a collection of theories, which appear to be quite disconnected, an in disagreement with each other? What are we to say of those who claim that the work of the founders of sociology was 'rarely cumulative'; that it was often characterised 'more by passion than by precision', by 'imagination rather than by order', and was 'sometimes not scientific on any definition. . .' and that these men 'did not spell out in any detailed way the precise nature either of sociological problems or of sociological analysis'? One can only gasp at the outrageous nature of such judgments.

We have seen in the most detailed way, the great consistency which existed among all the great figures of the nineteenth century - despite their differences of particular concepts and particular emphases; but, more especially, we have seen the completely demonstrable connections linking all these theorists in the ongoing argument of the century. Again, it is true that Marx appears something of an 'odd man out' here, but - even here - we have seen how similar his notions were to those of the other theorists underneath his metaphysical confusions and political polemics. But as for the rest: the thread which runs through Comte, Mill, Spencer, Ward, Sumner and Giddings is completely and utterly clear, and Giddings in a quite indisputable way can be shown to be a critical summation, a systematisation, of practically all the important elements of analysis which had been clarified before him. The cumulative nature of the work of the founders of sociology was perfectly clear, and the articulate statement of the orderly system and the related components of sociological analysis to be found in it was plain for all to read.

These and similar judgments are therefore such as completely to defeat understanding: especially when they are asserted by some of those who are teaching sociology, as well as others - economists, political scientists, members of the House of Lords, Vice-Chancellors, and the like - whose errors and superficialities of judgment can be more readily understood. The only conclusion there can possibly be is that people do not read and study the things they criticise: a fantastic and lamentable state of affairs! - especially among people who make public noises in supposed defence of standards of intellectual excellence.

However, our own concluding statement of the nature of the 'Foundations of Sociology' as accomplished by the end of the nineteenth century is clear beyond doubt. It has cost a good deal of study and effort, but the achievement of this basic clarity will be seen to have been well worth while. From this basis we can move on confidently to assess the 'Developments' of our own century; and, having done this, we shall then be in a position to clarify and throw into the wastepaper-basket a score of fallacies which are ruining the contemporary perspectives of the subject and breeding misunderstandings.